Border Sexualities, Border Families in Schools

Border Sexualities, Border Families in Schools

Maria Pallotta-Chiarolli

ROWMAN & LITTLEFIELD PUBLISHERS, INC.
Lanham • Boulder • New York • Toronto • Plymouth, UK

Published by Rowman & Littlefield Publishers, Inc.
A wholly owned subsidiary of The Rowman & Littlefield Publishing Group, Inc.
4501 Forbes Boulevard, Suite 200, Lanham, Maryland 20706
http://www.rowmanlittlefield.com

Estover Road, Plymouth PL6 7PY, United Kingdom

British Library Cataloguing in Publication Information Available

Library of Congress Cataloging-in-Publication Data

Pallotta-Chiarolli, Maria, 1960–
 Border sexualities, border families in schools / Maria Pallotta-Chiarolli.
 p. cm.
 Includes bibliographical references.
 ISBN 978-0-7425-1035-7 (cloth : alk. paper) — ISBN 978-0-7425-1036-4 (pbk. :
alk. paper) — ISBN 978-1-4422-0383-9 (electronic)
 1. Sexual minority students. I. Title.
 LC2574.P35 2010
 371.826′6—dc22   2009052239

∞™ The paper used in this publication meets the minimum requirements of
American National Standard for Information Sciences—Permanence of Paper for
Printed Library Materials, ANSI/NISO Z39.48-1992.

Printed in the United States of America

I am the rest between two notes,
which are somehow always in discord . . .
but in the dark interval, reconciled,
they stay there trembling.
And the song goes on, beautiful.

—Rainer Maria Rilke

This book is for those on the bi-borders and poly-borders: bisexual young people, bisexual parents, and polyamorous/multipartnered/multisexual families, particularly those who have participated in this research. To my dear inspirational friends Anne Hunter and Peter Haydon, and all the Australian poly and bi group leaders and members, this is especially for you for the love, support, and deep understanding with which you embrace humanity. I am humbled by your courage and vision.

Whatever is unnamed, undepicted in images, whatever is misnamed as something else, made difficult to come by, . . . under an inadequate or lying language, this will become, not merely unspoken but unspeakable.

—Adrienne Rich

Without the privileges, power, passports, special provisions, maps, tools, and language guides automatically bestowed upon heterosexual young people and monogamous heterosexual families, and increasingly being made available to gay and lesbian young people and same-sex couples, you are pioneers traversing the landscape, clearing pathways for future travelers.

And in memory of Alan McClare, the publisher who made this book possible as a pathway in support of those pioneers.

Contents

Acknowledgments

In my dedication, I have already thanked the amazing young people, families, and educators who have participated in this research. So I'd like to take this space to acknowledge the many people who have supported the development and completion of this project, which means supporting me!

This work has been inspired, mentored, and nurtured by two pioneer researchers, academics, and activists who know and understand the importance of passion in both our professional and personal lives. First, James Sears's interest and support from when I first mentioned the idea for this book in 1999 at the American Educational Research Association conference in Montreal has been unwavering, patient, and inspirational. It has been an absolute honor, gift, and pleasure to be working with and supported by such a pioneer scholar, mentor, and friend as James.

Second, I also wish to posthumously thank Fritz Klein for his pioneering work into bisexuality and his encouragement of my efforts in Australia. Meeting him, listening to his presentations, and indulging in the pleasure and privilege of conversation with Fritz in Sydney, 2002, at the Seventh International Conference on Bisexuality, are unforgettable gifts. Fritz is sadly missed, but what a legacy that I hope many of us will take forward!

I would also like to acknowledge two friends, collaborators, and colleagues who have undertaken research with me that also provided insight and data for this book's project: Wayne Martino and Sara Lubowitz. Working with such insightful and passionate people who are able to blissfully blend personal friendship and professional work is something I appreciate immensely. I look forward to further research collaborations with you but, more importantly, the ongoing joys of our friendships. I also wish to acknowledge my honors student, Erik Martin, who undertook specific research into bisexual young people's mental health and substance abuse. His passionate and thorough engagement with the research resulting in a first-class Honors thesis, and our subsequent joint publications, attest to the excellent caliber of his research prowess and skills of collaboration.

I have had the pleasure of meeting many incredibly dynamic and pioneering women who have inspired, mentored, and lightened the load with their camaraderie around issues of bisexuality and polyamory, and who have encouraged me to undertake my own research. They include Ryam Nearing, Deborah Anapol, Robyn Ochs, Wendy O'Matik, Melita Noel, Meg Barker, Elisabeth Sheff, and Serena Anderlini-D'Onofrio. Your own passionate work and queer feminism have sustained me.

I have also been beautifully supported by queer pro-feminist men who have transgressed the rigid boundaries of masculinity in their own endeavors regarding sexual diversity and family diversity. They include Bill Bruff, Bryan, Ron Frey, Ron Fox, Damien Riggs, Baden Offord, Christopher Mac-Farlane, John Ryan, Graham McKay, Wayne Roberts, Glenn Vassallo and Michael Wynter. In particular, it was the beautiful friendship with John Ryan that led me to the artwork and installations of Dani Marti, another visionary queer pioneer. Dani has allowed me to use his piece, *The Pleasure Chest*, on the cover of this book. It is a powerful work of secondhand beaded necklaces and Spanish rosary beads collected by Dani between 2000 and 2003. Its interweavings, diversity, and layering profoundly move me as a visual embodiment of what I am trying to convey in words. I also wish to thank Suzie Hampell and everyone at ARC One Gallery, Flinders Lane, in Melbourne, Australia, for representing Dani Marti and liaising so beautifully and smoothly for us.

Rowman and Littlefield sent me wonderful publishers and their team who patiently and confidently waited and watched and then accompanied the book to its completion with calm warm efficiency: Alan McClare, Art Pomponio, Evan Wiig, and Julia Loy. Just as the book was going into production, I received the very sad news of Alan McClare's passing. From the time I met Alan at the same AERA in 1999 where this book was an idea shared with James Sears, to the inspiring and encouraging conversations with Alan about the book at AERA in 2003, I had been excitedly anticipating celebrating the book's completion at AERA in 2010, and thanking Alan for his incredible gift of long-term patience, passion, and expertise. I waited too long. We have lost a beautiful man who combined personal respect and warmth with exemplary professionalism.

My immense appreciation also goes out to the reviewers who took time out of their busy personal and professional lives to navigate what was often a laborious manuscript, and provided insightful, encouraging, and critical commentaries: Mollie Blackburn, Amity Pierce Buxton, Loraine Hutchins,

Wayne Martino, and Geri Weitzman. And to Teresa Burnett for her meticulous indexing.

I also wish to thank the Faculty of Health, Medicine, Nutrition and Behavioural Sciences at Deakin University for an initial research grant to support me in beginning and developing this work, and my colleagues and leaders at Deakin University who provide the space and ambience within which to undertake this work. Also a huge thank-you to Adrian Kelly of Transcripts Plus for his sensitive and confidential transcribing of many interviews.

Finally, to my loved ones who have provided the immeasurable pleasures and groundedness of relationship, friendship, and family, as well as important distractions such as food and laughter, places to sleep, and reasons to party. Thank you for encouraging me to get on with my work, even if it's unclear or too clear, too queer or not queer enough. So many family, friends, and colleagues to thank over the years, and you know who you are, but in particular, Rob and Steph Chiarolli, my parents, Dora and Stefano, Bryan, Maria, Connie, Will Doherty, Madelaine, Kirsten, Jamie and Demetry, Sue and Mij, Alan Prefino, and the AGMC (Australian GLBTIQ Multicultural Council).

1

"Messing Up the School Sex Filing Cabinet"

Introducing the Research

> It's like the school's got an office where there's a filing cabinet in which you get put into the straight-A-achiever folder or gay-gruesome-B folder. But if you happen to be an X-file, forget it! You're alien! They don't want you in that office 'cause you mess up the school sex filing cabinet!
>
> —Marita, seventeen, bi student

> This one-size-fits-all model of family that schools endorse and erase the rest of us damages our most precious resource, our children, and wastes what so many of us as families could be contributing.
>
> —Nora, heteropoly mom

Educational institutions in Western countries, particularly in relation to health and sexuality education, are increasingly challenging heteronormative pedagogical practices and curricula in relation to gay and lesbian students and gay and lesbian families. Yet there appears to be minimal acknowledgment and application of queer educational theory and social and mental health strategies that call for sexual diversity and family diversity to be recognized as incorporating identities and structures beyond the gay/straight divide and beyond the monogamous heterosexual or homosexual couple framework. These absences and erasures in the "school sex filing cabinet" and the "one-size-fits-all model of family" leave some students and families feeling silenced and invisibilized, even within educational settings that purport to be espousing a multicultural multisexual pedagogical framework (Pallotta-Chiarolli, 1999a, 1999b, 1999c, 2002,

2005a, 2005b, 2006a, 2006b; Pallotta-Chiarolli and Martin, 2009). These border sexualities and families are

- bisexual students: this term will be used to define young people who are sexually attracted to both males and females, and/or identify as bisexual, and/or are sexually engaging with both males and females and identify themselves with such terms as "sexually fluid" and "sexually flexible";
- multisexual families: this term will be used to define parents and other family members who are "queerly mixed"—that is, of varying sexual identities, and who may also consider themselves to be in mixed-orientation marriages/relationships;
- polyamorous or multipartnered families: these terms will be used to define parents and other family members who are in openly negotiated loving/intimate/sexual relationships with more than one other person, whether they cohabit or live apart, and who are raising children together.

Throughout this book, the various terms above will be used according to which is more relevant and which is preferred by the research participant(s) being discussed or who are discussing their lives. In chapter 2, I will explore the above terms and identities in more detail and present any tensions or contradictions that may be evident such as between polyamory and various forms of religious and cultural polygamy.

In documenting the educational experiences of the above families and students, this book is a continuation of the need to challenge heteronormative constructions of adolescence, sexuality, and family in pedagogy, student welfare programs, school policy, and school cultures. It calls for the queerification of education (Letts and Sears, 1999) and student health promotion that acknowledges the existence, experience, and expertise of such border sexualities and border families. Indeed, the queerification of education also means addressing queer forms of heterosexuality in our school communities (parents, students, and teachers) such as heterosexual partners of gay, lesbian, bisexual, transgendered, or queer individuals, and heterosexual individuals who have more than one intimate partner.

> No child is born prejudiced, no child is born to hate. But our children will have to deal with the children of hate-mongers in schools, the children who are taught from birth that those of a different family life or sexual identity are *bad*. So many senseless hates, so much fear of the different . . . and our schools let it happen while proclaiming they're educating kids to take their place in the future. (Kathy, bi-poly mom)

Some readers may ask at this stage why I have combined research with bisexual students and research with polyfamilies. First, as will be explored in chapter 2, there is much theoretical overlapping territory. Queer theory, mestizaje theory, and borderland theory frame the lives of bisexual students and polyparents, as both groups live within, on the borders of, and beyond the gay/straight and same-sex/opposite-sex divides of sexuality, identity, and family. Second, there is much experiential overlapping territory: for example, some bisexual students seek polyrelationships and will be poly-parents of the future; some polyparents are bisexual or live with bisexual partners in mixed-orientation families.

Given that this research is one of the first of its kind, I have ensured that each chapter not only provides the research findings but also documents definitional, theoretical, and empirical work to date, including an analysis of some pertinent media, popular culture, and literary texts. This strategy allows for a thorough contextualization and analysis of the experiences of the participants, and also honors one of their major recommendations: that collations of this information be made available as a valuable resource for educators, health workers, families, and the students themselves. Thus, what may appear to be scattered and meandering material of various genres and styles, interwoven with research results that foreground the voices of the participants themselves, is a deliberate attempt to follow branches and threads that ultimately interweave in the sociocultural, educational, interpersonal, and personal lives of the research participants and those who connect and collaborate with them in educational and health systems.

This chapter will introduce the research and locate it within ongoing educational and sociological debates, research, and activism in regard to family diversity and sexual diversity. It will also discuss the research methodology in some detail because, being one of the first of its kind, this study raises significant questions in regard to accessing individuals and groups who remain largely hidden and acknowledging and honoring their concerns about representation, accessibility, and voice. Thus, the chapter will provide an overview of the research participants themselves, whom I have chosen to quote at length from their interviews, given their strong desire to be heard and to speak for themselves in the safe and yet powerful space of this text.

WHO ARE THE "X-FILES"? AND WHY STUDY THEM?

The world isn't heterosexual or homosexual, it's lotsasexuals.

—Wendy, fifteen, hetero daughter of bi-poly dad and hetero-mono mom

As Gibian writes about the "Almighty Power of Opposition," "Our entire Western system of thought is based on binary opposition; we define by comparison, by what things are not . . . [and by] entities that exclude each other" (1992: 5). Such dichotomous logics are being applied in constructing schools' sexuality and family files, which fail to consider those students and families who are being socially ascribed and are self-inscribing positions in the border zone between gay and straight sexual identities, and/or between gay and straight monogamously coupled families. In the words of bisexual singer/songwriter Tom Robinson, they are "simply trying to live a both/and life in an either/or world" (Bennett, 1992: 205), while finding themselves "caught in the teeth" of "dichotomous identity enculturation" (Entrup and Firestein, 2007: 99). Within our school communities, some children are being raised by "queerly mixed" border families:

- with bisexual monogamous or nonmonogamous parents,
- with parents of differing sexualities,
- with one or more parents in openly negotiated intimate sexual relationships with more than one partner.

My research is framed by a growing body of queer scholarship on bisexuality (see McLean, 2003; Anderlini-D'Onofrio, 2004, 2009a; Fox, 2004). As Angelides argues, bisexuality has been largely marginalized "and even erased from the deconstructive field of queer theory" (2006: 126). He calls for a "trinary-based deconstructive reading practice," which will make researchers more accountable in their use of "unstable terms" such as heterosexuality, homosexuality, and bisexuality (2006: 153). Indeed, in queer education theory and research, bisexual students and parenting in relation to education have not been explored to any significant extent (see McLean, 2005 for one such article). And yet, some young people are sexual border dwellers because they

- do not identify as gay, lesbian, or heterosexual;
- do identify as bisexual;
- do behave bisexually while adopting a gay, lesbian, or heterosexual label;
- do dismiss sexual labeling altogether, or use broader and more inclusive terms such as "sexually flexible" or "sexually fluid" (see Halperin, 2009).

By foregrounding the voices, perspectives, and experiences of the above border students and border families, this book will explore the kinds of negotiations, resistances, and meanderings they undertake in order to survive, if not thrive, within heteronormative, monogamist, biphobic, and polyphobic educational institutions. It will make visible the "non-normative intimacies" (Roseneil and Budgeon, 2004: 138) usually concealed in our school communities. It will interrogate "mainstream" hegemonic educational discourses of Identity, Truth, and Reality in order to demonstrate individual and family agency and strategies "to undo the logic and the clarity" of such constructs (Lionnet, 1989: 14). As Rasmussen states in relation to non-heteronormative identities in schools, educators need to "consider what it means to have certain faces that appear to be unrepresentable in particular pedagogical domains" (2006: 474). In undertaking the above explorations, I will provide some insight into the "huge, populous, prosperous, bustling world" (Rubin, 1984: 220) that inhabits the fluid, multiple space on the borders of simplistic and fixed identities of sexual duality, and opposite- and same-sex-couple families. Indeed, in using the school as a sociological setting, this research supports Roseneil and Budgeon's contention that "if we are to understand the current state, and, likely, future, of intimacy and care, sociologists [and educators] should decentre the 'family' and the heterosexual couple in our intellectual imaginaries" (2004: 135).

Likewise, Erera believes researchers "need to keep clear the distinctions between the institutionalized family, the ideology of the family, and the lives of actual families" (2002: 2). Her notion of "diverse families" is similar to my use of the terms "border families" and "border sexualities": families and individuals who are situated within and on the borders of mainstream heteronormative monogamist society and simultaneously in a zone of marginality and "deviance" constructed and defined by the mainstream Center. This insider/outsider positioning gives these border dwellers a dual and nuanced perspective on social environments such as a school site—"able to see that which is invisible to those with power and privilege. . . . They are better equipped to reflect on and examine critically social values, norms, and expectations" (2002: 202). Erera calls for research from the standpoint of these border dwellers rather than defining and analyzing them from the "traditional family lens": "Research has not kept pace with the rapid increase in family diversity, and, with some expectations, is still influenced by the traditional family paradigm. . . . This leaves us in relative ignorance about diverse families, which makes them seem more threatening" (2002: 213). As Carrington writes, "Texts, pedagogies, routines, behavioral expectations and curriculum design are based on presumptions of the [heterosexual] nuclear family as the baseline social formation. . . . We must give serious consideration to the implications of changing family forms and changing configurations of community if we are to provide educational experiences adequate to the needs of our students" (2001: 194; see also Lamey, 2003; Emens, 2004).

Hence, my research responds to Erera's and Carrington's call by interrogating the following from the standpoint of the "X-files," the border dwellers:

- how bisexuality may fall into the gap between the binary of hetero-sexuality and homosexuality that informs antihomophobic policies, programs, and practices in schools such as in health education, sexuality education, and student welfare programs;
- how "queerly mixed," multisexual, or polyamorous family structures and realities are being silenced in schools as they fall between the polarities of normative heterosexual monogamous families and non-normative but increasingly visible gay and lesbian families.

In undertaking this research, I was mindful of many sociologists' concerns that "there is far too much emphasis on the supposed deficits and problems with diverse families, and insufficient attention to their strengths. Those who have examined these families from their own standpoint have found strengths and abilities" (Erera, 2002: 213). Indeed, Erera finds that many of the problems experienced by "diverse families" are due to factors outside the family itself, including "discrimination, poverty, and inadequate societal support systems for families and children. The pressures, tensions, and problems they experience are, almost without exception, imposed by a social environment that does not accept or support them" (2002: 217).

This critique of the stripping of agency and the pathologization of border families is reiterated by some educational researchers in regard to non-heterosexual students. Rather than constructing queer young people solely as "wounded identities" always at risk, an "ethics of pleasure" requires that "a crucial counter-narrative" is made available that highlights the pleasure, agency, and power of non-heterosexual young people (Rasmussen, 2004: 456; see also Rasmussen and Crowley, 2004). My research was intended to explore the complex and multiple realities of border families and border sexualities: the wounds and risks in their lives, mainly due to external stigmatization and discrimination, and the pleasures, agency, and power in their lives, some-times experienced when resisting and overcoming external pathologization. Thus, it is important not only to understand how public "prohibition and disavowal are fundamental to the operation of [mono]heteronormativity," but also to understand how "recognition is fundamental to our survival" (Rasmussen, 2006: 482). This recognition and "address" must come not only from the external dominant "Center" but also from the "Other" them-selves, for, as Butler explains, "Those who gain representation, especially self-representation, have a better chance of being humanized, and those who have no chance to represent themselves run a greater risk of being treated as less than human . . . or indeed not regarded at all" (2004a: 141).

Thus, the aim of this book is to be a vehicle for representation and humanization, uncovering and "messing up" the absences and silences, misrepresentations and prejudices of existing school sexuality and family "filing" cabinets. It will do this by asking

- What are the problematic and/or empowering experiences and strategies of bisexual students and multisexual and polyamorous families in educational systems?
- What could schools be doing to promote healthy sexual, emotional, and social relationships for bisexual students and multisexual/polyamorous families in school communities?
- What recommendations/implementations do bisexual students and "queerly mixed" families suggest in regard to school curriculum, school policies, and student welfare in order to acknowledge and support family diversity in school communities?

"HAVE A NORMAL FAMILY LIKE STRAIGHTS HAVE": POSITIONING THE RESEARCH ON THE BORDERS OF STRAIGHT/GAY FAMILY FILES

I'm talking to people at a GLBTIQ conference about my latest research into polyamorous and multisexual families. The same gay father who has just applauded me for my work on same-sex families in schools looks very troubled and loudly says, "I don't think you should be doing this work. You'll alienate those you wish to persuade by shoving this polymorphous perversity polyamory crap in their face. It'll only justify their claims that two lesbians or two gay men can't have a normal family like straights have."

—from my research notes

With the gaining of more political power and sociocultural legitimation of gay and lesbian identities and families, there appears to be developing within schools what could be defined as a homonormative hierarchy based on what is constructed as the dominant or central within the marginal homosexual group: usually white, middle-class, monogamously coupled, exclusively homosexual parents (Klesse, 2007). I wish to state clearly here that my intention is not to position homonormativity alongside heteronormativity in terms of power within the wider society or within educational settings, but to consider difference, power, and hierarchy within the non-heterosexual margin as a consequence, reflection, and emulation of the workings of heteronormative monogamist discourses within the wider society (Riggs, 2007).

Family fundamentalists such as Kurtz (2000, 2003a, 2003b) have written extensively on their fears that legitimating same-sex marriage and families is a huge move along the slippery slope to legitimating polyamorous families. He uses his concerns for children's well-being as a major reason not to condone or promote such "inherently unstable" families and challenges "the idea . . . that tolerance of sexual minorities requires a radical remake of the institution of marriage" (2006: 19; see also Ceres, 2005). The success and power of such heteronormative discourses and systems of control and manipulation are evident in homonormative exclusionary and divisive measures applied to bisexuality and polypartnering within gay and lesbian family research and activism. In other words, some advocates of non-heterosexual marriages and families endeavor to reassure fundamentalists such as Kurtz that the slippery slope fears will not be realized, as only those relationships that are monogamous same-sex couples are "normal families like straights have," thereby assimilating to dominant heterosexual models and perpetuating what Hidalgo, Barker, and Hunter (2008) define as "the dyadic imaginary."

My research is thus positioned within and beyond ongoing debates regarding same-sex marriage and same-sex families as emulating and/or challenging heteronormative nuclear family constructs (see Goss and Adams Squire Stronghart, 1997; Rofes, 1997; Klesse, 2007; Riggs, 2007). For example, in reflecting upon whether same-sex marriage is a transgression of what constitutes "cultural belonging" or whether it is demonstrating "deservedness" of inclusion into a state-sanctioned fixed system, O'Brien arrives at the borders:

> Lesbians and gay men who seek marriage are thereby attempting to alter a landscape based almost entirely on the fissures of a gender binary. This is indeed radical. At the same time, . . . gender radical as it is, . . . same gender marriage is likely to perpetuate a status quo that favors one particular family form and concurrent set of cultural expectations and practices. (2007: 144)

Savin-Williams also situates his position on the border between the construction of gay people as having "a distinctive life course that reflects their 'queerness,' their sense of difference" or that "they are basically similar to straight people" by concluding,

> A differential development trajectories perspective allows that both notions are true and that remarkable diversity characterizes individuals with same-sex desire. They seek to adapt to mainstream culture even as they demand acceptance of their sexuality as normative and as they appreciate the increasingly gay quality of the culture . . . they simultaneously highlight their commonalities while challenging the stereotypes. (2005: 196–97)

From the discussion above, albeit brief for the purposes of this book, it is clear there is a growing body of debate, research, and activism addressing same-sex marriages and gay and lesbian families, and yet polyamorous and multisexual families have not been explored to any significant extent, particularly in relation to education. Polyamorous and multisexual families and communities are in the precarious position of lacking visibility and legitimation just as ethnic and gay/lesbian families and communities have experienced at various points in historical time (Attali, 2005). There are emerging power-challenging communities in Australia, the United States, the United Kingdom, and Europe (see Lano and Parry, 1995; Anderlini-D'Onofrio, 2004). However, there is no official evidence of any discussion or definition of polyfamilies within educational systems. "Queerly mixed" families therefore negotiate ways of participating within school communities and educating their children without any discernible formal or informal polyamorist discursive inscription or significant structural/cultural formations in schools. In other words, the school is a site of absence, silence, and isolation for children from multisexual and polyamorous/multipartnered families. As Goss argues, "We have to escape the tyranny of normativity even within the queer community," and he points out the lack of information on bisexual and transgendered families (1997: 13). This is particularly the case where bisexual and transgendered families are not monogamous or coupled, thereby contesting the "assumed dyadism of marriage . . . [and] do not rely on gender/sex binaries" (Hidalgo et al., 2008: 173).

Indeed, if the support of same-sex families "is made possible by a condemnation of all sex outside committed, monogamous relationships," then all that has been achieved is a heteronormative push for sexually diverse families "to mimic heterosexual relational structures" (Rudy, 1997: 200; Klesse, 2007; Hidalgo et al., 2008). Riggs explores how the neoliberal understanding of oppression is based on the need for the marginalized to be "included or provided space within existing legal, political and social frameworks, rather than challenging such frameworks themselves." Thus, the goal becomes "gaining equality *with* the dominant group," which can "promote assimilationism" (2007: 186). While Riggs acknowledges that "equality with" heterosexual monogamous marriages and families is an important goal, a lack of critical engagement and broadening of options beyond this form of activism continues to uphold heterosexual monogamous marriage and nuclear couple families "as the gold standard against which all relationships are measured" (2007: 189). Robson (1992) uses the term "domesticate" to describe what happens to same-sex attracted people who "accept the terms for belonging offered to us by the state . . . [that] may ultimately serve to further enshrine the existing forms of kinship that are available (and recognised) under heteropatriarchy, rather than creating a space for new ways of understanding ourselves and our relationships" (in Riggs, 2007: 191; see also Butler, 2004b).

Klesse refers to the delineation between "Good Homosexuals" and "Dangerous Queers" as being the machinations of heteronormativity with which some gays and lesbians are complicit (2007: 11). The title of Ocean's (2008) paper succinctly summarizes the disruptive potential of including bisexuality, particularly in its nonmonogamous forms, as feared by many same-sex marriage activists: "Bisexuals Are Bad for the Same-Sex Marriage Business" (see also Williams, 2008). Thus, what Pieper and Bauer (2005) and Ritchie and Barker (2006) call "mononormativity" involves the formation of new boundaries and borders between "the legitimate [heterosexual monogamous nuclear families] and the about-to-be legitimate [homosexual monogamous nuclear families] from those relationships and sexual practices which become more intensively inscribed as illegible [bisexual, multisexual, multipartnered families]" (Baird, 2007: 167).

I wish to state clearly that this book is not intended to undermine, displace, or negate the enormous work of gay and lesbian research, activism, and education campaigns to end homophobia and homonegativity in schools, nor to undermine, displace, or negate the significance of recognizing, affirming, and celebrating same-sex marriages and families in political, legal, educational, health, religious, and sociocultural systems and structures. Indeed, my own previous research and activism have been positioned within promoting sexual diversity education and fostering an antihomophobic school culture largely in relation to gay and lesbian children and same-sex families (see for example Martino and Pallotta-Chiarolli, 2003; Pallotta-Chiarolli, 2005b).

This book is also not intended to undermine, displace, or negate heterosexual monogamous families. Heterosexuality and monogamy should continue to be affirmed and celebrated, but should not be privileged or constructed as the only form of sexuality or relationship/family worthy of validation and attention within heteropatriarchal monogamist political, legal, educational, health, religious, and sociocultural systems and structures. Finally, this book is not intended to place bisexual and polyamorous individuals and their families and communities on a pedestal proclaiming their perfection with the purpose of recruiting new members. This would be merely another form of discrimination and inferiorization via simplistic representation, fetishism, and trivialization, thereby reducing bisexuality and polyamory to the level of trendification and exoticization for the salacious entertainment of the heteronormative Center. Rather, this book is about broadening, interrogating, and adding to ongoing debates and activism regarding sexual diversity and relationship diversity so that our work as educational researchers, policy makers and teachers does not merely assimilate or accommodate to the parameters still being set by a heteronormative Center, but transforms the very way we conceptualize, construct, and take action in regard to promoting healthy familial and sexual diversity. As Warner writes, "The impoverished vocabulary of the straight culture tells us that people should be either husbands and wives or (nonsexual) friends. Marriage marks that line. It is not the way many queers live. . . . Straight culture has much to learn from it. Queers should be insisting on teaching these lessons" (1999: 116).

Emens (2004) provides one example of such "lessons": eliminating the numerosity requirement (*one* woman and *one* man) which is still widely accepted as a requirement of marriage due to the persistent sociocultural, religious, economic, and political investments in the ideology of "supermonogamy," "the one-person-for-life ideal," even though it has largely been superseded by "serial monogamy," a linear progression from one exclusive partner to another. Indeed, whether the mainstream idealizes "supermonogamy" and practices "serial monogamy," there is a parallel system of "pretend monogamy" based on secret affairs outside the official monogamous union that are occurring concurrently.

Queer "lessons" also need to be learned in research. For example, in his study of gay men's polyamorous relationships, Bettinger (2005) discusses how most of the literature on gay male families has concentrated on the dyadic couple while occasionally noting that most of the men within these "dyads" were not monogamous. Singer also calls for better research to find out how many polyamorous families there might be, and how many of these are also raising children "to drive home that helping us [polyfamilies] is also 'pro-family'" (1996: 6).

Given the scarcity of educational research with families and students beyond sexual duality and relationship dyadism, I will now provide a detailed overview and analysis of my own research methods and processes. I hope that this will encourage further research that addresses the limitations of my own and extends the parameters of queer educational investigation and theorization.

"YOU FIND YOUR COMMUNITY WHERE THEY DON'T BOTHER TO LOOK": ACCESSING THE "X-FILES"

There's kids who live with all sorts of blended families, stepparents everywhere, adults everywhere, but if more than two of these adults happen to have sex together, even if they're so old and tired raising us kids that they hardly have sex anyway, but because they might or actually do IT every now and again, it's like they're from Pluto or from another galaxy. Meanwhile, we all know parents and teachers who call themselves monogamous and are cheating on each other but that's called normal. You do adultery and affairs on Earth but not honest polyamory.

—Alan, eighteen, bi son of heteropoly parents

How does a researcher go about accessing the "X-files" when they are officially constructed as nonexistent or at best insignificant in the current system of educational filing cabinets? Given the sensitivity and secrecy surrounding these issues, and therefore the difficulty in accessing participants, a variety of qualitative and ethnographic research methods were used in Australia and the United States. These included

- semistructured interviews with students, young adults, parents, and teachers;
- ethnographic methods such as participating in conferences and social events; collecting texts and documentation via attending social and support groups; participating in e-mail listservs of health groups, youth groups, GLBTIQ groups, and poly groups; analyzing popular cultural texts such as films, often referred to by research participants; and attending, presenting, and facilitating workshops and discussion groups at the "Loving More" polyamory conference at Harbin Springs in California in July 2001 and the Seventh International Bisexuality Conference in Sydney, 2002;
- analyzing some of the data from an e-mail survey conducted by Loving More magazine;
- analyzing e-mail postings on various bisexual, polyamorous, queer group listservs and e-mail correspondence with some of the members of these groups; and
- participating in the PolyResearchers e-mail listserv from its inception in 2006, which includes international academics, health/education professionals, and students discussing and debating resources and research.

Mindful of what Savin-Williams calls "clinical traps" wherein research recruitment and analysis flounder if they do not allow for the fact that "sexual behaviour, sexual attraction, and sexual identity questions do not always solicit similar populations" (2008: 135–36), I used very broad definitions of bisexuality and polyamory, and indeed worked on the premise of self-identification and self-ascription by my research participants. Throughout and everywhere, I asked to be connected to

- bisexual-identifying and/or bisexual-behaving young people at school or who had left school;
- parents of bisexual young people at school or who had left school;
- polyamorous parents or parents in multisexual families with children at school or who had left school;
- young people with polyamorous or multisexual families; and
- teachers and health/youth workers working with bisexual students and polyamorous families or multisexual families.

Sections of interviews from another Australian research project being conducted with Sara Lubowitz with women in relationships with bisexual-identifying and/or behaving men were also used if women discussed their children's schooling experiences (Pallotta-Chiarolli and Lubowitz, 2003; Pallotta-Chiarolli, forthcoming). Sections of interviews from a previous research project conducted with Wayne Martino on the diversity of masculinities in Australian schools were also used (Martino and Pallotta-Chiarolli, 2001a, 2001b, 2003). Specific research into bisexual young people's health was also undertaken simultaneously by my honors student (Martin, 2007) and further developed into separate publications (Martin and Pallotta-Chiarolli, 2009; Pallotta-Chiarolli and Martin, 2009).

Interview participants were given their transcripts to edit, veto, and add to in any way they wished. They were also given the option of choosing pseudonyms, and many did. In the interviews and group discussions, the following information was asked for but participants had the right to select which questions they responded to and were able to initiate or steer the conversations according to what mattered to them:

- Demographics such as age, gender, residential area, occupation, educational background, cultural identity and background, sexual identity, languages spoken, religious background
- Personal experiences, examples, opinions, recommendations regarding
  a. how schools could promote the health and well-being of bisexual young people and/or polyamorous parents and sexually diverse families;
  b. practical strategies, resources, and so on that should be in classrooms, in schools, in youth groups, parent groups, and local communities in fostering the health and well-being of bisexual young people and polyamorous parents and mixed-orientation families;
  c. examples of experiences of discrimination in school communities;
  d. examples of positive experiences in school communities;
  e. what was undertaken and by whom to overcome any negative issue or experience;
  f. recommendations/suggestions for further developing and promoting supportive school environments for bisexual students, polyamorous families, mixed-orientation families, and children from polyamorous and/or mixed-orientation families

The interview and discussion group research participants considered my long-standing participation in feminist, educational, multicultural, and queer communities as important in why they felt able to disclose details about their sexualities and/or families. Madison discusses research as "co-performative witnessing," wherein a researcher is "radically engaged and committed" (2007: 826). It is *"being there and with* as a political act in the excavation of subjugated knowledges and belongings for the creation of alternative futures" (2007: 829). I was seen to participate publicly through both the production of texts and speaking at activist, support, and social groups, and mainstream gatherings, such as within educational, religious, and health organizations and institutions. Since 2001, it was known that I had also been working on a novel for adolescents and young adults on the themes of polyamorous and bisexual families. Set within a multicultural multisexual Australia, the publication of *Love You Two* was met with widespread support from Australian and international poly and bi groups (Pallotta-Chiarolli, 2008).

A snowball sampling strategy was easily established as individuals known to me introduced other possible participants, who then informed others of my work, who then would contact me or just spontaneously tell me their "stories" as part of cafe conversations, party conversations, telephone calls, and e-mails. Friends in certain networks, communities, and organizations would direct potential participants to me or direct me to possible participants. E-mail list members would recommend participating in my research to others. While this type of sample is obviously biased in that it relies for its start on persons known to the researcher, the sample gradually enlarged to include individuals with diverse backgrounds and experiences. Snowball sampling was also effective as it is a "method that is suited to studies that focus on a sensitive issue or private matter" (Kowalewski, 1988: 214–15). This was especially pertinent as issues of trust and confidentiality were important in my research with "invisible" and/or marginal individuals and communities. However, particularly in relation to polyamorous families and young people, I am aware that my research methods were still ineffective in accessing larger representations of people of diverse socioeconomic, cultural, and religious locations, and transgendered identities. Noel points to the absence of closer examinations of "systemic privileges and benefits, particularly around such issues as: nationality, race/ethnicity, education, class, language, ability, age, gender, and sexuality" in much of the writing and research about polyamory, particularly in relation to how these variables impact upon "individual choice and personal agency" in the implementation of "multiple-partnership models leading to fulfilling relationships, families and communities" (2006: 604; see also Haritaworn Lin, and Klesse, 2006; Sheff, 2006, 2008). Most of my polyamorous research participants were "white, middle-class, college-educated individuals" who identified as male or female and with high levels of cyberliteracy, with which they were able to participate in social and support groups, particularly online, and thereby find themselves participating in my research (Noel, 2006: 615).

This discussion of how to diversify the range of research participants in "polyresearch" has been an ongoing theme on the PolyResearchers e-mail listserv. For example, Sheff talks about race, education, and class privileges that provide valuable buffers from the myriad potential negative outcomes associated with sexual and relational nonconformity. . . . The greater the resources, and the more privileges a person has to combat these potential losses, the more likely they are to engage in that risky behavior [and participate in communities, events, online groups and, subsequently, research projects]. . . . Perversity then becomes another luxury more readily available to those already in the dominant group. (2008: 16)

I hope that as polyamorous issues become more "known" and polyamorous people become more "visible," future research will be able to develop our knowledge of diversity within the label of "polyamory" beyond our current limitations, and the limitations of my research.

This leads to another issue that is relevant in effectively accessing "invisible" and/or marginal participants: the inclusion of the Internet in data-gathering methods. Many researchers are exploring how the Internet is redefining the "field" in fieldwork and expanding qualitative research beyond the bounds of real time, real space, and single locations via cyberspace, multiple time zones, and multilocations (Ito, 1996; Nardi, 1996; Eysenbach and Till, 2001; Hine, 2005). As with research being conducted with other hidden minorities (see Coomber, 1997; Hillier, Kurdas, and Horsley, 2001), the Internet has provided another reality for many polyamorous people and bisexual young people to communicate and substantiate each other's realities. As Klein and Schwartz state in their research using the postings on e-mail lists of married gay and bisexual men, "Chat rooms, newsgroups, and list-serves have revolutionized the lives of many people. . . . [They] have been able to share their stories safely and anonymously" (2001: 1; see also Peterson, 2001). As one list member commented to me on a polyamory listing,

> I've had more "real" communication in the last few weeks on this list with people like me and my family than I've had in total in my whole life. So I don't want to hear some white heterosexual married monogamous male psychiatrist tell me I need to get out into the community more. When the so-called community doesn't want to know you exist, you find your community where they don't bother to look. (Conrad, bi-poly dad)

A pioneering Australian study into the use of the Internet by same-sex attracted youth (SSAY) found that 85 percent of the young people reported that the Net

> played an important role in putting them in touch with others like them and 70% felt it played an important role in reducing their isolation. It offered a sense of community and support, especially when young people felt depressed or suicidal at some point (nearly 50%) . . . 62% of young men and 26% of young women found it important in facilitating Real Life contact and friendship with other SSAY. (Hillier et al., 2001: 1)

"Real Life" including school for many SSAY in the cited study "was a place in which most young people were hesitant to entrust their sexual identities, and Real Life encounters often loomed as threatening experiences" (2001: 2). A young bisexual person who I'd met via a bisexual listserv wrote the following to me in a personal e-mail:

> I hate it when these educational expert wannabes tell you that young people spend too much time on the computer and don't know how to talk to people in reality. Well, spend your money making schools safe for me to be able to talk about my life rather than wasting your funds on this kind of useless research. (Bryan, seventeen, bi student)

Then, perhaps realizing I might take this personally, being one of these "educational expert wannabes," he added, "So that's why I'm going to be part of your research, 'cause I think you might understand why I spend my time chatting to real peers on the Internet and not the fake shits at school." I hope this book demonstrates to Bryan and to all who participated in my research that I may have gained some understanding and am indeed calling on schools and their local communities to take action.

I am also calling for researchers that purport to address family diversity and same-sex attracted youth to also address the absences and misrepresentations about bisexuality, polyamory, and multisexual families in their own research. For example, Hillier and associates' study on Internet use by SSAY continually includes statements by and about gay and lesbian youth, as well as including a specific section on transgendered youth that has the following statement: "Many transgender people also identify as gay or lesbian and consequently experience both sexuality and gender-focused abuse and discrimination" (2001: 56). There is no statement that many transgender youth also identify as bisexual. Likewise, apart from a few quotations from young people who participated in the study where they discuss the "bi/gay/les rooms" (2001: 25), the only specific reference to bisexuality included in the whole report is the following quotation from a research participant, "Lex, 17 years":

> [The Internet] has allowed me to take control of my life, as opposed to being a "bi guy" and all the uncertainness/confusion/frustration that comes with that, I am now able to say to myself that I am gay, that's who I am, there's no way I can change etc so in that respect, the net, and the people I talk to on the net, has basically helped me to come to grips with myself. (2001: 22)

Although it is not the place of the researchers to dispute or deny the feelings of "Lex," there is no discussion by the researchers of alternative ways of representing bisexuality; how Lex's view does fit all too neatly into dominant discourses of sexual duality and bisexuality as "confusion"; and how this view could possibly be perpetuated in the Internet chat rooms, websites, and e-mail lists by listservers, organizations, and peers. The only comment that is made introduces Lex's words and draws attention to his experiences as an example of how young people "described the Net's influence in providing a space to . . . develop a stronger and more certain sense of self-identity," thereby inferring that a bisexual identity is weaker and less certain (2001: 22). The problematic consequences of these kinds of inferences and narrow representations on bisexual young people will be discussed in this book.

From 2000 to 2007, I read the e-mails posted to several polyamorous and bisexual listservs from the United States and Australia, following threads about schooling and education. On these lists, parents, families, young people, and activists shared their positive and negative daily experiences, asked questions, shared their hopes and fears, laughed and cried, labored and debated, relished and admonished over the daily realities of being border sexualities and border families. From the sharing of daily experiences with teachers to the sharing of the latest books, films, theories, and news items; from advising each other on how to deal with child welfare authorities to how to deal with religious fundamentalism in schools; from sharing where the next "meet-up," GLBTIQ youth dance party, or family day was being held in a specific city to making plans to lobby national governments, these lists were alive with discussion, debate, and dialogue. I think it is important to acknowledge the pioneers—list owners and list moderators—for having the wisdom and courage to begin the lists that are providing such support and social connectedness to so many young people and families whose health and well-being may already be severely compromised by the isolation and ostracism in their so-called real communities.

As a researcher, however, I was aware that working with e-mail postings to listservs requires a reconsideration of research ethics. Aspects of the technology and Internet-mediated processes of information gathering "generate new challenges that impact on the interpretation and implementation" of traditional research ethics codes (Clarke, 2001; see also Mann and Stewart, 2000). A major challenge is that Internet lists, catering so importantly for border sexualities and border families, inhabit borders themselves: "While the internet makes people's interactions uniquely accessible for researchers and erases boundaries of time and distance, such research raises new issues in research ethics, particularly concerning informed consent and privacy of research subjects, as the borders between public and private spaces are sometimes blurred . . . and communities may lie in between" (Eysenbach and Till, 2001).

For example, if a subscription or some form of registration is required to gain access to a discussion group, then most of the subscribers are likely to regard the group as a "private place" in cyberspace. Yet, simultaneously, the number of users of a community determines how "public" the space is perceived to be. A mailing list with ten subscribers is very different from a mailing list with a hundred or more subscribers, and, given that messages sent to mailing lists are sometimes also stored in Web-accessible archives, the actual number of people accessing messages may be greater than assumed and may be impossible to determine. Thus, a major question for researchers is whether privacy, anonymity, and confidentiality can be assured on the Internet. Most researchers concur that obtaining informed consent from all members of an online community is difficult (King, 1996). Indeed, seeking consent and announcing the presence of the researcher online may disrupt the group's interactions (Sanders, 2005). Thus, anonymity and protection of the members is considered to be the crucial factor (Hewson, Yule, and Vogel, 2003).

Well-known qualitative research theorist Denzin (1997; 1999), has presented himself as a "passive, lurking observer" in his research, as have Rafaeli and colleagues (1994), who decided that permission should not be sought for the use of publicly posted messages (see also Sanders, 2005). As Mann and Stewart report, "Debate about use of this material is active, with researchers beginning to rule not only that such sources sit within the public sphere of Internet services but that they can be freely referenced" (2000: 52; see also Jones, 1994). Unless there are specific guidelines for a mailing list wherein members must agree not to share information received on the list without express permission of the authors, it appears then that decisions about ethics in the online environment "are and will remain the responsibility of researchers themselves. Above all, the priority in qualitative research is to protect the well-being of participants" (Mann and Stewart, 2000: 63). According to Eysenbach and Till (2001), researchers must consider

- whether the research is intrusive and has potential for harm;
- whether the e-mail listserv group is perceived as "private" or "public" space;
- how the confidentiality of its members can be protected;
- whether and how informed consent should be obtained; and
- whether the intrusion of the researcher or publication of results has the potential to harm individuals or the community as a whole (see also McLennen, 2003).

Using Eysenbach and Till's (2001) checklist, I accessed several national and international listserv groupings over seven years, so a reader of my published data is unable to pinpoint which e-mail excerpts come from which listserv and when. Dates and times of e-mails as well as e-mail addresses are not included. As with the editing of interview and discussion group data, editing of e-mails included some obvious spelling and punctuation errors, and, to protect each person's confidentiality and anonymity, all names have been changed and specific references to places and identifying personal biographies discarded. I have never included a whole e-mail or e-mail discussion thread but paid particular attention to excerpting and separating e-mails from within one thread so that the whole e-mail I have read and worked with is never quoted. I have approached this research and the e-mail postings with the deepest respect for the young people and families in the listings, and I am undertaking this research in the hope that this material will help others struggling with similar issues in their schools and communities and to raise awareness within our educational systems. I have also wanted to promote and advertise the existence of these listings so that other young people and families are aware of their availability and efficacy as supportive spaces. Lastly, I have also occasionally sent in e-mails to these groups over the years, particularly to the group PolyResearchers, to advise of my forthcoming publications and events, and my previous publications and ongoing research is known to participants in the listings.

Another issue that arises, given the variety of research methods used and the enormous number on the Internet listservs, is the difficulty for researchers to provide a definite number of "participants" in the positivist modernist sense (Nielsen, 1997; Clarke, 2001). Thus, at best, the ninety-four research participants for this project can be broken down into

- bisexual and/or polyamorous young people in face-to-face interviews: sixteen
- bisexual and/or polyamorous young people in e-mail correspondence: thirteen
- multisexual and/or polyamorous parents in face-to-face interviews: eighteen
- multisexual and/or polyamorous parents in e-mail correspondence: twenty-two
- children of multisexual and/or polyamorous parents in face-to-face interviews: four
- children of multisexual and/or polyamorous parents in e-mail correspondence: ten
- bisexual and/or polyamorous teachers in face-to-face interviews: four
- bisexual and/or polyamorous teachers in e-mail correspondence: eight

"PASSIONATE SOCIOLOGY AND QUEER COYOTES": GIVING VOICE TO THE "X-FILES"

I actually got the courage to drop the word "polyamory" into a conversation with the principal at my kids' school. I was there for a parent information night and we got into this discussion about the families at his school. He was boasting about how the school accommodates all sorts of families, even, he said, *even* gay and lesbian families. The look he gave me said it all. He had no idea what I was talking about and started asking me what that "poly-what?" meant. And then I got frightened, I just froze, and had this vision of my kids being hauled into child welfare the next day or for psychiatric tests for abuse, and so I raced off pretending I needed to see another teacher. I avoided him for months and was so scared he was going to start asking my kids questions about their family and then trapping them into outing us.

—Naomi, hetero-poly mom with one hetero-mono
and one bi-poly male partner

Naomi's words above, constructed by her into a story, convey her fear and the mixed emotions of her attempt to speak to the principal. Thus, not only is she providing us with rich data in regard to the questions of this research, she is also allowing us to share her emotions, thereby experiencing something of how she feels being a polyamorous parent in a school. This book will present many such narratives, vignettes, and quotes from research participants as well as some of my own "stories" as a researcher. This method is in keeping with what Game and Metcalfe (1996) call "passionate sociology," which challenges modernist masculinist academic knowledge as "something dispassionate and disembodied, a product of the mind rather than the heart, body or soul" (1996: 4; see also Acker, Barry, and Esseveld, 1983; Du Bois, 1983; Lincoln, 1993). This research is a work of passionate sociology because "it celebrates an immersion in life, a compassionate involvement with the world and with others. It is a sociology concerned with the sharp and specific experiences of life; not seeking to dissolve these experiences in the pursuit of idealized abstraction, it wants to *feel* them" (Game and Metcalfe, 1996: 5; see also Usher, Bryant, and Johnston, 1997; Brew, 1998).

It is for these reasons that I have foregrounded the actual voices and stories of the research participants in what at times may be considered laboriously lengthy quotes and stories. However, this is a specific methodology whereby the researcher endeavors to represent the data "so that the humanness of these experiences is not lost . . . [and] must have the power to give the reader a [greater] sense of what it is that was experienced . . . than does the presentation of facts and information" (Goodfellow, 1998a: 105; see also Trinh, 1991; Goodfellow, 1997, 1998b).

As Naomi illustrates, people "lead storied lives and tell stories of those lives" (Connelly and Clandinin, 1990: 146). Denzin believes we need to keep in mind the distinction between "a life as lived, a life as experienced and a life as told" (1989: 30). Individuals construct narratives that are reflective, evaluative, "and also unconsciously selective . . . the act of constructing a narrative is identity work" (Duncombe and Marsden, 2004: 149). In this book, I use narrative and anecdote, and foreground many participants' voices strategically to offer a "complex sense of the lived" alongside and interwoven with "the reported" (Ely et al., 1997: 88). This way of presenting qualitative research findings "has power" because it allows "readers to enter into a vicarious experience." It brings readers "into the settings, characters, actions, dialogue and events of the research" and "let[s] our readers experience along with us the unfolding of the research story" (Ely et al., 1997: 64).

In order to give the reader an insight into the people behind the voices/ quotes, I have provided some information at the end of each quote according to what the research participant disclosed or wanted said about themselves. This always includes the name of the person (a pseudonym unless an interviewee wanted their real name used) and some of the following:

- age of young people and/or if they are the children of bi/poly parents;
- sexuality (e.g., bi, hetero);
- secondary school student (student) or university student;
- polyamorous or monogamous (poly or mono);
- relationship structure (e.g., group marriage, or specifying the partners of the participant);
- if they are teachers and/or parents.

Naomi's story also illustrates my use of standpoint epistemology, which describes and articulates issues and values from the perspectives of the participants (see McLennen, 2003; Homfray, 2008). Lugones (1990, 1994), a Chicana mestiza researcher from the United States, describes mestizaje research methodology or standpoint epistemology as "world-traveling" and "playfulness," suggesting that within a human rights framework of doing no harm and not condoning harm or abuse:

> Playfulness demands . . . a willingness to explore new behavior or attitudes without determining the "rightness" or "wrongness." It can also be used . . . to allow one to "try on" a different set of codes and rules in order to explore its own internal logic, sense of morality and context. At the end of a playful journey, one finds that the victims of arrogant perception are really "subjects, lively beings, resistors," [and] "constructors of [their own] visions." One can recognize and respect their independence and yet understand their interconnectedness with oneself. (1990: 204)

This question in regard to "rightness" and "wrongness," moral universality or relativity, arose in my work with participants in regard to whether I should accept their versions of the truth, and thereby see my role as one of describer, or to challenge them and thereby disrupt their evocations of their lived realities. In presenting the rationalizations and justifications of a group or person, I could be seen to be accepting these rationalizations and justifications. I could be accused of presenting a one-sided and distorted view. In line with mestizaje research methodology as exemplified by Lugones (1990) above, standpoint research methodology, and traditional social science methodology into "deviance," this research is not presenting a distorted view of "reality," but is presenting a view of the particular reality that engages the research participants.

Becker (1973) states that the viewpoint of conventional society toward so-called deviance is usually well known. Therefore, there is a need to study the views of those who participate in so-called deviant activities and lifestyles because in this way "we will fill out the most obscure part of the picture" (1973: 174). Becker then proceeds to query/deconstruct this stance: "I suspect that, in fact, we know little enough about the viewpoints of either parties involved. . . . We do not know what all the interests of rule enforcers are. Nor do we know to what extent ordinary members of conventional society actually share, to some degree, the perspectives of deviant groups" (1973: 174). This comment is particularly pertinent to many of my research participants who may appear within educational systems to be heterosexual young people in conventional heterosexual families, or adults who appear to be "ordinary members of conventional society" and then are revealed in this research to be bisexual and/or in multisexual and polyamorous families.

Indeed, my initial passion for undertaking this research arose out of the awareness of certain "real Others" who were not getting access to public and research spaces such as those of educational, sexuality, and family research. This was also a motivation for many of my research participants, as Jack, a bisexual polyamorous young man at university, explains:

> I don't want to do research into this. I don't want to prove this to you. It should be obvious, you know . . . when you offered me the opportunity to talk about this as a young bisexual, polyamorous man at university, it bothers me that I have to sit here and be a resource, that we have to number everything, that we have to tack it down, and if we can't prove it then it's not real, when to me it seems like these things are self-evident truths. It's so blindingly obvious . . . but you need to gather it. No one listens unless there is this solid weight. (Jack, bi-poly student)

Passionate sociology also asks that we consider the accessibility of our research. Again, this was an issue for my research participants, as Jack points out:

> The power that lies with academics and teachers and the majority of educational institutions lies in this really dense, inaccessible information. People say to me

there's a lot of information out there, and there is. I can walk into our library and find a pile of books on sexuality. I can walk in here [in your office], and it's all here, but where is the accessibility? Where is it in the media, and I'm not talking about goddamn queer is *Will and Grace*, you know, this standard night clubby, you know, upper-middle-class New York bullshit. Like, where is the fact that a young Australian male could like boys and girls, and maybe hey he wants to have a couple of different relationships at the same time, and it's not actually lying or cheating. (Jack, bi-poly student)

The powerful, emotive, insightful voices of the research participants such as Naomi and Jack, and the use of narrative and anecdote as accessible ways of knowing, are border research methods, as they border the poetic and the academic, the analysis and the story. Increasingly, ethnographic, anthropological, and other qualitative researchers are stating that research reporting can move beyond what they consider to be the dry and impoverished, inaccessible language of traditional academic writing. Researchers can choose to work from a place of acceptance of the emotional and intellectual dissonance, which is part and parcel of the process of trying to come to "know" social sites and their peoples (hooks, 1994b). As Altork states,

> We need to ask, first of all, whether we want to study a culture in a calculating, solely intellectual way, and then—when we turn to the task of bringing the culture to others—whether those whom we study would want to be represented in that way. Finally, if I dared, I would ask: who would want to read such an account? How many papers and articles have anthropologists read or listened to over the years from which every ounce of sensual and emotional content had previously been bled in the name of credibility? Do we really have to avoid lyrical description, subjectivity, and the personal voice in order to hold our place in the line-up of respected social scientists? (1995: 129)

Passionate sociology is also about empowerment and agency, as it aims to "unsilence the silenced" (Le Compte, 1993). As Butler explains, "Restriction on speaking is enforced through the regulation of psychic and public identification, specifically, by the threat of having to live in a radically uninhabitable and unacceptable identification. . . . The public sphere is constituted in part by what cannot be said and what cannot be shown. The limits of the sayable" (2004a: xvii). By foregrounding participant voices and perspectives, encouraging them to tell their stories, this research constructs participants as agents who uncover, keep covered, and discover in order to challenge the "limits [and costs] of the sayable." Through "uncovering" aspects of their lives, they assist research and the empowering of others in their situations, while simultaneously my role as a researcher is to maintain a "cover" for them in order not to harm families' and young people's lives within their everyday worlds. Situated on the border of uncovering and covering is "discovering" by participants about themselves and about others. Protected and strategic unsilencing allows participants to discover an empowering impetus and a growing confidence to continue to find ways of being agents in the negotiation of the tensions surrounding the issues of stigma and marginality in their lives, and to challenge the silence and denial regarding their locations within schools, the wider society and their communities of significant others. Thus, while undertaking research with the marginal within the marginal may appear to be risking "academic rewards" (Rubin, 2001: 712), this research is committed to the feminist research ethos that emphasizes "participant empowerment" (Yip, 2008: 7). Emancipatory research is not focused purely on "the contribution it makes to academic knowledge" but displays "particular consideration to the use that research may then be put to, or the effect it has on those being researched" (Homfray, 2008: 8). For example, at regular points throughout the years of this research, the various groups, listservs, and individuals who participated in my research were kept aware of my publications, and events and contacts I came across. This regular contact was put to good use by the groups themselves as part of their activist, social, and support objectives.

Here is an example of how the very act of participating in this research impacted upon an individual participant. Josie, a young bisexual woman, found herself crying during the interview and began to reflect on why:

> I think why I'm feeling emotional is that I don't often think about it [being bisexual]. I don't because it's something that even though I'm an open person, I still feel like it's something I don't understand yet and that's what scares me . . . because I don't know what's going on and I feel like is it fate, is it destiny, is it me, what's going on? (Josie, bi-mono)

As the conversation continued, Josie realized she had internalized the biphobic messages from society and was self-problematizing while never feeling confident enough to raise these issues with anyone before. As her words in the following chapters show, the interview became a space to think through these issues, to feel empowered, and to ask me for contact details of various groups and individuals she could access.

In summary, "passionate sociologists" working with people in the borderlands become a catalyst for border crossings: by empowering the border dwellers wishing to cross "la frontera" (the border) and by raising the awareness of those in the mainland of the existence and experiences of border dwellers. The role of these researchers can be described as what Valadez and Elsbree (2005) call "queer coyotes," serving as "mediators" in these queer border crossings, operating and navigating "within and outside the border of social interactions" of the dominant Center and the margins

(2005: 175; see also Naples, 2004). "Queer coyote" researchers have four characteristics in border crossing research:

- they operate in "secreto": they are secretive and protective of the research participants while simultaneously using the research process to help them move forward and cross borders;
- they know "los codigos": they know the codes of both the border zone and Center, and thus teach, explain, and work with the codes of each to the other;
- they have "la facultad": they can read different situations and contexts quickly and accurately, seeing into the deeper realities below the surface; and
- they express their sincere "compromiso": they have a commitment toward educational transformation and border pedagogy. "We are in union with other researchers who seek social justice for all groups and can make a difference for border dwellers" (Valadez and Elsbree, 2005: 176–77).

"WRITE THOUSANDS OF WORDS": AN OUTLINE OF THE FOLLOWING CHAPTERS

Josiah: You're kidding me; you're writing a whole book stating the obvious?

Maria: What's the obvious?

Josiah: That you can be turned on by both guys and girls and that your family may not be one mum plus one dad.

Maria: Well, sometimes people don't want to know the obvious.

Josiah: Well, write thousands of words and make it compulsory reading in this school.

—from my interview with Josiah, fifteen, bi student

The following chapter, chapter 2, will provide

- a theoretical overview of border theory and various other theories of multiplicity and insider/outsider/no-sider positionings, and how these theories are useful in understanding the social locations of bisexuality and polyamory;
- a more detailed explanation of terms such as bisexuality and polyamory and how these are being utilized and defined in this research; and
- an introduction to three broad performative strategies of "messing up" that I will use to "file" or classify the experiences and strategies of research participants with schools.

These strategies are

- strategies of passing: "getting the glass slipper to fit" (George, 1992) through normalization, silence, erasure, absence, mimicry, and assimilation in relation to school settings;
- strategies of bordering: "haciendo caras/making faces" (Anzaldua, 1990) through negotiating, balancing, weaving, maneuvering between the private world of home and public world of school; and
- strategies of polluting: being "the stranger, the undecidable" (Douglas, 1966; Bauman, 1988–1989) through noncompliance, personal agency, outing, resistance, and politicization by polluting the school world with one's bisexual and polyamorous existence. It must be stated here that "polluting" is used as a positive term of strength, agency, and empowerment, and is not intended to imply negative, insidious, harmful, or underhanded machinations. Indeed, Douglas (1966) refers to Jesus Christ and Martin Luther King as two "pollutants" who, via their noncompliance, innovation, and resistance to their dominant worlds, were able to initiate far-reaching empowering political, social, and legal outcomes.

These three strategies are framed by and impacted upon by three interweaving social processes of positioning that will also be explored in chapter 2. They are

- social ascription: being what external society and its systems, such as an educational system, demand from an individual and family;
- community acknowledgement: being what one's significant others positively affirm or negatively discourage, such as in a school community, gay and lesbian community, and ethnic community; and
- personal agency: being what the individual or family actually does despite the regulations and oppressions from both the wider society and one's communities.

Chapter 3 will explore the above theories and strategies in relation to bisexuality in schools, both bisexual students and students with bisexual parents. It will provide a comprehensive overview of the available literature, popular cultural texts, and research in relation to bisexual young people's health, well-being, and education before presenting the findings of my empirical research.

Chapter 4 will explore polyamorous, multipartnered, and multisexual families and their experiences in schools. As in chapter 3, it is important to collate and discuss any available literature, popular cultural texts, and research in this area before presenting my own findings.

Both chapters 3 and 4 will include recommendations made by research participants for policy, programming, and pastoral care in educational settings.

Chapter 5 will summarize the findings of the research and call for the need to move from models of difference and dichotomy to models of diversity and multiplicity.

2

"On the Bi- and Poly-Borders"

Theorizing Dichotomy and Diversity

I'm sitting in a café in inner-city Melbourne with two young university undergraduates who identify as bisexual. They're interested in the theories I'm going to use to try and "make sense" of their stories. I begin to explain the theories of border dwelling, the "undecideables," "the third space," "pollution theory," and am soon lost in an intellectual orgasm of words like metissage and mestizaje.

"Messy what?" the young man interrupts my cerebral pleasure, leaning forward.

I can't help laughing. "Mestizaje theory. It's about borderlands, intermixture and multiplicity."

The young woman laughs too. "Mesti . . . messy . . . how do you say it?"

I repeat slowly. "Mestizaje."

She laughs again and gives a thumbs up. "You mean, 'how messy-are-ya'?"

I raise my cup of coffee to her. "Well, exactly."

—from my research notes

This chapter is an overview of the theories and terms I use "in making sense" of participants' perceptions, lived experiences, and stories of those experiences. In presenting a discussion and exploration of the theories of mestizaje—"borderlands, intermixture, and multiplicity"—and some definitions of terms of identification, I hope to provide some theoretical and discursive tools with which "messiness" can be situated, understood, and articulated, but without reducing its multiplicity to simplistic,

29

dichotomous, and homogenizing meanings. Via theory and existing literature, I will

- define and outline bisexuality and polyamory;
- consider their positionings according to social ascription, community belonging, and personal agency; and
- present metaphors of passing (normalization), bordering (negotiation), and polluting (noncompliance).

Of course, should sitting in this chapter's café prove cerebrally cumbersome rather than pleasurable, I invite you to cross into the next two chapters where the results of my research are presented more directly.

THEORIZING BIFURCATION AND BORDER DWELLING

Aristotelian dualisms are common in contemporary Western discourses of social relations and identifications. These Western discourses have embedded in them dichotomous logics of "either/or" that tend to force relationships, identity-formations, and institutional structuring into bifurcated categories. However, the reality of contemporary social relations and identifications is not dichotomous but rather fluid, transitory, fragmented, episodic. Dichotomous logics of "either/or" do damage to the lived reality of people's lives, including the lives of bisexual young people and "queerly mixed" families who are part of the communities of our schools. The logics of bifurcation generate an interpretative terrain that reduces, erases, or distorts the lived complexities of individuals and families and intensifies harassment and oppression against anyone constructed as inferior or abnormal in the superior/inferior and normal/abnormal hierarchical dualisms.

The logics I utilize in this research that attempt to describe and interpret the complex realities of contemporary social relations and identifications without dichotomous reduction and distortion can be defined by the French term "metissage" and the Spanish term "mestizaje." Both these terms mean mixture and multiplicity, or as so aptly translated by the young people in the anecdote above, being "messy." As Bottomley writes, "We have no polite word in English like the French *meteque* or the Spanish *mestizo*, but people who celebrate being in-between . . . have indeed begun to take up some of the space created by multiple identities" (1992: 136).

In ancient Greece, the "metis" was an allegorical figure of "cunning intelligence" who practiced the "art of transformation and transmutation" in order not to be subsumed by dichotomizing systems: "Cunningly deceiving their oppressors, the oppressed artfully transform and transmute themselves in order to survive the power systems destroying them . . . [and] steadily eat away at the social-political-economic systems' scaffolding, transforming the oppressive society while no one is looking" (Worley, 2006: 517–18).

Mestizaje, or borderland theory, has been amplified and adopted by Latina/Chicana-American feminists of diverse sexualities, such as Cherrie Moraga (1981), Gloria Anzaldua (1987a, 1987b), Maria Molina (1994), and Maria Lugones (1994) in exploring the interweaving of ethnicity, gender, and sexuality. Mestizaje theory seeks to define identity as "metis," being in process, multiplaced, and shifting. Individuals locate themselves and are constructed by social, political, and cultural forces as being "mestizi," meaning located within, outside, on the borders, or "slipping between the cracks" of social, cultural, political, and educational groups and established discourses. Mestizaje persons within institutions such as education often find themselves challenging and being challenged by the discourses and political ideologies of what is binarily constructed as the powerful Center, such as the heteronormative monogamist Center, and the power-challenging or excluded Margins, such as the homonormative sexual duality Margin.

The realities of bisexual students and "queerly mixed"/polyamorous families in schools will demonstrate the powerful workings of bifurcation in dominant educational and youth health paradigms and discourses. I will utilize and draw from mestizaje theory to illustrate the complexities of borderland realities these dichotomous frameworks constrain, distort, and silence, as well as explore strategies and tools that attempt to move beyond traditional binary paradigms in the understanding of sexual diversity and family diversity (Rambukkana, 2004). Dichotomous discourses have constructed a borderland within which mestizaje persons such as bisexual youth and multisexual and polyamorous families weave and live their "multiple threads" or multiple realities by inhabiting "multiple lifeworlds" (Cope and Kalantzis, 1995), one of those being the world of school.

Thus, borderland theory is a tool in the deconstruction of a dominant ideology of bifurcation in order to make visible and explore the not-so-orderly identities that underlie Identity, the realities that are situated within Reality, the truths that are concealed by the Truth: "Like a fault-line, mestizaje uncovers what underlies social groups and what precisely they try to mask by repeating well-oiled discourses. At this point, classifications stumble, stories of origin skid out of control, and commemoratives become derisive or cynical, and there results an abyss, a nonmemory, and fractured identities" (Audinet, 2004: 135).

It is those border zones of "too much truth" (Derrida, 1981: 105) constructed as "unreal" or negated in dichotomous discursive boundaries in relation to sexuality and family, that will be explored (see also Trinh, 1991). Those border spaces exist as entities in themselves with all the dilemmas of weaving new patterns and constructing new discursive boundaries of identity, truth, and reality as they negotiate and resist the dichotomous patterns and discursive boundaries that exclude or distort them. These weavings and reconstructions make mestizaje "a fertile element," which, "even if disclaimed, makes society progress . . . opens up a new zone" (Audinet, 2004: 107). As Zerubavel writes, "We very often experience boundaries as if they were a part of nature. . . . It is we ourselves who create them, and the entities they delineate are, therefore, figments of our own mind. Nonetheless, our entire social order rests on the fact that we regard these fine lines as if they were real" (1991: 3).

Bisexuality and polyamory reveal the tenuousness of those "fine lines." For example, Goetstouwers (2006) found in his research that bisexual men appear to be seen by gay men as a challenge to their sense of security and fixity, of boundary and delineation, in regard to their own sexual identification and culture. Similarly, in her study of Australian women who had "relinquished" the sexual identity of lesbian after having relationships with men, McLean discussed the power of "discourses of authenticity" within the lesbian community (2008: 311; see Jeffreys, 1999, for an example of these discourses). The prevalence of these discourses raises questions about "the power of identity politics within sexual minority communities in shaping sexual identity boundaries," and the "perceived norms that create boundaries" and prevent "flexibility from being fully realised" (McLean, 2008: 311).

The explorations and weavings of metissage are framed largely by the discourses of power, regimes of truth, and sites of resistance and agency. "Truth" is understood as a system of ordered procedures or the production, regulation, distribution, circulation and operation of statements. Power is comprised of historical systems aligned across structures, institutions, rituals, practices, and individual lives, and the particular use of the products of these alignments, (such as knowledges and practices), to interrogate, regulate, supervise, train, and confine the behaviors and subjectivities of individuals and groups (Foucault, 1985; see also Bourdieu, 1977; Grosz, 1993). It is important to note the multiplicity inherent in Foucault's theory here: there may be two or more systems of power in conflict or convergence, each with its own "regime of truth." Hence, heteronormativity, homonormativity, and opposite-sex- and same-sex-couple families are three unequal systems of power that frame and marginalize bisexuality and "queerly mixed" families. However, power is also found in sites of resistance, struggle, and change as we shall see when we explore the agency and strategies bisexual students, multipartnered and multisexual families, and their communities and support organizations display in resisting and maneuvering around, within, and between these systems of power: "Mestizaje unfolds at the speed of individual adventures, but also at the speed of the collective" (Audinet, 2004: 146).

Unlike Zipkin who believes labels are "a necessary step to take before we get to the place where we don't need them anymore" (1992: 72), mestizaje theory does not argue for the need to do away with all frameworks, boundaries, identities, and truths. This absolute unfixedness would only be the other polar extreme of absolute fixedness, becoming another form of regimentation and oppression (see Weeks, 1987; Seidman, 1993). After all, most of the participants in this research have intentionally ascribed themselves labels such as "bisexual," "polyamorous," "queer," "married." Thus, my mestizaje theoretical analysis of the research data is situated within Butler's position: "I'm permanently troubled by identity categories, consider them to be invariable stumble-blocks, and understand them, even promote them, as sites of necessary trouble" (1991:14; see also Weeks, 1995). Mestizaje theory argues for the need to consider the reality of a third multiple space, a metissage borderland space, in which identity is multiple, plural, shifting, with multiple parallel processes of definition and dissection (see Trinh, 1990a; DeMunck, 1992; Keith and Pile, 1993; Sedgwick, 1993; Phelan, 1994; Heckert, 2005).

One of the strategies adopted by those in this third multiple space on the borders of various communities' insider/outsider positionings, and bifurcated classification systems, is the silencing of what those within the communities consider "taboo" and "unreal." First, this silencing is believed to prevent the undermining of the collective efforts and efficacy of the group's work, and second, it is hoped by the border persons that they will not be ostracized by the rest of the group, who may be the only allies they have. As Rust writes, "The fact that reality is not always as discrete as we wish it were leads us not to reject our categories, but rather to reject reality" (1992: 285; see also Soja and Hooper, 1993). Thus, bisexual students may remain silent when their realities are either ignored or subsumed into the gay, lesbian, or straight categories. Similarly, children from multisexual or heterosexually polyamorous families may see their realities as so far outside the discursive framework of the known and the spoken about families at school that they may align themselves with the children of heterosexual families or of gay and lesbian families, or may opt to leave any reference to their family lives outside the school gates. Indeed, many of the young people and families I worked with in this research could identify with the following description of border dwelling by Trinh:

> But every place she went
> they pushed her to the other side
> and that other side pushed her to the other side
> of the other side of the other side
> Kept in the shadows of the other
> (1990b: 328).

For many marginal groups, the existence of a mestizaje borderland space, or the marginal-within-the marginal, is often problematic as it can be seen to counteract their need for a united homogenous front in order to provide security and support for its members and a location to plan and implement strategies of resistance to the Central, mainstream power. For example, bisexuality and "queerly mixed" families have been considered as potentially dangerous to the gay and lesbian political agenda because of their very "messing up" of neat community unity and sameness. They problematize mainstream gay and lesbian strategic use of two arguments: first, the assimilationist argument to "seduce" or "tame" the dominant group with the "we are just like you" or "we will be just like you, not a threat to you" position, as seen in the same-sex marriage debates; and second, the argument of distinction and boundary maintenance that states that gays and lesbians are so distinct from heterosexuals there is no danger of "messing or "blurring" the segregationist boundary between them. Thus, there will apparently be no infiltration and pollution of the heterosexual side by deceptive and untrustworthy bisexuals and no reaping of heterosexual privilege by bisexuals who still wish to claim marginality alongside gays and lesbians. These two arguments are threatened by the reality of bisexuality and "queerly mixed" families. For example, when considering the "bisexuality reaps heterosexual privilege" contention, Angelides asks, "If bisexuality is a luxury with heterosexual privilege, is it not conceivable that such privilege provides it with potentially subversive possibilities for the infiltration of the economy of (hetero)sexuality?" (1994: 42; see also Angelides, 2001). As will become evident in my research, this subversive possibility is very pertinent to many bisexual parents who construct publicly proclaimed families with opposite-sex partners, thereby infiltrating the "economy" of heterosexual families.

Returning to the rigid conformity and uniformity that a minority community may operationalize as a means of inserting itself into the mainstream (Udis-Kessler, 1990; Pallotta-Chiarolli, 1995a), it is important to emphasize how this leaves individuals who had thought they were members of various communities questioning what happens when, "who I say I am may not coincide with the views of the group I claim, nor with the [external] others' views of me" (Pettman, 1986: 6).

With shock, sadness, and disillusionment, I witnessed an example of how "hegemonic gayness" (Dowsett, 1997), or what I call homonormativity, becomes operational when, in the late 1990s, bisexuals, as well as transgendered persons (other "X-files" who also problematize and "mess up" sex-gender dualities) were rejected as members of the Sydney Gay and Lesbian Mardi Gras. Applicants who indicated they were bisexual on their Mardi Gras application forms had to "state succinctly what special factors might persuade the board that [they] should be admitted." This exclusionary practice became an example of how fin de siècle Australian bisexual young people became aware of and challenged "classifications" and "commemoratives" (Audinet, 2004: 135; see also Savin-Williams, 2005). The following journalist in a queer paper voiced the concerns of many "dispossessed children": "The Sydney Gay and Lesbian Mardi Gras evolves from radical grassroots into a hegemony run by the dispossessed children of the establishment. There is an awful inevitability to social patterns, and queers haven't immunity from it" (McGregor, 1996: 39).

Bisexual support and activist groups raised their concerns at a New South Wales Anti-Discrimination Board (ADB) community consultation meeting. Bi Pride Australia founder Glenn Vassallo stated,

> Bisexuals feel our exclusion from Mardi Gras is a most obvious example of institutionalized discrimination. . . . This is happening because we are a minority group within the mainstream gay and lesbian community. . . . It is very similar to what has happened, and still happens, to gay, lesbian, bisexual and transgendered people in mainstream society. (in McQuarrie, 1999: 4)

A few years later, due to the effective campaigning of bisexual, transgender and other organizations, as well as other factors such as negative and bemused queer media reporting, and religious and political smugness in the heteronormative mainstream media, which of course relished this "divide and conquer" opportunity, bisexual and transgender applicants were "admitted" again. Indeed, by the thirtieth anniversary of the Mardi Gras in 2008, celebrating its evolution from a protest march, resulting in many arrests and police aggression, to a major cultural, political, and international tourist event replete with police marching bands, the bisexual Korean-American comedian Margaret Cho was honored with the title of "Chief of Parade" and led the parade in an open-top Saab.

I wish to draw attention to two other main factors for this reversal: declining membership numbers, and subsequent financial problems. One of the major reasons for these economic concerns was that many younger queers refused to become members of the Mardi Gras, and many bisexual young people refused to attend the events that were organized by an institution that refused them membership. The Mardi Gras was rapidly being seen as belonging to the older generation, so they took their partying and money elsewhere, often to straight spaces that were being queerified, or created their own "GLIBTQS" (gay, lesbian, intersex, bisexual, transgender, questioning, queer, straight spaces). As Savin-Williams states, "Gay adults have stopped listening to their gay children, to the new generation" (2005: 21). In response, bisexual young people undertook acts of "social creative defiance" (Lugones, 1994: 478) and constructed their own codes and locations for sexual/emotional engagement in response to such external hierarchical dualisms, negations, exclusions, and invalidations. These "playful reinventions" and "curdled behavior" (Lugones, 1994: 478) have been defined by Britzman (1998: 118) as "difficult knowledge [that] may be refused" by those in positions of power and gate-keeping.

An example of this social defiance is what one twenty-year-old gay male friend, Sam, wrote to me at the time:

> It's [Mardi Gras] getting more and more outdated and overpriced. It's run by these boring old conservative middle-class gay and lesbian liberationists who are just like my parents trying to tell me who I can hang out with and who's not family. I thought the whole point of the original Mardi Gras was to protest such bullshit sexuality discrimination so that the next generations like us could all mix and support each other. So I'm not going to go to any event where I can't even take some of my best friends, including straight mates with queer sensibilities. Yeah, some of my best friends are straight boys. Gee, Maria, it means you shouldn't go 'cause you're straight, but you're too queer for the straights and now too queer for the gays!

I remember how this last comment about me, and similar comments made by other friends at the time, made me aware of my own border positioning. I was often and am still labeled "queer straight" by many friends and professional colleagues, and I relish(ed) this mestiza label as defining a multiple site of interwoven identifications and community allegiances and memberships. Yet, in a situation such as the Mardi Gras Board implementing a biphobic and transphobic admission system, my mestizaje border zone became a site of conflicting identifications, allegiances, and memberships. In my personal and professional life, I was researching, teaching, and actively campaigning against homophobia and endorsing the importance of cultural events such as the Mardi Gras. Indeed, I had worked and associated closely with some of the instigators of such a regulatory biphobic/transphobic admission system as well as with proponents of the system who were otherwise outstanding leaders of the wider gay and lesbian community. Simultaneously, I was personally and professionally linked with bisexual communities around Australia and had always declared my work to be about sexual diversity and inclusivity rather than the construction of new sexual hierarchies. And yet here I was working and associating with gay and lesbian leaders who were ousting bisexual members from the leading national queer cultural organization. Meanwhile, my own heterosexual identity, marriage, and motherhood meant I was seen as being part of the "mainstream society," the heteronormative Center that framed and fueled such divisions and hierarchies within the Margins. Thus, for a few years, I experienced and had to negotiate the tensions and contestations around me, ensuring that I maintained my border status by both critiquing and supporting the various groups I was affiliated with and enduring their mixtures of criticism and support of me and my work.

As is evident in the above Mardi Gras example, mestizaje persons are not outside or in transcendence of dichotomous identity and community categories and epistemologies, but are located on the borderland of multiple possibilities in relation to these categories. Border dwellers complicate and interrogate binary classifications even as they acknowledge them in order to negotiate their own positioning and possibilities. Probyn's term, "outside belonging," tries to describe the notion of movement "in between categories of specificity" (1996: 9), of moving beyond these binaries to a recognition of fluidity, hybridity and intermixture, and heterogeneity within and between the opposites.

This notion of the "something else besides" is also found in Bhabha's work in relation to postcolonial diasporic cultures, and is highly pertinent in this book's discussion on family diversity and sexual diversity: "There is a sense of disorientation, a disturbance of direction, in the 'beyond': an exploratory, restless movement . . . here and there, on all sides" (1994: 1). Bhabha is interested in how subjects are formed in the interstices, in excess of the sum of the "parts" of difference (see also Burbules, 1997).

There is a need to explore and understand how these theorized possibilities translate or are reflected in lived mestizaje realities, such as in the school lives of my research participants, who inhabit the actual boundary, fence, interval, gap itself. There is a need to make visible the existence of mestizaje identities consisting of unclassifiability, impurity, hybridity, and fluidity without scissoring them into another state of fixity and homogeneity as living the New Truth, the Only Identity, the Universally Shared Reality. Hence, in this research, rather than upholding themselves as the New True and Only way of parenting that should be Universally adopted, poly parents speak of wanting equal affirmation alongside other family structures. This begins with an awareness of how they are currently "in between" normative and deviant constructions of family and an acknowledgment of how this "outsiders within" positioning influences their subjectivity and public identity and the way they parent and negotiate the public and private settings of their families.

One of these public settings is the school. The queerification of education requires addressing bifurcation and border dwelling because "the political effectiveness" of queer as metissage is "its polyvocality" (Angelides, 1994: 82; see also Angelides, 2001). Mestizaje queer theory, as described and applied to the lived experiences of the research participants in this book, problematizes static and preordained sexuality and family concepts and axes of identification within education in order to "incite border dialogues, to encourage boundary crossings, and [destabilize] categories" (Angelides and Bird, 1995: 4).

"TO BE OR NOT, OR BOTH OR NEITHER": BISEXUALITY AS BORDER SEXUALITY

When I think of my bisexuality, I think of Shakespeare. Now wouldn't my English teacher be happy? Well, actually no, the biphobe! I think of, "to

be or not to be, that is the question." Like Hamlet sitting on a fence trying
to decide, I'm supposed to decide to be straight or gay. Well, no way, I'll
stay on that fence checking everything out because I can see clearly from
there in all directions and if you want to get with me, you'll join me up
there. Some people reckon Shakespeare was bi. He wrote some stuff for
his male lovers, I've heard. But not one of my teachers ever talked about
that. No way! Would've made studying his stuff way more interesting.

—Marita, seventeen, bi student

Can human beings love both men and women at the same time? They
can if they can.

—Klein (1993: 6)

Bisexuality is both complex and fluid. It involves at least three dimensions:
behavior, attractions, and identity (Klein, 1993; Richters, 1997; Savin-
Williams, 2005; 2008). These dimensions do not map onto one another
in any simple or straightforward way, either at one point in time or pre-
dictively over time (Boulton and Fitzpatrick, 1996). Bisexuality rejects the
norm/deviance either/or model. It challenges binarily constructed assumptions of our society: the duality of gender, the necessity of bipolar relationships, the lack of viable alternatives to monogamy apart from what is
derided as "promiscuity." In doing so, bisexuals become suspect, or are seen
as cowards. Many who face this conflict succumb and pledge allegiance to
one of the politically legitimate categories, whether it be the dominant heteronormative or subordinate homonormative (Bradford, 2004).

Here is an example of a homonormative coercive stance on bisexuality:
its denial or exclusion from discourse in order to ensure an "inclusion" into
a "subculture": "Our disbelief in bisexuality works to women's advantage
. . . [because it] ensures their inclusion in the lesbian subculture" (Murphy,
1990: 88). Indeed, Jeffreys (1999) asserts that membership in a bisexual
subculture and allegiance to a bisexual politics is completely incompatible
with a lesbian feminist subculture and lesbian feminist politics because
of bisexual politics' "lack of any feminist critique of the construction of
love and desire and all their manifestations." Given that bisexual activists
consider the promotion of such a critique as actually one of their major
objectives, it is interesting to read the simplistic and stereotypical examples
that Jeffreys provides in support of her contention. She states that the "vast
majority of bisexual politics . . . is motivated by a sexual freedom agenda of
anything goes." She foregrounds the devastating effects on married women
whose husbands engage in secret sexual acts with other men, and frames
all forms of nonmonogamy and sadomasochism as examples of how "a bisexual politics privileges men and patriarchy." Jeffreys then concludes that
"even bisexual feminist activists who have a critique of heterosexuality and

seek to incorporate feminist ethics of love and sex into their relationships are distinguished from lesbian feminists by having chosen to love men" (1999: 284).

Hence, as exemplified by the above, the "concept of immutable sexual identity" is a political strategy that can be used by both the dominant and marginal discourses. "Bisexuals by their very existence sabotage that strategy" (Shuster, 1987: 66; see also Klein, 1993; Goetstouwers, 2006). Mass culture, history, and social sciences have left bisexuals hidden among heterosexuals and homosexuals. Bisexuals are claimed by either group based on even one "appropriate" relationship, despite historical and other research that reveals the range of mestizaje bisexual lifestyles (Shuster, 1987). As will be discussed further in later chapters, where bisexuality has been presented in popular culture such as film, the representations are similar to the earlier representations of gay men and lesbians as discussed by Russo (1987): demonization, pathologization, criminalization, and as objects of entertainment and humor.

And yet, the very label "bisexuality" with its "bi" prefix calls upon a binary or dual system of identification. Does this imply that individuals are two halves rather than one whole, and that bisexuality is "the best of both worlds" at best and "torn between two worlds" at worst? As Evans argues, "Two distinct Western cultures, gay and straight, . . . [and] the establishment of gay and lesbian 'ethnic style' communities strengthened the heterosexual/homosexual dichotomy . . . [which leads to] tensions of trying to live bisexual lives between cultures" (2003: 93). This, of course, is where the term "queer" has been reclaimed as endeavoring to include diversity, inclusivity, and multiple belongings without scissoring individuals *between* communities and homogenizing individuals *within* communities. The term "multisexuality" may be even more all-encompassing in mestizaje manner. For some theorists, however, bisexuality is considered to be an inclusive term that defines immense possibilities available, whether they are acted upon or not (Orlando, 1991; Wark, 1997; Diamond, 2008, 2009; Halperin, 2009).

There are differing definitions of bisexuality, some of which are framed by bifurcated logics:

- the conflict (either/or) models: bisexuality as largely transitional, "torn between two worlds" (Zinik, 1985);
- the synthesis (both/and) models: bisexual orientation as "the best of both worlds" (Klein, 1993);
- the Kinseyan continuum of sexuality based on binary opposition: heterosexuality and homosexuality at opposite ends. Bisexuality falls in the middle, sometimes as an incompletion, a split, or two parts or halves rather than a whole (Kinsey et al., 1948, 1953; Weise, 1992); and

- mestizaje models that insist the very power of what is defined as bisexuality is its unclassifiability and multiplicity, its being everywhere and elsewhere and nowhere (Wark, 1997; Angelides, 2001).

Bisexuality described in terms of the cultural conflict (either/or) and cultural synthesis/flexibility (both/and) models is grounded in binary structures. The "conflict model" views bisexuality as problematic, stemming from identity conflict and confusion; and the "flexibility model" views bisexuality as the coexistence of heteroeroticism and homoeroticism, as the successful integration of homosexual and heterosexual identities into a dual sexual orientation (Moore and Norris, 2005). The conflict model portrays bisexuals as anxious "fence-sitters," while the synthesis model describes bisexuals as experiencing the "best of both worlds." Underlying the conflict model of bisexuality is the notion that sexual orientation is a dichotomy and bisexuals are living in an inherently temporary or transitional stage that masks the person's true underlying sexual orientation. The flexibility model portrays the bisexual as somewhat of a chameleon, capable of moving easily between the heterosexual and homosexual worlds, which themselves remain unchallenged, fixed, and pure (Moore and Norris, 2005).

While the conflict model accurately predicts higher levels of conflict and confusion for bisexual individuals, it is important to not assume that this conflict is linked to underlying pathology. Instead, the links between individual conflict and external ascriptions and coercions need to be addressed. As Moore and Norris found in their research, despite higher levels of sexuality conflict, 85 percent of bisexuals "experienced their sexual identity in a fairly cohesive manner" (2005: 23; see also Diamond, 2009). The researchers conclude that it is "imperative for professionals to recognize the error in assuming bisexual identity represents pathological disturbance and, as such, requires clinical intervention." It would be more useful to address the cultural factors that "may inhibit positive bisexual identity development," such as providing and promoting school and work-based sensitivity training, mentoring programs, and media visibility campaigns (Moore and Norris, 2005: 23).

Although I will be presenting bisexual students who frame their sexualities within the conflict-synthesis continuum or mestizaje models, bisexuality as mestizaje is the framing definition being used in this research. In other words, bisexuality is fluid, meaning different things to different people identified as or identifying as bisexual, or behaving bisexually even if they do not identify as bisexual (Savin-Williams, 2005; Diamond, 2009; Halperin, 2009). Indeed, based on their empirical and longitudinal investigations, researchers such as Diamond combine the bisexuality as a "third orientation" and bisexuality as "heightened fluidity" models, concluding it is "a stable pattern of attraction to both sexes in which the *specific balance* of same-sex to other-sex desires necessarily varies according to interpersonal and situational factors" (2008: 12).

"CHOOSING NOT TO CHOOSE": MULTISEXUAL AND POLYAMOROUS FAMILIES AS BORDER FAMILIES

They say polypeople can't make a choice, that we have to choose. Okay, I'm choosing. I'm choosing not to choose. I'm not going to ditch one loved one just because I love someone else. That's called serial monogamy, more like serial heartbreak! And what it does to kids! I know from divorced friends that they often don't stop loving the person they ditched for the new loved one. But they think they have to make a choice.

—Naomi, hetero-poly mom with one hetero-mono and one bi-poly male partner

In an age when homosexuals demand church weddings and some cities have passed domestic partners ordinances which extend special privileges to same sex or unmarried couples, nonmonogamy is still so socially unacceptable that we don't even have a widely understood *name* for it. This may be because variations in relationship orientation are perceived as even more of a threat to the established social order than variations in sexual orientation.

—Anapol (1992: 80)

Social policies, including educational policies, inscribe the heterosexual monogamous married unit as the heart of the organization of the social field, and there are punishments and restrictions for those who do not conform or, as Brosnan writes, if we try "pulling the family out of the closet" (1996: 53). Nevertheless, historical, anthropological, cross-cultural, and contemporary accounts and research continue to reveal the diversity of marital and nonmarital relationships:

- Sexual/loving partners do not always live together.
- Sexual partners are not always in "romantic" love.
- Loving partners are not always sexual.
- Marital partners may have partners who are not their spouse.
- Sexual/loving partners may not be heterosexual (see Buxton, 1991, 2001, 2004, 2006a, 2006b, 2007; George, 1992; Pallotta-Chiarolli, 1995a).

Multipartner or polyamorous relationships combine traditional concepts of commitment, love, and "a lifelong intention to support each other in whatever ways seem appropriate" with marginal concepts of sexually and lovingly relating to more than one person at the same time with all partners fully aware of this (Taormino, 2008). Multipartnered and/or multisexual families are part of school communities, whatever particular form, label, or identity they may use, such as polygamy, polyandry, polyfidelity, polyamory, or responsible nonmonogamy. Sensationalized stereotypes about nonmonogamous relationships, and the reiteration of one or two simplistic representations of nonmonogamy to represent all nonmonogamies, conspire with silence about diverse partnering realities to perpetuate ignorance; external stigmatization; and internalized doubt, shame, and hatred. For example, mainstream Western heteromonogamist representations tend to focus on patriarchally imposed polygamies that are abusive to women and usually linked in the media to religious-based polygamies such as Mormon and Muslim polygamies or non-Western polygamies such as African polygamies. Queer-based polygamies, women-centered polyandries, as well as noncoercive and nonabusive religious and non-Western polygamies are underrepresented. "Every TV show, every book, every movie, every play, every greeting card, every commercial, and every love song reinforces the monogamist ideal . . . [and] less than 10% of family therapists approached by Beyond Monogamy was willing to offer services supportive of the [nonmonogamist] lifestyle" (Turney, 1993: 4).

For the purposes of this research, and as far as it is possible for me as a researcher to ensure that no form of gendered subjugation or abusive, coercive, or state- or religion-imposed nonmonogamy exists within the families of my research participants, my aim is to present only those forms of multipartnering that are based on gender equity, love, choice, and agency among its individuals, whether they be hetero-poly, queer-poly, religious-poly, or cultural-poly. These individuals inhabit border locations within, between, and beyond the binary hierarchy of lifelong marital monogamy and noncommitted, nonmonogamous sexual encounters (Rambukkana, 2004), as well as between patriarchally imposed monogamy and patriarchally imposed polygamy. For example, research with multipartnered women finds that they

> spoke of viewing their own lives from these two different angles, from both the vantage point of the married woman in her position of conventional goodness, and from that of the outlaw roaming some uncontaminated, unformulated lawless region . . . and the resulting image was clearer and more whole; it had more depth and dimension than either snapshot on its own. Looking at themselves from both inside and outside the frame, they felt they could begin to reassess their lives and their relationships more honestly. (Heyn, 1992: 262; see also Botwin, 1994; Mroczek, 1994)

Yet, despite such feelings of self-affirmation and self-actualization, identifying as a polyamorist or belonging to a polyfamily is a site of external sociocultural absence, silence, and individual isolation: "Everyone from feminist scholars to men's magazines has enshrined monogamous commitment . . . as if there were no sensible middle ground between marriage and bacchanalia. . . . As if it were humanly impossible to be devoted to two [or more] lovers" (Talbot, 1992: 68).

Indeed, none of the differences and issues outlined above in relation to imposed and chosen, culturally diverse and religiously diverse nonmonogamies, and their underrepresentations and misrepresentations in mainstream media, are being adequately addressed in most Western educational systems despite the diversity of families that constitute the communities of its schools. And yet theorists such as Weeks (1998) believe that families of choice, the varied patterns of domestic involvement, sexual intimacy, and mutual responsibilities, are increasingly displacing traditional patterns of marriage and family.

There are, of course, constraints—economic, social, cultural, gendered, personal—that severely limit free choice. As this research will show, and as I have discussed in the previous chapter, it is easier for some people to adopt marginalized family lifestyles than others (Haritaworn et al., 2006; Noel, 2006; Sheff, 2008). No matter how easy or difficult it is to publicly come out, stepping onto the monogamy/"promiscuity" borders as a polyamorist requires a coming out to oneself, similar to the coming out based on non-heterosexuality. This often entails people realizing they are polyamorous or desiring a polyamorous relationship style before they have met other polyamorous people or, indeed, are even aware of the label and discourse; locating resources such as local groups and online lists; and determining how "polyfluid" one is or is able to be, meaning where a person feels able to situate himself or herself along a continuum between lifelong monogamy with one partner and lifelong nonmonogamy with multiple partners (Weitzman, 2006).

Multipartnerists, or polyamorists, feel that existing terms such as "adultery," "cheating," "affair," and "extramarital" are deliberately negative and inappropriate when applied to their relationships. Hence, since the 1970s there have been inventions of labels, such as polyamory, polyfidelity, group marriage, intimate network, multilateral marriage, and what I call multipartnering, that focus on the idea of multiple relationships without the connotations of negativity, deception, and pathology (Francouer, 1972; Constantine and Constantine, 1972; Anapol, 1992; Nearing, 1995; Zell, 1992, 1996). Indeed, most theorists agree that successful nonmonogamous relationships of any kind have built-in rules and boundaries that provide emotional, mental, and sexual safeguards, which make outside sex "very predictable and orderly" (Blumstein and Schwartz, 1983: 289). Nonmonogamous relationships are made up of "policies of territory, time allotment and veto power" (Prineas, 1995: 23). Mixed marriages between monogamists and nonmonogamists would particularly involve very specific boundaries and negotiations. Thus, border families incorporate border negotiations within their structures as well as negotiating how they will border external societal structures.

Some theorists, in advocating polyamory, believe there may never be a "crisp scientific definition" since polyamory/multipartnering is, by its very nature, "a process hard to bolt to the floor" (West, 1996: 21). In considering individuals' "monogamy orientation" (Burleson, 2005) or "relationship orientation" (Weeks, 1998), theorists such as Weitzman (2006) are constructing monogamy/nonmonogamy as existing along a continuum similar to sexual orientation and gender (see also Burleson, 2005). However, in ways similar to how bisexuality and multisexuality are understood within the mestizaje paradigm, West (1996) calls polyamory a "mixed model," for the word "continuum" is too linear to encompass its diversity. Kieffer describes polyamory as "patchwork intimacy . . . a rather complex and variegated pattern or conglomerate of intimate relationships and experiences" that cannot be molded into a singular and all-encompassing definition (1977: 277; see also Johnson, 1991; Trudinger and Frey, 1995/1996). For example, some multipartnered relationships adhere to "gender monogamy" whereby partners may not have intimate relationships with anyone of the same gender as their primary partner (Buxton, 2006a; 2006b; Weitzman, 2006).

Multiple partnerships need not mean conflict between lifelong monogamy and dishonest, secretive nonmonogamy or the synthesis of the two polarities of marital monogamy and so-called promiscuity, as in serial monogamy, but an actual invention of new meaning into mestizaje relationship models such as multipartnering. Instead of meaning deriving from dualistic coercions, meaning derives from multiple options. In dealing with personal identity as a nonmonogamist, multipartnerist, or polyamorist, three modes of intersection are evident:

- experiencing conflict between the polarities resulting in an either/or choice, or coerced decision (either get married and try to live a heterosexual monogamous lifestyle as a pretend monogamist with occasional lapses defined/normalized as "affair" or "adultery," or resist marriage/committed relationship altogether);
- negotiating and synthesizing elements of both polarities resulting in a location along a continuum between the two binaries (such as serial monogamists and public monogamists/closet nonmonogamists); and
- moving beyond the polarities to construct a mestizaje identity that is multiple, fluid, beyond binaries and dualities (such as married and unmarried polyamorists and polyfidelists of varying sexualities).

Most theorists who have written positively about nonmonogamous alternatives have done so within a framework of binary synthesis, proposing the need for a "middle ground between the free love/do your own thing doctrine of the sexual revolution and outmoded lifelong monogamy" (Anapol, 1992: ix). Monogamy and "promiscuity" are positioned on a continuum rather than being a dichotomy, as most people are somewhere in between. Very few people have one lifelong relationship and very few have never had an exclusive relationship for at least a brief period of time. Hence, "responsible nonmonogamists" are constructed as making both/and choices in an either/or world: "Without the synthesizing energies of the third, we are left alternating between two irreconcilable polarities" (Anapol, 1992: 149).

Where a notion of a borderland is constructed, it is polyamory's positioning as a site of in-betweenness. By choosing a multipartner relationship, Anapol (1992) believes an individual is placing oneself "in the center of the cyclone" confronting "opposing forces" from the powerful monogamous heterosexual marital mainstream (which in reality involves many husbands and wives having secret extramarital relationships) and the power-challenging nonmonogamous, nonmarital marginality (which in reality usually involves serial monogamy or a linear progression through a series of monogamous or pretend monogamous relationships). Nearing also speaks in terms of a synthesis model, albeit hierarchical, when she writes that multipartnerships are really "taking the best of the old ways and evolving something new and improved" (1992: 82). She regards herself as having "been blessed" with loving partnerships that have lasted for twenty-three, fifteen, and two and a half years concurrently. She defines her position as "like a creature who is most comfortable in a tribal band, living with the benefits and responsibilities of overlapping circles of love" (1996a: 4).

Multipartnerists or "responsible nonmonogamists" believe their "time has come" and are calling for identity and community constructs and classifications with which to establish a history of activism and discursive possibility (Anapol, 1992: x; Anderlini-D'Onofrio, 2009a; Barker and Langdridge, 2010). Supportive networks for "ethical nonmonogamists" are springing up in Western countries, providing an expanding field of labels, histories, and validation (Anderlini-D'Onofrio, 2004; Anapol, 2010). This movement is at a historical point in time where gay liberationists, feminists, multiculturalists, and Indigenous activists have all previously been: at the beginning of a long road to public awareness, acceptance, and validation in sociopolitical structures. Research by Beyond Monogamy in Australia, founded by Carl Turney, found that the single most common group is a threesome with one woman and two men followed closely by a foursome of two couples. Many of these have children. Mostly due to social pressure, such groups rarely live in the same house (Turney, 1993). However, Turney believes that "Whether realising it or not, most people have been slowly

and steadily moving in the direction of polyfidelity," with increasing sociocultural discourses affirming social freedom, independence of partners, and
sexual diversity (1993: 27).

In Australia in the early 1990s, Carl Turney's television and other personal appearances, newsletter publication, pamphlets, and other resource
materials with names of contact persons and contact groups around Australia led to the creation of small secretive networks in most Australian
states. Originating in Perth, Western Australia, Beyond Monogamy Inc. was
for three years one of the world's twelve nonprofit educational support as-
sociations for those involved in "honest, balanced, intimate relationships
of three or more adults" (1993: 27). It offered regular social meetings; a
lending library; referrals to qualified marriage counsellors, doctors, and
lawyers; a speakers bureau; and personal consultations. By early 1993, Beyond Monogamy Inc. had a mailing list of more than 100 singles, couples,
threesomes, and foursomes either interested or involved in nonmonogamy.
After several years of campaigning, often in isolation, the level of personal
stress and social hostility led Turney to adopt a less public stance. His and
other fledgling networks in Australia were forced to go back into the closet
until in 2000, Turney and Tim Payne started a second Beyond Monogamy
group from Melbourne, which ran for approximately three years.

Today, the term polyamory is surfacing again in Australia, with increasing
strength and publicity, as an attachment to bisexual community networks
such as the Sydney Bisexual and Polyamorist Network. The year 2000 also
saw the start of the online mailing and discussion list PolyOz which at the
time of writing has 700 members. In 2004 Anne Hunter and Peter Haydon
ran some polyamory workshops at Confest (Australia's "Burning Man"; see
www.dte.org.au/) and observed a need for a safe social space specifically for
poly people. PolyVic was created and incorporated and began having regular monthly socials and discussion groups. Flowing on from that and with
the help of the PolyOz network, a number of poly groups began meeting in
many of the state capital cities and some regional areas such as PolySA and
PolyWA. These groups maintain active listservs as well as organize regular
social and support functions. Some of these functions include picnics and
other day events for polyparents and their children. Currently there are
active social groups in Melbourne, Sydney, and Adelaide that run regular
monthly socials and discussion groups. There are less regular social groups
in Bendigo, Perth, and Canberra, and at the time of writing there has been
a lot of interest but as yet few actual meet-ups in northern New South Wales
and southern Queensland.

At the time of writing there hasn't been much political activity on the part
of the current poly groups. However, media interest is on the increase in Australia. The poly community has been wary about engaging with some of the
more sensationalist current affairs programs, but there have been radio inter-

views, newspaper articles, and a six-minute documentary—*Poly People*—that screened at the Melbourne Queer Film Festival in 2009 and featured Anne Hunter from PolyVic and the founders of the Sydney Poly group.

In relation to PolyVic, Anne Hunter writes,

> PolyVic is a deliciously warm friendly cuddly bunch with a Google list membership of almost 200. Average attendance at socials is 30–50, and at discussion groups 20–30. We have an age range of roughly 20–60 with a bulge in the 30s. Relationships cover the poly spectrum from polyfidelity to comfortably casual. . . . We pride ourselves on being extremely queer-friendly and welcoming of anyone who is poly-open, whether or not they identify as poly. Inclusivity is highly valued. There is a higher-than-average level of education and IQ, especially emotional intelligence—which I guess is necessary for survival in poly relationships. We're predominantly middle-class, of mixed ethnicities but with a leaning to white-Caucasian. As is common there is a significant overlap between the poly, bi, queer, kink, gaming and geek communities. . . . We're lucky in that we have found a really friendly inner-city pub with a pleasant upstairs room in which we hold events. We also have family picnics every second month, and more ad hoc events like weekends away, all of which contribute to our current thriving community. (personal communication, October, 2009)

Musician and seasoned traveler Penelope Swales, who has toured numerous poly communities in the United States, observes some of the differences and similarities between Australian and U.S. polygroups:

> I think the biggest difference is in numbers. But in terms of actual poly culture I was quite surprised at how similar people were. . . . At least in some parts of the United States there is a larger critical mass of poly people, which makes for more viability and vibrancy. I came across a lot more dedicated poly households in the United States. But in other areas like the Midwest I was basically coming across little pockets of half-a-dozen or so poly people who seemed to be struggling with the isolation in their little area. . . . New York is like a much bigger version of Melbourne, and Seattle and Portland—there's enough poly people up there that people who aren't poly are quite aware of the poly community. . . . As far as cultural similarities are concerned I guess—since the advent of the Internet there's been quite a lot of exchange. So I found poly people had similar interests and often similar attitudes, similar humor, similar jokes. . . . Probably both in the States and in Australia computer geeks tend to dominate, partly because the Internet is the easiest way to facilitate the community. And having the shared language and a lot of Australia being quite heavily informed by American culture means there's quite a lot of cultural traffic between the two communities. I suppose maybe the most obvious difference is that poly people in the States seem quite comfortable identifying as poly, whereas in Australia people are a little bit more wary. There's more formal poly culture in the United States in terms of regular conferences, retreats, workshops, cuddle parties, Pride Days, etc., than there are in Australia—again

it partly comes down to numbers. There are more people prepared to take on the organizing, and more people who are going to go if they're organized. (Interview with Penelope, courtesy of Penelope Swales and Anne Hunter, October, 2009)

Similar increasing inroads are being made in the media, socially, and on the legal scene in the United Kingdom and in Europe, led by academics and activists such as Meg Barker (see Barker and Langdridge, 2010). For example, over 200 people attended the London Polyday event in August 2008, and by October 2008, a Google search found there were 1.6 million international Web pages on polyamory.

So how many self-identified polyamorous people are there? Due to the stigmatization and invisibility of polyfamilies, it is difficult to provide a conclusively quantifiable response. Weitzman (2006) has collected some statistics from previous research undertaken by a variety of researchers, and together with discussions on the PolyResearchers listserv, the following summary can be made at this stage:

- 20–28 percent of lesbians are polyamorous;
- 65 percent of gay men are polyamorous;
- 15–28 percent of heterosexual couples have some understanding around nonmonogamy;
- Loving More magazine has a database of 13,000 people and 5,000 people responded to its online survey in 2002, of whom 51 percent said they were bisexual. These figures have led to an estimation of 50,000 poly-identified people living in the United States;
- PolyMatchMaker.com, the leading poly personals site, currently has around 7,000 members.

But what about those who may not have heard of the label "polyamorous" and are living it? Taormino (2008) presents the findings of the Janus Report (1993), which sampled 1,800 people. Twenty-one percent said they participated in an open marriage. She also refers to the 2007 survey by Oprah.com of over 14,000 people, 21 percent saying they were in an open marriage. In relation to young people, Chihara sees the Internet as "instrumental in spreading the polyamorous word." Polyamory.org has a private "Under 30" mailing list with more than 150 members ranging from teenagers and older (2006), while researchers such as Larsen (1998) report an increase in polyamory among young people seeking alternatives to the disillusioning experiences of "pretend monogamy" and "adultery" they witnessed within their own families.

Again, similar to ways gay men and lesbians were stereotyped and presented in popular culture until recently (see Russo, 1987), individuals with more than one partner have been subjected to, and overwhelmingly still are, to demonization, pathologization, criminalization, and being made objects of entertainment and humor. However, recently, information about media personalities such as Tilda Swinton, Will and Jada Pinkett-Smith, and Dolly Parton, as well as "the ordinary citizen and family" who live multipartnered lifestyles, is becoming more available via newspaper and magazine reporting; Internet resources including online communities and organizations and the YouTube Poly comedy "Family," based on the life of its polyamorous film-makers, "3 Dog Pictures"; TV programs and talk shows such as the HBO series *Big Love*, an episode of *Ally McBeal* where Heather Locklear's character was on trial for being married to two men; documentaries such as *When Two Won't Do* and *Three of Hearts*; and popular films such as *French Twist*, *Bandits*, *Ordinary Decent Criminal*, and *Take the Lead*. Given increasing examples such as these, as well as polyamory becoming a storyline in mainstream TV series such as *Hollyoaks* from the UK, it is predicted that there will be an exponentially increasing acceptance and normalization of multipartnering (Newitz, 2006). As we shall see in later chapters, where some of the above examples and others will be discussed in further detail, polyfamilies are calling for more positive texts and media resources to be made available about their families to the general public and in schools alongside texts for children and teenagers about same-sex families (see for example Pallotta-Chiarolli, 2008).

Another branch of polyamory is the multisexual or mixed-orientation families where two or more parents identify as differing sexualities. Page (2004) found that 33 percent of her bisexual sample was involved in a polyamorous relationship, while 54 percent considered this type of relationship ideal (in Weitzman, 2006). Buxton's (1991, 2001, 2004, 2006a, 2006b, 2007) role as director of the Straight Spouse Network, her subsequent research, and other research studies (Pallotta-Chiarolli and Lubowitz, 2003; Pallotta-Chiarolli, forthcoming) conclude that many heterosexual partners do not necessarily want a relationship to end if a partner identifies as gay, lesbian, or bisexual. There may be a strong bond that both partners do not wish to break, and they come to see themselves as life partners in a mixed-orientation *mestizaje* partnership that not only deconstructs and broadens the meaning of marriage but also interrogates the binarily constructed heterosexual/homosexual divide. Partners in gay/straight or bisexual relationships must deal with the issue that the outside worlds, whether they are heterosexual or homosexual worlds, will rarely consider the relationship valid, as it does not fit neatly into the prescribed dualism of heteronormative marriage or homosexual relationship (see for example Nahas and Turley, 1979; Gochros, 1989). In her study of gay men and straight women in intimate relationships, Whitney (1990) found that many women deliberately chose gay-identifying men as partners and co-parents, hence

deliberately choosing to enter the borderland of ambiguity and unclassifiability (Anzaldua, 1987a). A research participant in Buxton's research into
heterosexual women married to gay- or bisexual-identifying men stated,
"Our relationship has internal validity regardless of outside standards. . . .
It took a while for us to write this script for ourselves. We've survived seven
years of marriage by tolerating the ambivalence of what we are and what
could happen" (1991: 231–34).

Indeed, the available research finds that most people pretend to the
outside world to live conventional lives: "It's safer to appear to be just like
everything else. We can't know how many secrets exist behind the appearances" (Whitney, 1990: 227). As Gochros writes,

> Just a decade ago interracial marriages were "unthinkable" and usually failed
> not because of the partners' biological racial differences, but because of the
> isolation, stigma, and lack of support they received. Today they are more ac-
> cepted and relatively viable. . . . Similarly, it can be expected that as acceptance,
> information, and support increases, the problems I have described [about
> multisexual relationships] will decrease. (Gochros, 1989: 251)

The availability and use of an empathic, knowledgeable support system
or community is an important issue for multisexual families (Gochros,
1989; Buxton, 2001, 2004, 2006a, 2006b). Almost all heterosexual wives
with bisexual male partners in research studies report a strong sense of
isolation and panopticonic fears: "The more isolated they felt, the more
stigmatized they felt; the more stigmatized they felt, the more they isolated
themselves" (Gochros, 1989: 109). Bisexual partners in marital relationships need to negotiate and border a major paradox: the contradiction
between the heterosexual public identity, which places them comfortably
in the mainstream of society with an affirmed marriage, family, and social
identity, and their stigmatized and forbidden homosexual desires and behavior, which would position them outside this Central zone (Brownfain,
1985; Weinberg, Williams, and Pryor, 1994; Joseph, 1997; Pallotta-Chiarolli
and Lubowitz, 2003).

Greater knowledge about "queerly mixed" and/or polyamorous partnerships in history is providing alternative models and frameworks of relationship realities and possibilities that have long remained concealed beneath
the veil of "official" biography. For example, Foster and associates (1997)
have researched and compiled a collection of biographies of threesomes
from ancient times to today (see also Roiphe, 2007). Vita Sackville-West,
a writer, and Harold Nicolson, a politician, in early twentieth-century
England have had their multisexual polyamorous relationship discussed
in biographies, one of them written by one of their sons, Nigel Nicolson
(Nicolson, 1973; Glendinning, 1983). Cook (1993, 1999) discussed First
Lady Eleanor and President Franklin Roosevelt's marriage and their outside

partners in her biographies, including Eleanor's relationships with both journalist Lorena Hickok and police sergeant Earl Miller. Another example is the creator of the Wonder Woman comics, William Moulton Marston (who also invented the lie detector!), who lived with two women, his legal wife, Elizabeth Holloway, and second partner, Olive Byrne. They raised their children together, and Wonder Woman was based on his two partners (Daniels, 2004).

A contemporary figure is the multipartnered feminist Patricia Ireland who was president of the United States National Organization of Women (NOW). Commuting back and forth, Ireland lived in Florida with James Humble, her husband of nearly thirty years, who is a painter, and also in Washington with a woman who did not want to be identified because she feared losing her job. Ireland constructs herself as a mestiza border dweller in the following:

> Ireland says it is her very ability to be all things to all people that makes her the right leader for these contradictory times. . . . "I'm a hybrid," Ireland says." I want to do everything. I don't see why I can't have my cake and eat it too." . . . She declined to label herself either a lesbian or bisexual. . . . "What I have described is who my family is, not my sexuality," Irelands says. . . . She hopes the discussion of her personal life will dispel the myth that most Americans live in traditional families. "There's still this concept of Mom, Dad, Dick, Jane, Spot, Puff," she says. "But there are really all kinds of arrangements people make in their lives." (In Gross, 1992: 16, 38)

As the participants in my research say, these biographies are a powerful way of inserting these issues into the mainstream, including an educational mainstream, that is interested in celebrities, popular cultural icons (see for example Dolly Parton's autobiography, 1994), and the lives of famous historical figures. Certainly, it is interesting to note that much of the academic, personal, and self-help texts on polyamory are being written by women (Pallotta-Chiarolli, 2004). Jackson and Scott trace this development to the feminist deconstruction of heteropatriarchal monogamous marriage that was "widely discussed in the seventies," and indeed raise their concerns that since then, "the critique of monogamy has become so muted as to be almost inaudible" (2003: 28). Sheff (2008) believes polyamorous women are at the forefront of the movement because polyamory is actively opposed to androcentric "unequal gendered access to multiple partners," which has historically been the dominant form of nonmonogamy, both within mainstream societies and within the early "free love" and "sexual revolution" movements. Other theorists point to the lack of data and discussion from heterosexual men as being due to the impact of hegemonic constructions of masculinity in silencing men's "nonsecret negotiated nonmonogamy" with their women partners, particularly if it is the women partners who are nonmonogamous rather than the men (Jamieson, 2004; Ley, 2009). Both the living of polyamorous gender-equitable relationships and its public discussion constitute a surrendering of traditionalist masculinist power and privilege based on androcentric "private nonmonogamy," while "having" monogamous women partners as their possessions is a symbolic honor. Ley (2009) uncovers historical and contemporary examples of "cuckoldry," or men with "hot wives" who have transgressed this dominant construction of heteropatriarchal masculinity: they are monogamous heterosexual men who love, affirm, and celebrate their nonmonogamous heterosexual or bisexual wives. Indeed, these men have sometimes explored their own sexualities with other men if their wives have wanted them to for their own erotic pleasure. Ley (2009) refers to this as "forced bisexuality," which these heterosexual-identifying men find extremely arousing as it is a form of submission and "sissification," or forced feminization, to their dominant wives and their wives' male lovers.

PROCESSES OF POSITIONING BI- AND POLY-BORDERS

It's like everyone has an investment in who you are, you know. You are just all of you, parent, partner, worker, a member of your church and your neighborhood and your country, you know? And of the polycommunity of course. But it's like your kids' school, your boss, your church, your neighbors, your laws, your polypeers are all telling you what you should be. And what they don't want you to be, or what they don't want to see you being, you know? So, you know, somewhere in all those "shoulds" is you. All the bits of you.

—John, hetero-poly dad with two hetero-mono partners

Border dwellers are faced with the inability of carrying their multiple realities into all their sites of existence at all times. Each site, such as a school, requires certain "truths" be concealed and certain "lies" be lived if they are to be positioned within it. In order to understand the borderland locations of bisexual students and polyamorous families, it is necessary to examine further the very processes of positioning and how these impact upon, and are impacted upon, by strategies of passing, bordering, and polluting.

"They Say, Therefore I Should Be": Social Ascription and Hierarchies of Deviance

I think being bisexual, people think of you as being weak and kind of flaccid or unable, but . . . [being bisexual] just feels like a natural process and sometimes I focus on just who I am but society makes me think I'm really confused.

—Josie, bi-mono

Social ascription refers to the classifications and controls imposed on one by the powerful Central discourses within a society, as upheld by institutions such as education, religion, and law: "The barracks stands by the church stands by the schoolroom . . . surveillance depends [upon them] for its strategies of objectification, normalization and discipline" (Bhabha, 1990a: 86).

Foucault (1977) uses the panopticon model as symbolic of this power of the wider social order. The panoptical prison placed one guard in the center who surveilled all the prisoners night and day. One effect of constantly being watched was that prisoners began to watch themselves. In other words, the external guard's gaze began to be internalized in each prisoner, who took on the responsibility to supervise himself. The panoptical gaze is the self-surveillance of those who have been conditioned to being watched, evaluated, and regulated. The panoptical gaze produces control through normalization in both guards and prisoners. Even if there is no "guardian" present, the power apparatus still operates effectively, as the "prisoners" have internalized the norms. As Kazmi (1993) explains, it is not necessary that anyone should actually occupy the guard tower. It appears that each person is his or her own panopticon, an external monitor of self and others.

Hierarchical, continuous, and functional surveillance, as felt by all participants in this research, is organized as multiple, automatic, and anonymous power. This enables the disciplinary panopticonic power to be everywhere and always alert, since it leaves no zone of shade and constantly supervises the very individuals who are entrusted with the task of supervising. Disciplinary power is therefore exercised through its invisibility; at the same time it imposes on those whom it subjects a principle of compulsory visibility which assures the hold of the power that is exercised over them. "It is the fact of being constantly seen, of being able always to be seen, that maintains the disciplined individual in his subjection" (Rabinow, 1984: 199). The panopticon is "at once surveillance and observation, security and knowledge, individualization and totalization, isolation and transparency" (1984: 217). Power is made visible not by public display of its source and origin, but by the objectification of those on whom it is used, and through the formation of a body of knowledge about these individuals. Mestizaje persons such as bisexual young people and "queerly mixed"/polyamorous families are particularly aware of how their multiple realities are subjected to the panopticonic gaze. This leads to their scripting performances of normativity: scissoring, simplifying, and homogenizing their selves and their lives, finding the "ready-made code and having to accommodate oneself to it" (Trinh, 1991: 136), as occurs in school communities.

Nevertheless, within this system, panopticonic conformity to social norms can be beneficial, gratifying, profitable, and pragmatic. Conformity to a set of norms is a means of maintaining status. For example, "deviant norms" such as being gay or lesbian or in a same-sex relationship can even become acceptable because they make deviants easily defined and located, and thus detached and distanced from those subscribing to "normal norms," who of course are doing the defining by utilizing these dichotomous logics (Gibbs, 1981). Seidman (2001) refers to a normalizing logic that recognizes gay identities but only on the condition that every other key aspect of the gay self exhibits what would be considered "normal" gendered, sexual, familial, work, and national practices: "Only the homosexual who is a mirror image of the ideal heterosexual citizen is acceptable" (2001: 325). Thus, to be a monogamous gay man married to another monogamous gay man and raising children in a middle-class suburban home is more "normal deviance" than nonmonogamous polyamorous gay parents who display "deviant deviance."

Panopticonic conformity can also be called "passing": self-regulation and normative performativity as a strategy of assimilation to social ascriptions in order to avoid discrimination and harassment (Kroeger, 2003). Passing establishes hierarchies within the deviant group as group members attempt to deal with the either/or alternatives constructed by social ascription: those who can pass as the Same as the dominant group or those who can be a recognizable and acceptable Other that the dominant group can distinguish itself from as superior and normal. A major function of social ascription is the maintenance of social cohesion and boundary demarcation as a result of the labeling and containment of the transgressor or pollutant. Thus, dichotomous transactions taking place between "deviant" persons on the one side and agencies of control on the other are boundary-maintenance mechanisms (see Schur, 1971; Sagarin, 1977). Indeed, many institutions built to inhibit deviation actually operate in such a way as to perpetuate it, such as monogamous marriage and adultery constructed as a hierarchical dualism, which depends upon the very social demarcations of what constitutes a "true" relationship and what constitutes deviation from that "truth." Of course, this discussion of social cohesion, boundary-demarcation, and deviation is highly pertinent to the question of my research: what happens to those who straddle the border zone, blurring and messing up boundary-markers, as they are able to pass as the Same as the Center, and because of this very ability, are seen as an unacceptable Other by both the Center and the central Margin?

One of the costs of panopticonic passing to socially ascribed norms of the heteronormative monogamist Center on the nonheterosexual Margin is the construction of internal hierarchies: Do gays and lesbians ally themselves with the Center in opposition to bisexuals and polyfamilies, thereby climbing a few more steps out of the panopticonic prison in order to gain legal, political, and socioeconomic rewards; or do they ally with the "deviant" bisexuals and polyfamilies and thereby experience even more stigmatization, policing, and the refusal of the Center to grant mainstreaming rewards? This dilemma is presented with sinister eloquence in the following:

> The worst aspect of passing—that you become what you imitate, and that disdain for your own kind, the member of your own kind who is too conspicuous or too courageous to try to pass, enters into your heart and you become a traitor, denying like Peter when the moment comes to declare your real allegiance, or keeping silent. . . . We were like mice that have been brought up with cats and are not eaten. First we enjoyed the luxury of not being eaten; then we became cats ourselves and were stricken with terror at the idea that we would be taken for mice, that the us in us *showed*. In some cases, some of us became more ferocious toward mice than cats in order to show that there was no mouse in us. The less extreme simply adapted so perfectly and felt so comfortable, that they saw no reason for changing . . . [and] gratefully accepted our position in society as honorary cats and took our nourishment from the masters . . . to eat cat food. (Meigs, 1983: 32–33)

Despite the costs of being on the Margins of a socially ascriptive Center or being socially ascribed a border-deviant position within a Marginal location, there are some insights and understandings that come from refusing to pass or passively self-police according to panopticonic policing. The Margins reveal the shape, the texture, the meaning of the Centers; what is rejected or controlled speaks loudly about the rejecter and controller (Giroux, 1993; Erera, 2002; see also Babcock, 1978; De Certeau, 1986; Stallybrass and White, 1986; Hastings, 1995). As will become evident in the following chapters, the research participants in this study had many insights and understandings that came from having to deal with, resist, and negotiate social ascription and panopticonic policing. For example, from the polyamorous border, the official marital monogamism of the Center and the marital monogamist aspirations of the gay and lesbian Margin can be seen as surfaces underneath which secretive nonmonogamy flourishes. From the bisexual border, the official heterosexuality of the Center and the increasingly tolerated deviance of a homosexual Margin can be seen as surfaces underneath which diverse forms of bisexual behavior occur. Hence, borders are sites from which we see the instability of social categories, their temporal and spatial shifts and fluctuations. They are the metissage zones of unpredictability at the edges of discursive stability, where contradictory either/or discourses overlap, or where discrepant kinds of meaning making converge in both/and manner. A major task of mestizaje thinking is the understanding of the multiple fluid subjectivities within the Margin and within the Center: fragmenting such unitary static polar positions; preventing the Margin from being determined and defined by the Center; and, indeed, fragmenting and destabilizing the unitary stasis of the Center (Deleuze, 1989).

"They Say, Therefore I Must Be": Significant Others and the Politics of Community/Ghetto

I don't belong in the gay community because that's just it, you know, it's the gay community. I want to belong there but not do their gay ghetto thing, their biphobic politics. But I don't belong in my ethnic community either because of my bisexuality. I'm not going to slice myself up to be the bits each community wants me to be. But it is hard, yeah, because there are bits of me in each community.

—Salvadore, bi-poly dad

Mestizas belong even where "their own people" deny it.

—Phelan (1994: 66)

In a racist, misogynist, and heteronormative society that has despised and devalued certain groups, it is necessary and desirable for members of those groups to adhere with one another and celebrate a common culture, heritage, and experience. This grouping is usually referred to as a "community." For example, the transition from being homosexual to being gay is seen as "enculturation" into a "gay community," involving the "learning of a lot of social skills" in the "homosexualization" of life (Dowsett, 1997: 162–163). Part of this learning can be problematic as individuals negotiate the identities with which they have come into the community, deciding what needs to be shed and what needs to adopted: "Not only do poofs and dykes come out, we also come IN to the gay community, . . . [which] can be accompanied with a fair bit of angst and a frenzied attempt at repackaging ourselves" (Smart, 1994: 9).

Identity politics and the communities they represent struggle with the need for labels around which to call for civil rights, while simultaneously developing discourses and institutions for bringing differently identified groups and individuals together without suppressing or subsuming the differences within, the metissage (Epstein, 1987). As discussed earlier, in its drive to invert the hierarchical privilege of powerful Central groups, a particular Marginal group may inherit the symbolic terms of hierarchy and become a place of production of new hierarchies (Pettman, 1992; see also Young, 1990a). Within these dichotomous logics, "self-professed radical alternatives" may promise liberation but offer "new forms of hegemony instead" (Dirlik, 1987: 50). For mestizaje persons, such as bisexual young people, the sanctuary offered by the gay and lesbian community can also be a prison. The "multiple within" realities of metissage or the existence of "edge identities" (Bersten, 2008) call for the following questions to be addressed: How does one use the word "community" without meaning homogeneity; and where and how are the boundaries of exclusion and inclusion of a community drawn? How do we construct a supportive "community" and an effective "identity politics" without collapsing membership into an inclusion/exclusion paradox?

The bisexual community is itself a minority sexual community often excluded from another sexual minority community, the gay community, and indeed excluded from the dominant heteronormative wider society as well. The polyamory community also has been debating and defining its borders and boundaries. For example, there is general acceptance of polyfidelitous families whose members are nonmonogamous only within a closed circle of people. However, there is great debate over whether swingers can be included—having multiple sexual partners when one is at a swingers' club with one's lifelong partner is not considered by most polyamorous people as the same as being in emotional, daily, familial relationships with more than one other person (Nearing, 1995; Easton and Liszt, 1997). Thus, there appears to be a developing delineation between "good, respectable polyamorist" and "bad, promiscuous polyamorist" (Petrella, 2007).

Thus, whether the goal of a community is to assist individuals in conforming to more normative behavior or to challenge the attitudes of a hostile society, difficulties and contradictions will manifest themselves within that community in relation to how it will present itself to the wider society and how it will deal with internal differences. Goffman (1973) uses the phrase "concern with in-group purification" to describe the efforts of stigmatized persons to "normify" their own conduct and also clean up the conduct of mestizaje others in the group (see also Adam, 1978; Adler and Adler, 1994; Petrella, 2007). As Giroux writes, identity politics "enabled many formerly silenced and displaced groups to emerge from the margins of power and dominant culture to reassert and reclaim suppressed identities and experiences; but in doing so, they often substituted one master narrative for another, invoked a politics of separatism, and suppressed differences within their own 'liberatory' narratives" (1993: 3).

Freire (1972) also explores the operation of dichotomous logics in the way the oppressed often emulate the strategies of control adopted against them by their oppressors. Indeed, as experienced by some research participants in this study, "normative deviants" such as gays and lesbians were sometimes positioning themselves alongside the "normal straights" in bullying "abnormal deviants" such as bisexual people or polyamorous relationships: "When homophobia ceases to exist among our enemies, queers will perfect it for decades to come" (Bashford, 1993: 67).

Is it possible to accommodate for mestizaje difference and maintain the cohesion necessary to undertake political and sociocultural struggles? Young (1990a, 1990b) calls for a politics of difference beyond community, while Burbules (1997) calls for a model of diversity rather than difference. In other words, considering each group's oppression as unified, homogenous, and distinct fails to accommodate the similarities, overlaps, and diversity of oppressions of different groups, and falsely represents the situation of all group members within one group as either completely the same or completely different. This is very pertinent to the somewhat divisive debates about same-sex marriage within the gay and lesbian community over whether to have polyamorous people's constructions of marriage included. How broad, optional, and multidefinitional does the meaning of marriage need to become to accommodate the various relationship permutations within queer communities?

Yuval-Davis's (1994) idea of "transversal politics" recognizes the specific positionings of those who participate in a community as well as the "unfinished knowledge" that each such situated positioning can offer. Hence, identity politics is not an end in itself; "it is a precursor to further, more broadbased and hence more effective, activity" (Adams, 1989: 26; see also Squires, 1992). This is a framework that constructs "community" and "identity politics" as strategic tools and sites of arrivals for border travelers in preparation for future departures. Communities are not meant to be fixed and homogenizing entities and constructs that restrict further journeys. Thus, in relation to this research, the "slippery slope theory" suggests that the achievement of one social and legislative change, such as allowing same-sex couples to marry, opens the doors for other changes, such as allowing people to marry more than one other person. Interestingly, as presented in the previous chapter, this is exactly what objectors to gay marriage are foregrounding and fearfully predicting will occur (Kurtz, 2000, 2003a, 2003b, 2006).

"I Say, Therefore I Am": Personal Agency and the Strategies of Inner Place

> I am bisexual, I am polyamorous. I let everyone know just like they know I'm a mother. All those parts of me fit each other part and I don't care if those who like my sweet mummy me want to vomit at the polybi me. I don't care if I muddy their water, pollute their world.
>
> —Cate, bi-poly mom

> I did it, and I didn't die. I didn't even languish. Quite the contrary—I flourished. And with every fresh act of daring against the taboo, I blossomed more. Instead of hiding all scrunched up in my fearful skin, clinging to it, I began to slough it off and stand up straight, clear and clean, my strong new skin gleaming in the sunlight.
>
> —Johnson (1991: 9)

Constructions of social relations with no room for personal agency but only for "social puppets on fine, flexible wires dancing across stages not of their own making" are problematic (Boden, 1990: 193). As will be very evident in this research, people are, and always have been, active agents in the constitution of their unfolding social worlds (Edwards, 1988; Nicholson, 1990; Davies, 1991; Davis, 1991; Butler, 1993; Chambers, 1994). Borderland mestizaje theory states that within structural and discursive frameworks and panopticonic processes can be found some degree of individual agency and action. Rather than seeing socialization as a "printed circuit" in which persons are programmed to behave in the "right way," agency can be found in "the daydreaming and the questioning, the funneling and the digging, the adopting of now this stance and now that stance, the recurrent problems and the turning-points" (Plummer, 1975: 14). Framed by panopticonic regulations, socially ascribed meanings, and community rules for belonging, a mestizaje person's border life is "an emergent, situated, negotiated one where considerable variation becomes possible" (Plummer, 1975: 50).

The strategy of polluting will be explored in this book as a metaphoric description of agentic and innovative actions by bisexual young people and multipartnered families in schools. Nevertheless, research participants will also explain how passing and bordering can hold different forms of polluting, subversive power. Certainly, agentic practices and discursive knowledge always exist within determinate historical and spatial bounds. However, if agents were unable to originate new forms of activity then "it would be impossible to account for the extraordinary variation in social conduct that has been exhibited in the course of human history" (Cohen, 1987: 291; see also Jackson, 1978; Sewell, 1992). For example, the construction of cyber communities, Internet chat rooms, and the production and development of independent media and resources by polyamorous individuals and groups are forms of pioneering agency that are major contributors to increasing social and legal recognition.

Certain circumstances tend to influence the level and nature of agency. Actors need to have access to knowledge of their social locations, the modes of articulating this knowledge, and the means of disseminating knowledge. If enough people or even a few people who are powerful enough act in innovative ways, their action may have the consequence of transforming the very structures that gave them the capacity to act. Hence, agency is collective as well as individual (Sewell, 1992). For example, new labels can be constructed to define new forms of relationships. The word *polyamory* was only constructed in the early 1970s by Morning Glory Zell (Zell, 1992; Zell and Zell, 1996). In my own research, I use neologisms such as multisexual, multipartnering and "queerly mixed" to endeavor to define new, shifting, and evolving forms of relationships and families.

According to mestizaje theory, living in the borderlands itself is agency, a challenge to the contrived fixity, orderliness, and homogeneity of various groups and communities, as Lugones explains:

> Code-switching; categorical blurring and confusion; . . . announcing the impurity of the pure by ridiculing his inability at self-maintenance; playful reinvention of our names for things and people, multiple naming; caricaturing of the fragmented selves we are in our groups; revealing the chaotic in production; . . . undermining the orderliness of the social ordering; marking our cultural mixtures as we move; . . . Thus curdled behavior is not only creative but also constitutes itself as a social commentary, . . . an act of social creative defiance. (1994: 478; see also Erera, 2002)

Living on the borders requires stigma management (Goffman, 1963), a form of agency pertinent to mestizaje persons (see also Adler and Adler, 1994). Stigmatized people's lives are characterized by a constant focus on intertwined processes of concealing, passing, information control, and revealing. "Disidentifiers" such as props, actions, or verbal expressions are used to distract and fool those who would scrutinize and ostracize so that they believe border dwellers do not have the deviant stigma. Leading a "double life," maintaining two different lifestyles with two distinct groups of people that both have significant meaning and connection for an individual—one group that knows about their deviance and one that does not—is also another form of agency. Agency is evident in the very negotiation of many "homes" or "worlds," such as the worlds of home and school (Evans, 2003). Both resisting and desiring identification and membership in various worlds, border dwellers construct a new identity and a new "home" that allows them to journey between, within, and beyond these worlds.

Thus, disclosing deviance is not the only form of agency. Truths that are silent are difficult to police and therefore also negative or dangerous to the dominant discourse (Aruna, 1994; Kroeger, 2003). Silence frequently means that the Other against which the dominant discourse mounts a defense is invisible precisely because it is immune to discursive appropriation (Ryan, 1993). Thus, passing can be as agentic as polluting, as people may "pass in order to bypass being excluded unjustly in their attempts to achieve ordinary, honorable aims and ambitions" and in order "to be more truly themselves" (Kroeger, 2003: 2). If a border person or border family is not "passing by default" but, instead, "passing deliberately," passing can become a subversive act (Samuels, 2003: 243). Rather than being an act of assimilationism, passing becomes an act of defiance, a performance on the very stage of social scrutiny and surveillance.

The above strategies of personal agency exemplify Foucault's belief in "the plurality of resistances": "resistances that are possible, necessary, improbable; others that are spontaneous, savage, solitary, concerted, rampant, or violent; still others that are quick to compromise, interested, or sacrificial" (1978: 96). In his later work, Foucault elaborated a notion of situated agency, making use of concepts such as self-reflexivity and ethics. Critical reflexivity involves the self questioning what is held to be "universal, necessary, obligatory." This kind of interrogation opens up a space for experimentation; reality is confronted with liberty and possibility. As many of the young people and families in my research show, the self must "grasp the points where change is possible and desirable, and . . . determine the precise form this change should take" (Foucault, 1984: 46). Thus, an analysis of personal agency must not dispense with the analysis of normative and normalizing ascriptive structures in identity formation and fluctuation. Foucault's notion of situated agency acknowledges that even critical skills and practices of resistance are themselves socially produced and constrained by cultural discourses. They are not simply the result of some "inner space" that transgresses the outer world. In relation to situated agency, questions arise in understanding why bisexual students and polyamorous families select certain actions and strategies of passing, bordering, and polluting as well as why they believe they need to undertake these actions. What are the various sociocultural, legal, and political discourses about family, sexuality, and schooling that frame the kinds of strategies border dwellers undertake and their belief in the need for specific types of strategies? How do they utilize the gaps, silences and distances between their various worlds and their "regimes of truth" to construct borders within which they can construct new "truths"?

In summary, being on the borders allows for mestizaje agency in relation to action, identity, and community allegiance. Passing, bordering, and polluting (normalization, negotiation, and noncompliance) happen simultaneously and in interwoven ways. Being located in the borderland involves a straddling of various political and social groups, drawing the best from each into a personal political system and remaining detached enough to be able to critique and challenge these very groups. It means working effectively for the issues of various groups according to one's own needs and beliefs, but refusing to be drawn into internal conformist factionalism. Being located in the borderland means acknowledging that while one is actively pursuing this metissage personal agency, choosing from the political, legal, economic, social, and cultural options available to one at a particular historical, economic, political time, there are external forces and discourses from both power-challenging minority communities and the powerful Center of the wider society constantly trying to pinpoint, locate, fixate, label, construct, and ascribe an identity that is acceptable and useful to them.

SOME METAPHORS OF MIXING AND MESSING: PASSING, BORDERING, AND POLLUTING

In endeavoring to articulate and understand metissage, theorists constantly use spatial, temporal, and other metaphors. Indeed, the very definitions of metaphor are based within notions of fluidity, shifting, and multiplicity (Derrida, 1982; Van Den Abbeele, 1992). "Metaphor" comes from *meta-phorein*, meaning to transfer or transport. This definition is very applicable to the use of metaphor as a literary or narrative device and conceptual strategy to articulate the shifts and unfixedness inherent in the lives of multiplaced/denied-a-place persons such as bisexual young people and "queerly mixed" families in schools. Through this linguistic device, there is an attempt at identification and description as well as an acknowledgment of the elusiveness and ambiguity of the subject and this very endeavor. For example, the hegemonic response to mestizaje ambiguity can be metaphorically illustrated by language pertaining to the abhorrence of viscosity and ambiguity. The way persons are "revolted by the sticky, an intermediate state betwixt and between the solid and the liquid" is discussed by Zerubavel (1991: 36). Similarly, "ambiguous creatures that straddle the boundaries of our conventional categories," such as the bat, "a sort of combination of a bird and a rat," are perceived with fear and anxiety. Interestingly, as a strategy of resistance and reclamation, the bat is often used metaphorically by bisexual communities to depict bisexual persons. Indeed, the vampire as part human/part animal and bordering life and death, is often a popular cultural image of a bisexual person, particularly in film. Other animals of metissage that are often considered abhorrent as they challenge the comforting distinction between order and chaos are reptiles that inhabit both land and water and insects that "dwell in cracks that are zones of separation and that, as parasites, are both part of and separate from us" (Zerubavel, 1991: 36).

As has already been presented in relation to social ascription, community belonging, and personal agency, in this research I am utilizing mainly three kinds of metaphors to explore and explain the border existences of bisexual young people and multipartnered families. These are "passing," "bordering," and "polluting." The following chapters will explore how these metaphors can assist us in understanding the experiences of border sexualities and border families by foregrounding the voices of these border dwellers and applying the metaphors. In the rest of this chapter, a more theoretical analysis of these metaphors themselves will be undertaken.

Metaphors of Passing

> You pass as straight, you pass as monogamous, you pass, pass, pass, so they'll leave you alone so you can pass through your life, raise your kids, enjoy love, with some peace.
>
> —Salvadore, bi-poly dad

> Wherever there is prejudice and preconception, there is passing.
>
> —Kroeger (2003: 4)

(a) The Closet and the Clothesline, or "Do You Want to Play Show and Tell?"

> I won't hang us out on the line for the world to shit on us. Until my kids can be guaranteed that they can do a "Show and Tell" at school about their family without any harassment, we're not showing or telling anything. That way, we can live and love the way we want and the school has no power over us.
>
> —Naomi, hetero-poly mom with one hetero-mono
> and one bi-poly partner

A well-known metaphor is the gay-liberationist construction of the closet as allowing for "passing" while concealing a deviant secret, set alongside my metaphor of the clothesline, where all is supposedly clean and on display—or polluting the visual/visible landscape. Kroeger provides a succinct definition of "passing":

> Passing involves erasing details or certain aspects of a given life in order to move past perceived, suspected, or actual barriers to achieve desired ends. . . . [It is] the act of creating, imposing, adopting, or rejecting a given identity and the way society rewards and personalizes people when they do. It is about not only crossing individual boundaries but also the anxiety this provokes. (2003: 8)

The relationships between passing (the closet) and polluting (the clothesline) are intertwined with the multiple within the closet and the multiple on the clothesline, and the fact that the "garments" on each travel between, within, and beyond both closet and clothesline. Both the closet and clothesline conflate a person as both Marginal and Central, as "*the* open secret" within a heteronormative culture (Sedgwick, 1993: 246). Sedgwick's (1990, 1993) "epistemology of the closet" has focused scrutiny on those who inhabit the clothesline who are more related to the closet than they would wish to think. They may not disclose any same-sex desires to themselves, let alone to others, thereby being closeted while inhabiting the clothesline. And of course, adultery, affairs, and cheating could be said to be a way of living with closets while existing on the clothesline of heterosexual marriage.

"Outing," or moving onto the clothesline, can also be a form of closeting. Revealing one's border sexuality and/or border family to a Central institution such as a school can result in stigmatization and stereotyping, which can again lead to a closeting:

> When you have spent your whole life in the closet, everyone you know, either personally or professionally, knows you as someone other than who you are. In coming out, you run the risk of losing all control, all ability to predict how everyone in your life will feel about you, interact with you, think of you. (McDonald, 2001: 166)

Thus, as Fuss writes, "Coming out was also simultaneously a closeting" in two ways (1991: 4). First, disclosure leaves people vulnerable to the simplistic ascriptions applied to them and with which they will be permanently labeled and classified at the school. Second, the *out*come of disclosure may encourage them to "closet" any future information about their lives in the Margin in order to avoid further public humiliation and pathologization. Yet, it also avoids further engagement and potential future affirmation by the wider school community with the intricacies of their lives.

Concealment as a strategy of survival is a form of personal agency, albeit fraught with self-problematization and tensions:

> When was the first time I noticed I had the gift of making myself invisible? . . . It was a self I erased myself, or was it that I was being erased? I don't know. The only thing I know was that I was still there. I knew that I was there, but nobody saw me. . . . Can they feel the *not* seeing me? or am I the only one who feels it because I know I'm there; because I am there, aren't I? (Lizarraga, 1993: 32)

Where in this ambiguous heterotopic space, in this wearing of a label, in the camouflage and the performance, does one identity leave off and the other begin? This sense of living "dissociated lives," structured by a "radical dissociation" (Eribon, 2004: 104) between a "presentable self and another reality hidden," also posits the closet as a multiple-within heterotopic space, a fluid counter-site that is "at once protective and obliterating, ordinary and alienating" (Persson and Richards, 2008: 79; see also Seidman, Meeks, and Traschen, 1999); allows for the existence and development of safe communities and networks; and has shifting, porous, and permeable borders as disclosure increasingly occurs strategically and cautiously (Foucault, 1986). As Worley explains, "As long as those who oppress, enslave, and colonize believe they are in control, believe they know what is going on, and view the other as transparent, the oppressed may steadily eat away at the socio-political-economic system's scaffolding, transforming the oppressive society while no one is looking" (2006: 518).

For a mestizaje bisexual student or a student from a polyamorous family, being in the closet is being both inside and outside at the same time. It is where the multiple-within of one's sexuality or family can be lived with minimal scrutiny and ascription, where there can be an effacing of limits and a radical confusion of identities. This concept of the closet as a political strategy is discussed by many mestizaje border dwellers such as Aruna, a lesbian of Tamil and Malaysian backgrounds: "Even as I am suspended between borders, between definitions, . . . I survive by remembering that going in and out of closets is a strategy for working to remove the conditions that make my closets necessary in the first place" (1994: 374). The closet, or passing, represents a possible mode of evading "other more undesirable forms of governance" such as rigidly being hung up on the clothesline to be buffeted by wind and rain and heat, and it is used in order to "assert a degree of control" over life. Mason calls this the "discourse of silence" but does acknowledge that growing visibility more effectively and quickly subverts the "regime of regulatory power" that renders certain sexualities "both unseeable and unknowable" (1995: 87).

Fisher believes the closet can be understood "not as a place for stillness and hiding but as a technology that enables action and investigation. . . . [I]t is not only necessary, but also empowering to retreat into the closet in various situations" (2003: 179). What Fisher calls "renters of hidden and unseen spaces, transitory occupants of dynamic closets" are able to "regularly travel across a trajectory of 'official' locations" (2003: 189):

> As skillful tacticians, we do not stay or remain fixed in the closet. Rather, it is our personal unfixed and fluid movement in and out of closet doors that offers us a certain currency in the social world . . . "escaping prediction" and "making do" in a world that enforces real consequences associated with sexual deviance and their betrayal of social norms. . . . It provides us with opportunities and possibilities for moving across flexible locations and ambiguous categorizations. (2003: 190; see also Persson and Richards, 2008)

Kroeger's study of passing also critiques its dominant construction "as a cop-out, with the passer complicit in the system that made it necessary to pass in the first place." She sees passing as providing possibilities for "effective if slow-moving means of hastening social change" (2003: 3). In the face of "oppressive and unfair" systems, passing may at times be more effective than protesting because the former would enable the passer to "meet his [or her] personal aspiration in the here and now" (2003: 132). Passing can thereby become a strategy for political action because, if it permits a person to gain some "standing" and stability, including economic stability, these can then provide access to future "power to be an agent of change" (2003: 133). Thus, although passing may sometimes be and feel like a "dissonant interjection" for border dwellers, it may serve the "purpose of smoothing a path of transition to a new and desired position or location" and therefore be a "dissonant smoothing" (2003: 210). It is a method of circumvention and subversion rather than opening oneself to persecution and imposed passivity. Kroeger also documents sociocultural shifts whereby "condemnation now falls less on the passer and more on the individuals and institutions whose policies, attitudes, or practices made the deception necessary in the first place" (2003: 217). Persson and Richards also argue that universally constituting "disclosure" as therapeutic and "healthy" tends to individualize stigma "and foreclose any consideration of the complexities of stigma as socially produced and lived, let alone any enabling or productive aspects of non-disclosure" (2008: 76). Thus, passing may be a powerful strategy for the passers in the immediate here and now, and in hindsight or retrospect, when the passers have reached a position of power where they can disclose their past acts of passing, this becomes another form of agency: pollution of the present by disclosing a past of passing. Nevertheless, the everyday living of "relationship concealment" in the present, which may be "outed" as the past in the future, can have harmful consequences in the present for personal and relational well-being, such as mental health issues including anxiety and fear and other personal health effects. "Relationship concealment" can also undermine relational commitment by constraining cognitive and emotional interdependence due to restrictions on being together, undertaking desired activities, and sharing experiences that are relationship-enhancing, particularly as regulated and repressed in public settings (Lehmiller, 2009).

Particularly in relation to polyamorous and multisexual families, concealment and passing strategies have been used so effectively that "there is much to see where traditional social science has failed to look" (Fisher, 2003: 173). As Brown writes, "The world produces the closet, and the closet itself produces a world" (2006: 323). In the following chapters, four major concealment/passing strategies will be evident in bisexual young people and polyfamilies in schools (Richardson, 1985):

- withdrawing: an either/or strategy that requires giving up a part of one's identity in a given school context;
- compartmentalizing: a both/and strategy which allows a person to place every different role into a different "airtight cubicle" in order to have the best of all worlds (Richardson, 1985:73);
- cloaking: a both/and strategy that involves people appearing to be "conventional, legitimate" which they both are and aren't (Richardson, 1985:74). This camouflage means using words like "auntie" or "family friend" to describe a polypartner; and

- fictionalizing: a metissage strategy, which involves performance, deception, and omission, constructing gaps and filling in gaps with creations and fantasies.

(b) The Metaphor of Performance

> I deserve an Academy Award! Every day I go to school and perform the straight boy. Every weekend I go to gay events and play the gay. It gets a bit freaky, like I'm not getting to be the bi boy, which you know is the role I really want to play. So it's like I play all the supporting roles but the lead role of Bryan the bisexual boy I don't get to play.

> —Bryan, seventeen, bi student

> The production of social life is a *skilled* performance.

> —Giddens (in Cohen, 1987: 286)

Social roles are played out according to scripts and discourses that have framed an individual's life since birth. Thus, the participants in my research are social performers who know the lines in the "dominant" drama of heterosexuality and the heteromonogamous family and are able to "take licence with the play, acting it in a variety of styles, substituting lines and switching characters" (Cohen and Taylor, 1976: 64). This type of script manipulation means mestizaje persons not only monitor their own performance of the script, but also display a variety of styles in that monitoring. Script switching, script evasion, and juxtaposition are standard elements in many "dramatic models" (1976: 66). Performance defines the kinds of passing strategies and "cultural gestures" mestizaje persons adopt in order to belong to diverse and often oppositional communities and negotiate the required identifications: "constantly changing costumes and roles, learning and adhering to a complex matrix of conventional behavior, and working hard to maintain their performance in each ongoing situation without undermining or threatening their *different* behaviors in *other* social situations. . . . Individuals must absorb the social conventions, must practice, rehearse, and maintain their performances" (Meyrowitz, 1985: 2).

One strategy is information control, by which mestizaje persons prevent others from discovering other facets of their identity and other communities they belong to. In part, this may be done by constructing and selectively presenting/performing only certain aspects of one's self to an audience (Plummer, 1975). Anzaldua (1990) uses the metaphor *"haciendo caras"* as a performance/passing strategy of mestizaje persons and points out both the ascribed and agentic elements of this strategy:

> *Haciendo caras,* "making faces" means to put on a face. . . . Some of us are forced to acquire the ability, like a chameleon, to change color when the

dangers are many and the options few. . . . Between the masks we've internalized, one on top of another, are our interfaces . . . between the masks
that provide the space from which we can thrust out and crack the masks
. . . we begin to acquire the agency of making our own *caras*. (Anzaldua,
1990: xv–xvi)

Another version of *haciendo caras* is what Hochschild calls "emotional
labor," or "emotional management." This involves inducing or suppressing one's feelings in order to "sustain the outward countenance
that produces the proper state of mind in others." Feelings are managed
"to create a publicly observable facial and bodily display" (1983: 7).
In this way, one or both of two desired outcomes or "exchange values"
and "use values" may be achieved: "pain avoidance" and "advantage-
seeking" (1983: 36). However, Hochschild also points to inherent dangers in these forms of "emotion work" or performance: first, at some
crucial points in life, the fusion or estrangement between the "true self"
and "acted self" will be tested; and second, the "false self," which is a
"sociocentric, other-directed self," may set itself up as the "real self" so
one's "inner self" never emerges (1983: 136). Hence, Hochschild's call
for a "healthy false self," which enables discretion and safety while allowing the emergence of the "true self" when there is minimal danger
(1983: 195). Of course, the whole dichotomous construction of "true"
and "false," "inner" and "acted" selves can be problematized as drawing
upon essentialist discourses of an authentic self removed from sociopolitical and sociocultural contextualization.

Some theorists such as Butler (1991) consider parody the most effective
strategy for subverting the fixed "binary frame." Parody is a form of passing, as it requires a mimicry and "repetition" of what and who is being
observed (see also Bordo, 1992). Thus, polyfamilies will perform a parody
of couple families and bisexual students can parody or mimic gayness and
straightness. The critical task for power-challenging movements and border
dwellers is "to locate strategies of subversive repetition" and to "affirm the
local possibilities of intervention through participating in precisely those
practices of repetition that constitute identity and, therefore, present the
immanent possibility of contesting them" (Butler, 1990: 147; see also Lugones, 1994).

Metaphors of Bordering

They say I'm a fence-sitter. Crap. I don't sit on a fence and do nothing. I
use the fence to get a good look at what's on all sides before I make my
moves.

—Marita, seventeen, bi student

Living as we did—on the edge—we developed a particular way of seeing reality. We looked both from the outside in and from the inside out. We focused our attention on the center as well as on the margin. We understood both . . . a mode of seeing unknown to most of our oppressors that sustained us.

—hooks (in Trinh, 1990a: 341)

(a) The Borderlands and Mestizaje

Crisscrossing more than one occupied territory at a time, she remains perforce inappropriate/d—both inside *and* outside her own social positionings. . . . A trajectory across variable praxes of difference, her (un)location is necessarily the shifting and contextual interval between arrested boundaries.

—Trinh (1991: 4)

In Anzaldua's (1987a, 1987b, 1989) work, the border zone becomes the site of much activity, agency, resistance, and creativity. As the next two chapters will illustrate, borderland theory resonates with the experiences of bisexual young people and "queerly mixed"/polyamorous families. In a constant state of transition, the prohibited and forbidden are the inhabitants of the borderlands, those who cross over, pass over, or go through the confines of the "normal" (Anzaldua, 1989: 194; see also Kamuf, 1991; Trinh, 1992; Lugones, 1994; Colker, 1996).

Anzaldua also utilizes the term *nepantla* to theorize liminality, and those who facilitate passages between worlds she names *nepantleras* (in Anzaldua and Keating, 2002: 1). Nepantla is a zone of possibility, where nepantleras are exposed to new perspectives and knowledge. It is an in-between place of constant transition: "Nepantla is the site of transformation, the place where different perspectives come into conflict and where you question the basic ideas, tenets, and identities inherited from your family, your education, and your different cultures" (2002: 547–48).

Thus, Anzaldua's work is pertinent to border sexualities and border families for it is about multiple divisions, and the borderland itself is a place of creative hybridity, as we shall see in the next section on border dwellers as agentic polluters. Mestizaje and nepantla theories "create new categories of identity for those left out or pushed out of existing ones" (McLaren, 1993: 142). The border is a metaphoric space of reflection, resistance, and transcendence where one can find "an overlay of codes, a multiplicity of culturally inscribed subject positions, a displacement of normative reference codes, and a polyvalent assemblage of new cultural meanings" (McLaren, 1993: 121).

(b) The Margin Metaphor

> When you're a fringe dweller, you're on edge all the time, waiting for the
> principal to call you up and tell you they got child welfare on to you.
> Waiting for your kids to come home bruised because they got bashed
> for having you as parents. When you're on the fringe of what society ex-
> pects, you're always on edge about what will happen to you. So you slink
> around corners, you know, like avoid going to school events, avoid your
> kids' friends coming over. It isn't healthy. But you also see how unhealthy
> some "normal" families are, so in the end, you know, you stay on the
> fringe 'cause it's safer and you get to live your family life at home the way
> you want without getting sucked into the whirlpool in the center.

> —John, hetero-poly dad with two hetero-mono partners

Although John's experiences of marginality above mainly present the impact of panopticonic fear (see Golovensky, 1952; Stonequist, 1961), constructs of the Margin can also be agentic, as the Margin can be a border site
of survival and nurturing and radical possibility. It is a "space of refusal,"
where one can "say no to the colonizer, no to the downpressor" (hooks,
1999: 341; see also Gunew, 1994; Erera, 2002). This insider/outsider bordering, or what Rutledge (2005) calls "dual marginality," of mestizaje persons, such as bisexual young people and "queerly mixed" families in this
research, means they often dwell both in the Margin and the Center and on
the borders between (see also see also hooks, 1994a, 1999; Billson, 2005;
Bersten, 2008). Indeed, border dwellers learn to survive by utilizing the ar-
tificial chasm between Margin and Center as the space that is "unknown" to
the oppressors from both the Center and the central within the Margins.

Metaphors of Polluting

> There's too much of me . . . I can't fit into a Tupperware plastic version of
> a married wife and mother. I'm not a tidy meal sealed in plastic. I leak, I
> ooze out, I'm a messy mixture.

> —Naomi, hetero-poly mom with one hetero-mono
> and one bi-poly partner

As explained in the introduction, "polluting" is used as a metaphor of
strength, agency, and empowerment, and is not intended to imply negative, insidious, harmful, or underhanded machinations. Indeed, it is only
through polluting existing and residual "Tupperware plastic versions" of
systems and structures that emergent and empowering systems and structures can evolve. It is via "messy mixtures" and their noncompliance, innovation, and resistance to their dominant "sealed in plastic" worlds, that far-
reaching, empowering political, social, and legal outcomes are initiated.

(a) Pollution and Impurity

The metaphor of pollution is often used to represent the disordering of orderly systems of classifications, replete with their distinctions between categories. Thus, it is very applicable to bisexual young people and multi-partnered families in this research. "Where there is dirt there is a system," the anthropologist Douglas writes about "pollution theory," as dirt is "simply the by-product of a systematic ordering and classification of matter" (1966: 2–3). Defining a person, idea, or action as a pollutant or metissage is its condemnation, as it is "likely to confuse or contradict cherished classifications" (Douglas, 1966: 48). She uses Sartre's (1943) essay on stickiness to explain her theory. Viscosity, he says, repels because it is a state halfway between solid and liquid (see also Zerubavel, 1991). "Danger lies in transitional states, simply because transition is neither one state nor the next, it is undefinable" (Douglas, 1966: 95–96).

Border metaphors teach that there is always a polluting excess, a supplement beyond fixed and normative poles that can never be subsumed. Mestizaje persons are seen as the excess or unable to be fixed and incorporated (Derrida, 1978, 1981; Burbules, 1997):

> What has happened, if it has happened, is a sort of overrun [debordement] that spoils all those boundaries and divisions and forces us to extend the accredited concept, . . . [but] it still will have come as a shock, producing endless efforts to dam up, resist, rebuild the old partitions, to blame what could no longer be thought without confusion, to blame difference as wrongful confusion! (Derrida in Kamuf, 1991: 256–57)

Bersten writes about the seepage of "edge identities," which negotiate multiple partial subjectivities in the interstices of multiple marginalized communities: "The fear, the liminal panic, inspired by the edge identity is a fear of the borderless, infectious. There is no clarity; . . . we seep beyond, always" (2008: 25). These notions of pollution—seepage, impurity, and defilement—are applicable to polyamorous parents as they pollute the socially sanctioned construction of monogamous marriage and nuclear parenting, creating spaces of agency, innovation, and possibilities.

(b) The Undecidables

> How can a school classify me and my family? Frankenstein's monsters? Edward Scissorhands? They don't know what to make of us, what to call me. But we're there and they have to deal with us.
>
> —Mateusz, sixteen, bi son of bi-poly dad

Derridean differance can refer to structures and movements that cannot be conceived on the basis of the either/or opposition of presence/absence.

Derrida defines these as "undecidables" (1981: 71). *Differance* describes the way categories are always attempting to "hold down" a meaning that can never be fully expressed. "There are only, everywhere, differences and traces of traces" (Derrida in Culler, 1982: 99). Thus, Derrida's "undecidables" are located within the third space of *differance*, the space of ambiguity where is found the *supplement*: a word standing for both an addition and a replacement, the outside that enters the inside, the difference that turns into identity, and thus "is neither a plus nor a minus, neither an outside nor the complement of an inside, neither accident nor essence" (Derrida, 1981: 42–43). In his study of migration, culture, and identity, Bauman uses the Derridean definition of the "undecidable" to represent any identity that "calls the bluff of the opposition" between mainstream and marginal (1990: 145): "Undecidables . . . their under-determination is their potency: because they are nothing, they may be all. . . . They brutally expose the fragility of a most secure of separations. They bring the outside into the inside, and poison the comfort of order with suspicion of chaos" (Bauman, 1990: 146).

These metaphors of impure "undecidables" aptly apply to bisexual young people and "queerly mixed" families: "They are that third element which should not be. The true hybrids, the monsters: not just unclassified, but unclassifiable. . . . They question oppositions as such, the very principle of the opposition, the plausibility of dichotomy. . . . They unmask the brittle artificiality of division" (Bauman, 1990: 148–49; see also Bhabha, 1990b).

At the macro level, Bauman (1973, 1990, 1997) argues that societies and institutions such as educational institutions "can be understood in terms of their need to establish an order or structure" and thus alleviate the "slimy" or "the stranger that threatens the stability and coherence" of the social order inherent within or framing the institution. This is accomplished by "suppressing and excluding any individual or group that comes to symbolize disorder or ambivalence" (Marotta, 2002: 38). The imposition of order and purity on a "chaotic world" leads to "exclusionary practices," and paradoxically, in seeking "to eliminate chaos and ambivalence" and pollutants, the push to purity "reproduces them" (Marotta, 2002: 39). Pollutants such as bisexual young people and polyamorous families are agentically "embracing ambivalence, contingency and uncertainty and thus transcending boundaries" (Marotta, 2002: 40). In this way, they are agents in the reconstitution of the social order.

(c) The Stranger

> It's like you're a stranger coming in to this new land, or new planet because what they see as normal and obvious, you question. You go, "why is it like that?" "Who said it has to be this way?" "When did this start be-

ing that way?" And they have no answers because they can't see anything else but what they live. And if you do it enough at school, they call you strange, freakazoid, schizoid.

—Andrea, seventeen, bi student

There are friends and enemies. And there are *strangers.*

—Bauman (1990: 143)

The metaphor of the stranger depicts a potential wanderer with the agentic characteristics of mobility, freedom from convention, and abstract relations (Simmel, 1971). The stranger is not rooted in the peculiar attitudes and biased tendencies of the group she or he encounters and may seek to belong to. The stranger's freedom from conventions contains "all sorts of dangerous possibilities," since strangers such as bisexual young people and "queerly mixed" families are not confined in their actions by "custom, piety, or precedents" (Wood, 1934: 250).

The stranger challenges a group's or institution's "thinking as usual," which functions "to eliminate troublesome inquiries by offering ready-made directions for use, to replace truth hard to attain by comfortable truisms" (Schutz, 1944: 501). The stranger questions nearly everything that seems to be unquestionable or "taken-for-granted" (Schutz, 1944: 507). As a mestizaje person, "the cultural pattern of the approached group is to the stranger not a shelter but a field of adventure, not a matter of course but a questionable topic of investigation, not an instrument for disentangling problematic situations but a problematic situation itself" (Schutz, 1944: 506). The stranger remains a permanent "slimy," always threatening to wash out the boundaries vital to identity (Bauman, 1988–89: 11). The "foreigners" are never simply torn between here and elsewhere, now and before, but instead belong nowhere and everywhere (Kristeva, 1991), and from this location can resist, negotiate, and transform the "fixity" and "rigidity" around them through noncompliance.

This chapter has undertaken three theoretical discussions: defined and outlined bisexuality and polyamory; considered their positionings according to social ascription, community belonging, and personal agency; and presented metaphors of passing (normalization), bordering (negotiation), and polluting (noncompliance). The following chapters will undertake a more detailed investigation of the research participants' experiences and perceptions of schooling in relation to the above theoretical discussions by foregrounding the voices and narratives of the participants themselves.

3

"We're the X-Files"

When Bisexuality "Messes Up" Sexual Dichotomy in Schools

One evening, as we wait for my daughter Steph's computing class to begin, three girls around twelve years old come cheerily in to collect some material for their next class. They look confident and speak assertively, arms and hair swinging. I notice Steph has taken my hand and is squeezing it.

I look across and notice a faint shy blush on Steph's face. "What's up, Steph?"

Steph is still staring at the girls. She whispers, "Which one do you like?"

"All of them. They look like really nice, smart young women."

Steph persists. "No! I mean, which one do you *like?*"

"Which one do *you* like, sweetie?"

Steph nods her head toward the long-haired girl in jeans and t-shirt who's doing most of the questioning in articulate computer-speak. "Do you like her too?"

"Yes, I do," I reply.

Steph smiles slightly, pleased, still not taking her eyes off the girl.

"What're you feeling, Steph?"

Steph smiles shyly. She shrugs and looks at me with embarrassment. I squeeze her hand. "It's okay, Steph. She's gorgeous and if you think that, that's fine. Enjoy those feelings, there's nothing wrong with them."

—Pallotta-Chiarolli (1999c: 78)

I remember this incident for the frankness, simplicity, and awe with which an eight-year-old girl, my daughter, recognized her attraction for an older girl. I remember the wonder in her eyes, the blush on her cheeks, and the way her warm little hand squeezed mine. Until then, Steph had had crushes on boys and had never expressed an attraction for a girl. And she has never expressed an attraction for a girl since then, even though as parents we had always let her know that whatever her sexuality would be, we would celebrate it and support her.

I also remember the slight embarrassment and a lack of words to describe whatever she was feeling for this older girl, despite growing up in a family and various communities where sexual diversity and family diversity were given labels, acknowledgment, and affirmation. I realized at that point that the heteronormative world unfortunately framed and leaked into our family and communities, and I have documented (Pallotta-Chiarolli, 1999c, 1999d; Curran, Chiarolli and Pallotta-Chiarolli 2009) how that world insidiously manifested itself in her school settings. That evening, she still sought a parent's affirmation that what she was feeling was wonderful, natural, and to be enjoyed, despite being told this for her whole childhood life. And yet, I also felt some satisfaction and encouragement that, as parents, we had provided a space or sanctuary within our family and communities that at least allowed Steph to have such an open conversation with her mother, and indeed, led her to assume her mother would naturally be experiencing similar attractions.

ON THE BORDERS OF SEXUALITY RESEARCH: INTRODUCING THE "X-FILES"

I can't wait to leave school so I can get educated.

—Marita, seventeen, bi student

Bisexuality and bisexual young people reside on the borders of sexuality research. Heath (2005) refers to the "silent B" in much GLBT research. The most basic questions that motivate and gain major funding in both quantitative and qualitative gay and lesbian research, such as "how many?" and "who are they?" remain unanswered and underresearched in relation to bisexual-identifying and bisexual-behaving young people (Pallotta-Chiarolli, 2006a). The available evidence does suggest that bisexuals are more numerous if we take into account not only identifying as bisexual but behaving bisexually throughout the life span. For example, in the United States, the Centers for Disease Control and Prevention's National Center for Health Statistics found that 14 percent of young women and 6 percent of young men in their late teens and early twenties reported at least one same-sex encounter (Mosher, Chandra, and Jones, 2005). They also found that 1.8 percent of men and 2.8 percent of women aged eighteen to forty-four gave their sexual preference as bisexual. Taking identity and behavior into account, Owens (1998) estimates lesbians and gays at 6 to 10 percent of the adolescent population and bisexuals at less than 30 percent. Thus, although there appears to be a significant number of bisexual-identifying and/or behaving young people in our school communities, if actually not more than gay and lesbian young people, they are the group that receives less research attention.

The exact number of bisexual youth is difficult to determine for two main reasons. First, due to the label itself being stigmatized, many young people may feel coerced to identify as either heterosexual or homosexual in research. Second, the figures vary depending upon whether the research has been conducted using sexual identity and/or sexual behavior as the defining criteria (Fox 2004; see also Russell and Seif, 2002). For example, many heterosexual-identifying young people who have one or more same-sex experiences would tick the "heterosexual" box in a survey. In other cases, researchers have actually decided which kind of "bisexual" young person they will include in their studies. For example, despite young women identifying as bisexual and being recruited from GLBT young people's community groups for his research, D'Augelli chose to only include those young women "whose sexual orientation was not more heterosexual than lesbian" in order to "create a more homogenous sample of females" (2003: 12; see also Diamond, 2008). Thus, young women identifying as bisexual, having sex with other young women, attending GLBTIQ community groups, but stating they were "mostly heterosexual" or "unsure," were excluded. This is despite the researcher stating that the cohort contained "self-selected samples of lesbian and bisexual females who . . . are sufficiently open about their sexual orientation to attend groups for lesbian, gay and bisexual youth" (D'Augelli, 2003: 27).

The importance of undertaking research in order to inform health and education policy has always been a given, and yet this connection has largely remained ignored in relation to bisexual young people (Pallotta-Chiarolli, 2005a, 2006b). Research conducted by the Ontario Public Health Association in Canada (see Dobinson, 2003, 2005) and a study conducted in the UK (see King and McKeown, 2003) found bisexual people have worse mental health than their homosexual or heterosexual counterparts. Other studies also consistently report that bisexual youth have higher rates of suicide attempts, substance abuse, and overall health risks (Eisenberg and Wechsler, 2003; Goodenow, Netherland, and Szalacha, 2002; Robin et al., 2002; Udry and Chantala, 2002; Ford and Jasinski, 2006; Warner et al., 2004). In Australia, the importance of bisexual-specific research became evident when Jorm and associates (2002) publicized their alarming findings into Australian bisexual youth health. In the same year, the Australian Medical Association released a position statement, "Sexual Diversity and Gender Identity" (2002), that includes a statement finally acknowledging how recent studies report that bisexual people have worse mental health than their homosexual or heterosexual counterparts. This was accredited to more adverse life events and less positive support from family and friends, as well as possibly being at greater risk of sexually transmitted diseases (STDs) due to a lack of targeted health promotion activities.

Yet, in spite of these findings, "as gay and lesbian issues have begun to reach Australian health policy machinery, bisexual people have been almost completely excluded" (Heath, 2005). For example, Heath (2005) refers to how the Ministerial Advisory Committee on Gay and Lesbian Health in Victoria (MACGLHV) notes the lack of research on the sexual health needs of "bisexually active" people. However, it proposes "nothing to rectify this situation." Rather, it calls for the establishment of a health and well-being policy and research unit that would "focus on gay and lesbian health but address bisexual, trans and intersex health issues insofar as they overlap with those of gay men and lesbians" (Ministerial Advisory Committee on Gay and Lesbian Health Victoria, 2003: 149). This notion of overlapping can be deployed to deny or marginalize bisexual specificity according to its inclusion within or pertinence to gay and lesbian health (Volpp, 2010). At state policy level, this is a highly problematic example of "exclusion by inclusion" (Martin and Pallotta-Chiarolli, 2009; Pallotta-Chiarolli and Martin, 2009). By 2009, the MACGLHV had been renamed the Ministerial Advisory Committee on Gay, Lesbian, Bisexual, Transgender and Intersex Health and Wellbeing (known as GLBTI MAC), and published *Well Proud: A Guide to Gay, Lesbian, Bisexual, Transgender and Intersex Inclusive Practice for Health and Human Services.* Thus, in both title and objectives, this document is more focused on diversity and specificity within the queer communities, such as listing bi-specific organizations and services. However, "overlap" is still evident in its health issues and needs sections on "gay and bisexual men" and "lesbian and bisexual women."

Internationally, in the research that does exist, bisexuality is largely subjected to one or more of four types of problematic representations in sexual and emotional adolescent health and education research, and in the wider populist culture:

1. Underrepresentation

This invisibilizes bisexual young people. In their review of "scholarly attention previously given to mental health among bisexual individuals when compared to homosexual and heterosexual individuals," Dodge and Sandfort found that the number of articles that present "relevant information specific to bisexuals in terms of mental health is a miniscule proportion of the published literature on sexual orientation and mental health" (2007: 41; see also Volpp, 2010). Indeed, Diamond argues that many studies of same-sex sexuality "have specifically excluded bisexually identified individuals over the years for the sake of conceptual and methodological clarity," rather than exploring the messiness/metissage of sexual diversity (2008: 5). She found that from 1995 to 2005, only 19 percent of journal articles published on same-sex sexuality included the words "bisexual" or "bisexuality" in the title, abstracts, or subject headings. Although this is an increase from 3 percent in the 1975–1985 timeframe, it is still "somewhat ironic" given that "bisexual patterns of sexual attraction and behavior are more common than previously thought" and more common than exclusive same-sex patterns (2008: 5; see also Diamond, 2009).

As discussed earlier in relation to the MACGLHV, a particular method of invisibilization is what can be called "exclusion by inclusion" (Martin and Pallotta-Chiarolli, 2009; Pallotta-Chiarolli and Martin, 2009). This is evident in the way educational and health organizations focusing on same-sex attraction gain funding for projects that appear to be inclusive of bisexual young people by including bisexuality as a category in their project outlines and submissions, but they do not follow through with bisexual-specific recommendations, outcomes, and services for youth (Malinsky, 1997; Russell and Seif, 2002; Ryan and Rivers, 2003).

There are many of these examples of bisexual "exclusion by inclusion" in international health research (Hughes and Eliason, 2002; Cabaj, 2005; Parsons, Kelly, and Wells, 2006). In 1998, Garofalo and associates found lesbian, gay, and bisexual (LGB) young people were three and a half times as likely to have attempted suicide during the past year or be victims of forced sexual contact, and they were more likely to engage in risky behaviors such as alcohol and drug abuse than were heterosexual youth. Although it was noted that 78 percent of the sample identified as bisexual, there was no comment upon how this high proportion might affect the findings. Ten years later, "exclusion by inclusion" research based within the sexual bifurcation discourse was still being undertaken and published, albeit more often problematizing these research methods and sexual binary systems of classification. For example, Hatzenbuehler and others (2008) explored alcohol use among LGB and heterosexual young adults that demonstrated higher rates of alcohol consumption among what they call "nonheterosexual" young men and women. They concluded that "minority stress" would add to the consumption of alcohol among LGB adolescents and young adults "in order to cope with stress related to having a stigmatized identity" (2008: 88). However, as they conceded, they did not analyze their data to determine how different types and levels of "minority stress" within the LGB grouping may have impacted upon individual alcohol consumption levels. After acknowledging that the combination of "individuals with same-sex and both-sex orientations . . . obscured important within-group differences among LGB students," the researchers recommend that future studies "should oversample bisexuals, especially in light of recent findings" that they are at higher risk "for substance use and abuse" (2008: 88).

2. Misrepresentation

This occurs via media and popular culture stereotypical constructions, societal presumptions, and prejudices (Boulton and Fitzpatrick, 1993, 1996; Bryant, 1996, 2005a, 2005b; McLean, 2001, 2003). "Female bisexuals are often tossed into the script as erotic grist for the heterosexual male target audience. Male bisexuals are excluded for the same reason . . . [or are] included to heighten the perversity of the sinister character" (Bryant in Alexander, 2007: 117). Where historical bisexual characters are filmed, their same-sex relationships are usually written out of the script (Bryant, 2005a). For example, in the film *Troy*, the loving relationship between Achilles and Patroclus is reduced to that of friends and cousins.

Bisexual young people grow up seeing very few bisexual characters in the media and those they do see encompass negative bisexual stereotypes such as criminals, murderers, AIDS carriers, and vampires—and they usually end up dead. For example, in *Dallas Doll*, the bisexual deceptive and manipulative Dallas "parasitically insinuates herself" into the life of the Sommers family (Watson, 2008), seducing the father, mother, and son. Thus, she constructs a polyfamily by destroying the love, cohesion, and connections within the original nuclear heteronormative monogamist family. Via this deliberate fragmentation, Dallas is able to take their land, establish a Disney-like golf course, and become wealthy. In the end, however, the rather "alien" Dallas is whisked away by "real" aliens in a UFO. Whether she has died or been taken by the aliens to join them in outer space remains ambiguous. Although this characterization and plot regarding Dallas is highly problematic and complicit with prevailing stereotypes of bisexuals as "sexual vampires," "aliens" out to entrap "anything that moves," or as the "all-too-convenient trope by which the dramatic tension of the stereotypical love triangle is heightened" (Andre in Alexander, 2007: 120), Watson (2008) argues that the disintegration of the middle-class heteronormative monogamist family also proves to be liberatory and transformative as its members are given greater agency to determine what they want their lives to actually be. This is particularly the case for the mother, who establishes the exhilarating independent life on a farm that she had once experienced in her childhood. Watson's critique can also be applied to the *Rocky Horror Picture Show*, wherein it is the bisexual Dr. Frank N. Furter, a self-proclaimed "sweet transvestite" from the planet of Transsexual in the galaxy of Transylvania, who is killed at the end of the movie by his own servants. He seduces both Brad and Janet, a newly engaged middle-American heterosexual young couple, who arrive at his castle symbolically lost on a stormy night. The seduction may be deceptive, but it does awaken their sexualities and insights so that they leave the castle far wiser and with greater depths to their characters.

There are also films that present images of bi-eroticism but either fail to mention the word "bisexuality," as in *Chasing Amy*, or fail to develop a character's life as bisexual, particularly if the character is male (Yescavage and Alexander, 2003; Bryant, 2005b). Andre refers to this as "bisexuality and bi-eroticism as 'implications' in people's lives, and without exposition" (in Alexander, 2007: 120). For example, bisexuality may be constructed as a temporary "phase" or experimental, as in the films *Threesome* and *Just One Time*, with a return to the more "mature" and "authentic" monosexuality (straight or gay) and/or marriage by the end of the film.

In Gregg Araki's *Splendor*, we actually see a woman express her "femantasy" to her two male partners, Simpson's (2006) term for a woman's desire to watch men have sex with each other. Even though the three of them do make love, with one screen kiss between the men, and set up a long-term relationship as a polyfidelitous triad, replete with twin babies, the men are presented as engaging sexually with the woman, not with each other, even though there is a growing "bi-affectionate" emotional intimacy between them. Interestingly, *Splendor*, by gay-identifying director Araki, was a homage to the actor Kathleen Robertson, whom he had previously cast as a lesbian in his earlier film, *Nowhere*, and with whom he had a relationship for two years.

Splendor also follows Araki's more violent movie, *The Doom Generation*, which is part of his youth trilogy. This latter film has been the subject of much debate: Is it "cinematic trash" or a "cultural treasure"? Indeed, as Watson (2008) concluded with *Dallas Doll*, some cultural analysts such as Hart (2005) see it as bordering/being both. It is a road movie about Amy and Jordan, young "druggies" who get involved with a bisexual named Xavier who, in common metaphoric representations of bisexual people, is presented as a drifter: rootless and going nowhere. He has also just shot a Korean convenience store owner, and from there the three unwittingly commit a series of murders. Thus, we have what could be surmised as the typical bisexual criminal introducing a somewhat fragile, somewhat naïve heterosexual couple to "the dark side" of crime and murder. And yet, simultaneously, Xavier challenges the couple's ideas about the gay/straight duality (Hart, 2005). Indeed, the film explores the attraction between the two young men and their relationships with Amy. There are several erotic scenes between Xavier and Amy intended to entice Jordan to join in. The film ends with the brutal killing of Xavier and Jordan, with Jordan's penis being severed and placed in Xavier's mouth, by neo-Nazi gay-bashers. This occurs just as the two young men are about to consummate their sexual relationship without Amy present. Hart argues that despite the "unexpected, remarkably brutal bloodbath" at the end of the film, "it effectively represents Araki's way of making an incredibly powerful statement about the repressive nature of hegemonic ideology in the United States in relation to bisexual men and other nonheterosexual individuals" (2005: 54–55). Indeed, Araki has given his three characters the surnames of Red, White, and Blue. Hart concludes,

> Paradoxically speaking, even cinematic works that appear on their surface to be trash can contain substantial cultural value as they lead their viewers to stretch beyond their comfort zones. . . . [Araki's films with] their intentionally raw depictions of extreme aggression, angst, nihilism . . . [and] dysfunctional young people striving desperately to forge any sort of meaningful relationship with another . . . vividly and powerfully embody the very undercurrents of anarchy, disorder and (sexual) otherness that civilized societies of all kinds have, for generations, been striving to repress at virtually any cost. (2005: 67)

There have been some recent shifts in representations of bisexuality that do not depend on negative, antisocial stereotypes or the horror/science fiction genres in order to make a point about the need to disrupt heteronormative monogamist constructions of sexuality and relationships. One example is the film *De-Lovely*: after a cinematic history of married bisexual men being portrayed as deceitful adulterers, this Cole Porter biopic is the first mainstream film in which a bisexual man actually tells his wife about his attraction to men before they are married. Another example is the French film *French Twist* which uses humor and tenderness in its story about a straight housewife/mother with an adulterous husband. She falls in love with a butch lesbian yet realizes she is still in love with her husband. Together, the three of them raise the two children, and indeed, the lesbian character becomes pregnant by the husband after a one-night stand. By the end of the film, the husband has ceased his secret adultery, is seen caring for the new baby and kissing the two women who are nursing the new baby in bed. And in a final "twist," while trying to find a new house for the expanding family, the husband meets a man with whom there is a strong suggestion of future intimacy. Thus, the film has mapped a progression or a set of "twists" from heteropatriarchal pretend monogamy and sexual dichotomous fixedness to a mestizaje reality of bisexuality and polyamory that "models the expanded [multisexual] families one finds in polyamorist communities around the world" (Anderlini-D'Onofrio, 2009b: 353–54; see also Anderlini-D'Onofrio, 2009a)

This leads me to another major absence in popular culture: positive representations of bisexual parents, particularly fathers. Again, even if a character may be read as a bisexual parent, the label "bisexuality" is absent or the parenting storyline is a subplot. For example, *A Home at the End of the World*, based on the novel by Michael Cunningham (1990), has "sex, drugs, and polyamory, but it doesn't have a man who calls himself bisexual" (Bryant, 2005b: 311). Nonetheless, two men start as close teenage friends, become lovers, are both eventually involved with the same woman with whom they have a child, and move to the country to raise her as very loving fathers. Another example, *Brokeback Mountain* has sparked ongoing debate regarding whether Jack and Ennis are married gay men or married bisexual men, given that they are shown proactively establishing sexual and loving relationships with women after they have acknowledged their love for each other (see for example Pitt, 2006; Watson, 2008). Nevertheless, both men are portrayed as capable fathers who wish to maintain loving relationships with their children as well as their authority as fathers. In particular, Jack's authority as a father is challenged by his father-in-law, who appears to suspect that Jack is not "a real man." We see Jack asserting his position as head of the household, much to the delight and approval of his wife. In relation to Ennis, after losing much contact and access to his daughters after the divorce and his ex-wife's remarriage, the film ends with his adult daughter coming to find him in the caravan, where he lives alone, to invite him to her wedding.

In *Priscilla, Queen of the Desert*, the drag queen character, Tick, could be called bisexual, as he has a wife and a son in Alice Springs (Hunn, 2002). Indeed, it is his wife's nightclub he travels to through the Central Australian desert by bus with two fellow drag performers in order to financially support her with the drag show. And it is his son with whom he reestablishes a relationship and takes back to Sydney to live with him. His son actually soothes his father's anxieties about how he will cope with living in Sydney's gay culture. Part of the reassurance that he will be a good father occurs when his son lets him know that his mother has told him all about Tick and his lifestyle in Sydney, and "it's not a problem." These later scenes contrast with Tick's earlier reluctance to admit the existence of a wife and son, which "is vindicated by the shock responses of his co-travellers," the gay Adam and transsexual Bernadette (Watson, 2008). Also of interest is that although the film skirted around naming and developing the bisexuality and fathering role of Tick, the character was based on well-known Sydney drag queen, Cindy Pastel (aka Ritchie Fingers), whose son grew up in Sydney with his father and whose mother eventually joined them there. Upon recently retiring from performing, Pastel explained in an Australian gay newspaper interview,

> The Priscilla thing didn't really work in my favor . . . after it came out to the world that I was bisexual. Had it not been advertised that I was bisexual I probably could have gone on just as a typical person who got on with their life and didn't need labels. . . . It's time now to pull away from the scene because I just don't feel like I fit in. (Lamont, 2008: 5)

Hence, in this specific intersection of art and life, it appears that art presented the border possibilities that were not available to Tick in his real life. Indeed, the filmic portrayal and publicity of this reconciliation of multiple worlds at the border problematized his border reality as a bisexual father/drag queen in Sydney.

One other film that presents a father whose bisexuality is not revealed until his blackmailing gay partner turns up at his funeral is the dark comedy, *Death at a Funeral*. We see the adult offspring struggle to connect the image they have of their father as a dedicated "decent" father who adored their mother with the new images of their father in typical costume gay dance-party attire in the arms of his male partner, which they find abhorrent. Indeed, the dead man's wife is earlier depicted wondering how she will live without her very considerate and loving husband. The slapstick humor involved in the events that ensue, such as trying to conceal this new information about their father's other life in order not to discredit him in front of his family and friends, and trying to conceal the accidental death of the male partner by placing him in the coffin with the father, give way to a sobering eulogy delivered by one of the sons. In this eulogy, the father is described as inspirational to his children in teaching them to aim for their desires in life, and whether they succeed or fail, the importance is in the endeavor. Words like "decent" and "loving," which had been applied to the father before his bisexuality was dramatically and comically exposed, are reclaimed and reaffirmed in the eulogy. Indeed, new descriptions such as "exceptional," "understanding," and "good" are added. In addition, the man's family and friends are asked to gain wisdom and reestablish commonality in accepting the complexities, chaos, and confusion of life, love, and being human. Again, Hart's (2005) theory is substantiated: that through such humor, shock, "grossness," and mockery, which effectively engage a mainstream voyeuristic audience, can come opportunities for moral lessons and cultural interrogations.

Another dominant misrepresentation in the media and mainstream society is "bisexual men as AIDS carriers" (Worth, 2003). All the bisexual young men in my research were aware of this and other misrepresentations (Pallotta-Chiarolli, 2005a, 2006a; see also Eliason, 2001) either through what they heard in their local communities or through their own reading:

> When I was doing my AIDS research, I came across this survey done in England with school children aged something like thirteen to eighteen and it was talking about AIDS and it was talking about who's to blame. . . . They divided it up into high blame, middle blame and whatever, stuff like that. But one of the high blame said stuff like it's the murderous bisexual males that we should kill because they're the ones who have spread it to our innocent heterosexual community. It's almost like if they're gay, they'll never change and we'll just

let them sort of kill themselves off with this AIDS disease, but these bisexual males, they spread it to us and we really have to stop them. (Benjamin, nineteen, bi university student)

In young women's magazines, the readers, presumed to be heterosexual young women themselves, are advised that all bisexually active young men are secretly engaging in sexual relations with other young men; having a bisexual boyfriend is "dangerous" and "risky," as all women in relationships with bisexually active men are unaware of or have no say in their partner's sexual identity and sexual practices, and therefore are at high risk of contracting STDs; they are also informed that bisexual men are predatory and will have sex with "anything that moves." Jack, a bisexual polyamorous young man, recalls the responses of many heterosexual males to him that illustrate the impact of this last kind of representation:

The amount who affirm to me their heterosexuality—I don't need to know, I don't care. And they say, "Oh, no, but I'm straight, straight." In case I was going to molest you because all bisexuals molest people. Now that they've said that, they are somehow safeguarded: "He can't touch me." Against this imaginary threat to their sexuality. (Jack, bi-poly university student)

In relation to bisexuality and young women, the main myth is that most girls are transient bisexuals, "trendy bisexuals" (Burleson, 2005), or what Marita, a seventeen-year-old bisexual young woman, calls the "drunk-on-a-date bisexual," experimenting or "phasing" with sex with other girls, usually for the "normal" titillation of their heterosexual boyfriends, before returning to or restoring one's true "normal" (sober?) heterosexuality (see Herdt, 2001; Atkins, 2002; Russell and Seif, 2002; Fahs, 2009). Katy Perry's "I Kissed a Girl" is a recent pop song with an accompanying video clip, both very popular with adolescents while incensing many lesbian and bisexual activists, as it all too conveniently fits these normative stereotypes. Although the whole song is about the act of kissing a girl, the video clip does not have one kiss between Katy Perry and other girls. Instead, there are lots of scenes of hyperfeminine girls attired in standard masculinist porn lingerie and burlesque outfits parading, posing, and pouting for the camera rather than for each other. The clip ends with Perry waking up in bed next to her boyfriend, as if waking up from a troubling dream. As she looks across to him, her facial expressions are those of relief and comfort that it was just a dream and she is safely in a hetero bed with her hetero man. While the lyrics say she liked kissing a girl and hopes her boyfriend doesn't mind, Perry winks flirtatiously at the camera as if knowing that most boyfriends will indeed not mind it at all. Other lines emphasize that kissing a girl is part of her "experimental game" and not related to love, thereby undermining and negating the potentialities of deeper, committed, and long-lasting relationships between women. This kind of heteropatriarchal framing of same-sex attractions and delineation of how these attractions can be deployed contribute to the "erasure of bisexuality as an authentic sexual identity" and create "uneasiness" for those women identifying as such (Thompson, 2006: 57). However, Thompson argues that even though girls' same-sex attractions and practices from childhood are reinscribed through heterosexual and masculinist norms of desire and female objectification, they simultaneously undermine them by "creating a space for same-sex desire and same-sex sexual play in the lives of young girls" (2006: 57). Thus, popular cultural representations such as Perry's song and video clip may be situated on a complex border where they may be suggestive of same-sex possibilities for young women even while undermining or confining them to comply with hetero-masculinist norms.

Two films, *April's Shower* and *Imagine Me and You*, explore women's bisexualities without pandering to the heteropatriarchal constructions discussed above. Although problematic in their absence of the term *bisexual*, these two films clearly disrupt three dominant assumptions regarding women's interpersonal and sexual lives: the significance of heteronormative rituals and structures such as weddings and bridal showers; the homonormative constructions of lesbian sexualities as fixed and stable; and the inevitability of women who have sexual relationships with other women leaving the female partner in order to establish a more "real" and loving relationship with a man. As Hagen summarizes, both films present female bisexuality "as a vehicle for women to learn to follow their hearts rather than blindly conform to social norms" (2008: 347) via following the dilemmas and conflicts the protagonists experience "between their interests in conforming to the standards of a heterosexist society and engaging in a same-sex love that is not socially and legally legitimized" (2008: 349). In each film, the bride-to-be, April, or recently married bride, Rachael, leaves her male partner, whom she still loves, to be with the woman she loves more. Thus, bisexuality in women is seen as being about love and emotional commitment as much as about sexual action. Interestingly, in *April's Shower*, the one woman who appears to be the only "real" lesbian finds herself sexually attracted to and beginning a relationship with a man with whom she also shares other passions such as painting and food ("prosciutto and figs").

Thus, a major misrepresentation that has been discussed so far is explicit sexual mainstream representations of bisexual young women as "Penthouse bisexuals" (Burleson, 2005): they emulate the "hot bi babe girl on girl action" that is a staple of "straight male porn" and indeed, impact upon what young men come to expect and demand from girls:

Guys sometimes want to know which I like better, men or women, and when I answer both equally, the first thing they say is "then let's hook up the threesome," and I say, "OK, let's find a guy we both like," and that gets them every time. The thing is, they don't bother to ask if I'm even into threesomes and what kind, it's just like my bisexuality's there at their command, like, for them to control. (Katrina, eighteen, bi student)

Katrina's experiences are an example of how cultural constructions of women's bisexuality are based on heteropatriarchal fantasy. Fahs (2009) refers to "public performative bisexuality" expected from women who internalize heteropatriarchal cultural scripts regarding women's sexualities, particularly as it is proliferated in the media and popular culture. In her research, she found "the demand for conformity to performative [hyperfeminine] bisexuality [on young women] was striking" (2009: 444). It needs to be stated that this is not to deny or repress women's erotic pleasures should they enjoy or desire "performing bisexuality" for male partners. What is of concern is the lack of a woman's agency in scripting and staging her sexual encounters with women and what role men will play in these encounters—and indeed what same-sex action she might desire between the men. What is of concern is the high level of coercion, scripting, and staging by men that women experience in "male-dominated, male-controlled, male-observed" same-sex eroticism constructed as men's entertainment (2009: 446). It reminds me of a situation that arose when my best girlfriend and I exchanged a hug and kiss while waiting for coffees to be served at a café counter. We heard some snickers and looked over to find two young men who were serving behind the counter, leaning back into each other with arms folded as if reclining on an armchair watching TV, staring at us with surly smiles. "Do it again for us," one of them commanded, with what was meant to be a sexy sneer. "Okay," I said, "but you do it first for us," and I pointed to the man next to him, performing my own leery sneer. "No way," and they both jumped a few feet away from each other (Pallotta-Chiarolli, 2006c).

In my workshops with adolescent girls in schools, I am often told about girls "dirty dancing" or "pashing at parties" to "turn on" boys or at their boyfriends' requests. While I emphasize that girls should be able to kiss and be sexual with other girls as they desire, I question the gendered power dynamics at play there, and the role of boys as puppeteers in these situations. And when I ask girls what would happen if they should ask their boyfriends to "make out" with another guy the girls think is "hot," the usual responses are, "No way, you just don't ask that," or "No way, he'd dump me 'cause he'd think I was a freak," or "No way, he wouldn't do that for me." As Fahs writes, "For women, the rules are clear: either choose a man for a sexual partner, or choose a woman with a man's approval" (2009: 447).

Thus, alongside the misrepresentation of all bisexual girls wishing to perform for "straight men's pleasure" is the misrepresentation and underrepresentation of what could be called "hot boy on boy action" for "women's pleasure" or what Simpson (2006) terms "femantasy." While bisexuality is constructed as "an enhancement of a woman's femininity and sexual desirability for men," men's masculinity and desirability to women is constructed as undermined if they are interested in other men, as supposedly women do not fantasize over "men on men." Yet there are "girlfags" who are sexually attracted to queer men, and who seek bisexual men because they bend gender rules in bed, in parenting, and in other facets of relationships, politics, and culture (Julz, 2005).

> If you're a man who loves women, admitting a sexual interest in other men—or even failing to mention how uncomfortable/ill the very idea of it makes you feel—can apparently cost you your virility. . . . Women are beginning to talk about their interest in boy-on-boy romance—something I've only slightly-tongue-in-cheek(s) dubbed "femantasy"—as loudly as men have for years bragged about their interest in girl-on-girl action. Some are even trying to persuade their boyfriends to return the "lesbian" favour so often requested of them in the past. (Simpson, 2006; see also Davies, 2005)

"Femantasy" is very evident in two fiction genres, written predominantly by heterosexual females and proliferating via the Internet, which specialize in men having explicit sexual relationships with each other. First, slash fiction, and its sub-branches slash art and slash vidding (visuals cut and pasted from video-clips such as YouTube), often rewrites and reinscribes mainstream media heterosexual male characters and storylines into same-sex and bisexual characterizations and storylines (Cicioni, 1998; Jenkins, Jenkins, and Green, 1998; Davies, 2005). For example, the "Kirk/Spock" stories based on the *Star Trek* characters remain an important slash fiction fandom, while new slash fandoms have grown around other television shows (e.g., *Starsky and Hutch*), movies (Harry Potter and Draco Malfoy), and books with sci-fi or action adventure roots (Woledge, 2005). At the time of writing, the Holmes/Watson relationship as performed by Robert Downey Jr. and Jude Law in *Sherlock Holmes*, with its quite mischievous queer subplot, is beginning to be discussed as the "perfect" male couple with which to script slash erotic and porn fiction, and provides "girlfags" with ample femantasy lead-ins. Femslash is a subgenre of slash fiction which focuses on romantic and/or sexual relationships between female fictional characters, but interestingly, there is less femslash than there is slash based on male couples: it appears that heterosexual female slash authors generally do not write femslash (Thrupkaew, 2009).

Second, slash-like "femantasy" fiction is written in various Japanese anime, or manga, fandoms, including cartoons, comics, video games, and fine art, and is referred to as *shounen-ai, yaoi*, or "BL" (boys love), for homoerotic, homopornographic, and homoromantic relationships between male characters (McLelland, 2000; Nagaike, 2003; Zanghellini, 2009). A subgenre is *dojinshi*, which parodies and subverts mainstream male popular culture identities such as film actors and their characters. All these genres are differentiated from *gei comi*, which is by gay men and for gay men (Mizoguchi, 2003). Yaoi has become an umbrella term in the West for women's manga or Japanese-influenced comics with male-male relationships. Indeed, as Japanese yaoi gained popularity in the United States, American women artists began creating original English-language manga for female readers featuring beautiful male-male couples referred to as "American yaoi" (Lewis, 2006; Wood, 2006).

Globally, the yaoi fandom is viewed by many cultural analysts as a "refuge" from mainstream misogynistic culture (Cicioni, 1998; Suzuki, 1999; Thorn, 2004; Davies, 2005; McLelland, 2006). However, it is also telling that from a heteropatriarchal perspective, it has been criticized as allowing girls to avoid adult (read: heterocentric and heteropatriarchal) female sexuality, as it creates and explores greater fluidity in perceptions of gender and sexuality, thereby rejecting "socially mandated" gender roles (Nagaike, 2003; McLelland, 2006). Suzuki (1999) sees "BL manga" emerging from girls' contempt and dislike for masculine heterosexism and from an effort to define "ideal relationships" among men. Hashimoto (2007) has called yaoi a form of empowering "female fetishism." Mariko Ōhara, a science fiction writer, has said that she wrote yaoi Kirk/Spock fiction as a teenager because she could not enjoy "conventional pornography, which had been made for men," and that she had found a "limitless freedom" in yaoi, much like in science fiction (McCaffery et al., 2002). Thorn suggests that yaoi and slash fiction fans are discontented with "the standards of femininity to which they are expected to adhere and a social environment that does not validate or sympathize with that discontent" (2004: 169). Likewise, slash fiction writer Raven Davies talks about the readers of slash fiction being "left unfulfilled by mainstream heteronormative entertainment. They all suffer from the same tired boy-plus-girl story formulae, concocted by those fearful of pushing a few harmless buttons" (2005: 198).

Overall, the various genres of "femantasy" highlight that as women have gained greater economic power and queer feminist understandings and assertiveness over their sexual desires, commercial demand for the sexualization of men, including "boy on boy action," may correlate. Some men and feminists, such as those who critique "femantasy" genres may think this is degrading, and certainly yaoi and other pornography exploiting men is subject to traditional feminist criticisms, particularly in the depictions of male rape and pedophilia, as another example of the objectification of human beings via sexual caricatures, the creation of unrealistic sexual and physical expectations, and the consequent negative body images and interpersonal abusive expressions (Mizoguchi, 2003; McLelland, 2005; Zanghellini, 2009). Both slash fiction and the yaoi genre lack empirical research into women's motivations and desires, as well as their rewards from constructing and consuming these genres. And yet, as McLelland asks, why is there such a curiosity and an "incredulous 'Why?'" into why women would enjoy male-on-male fellatio, anal intercourse, and other sexual acts and romantic expressions when "few people react with surprise to the fact that male pornography is full of 'lesbian sex'" (2006).

What also remains as yet unresearched is how many critics of "femantasy" are as stridently critical of cultural representations of "straight men's girl-on-girl fantasies." For example, in 2009, Calvin Klein released a new jeans marketing campaign that included billboards and advertisements featuring three young men and a young woman, all half-clothed and entangled, lounging over a couch in a way that suggested they were taking a languid break from an intimate foursome. Indeed, while the girl kisses one of the boys, another boy lies at their feet and appears to be either undressing or putting his jeans back on. James (2009) reported on how many people passing a fifty-foot-tall billboard in Manhattan found the ad "outrageous" and "disgusting" for adults and their children. It would have been a researcher's delight to ask these passersby whether they responded similarly to the numerous advertising campaigns featuring two or more young women entangled and half-clothed, and also the more often seen marketing and media campaigns that feature two or more young women with a man (who is sometimes much older than the women). Interestingly, James reports that "younger consumers" were "less judgmental" and as one twenty-eight-year-old teacher said, "I think that many younger people are OK with threes and fours. . . . In college, many people engage in threesomes either with their friends, strangers, or even their main partner and then a friend" (2009). A spokesperson from Loving More, a polyamory organization, pinpointed that what critics were upset about was the homoeroticism between the young men, that "it's extremely confronting for people. It pushes the cultural input button" (2009).

Setting aside media, popular cultural, and youth cultural examples, misrepresentations and assumptions are also apparent in research. For example, the emphasis in some research becomes explaining or rationalizing bisexuality in young women as being predominantly due to the desire for same-sex sexual contact occurring within a coercive heterosexual framework (D'Augelli, 2003). I agree it is important to acknowledge how some of the heterosexual experiences "were coercive and nonconsensual" rather than chosen or desired by same-sex attracted young women, and how the impact of the "lower visibility of lesbians in society" could be seen to "slow down identification as lesbian, and it may well be that the onset of sexual behavior with other females is a crucial step for bisexually identified youths to move to lesbian identification" (D'Augelli, 2003: 25). Nevertheless, researchers need to ensure that these discourses of what I call "pre-lesbian bisexuality" are not constructed as depicting the universal story for all bisexual young women and do not prevent the research and questioning needed with young women whose lives are not represented within such discursive frameworks of coerced heterosexual activity.

The construction of bisexuality as transitional is often the only discourse articulated by some researchers (Entrup and Firestein, 2007). In a fourteen-city study of LGB youth, Hershberger, Pilkington, and D'Augelli found that bisexual youth were more than five times as likely as lesbian and gay youth to have attempted suicide more than once. Interestingly, in the analyses of these findings, the researchers reveal their own constructions of sexuality as fixed and stable, with bisexuality depicted as a transitional phase, when they conclude, "It might well be that those identifying as bisexual experience unusual stress until their self-identification has stabilized" (1997: 492–93).

Likewise, in some research, bisexuality may be problematized even if there is no evidence of its links to health and well-being concerns (Miller et al., 2007). For example, Cochran and Mays (1996) found that while the majority of young lesbians and bisexual women did not use barrier protection during oral sex with women, those participants who do use barriers are most likely to identify as bisexual. Despite such findings, Cochran and Mays still reported that "high-risk sexual experimentation . . . is most likely to occur among teenagers who do not yet consider themselves to be lesbians" (1996: 85). As Miller and partners state, researchers need to be aware of "unintentional implications that bisexually identified clients are not 'yet' gay or lesbian and/or are necessarily engaging in high-risk behavior" (2007: 42).

3. Outdated Representation

This situation has arisen due to the lack of current research that engages with shifting discursive and societal constructs of bisexuality, particularly among adolescents and young people. Entrup and Firestein refer to the "TNG: The Next Generation," whose sexuality is "characterized by fluidity, ambisexuality, a reluctance to label their sexuality, and an interest in the sacred" (2007: 89). Young people's polyamorous and multisexual relationship negotiations and partnering preferences lack sufficient current scholarship (see Pallotta-Chiarolli, 1995a, 1995b, 1996, 2005a; Anderlini-D'Onofrio, 2004; McLean, 2004; Chihara, 2006). For example, Rambuk-kana writes about the formation of the discussion and social group, the Trent Polyamory Society, in his university, "Canada's Outstanding Small

University," the rationale and goals of the group, and the diverse reactions from other students (2004: 143). As the following university student explains,

> I've had a short but very wonderful relationship with a guy last year, but we never considered each other boyfriends and he was in a long-term relationship with a girl. She got me together with him. They are polyamorous. They use the term "ethical sluts" about themselves. . . . The sort of relationship which I'm in at the moment is with a woman who's also involved with a couple who I'm friends with and we all went out last night and she was kissing all of us, and there was nothing weird about that for us. (Jack, bi-poly university student)

A recent documentary, *Bi the Way* has the subtitle of "a documentary about the whatever generation" while the blurb declares that "a new sexual revolution is here . . . [with] a generation that has embraced sexual ambiguity in a style entirely its own." The documentary is a road trip throughout the United States exploring teenage and young people's bisexualities and the dilemmas they face in living out their realities, particularly young bisexual men. Bryant (2009) reviews the documentary as very "watchable" but comments on the absence of "happy, well-adjusted bisexuals going about their daily lives, and it doesn't talk about the organizations and events that are available to bisexual people" (2009: 459). It does, however, include many "adult experts," such as psychologists, sex researchers, and historians, as well as two "notorious biphobes" (Bryant, 2009: 458). Likewise, *The Bisexual Revolution* is a documentary that explores the history of bisexuality in popular culture and youth cultures.

Four other areas in need of substantial research and updating are young people's queering of bi/sexuality (Russell and Seif, 2002), the experiences and perspectives of young people growing up with bisexual parents (Garner, 2004), culturally diverse expressions and classifications of bisexuality (Hutchins and Ka'ahumanu, 1991; Dobinson, 2005), and the experiences of bisexual refugees who are significantly less successful than other sexual minority groups in obtaining refugee status in Canada, the United States, and Australia (Rehaag, 2009).

Many young people reject the "tripartite system of stable identities" altogether (Russell and Seif, 2002: 76; Savin-Williams, 2005). What Angelides (2006) calls the "trinary" labels of gay, lesbian, and bisexual are seen by some young people, like seventeen-year-old Andrea in my research, as "leftovers from the seventies and eighties sexual cultures, real retro," when fixed and essentialist notions of sexual orientation were used to imitate ethnic minority models in civil rights campaigns in order to begin to make some political and legislative inroads (Epstein, 1987). Indeed, Savin-Williams created some controversy with his assertion that

I believe that the gay adolescent will eventually disappear. Teens who have same-gendered sex and desires won't vanish. But they will not need to identify as gay. . . . Disconnects between behaviour, identity, and sexual orientations already coexist for many teens . . . [and] integration and normalization of homoeroticism, [is] resulting in the near disappearance of the gay adolescent and the emergence of sexually diverse young people. (2005: 21–22)

Some bisexual-behaving young people in my research defined themselves as "queer," a defiant reclamation of a previous era's medical and sociocultural labels of deviance. Other terms that are increasingly being used by or applied to young people are "heteroflexible," "not quite straight," and "mostly straight," particularly in relation to young women (Thompson and Morgan, 2008). Other young people refused to be sexually labeled at all. Andrea refers to herself as a "UFO, an unidentified fucking object." Thus, alongside young people feeling like marginal "X-files" in wanting to claim a bisexual identity, there are young people who stridently claim their right to be "UFOs" or what I call "Y-files," as in "(Wh)Y should sexuality be labeled anyway?"

4. Homogenized Representation

This is apparent where the diversity within youth groups, youth subcultures, and categories such as sexual categories is not acknowledged or explored, or it is deliberately homogenized (D'Augelli, 2003). Skott Freedman was America's youngest bisexual singer/songwriter/activist in 2002, and a regular on the U.S. college circuit with his lecture, "Battling Biphobia and Bringing Bisexuals Back to Both Communities" (see Tor, 2002). He sees his bisexuality being as much a part of his music as is his being Jewish. As he wrote in his e-mail interview, "When I speak about bisexuality, though, I do make sure that they keep in mind I am 'a' bisexual, not 'the' bisexual. Every person is different and it gets dangerous when we begin generalizing."

Very rarely do we read of class, ethnicity, geographical location, gendered expectations, disability, and other factors that impact upon a bisexual young person's decisions, negotiations, and experiences (Pallotta-Chiarolli, 1995a, 1995b, 1996, 1999b, 2005a, 2006a; Herdt and Boxer, 1995; Ryan and Rivers, 2003; Fuji Collins, 2004; Firestein, 2007; Volpp, 2010). For example, Paul and associates (2002) found that the highest prevalence of suicide attempts among nonheterosexual males was among Native American respondents and bisexual or nonidentified respondents. Likewise, Goodenow and others (2002) found in their research that bisexually active males were more likely than others to be members of ethnic minorities and were less likely to attend urban schools. Geographical isolation and living in a rural environment may have an exacerbating effect on the lack of social support for a bisexual young person, although there is no available literature in this specific area (Martin,

2007). Michelle, a young bisexual research participant who was part of a rural community for a significant proportion of her life, referred to difficulties in growing up and being quite isolated in relation to her sexual orientation, support groups, and health services: "I think I'm quite passionate when it comes to people living in rural areas . . . I think it's more difficult to get access to even social groups and support groups. . . . I never had access to any of that . . . it was just nothing" (in Martin, 2007: 32).

"EVIDENCE OF BI KIDS": AN OVERVIEW OF THE AVAILABLE RESEARCH

Within education, the pattern of scant research on bisexual diversity outlined above is easily evident. As Bryan states, "It's simple bullshit logic! They don't have evidence of bi kids in schools because they don't want to find it and so don't write their research looking for it" (Bryan, seventeen, bi student).

Owens discusses how heterosexism "formalizes a societal dichotomy of heterosexuality versus homosexuality with little room for bisexuals" in educational research (1998: 55; see also Russell, Franz, and Driscoll 2001; Russell, Seif, and Truong, 2001; D'Augelli, 2003). Indeed, most of the information on bisexuality has been obtained from studies with adult samples, and it is "unclear to what extent a separate bisexual cultural identity is consolidated during adolescence" (Ryan and Rivers, 2003: 105; see also Boulton and Fitzpatrick, 1996; Russell and Seif, 2002).

Thus, we seem to mainly rely on research with adult samples to provide indicators of some of the experiences and concerns during adolescence and within school settings for bisexual youth. For example, Galupo, Sailer, and St. John (2004) found that bisexual women participants in their research were much more likely than lesbians to feel as though their sexual identity was invalidated within friendships with heterosexual women, being either ignored or not taken seriously. There was a "tendency not to discuss attraction to women" which was viewed by bisexual participants "as a routine sacrifice" in order to maintain the friendships (2004: 46). Bisexual participants indicated that they discussed "their sexual interests and behaviors more explicitly with their heterosexual friends when the partner is male" and if they did describe their sexual activity with women, it was often in ways that undermined the importance of these relationships. Thus, "some bisexual participants felt as though their friends' support of the relationship was contingent upon the partner being male" (2004: 47). In a later article, Galupo (2006) also discussed how there was less opportunity and also less preference for bisexual men and women to have strong friendships with other bisexual people, thereby raising the issue of internalized biphobia as it shapes friendship patterns. Herek (2002) reports on a 1999 national survey in the United States with 1,335 respondents, where ratings for bisexual men and women were lower than for all other groups assessed—including religious, racial, ethnic, and political groups—except injecting drug users. Heterosexual women rated bisexuals significantly less favorably than they rated homosexuals, regardless of gender, whereas heterosexual men rated male targets less favorably than female targets, regardless of whether the target was bisexual or homosexual. An earlier study by Eliason (1997) had also found that bisexual people were less acceptable to heterosexual people than either lesbians or gay men. Further, bisexual men were less acceptable than bisexual women, particularly for heterosexual men. In regard to my research, and given that friendships and peer group relations are of high significance to most adolescents, to what extent would the contingencies and shifting group allegiances impacting on adult research participants have impacted upon them since adolescence, and to what extent do they impact on bisexual young people in their friendships with heterosexual peers at school today?

In regard to health and well-being research, the cohorts are also mainly adult bisexuals. In their UK study, King and McKeown (2003) found that bisexual men experienced higher psychological distress than gay men, such as worry, depressive ideas, depression, sleep problems, fatigue, concentration difficulties, and irritability, and they were more likely to have used recreational drugs; and both bisexual men and women were less at ease with their sexuality than homosexual men and women. Gay and lesbian participants were "more likely to be open about their sexuality to parents, siblings, friends, colleagues, GPs, and mental health professionals than bisexual men and women." In particular, bisexual women were less likely to report that they had received a positive reaction from siblings and mental health professionals. Similarly, Page found that

> bisexual women and men seek help for sexual orientation issues less frequently and rate their services as less helpful with sexual orientation concerns than gay and lesbian participants in comparable research. . . . Participants urged providers to validate bisexuality as legitimate and healthy, to be accurately informed about bisexual issues, and to intervene proactively with bisexual clients. (2004: 139)

Bisexual research participants were more likely to report that clinicians "*invalidated and pathologized*" the sexual orientation of the client by either assuming the client's bisexuality "was connected to clinical issues when the client didn't agree, or assumed that bisexual attractions and behavior would disappear when the client regained psychological health" (Page, 2004: 139; see also Dobinson, 2003; Page, 2007). However, Townley (2005) reports on research in the UK that shows how despite widespread prejudice and stigma, bisexual people believed they engaged in enriching relationships and being bisexual offered opportunities for enhanced self-esteem. The following questions arise then: To what extent do bisexual young people feel invalidated and pathologized by families, health services, and educational systems, particularly health services provided within schools; and to what extent are they able to develop healthy self-esteem and engage in healthy relationships at school despite such invalidation and pathologization?

In regard to risk-taking behaviors, Drabble and Trocki (2005) found that bisexual women were more likely to drink heavily, use drugs, and smoke as compared to both heterosexual women and lesbians (see also Midanik et al., 2007). They believed there is "some evidence" that these behaviors were linked to coping with the stress of marginalization in relation to both heterosexual and lesbian communities (see also Fox, 2004). Rothblum and Factor (2001) and McNair and others (2005) found that bisexual women had poorer mental health than heterosexual women or lesbians on almost all measures, while Koh and Ross found that bisexual women were far less likely to be out, and "significantly more bisexual women used illicit drugs . . . [and] reported a greater frequency of having had an eating disorder" than heterosexual women or lesbians (2006: 40). Indeed, bisexual women who were out to a majority of family, friends, and coworkers had a twofold increased risk for having had an eating disorder compared to heterosexual women. The researchers point out that there is no other existing data on bisexual women and eating disorders, particularly in relation to "outness." Again, in relation to the positives and problematics of being out, Koh and Ross found that while lesbians who are "undisclosed" are more likely to have "reported suicidal ideation occasionally or very often compared to heterosexual women," bisexual women who were out were "twice as likely to have reported suicidal ideation occasionally or very often compared to heterosexual women" (2006: 46). Thus, for lesbians, "outness" can be associated with more positive mental health, while for bisexual women, it makes them more prone to discrimination and therefore "increased emotional stress" (2006: 50). Koh and Ross (2006) call for further research into how lesbians and bisexual women may experience disclosure and closetedness differently, with subsequent differing implications for mental and emotional health. Indeed, further research is required into how and why disclosure and closetedness affect the mental and emotional health of young bisexual people. Likewise, given the high rates of eating disorders among adolescent girls, are there links to feeling marginalized as bisexual, and if so, how prevalent is this linkage?

In relation to bisexual men, Wold and associates (1998) found that they were more likely to have drinking problems (see also Midanik et al., 2007), and were three times as likely to have unprotected sex with their female partner as their male partner. Indeed, 74 percent of the men did not discuss their HIV status with their female partners. In more recent research by Dobinson (2005), bisexual male participants said they did not receive appropriate information about sexual health from health service providers, and indeed, were recipients of inappropriate jokes and comments, voyeurism and pathologization from these providers. The participants called for the development of separate or bi-specific health and community services for bisexuals as well as better competency and sensitivity training for providers in GLBTIQ and mainstream services. Some of the bi-specific services they called for included counseling/mental health services, coming out groups, telephone support services, the development of bisexual social spaces, as well as undertaking a large-scale media and public information campaign. Interestingly, and pertinent to my research, Dobinson's participants called for the establishment of services and programs specifically for bisexual young people, including a helpline, mentoring programs, and support groups: all too obviously lacking in their own youth. Thus, the question arises: What kinds of services do young bisexual people want, and how can these be provided in a school setting?

In summary, given the limitations in research I have discussed above, the available recent studies about bisexual young people are pointing to higher rates of anxiety, depression, and other mental health concerns as compared to homosexual and heterosexual young people (D'Augelli, Hershberger, and Pilkington, 1998; Jorm et al., 2002; Udry and Chantala, 2002; Ryan and Rivers, 2003):

> I vaguely remember waking up in the mornings and I used to think, like, how can I get through another day with everyone being so horrible to me all the time. . . . I did think I'm really depressed, everything is really awful and I thought about suicide. (Rowan, nineteen, bi student)

> I became quite depressed, quite anxious about my sexuality. . . . I was crying continuously, I couldn't sleep. This went on for about two weeks. I had to go and stay with my dad because I wasn't eating, I wasn't showering, yeah, I was just not doing anything—I couldn't look after myself, I couldn't function. And I know that it did stem from me questioning my sexuality, and I thought it was the end of the world. (Michelle in Martin, 2007: 34)

Research also shows that bisexual young people have more current adverse life events, greater childhood adversity, less positive support from family, more negative support from friends, and a higher frequency of financial problems (Jorm et al., 2002). Saewyc and others (1999) found that bisexual teenage girls were twice as likely to report unwanted pregnancies, while Hunter (1996) found that bisexual youth and those who are still exploring their sexual identities reported negative attitudes about their sexuality, as compared to self-identified lesbian and gay youth. Bisexual youth also had less information about sexual orientation and about lesbian and gay communities, which may increase isolation, affect self-esteem, and promote risky behaviors.

The available research also points to greater learning difficulties among bisexual young people. These poorer learning outcomes are of course linked to the feeling of emotional and mental disconnection and anxiety at school, which interfere with learning. Russell, Seif, and Truong (2001) found that boys who identified as bisexual experienced greater school difficulties, while boys who identified as exclusively same-sex attracted did not differ from their heterosexual counterparts on school outcomes. There appeared to be links between feeling disliked by their peers, participating in delinquency, substance use and abuse, sexual risk taking, and the depressed academic performance of boys with bisexual attractions. Likewise, both girls and boys who were bisexually attracted reported negative feelings about their teachers, which impacted on the pragmatics of learning such as "paying attention, getting homework completed, and getting along with other students" (2001: 120).

In a large school-based sample, Goodenow and associates (2002) found that bisexual young people reported higher levels of sexual risk and injecting drug use than heterosexual or gay-identified peers. They also found that bisexually active adolescent males report especially high levels of AIDS risk behavior. The researchers theorize that as members of neither the heterosexual majority nor any visible gay community, bisexual young men may function outside the normative constraints of either group. Socially marginal, they may experience isolation, loneliness, and stress, leading to increased levels of "acting out" and risk behavior. Interestingly, Goodenow and others found that bisexual young men also reported lower rates of AIDS education, even after school absence due to fear as a variable had been controlled in the research. One plausible explanation provided by the researchers is that standard classroom instruction does not address the concerns and questions of many young men who have sex with men and is therefore dismissed, discounted as irrelevant, or entirely forgotten.

Another possible explanation, however, is that HIV/AIDS education is constructed as being for straight and gay young men. In deflecting or rejecting the label of "gay," young men who have sex with men but who identify as heterosexual may ignore or avoid HIV/AIDS education as it is "not about them." Certainly, GLBTIQ community services provide HIV/AIDS prevention education, and, although some community-based HIV/AIDS prevention interventions targeted toward sexual minority youths have demonstrated effectiveness, these approaches have not been used, or been permitted to be used, in school settings due to homophobic limitations and boundaries. Given the stigma attached to nonheterosexual identities, it would be unrealistic to assume that young men who do not identify as gay would join gay support groups, apply for gay-related medical services or social services, or participate openly in HIV-prevention activities aimed at gay youth. It is possible, however, to make mainstream classroom instruction more inclusive and more culturally appropriate for sexual minority adolescents who border or reject the duality or tripartite classification system of sexuality.

In relation to the links between harassment and violence and the mental health and risk-taking behaviors among bisexual young people I have discussed above, a few studies have pointed to various concerns. Research conducted by Robin and partners (2002) illustrates how behaviorally bisexual students are more likely to report suicide attempts, drug use, unhealthy weight control practices, and being harassed and injured by others. Udry and Chantala found a stronger link between bisexual adolescent males' and females' substance use and "delinquent behavior" as compared to heterosexual and homosexual cohorts (2002: 91). Indeed, while bisexual adolescent males were more likely to report "selling sex for drugs or money," bisexual females had higher rates of suicidal feelings, depression, and victimization, including being attacked or being in a physical fight. Thus, bisexual adolescent females emerged as the highest risk group, as their delinquent/rebellious behaviors were accompanied by extreme emotional distress. The researchers concluded that bisexual adolescents were a "priority group for both research and clinical attention, because we have obviously failed in the past to recognize them as a high-risk group." Interestingly, they also question "what kind of public health effort would be appropriate," and "what the political acceptability of such an effort might be" (2002: 91).

Similarly, in analyzing data from the National Longitudinal Study of Adolescent Health in the United States, Russell, Franz, and Driscoll (2001) found that young people who reported attraction to both same- and opposite-sex persons were at greater risk of experiencing, witnessing, and perpetrating violence than young people who were attracted to same-sex persons. These findings were supported by a Canadian study from the Centre for Justice (Beauchamp, 2004), which found that rates of violent victimization were 2.5 percent higher for gays and lesbians than heterosexuals, and 4 times higher for bisexuals. The study also found that 15 percent of gays and lesbians and 28 percent of bisexuals reported being victims of spousal abuse in comparison to 7 percent of heterosexuals. Of demographic significance is that a higher proportion of bisexuals were under twenty-five, single, students, and low-income earners, thus reflecting the generational shifts in sexual labeling. Linda was a bisexual young woman in my research who had come out at school, and then found she had to leave school early after harassment and bullying led to suicide attempts:

> I got thrown downstairs, punched and threatened with rape by boys for coming out as bi. They said raping me would take away the lesbian parts. I'd tried

several times to complain to the principal. I reported what these guys were doing, but all he said all the time was that since I'd done this foolish thing and
come out, he could guarantee no protection; I'd brought it on myself. So when
these losers saw my complaining wasn't getting me anywhere and they weren't
getting in trouble, they got worse and worse. (Linda, seventeen, bi student)

In relation to substance abuse, there were several instances in Australian
research conducted with bisexual young people by Martin (2007) and
published in Martin and Pallotta-Chiarolli (2009) and Pallotta-Chiarolli
and Martin (2009) where drug and alcohol use was seen as a way of coping
with discrimination and marginalization. Sam talked about his use of anti-
depressants, (although this was a licit, maintenance dose), and related it to
"not feeling that there's any comfortable place to rest in terms of my identity." He also gave details about alcohol, marijuana, and mental well-being:
"With alcohol and marijuana, I think it's more about a sense of numbing
because . . . there's often a lot of problems that they don't have the tools to
address, and if they're queer in particular, I think there's a lot of reasons to
want to repress that" (in Martin, 2007: 42).

Other participants in Martin's research, such as Victoria, stated how their
excessive drinking and marijuana smoking were most likely caused by loneliness as a result of not having much emotional support from their families
and friends to "kind of escape the reality of being home" (2007: 42). Michelle explained: "When I was starting to question my sexuality, there was
no way at that stage I felt I could talk to my friends that I was socializing
with then, so it was much easier to have a drink, and just try and relax that
way and forget about it" (in Martin, 2007: 35).

The assumed "overlap" between bisexual people and gay/lesbian communities has been problematized in research into bisexual young people's
health, including by Martin's (2007) research participants. Balsam and
Mohr (2007) found bisexual young people experience higher levels of
identity confusion and lower levels of both self-disclosure and community connection in comparison to their gay and lesbian peers, which may
increase isolation, affect self-esteem, and promote risky behaviors such
as alcohol abuse. There appears to be some sense of normalization of
drug use and risk-taking behaviors among gay and lesbian communities,
within which bisexual young people may try to socialize (Howard and
Arcuri, 2006):

They might become part of the gay community, and because it's a bit of a
monoculture type of club, so when they do that that's when they get confronted with drugs. . . . So if they start then going to those clubs, then they'll
be confronted with ecstasy users, and then they might come across ecstasy
and might experiment. (Mike, youth health/community worker, in Martin,
2007: 38)

Thus, socially supportive environments may provide a buffer against stress and related effects, but at the same time, even when bisexual young people are able to socialize with gay and lesbian young people, away from heteronormative spaces and homophobic surveillance, there is often a strong internalized awareness of having been rejected by heteronormative mainstream spaces and institutions, which forces them to seek out alternative minority group spaces that they may also not feel completely at ease in. If peer groups (such as those within the gay party scene, for example) are involved in drug use, being in such an environment may also encourage an individual to use drugs in association with their friends (Howard and Arcuri, 2006). Sam discussed his use of crystal methamphetamine and other drugs among queer youth as being linked to the desire for "intense conversations" and their ostracism from the heteronormative "mainstream": "Yeah, with the stimulants it's certainly sensation seeking. If you feel more sensation life feels more meaningful, in a lot of senses because especially for queers and I include bisexuals and gays and lesbians, and trans people—the common dialogues of religion and politics reject them. They don't have a home in mainstream" (in Martin, 2007: 39).

There is little research directly attributing substance abuse to rejection from mainstream dialogues and discourses, although Hawkins (2002) explains that alienation from the dominant views of society, low religiosity, and rebelliousness predict greater substance use in adolescence. Thus, bisexual adolescents and young people may turn to more alternative youth subcultures in order to express their sexuality because being bisexual in a heteronormative society may put them on the margins or outside of their everyday friendship and support networks at school. Indeed, Cotterell emphasizes that "having friends and being included in the group are among the most important concerns of adolescents" (1994: 259). This was supported by Martin's bisexual adolescent and young adult research participants, such as Sam who stated that "being socially connected is really important to your mental, physical and spiritual health" (2007: 40). Thus, social pressure exists and perhaps is exacerbated within mainstream friendship support networks such as those at school and in local neighborhoods in relation to those who are bisexual. Youth health/community worker Mike also explained how they may seek other youth subcultures within which to express their sexual identities:

I would say for the experiences of the young people in my youth group that those who identify as bi, particularly younger ones, they do have more drug and alcohol problems. So therefore one girl was recently hospitalised from drinking too much, and the guys tend to be using those types of harder drugs. They tend to present as more instances of self-harm, and they tend to be "emos" or "Goths, they're "bi emos" or "bi Goths." . . . So maybe that's one way they do cope. So because of that they tend to lean toward more of that depressive, self-harming type of persona that will be involved in more alcohol and drug use and abuse. (in Martin, 2007: 41)

Recent research on increased rates of self-harm and attempted suicides in the Goth youth subculture states that it is unsure whether this is normative behavior within this subculture or whether young people with a propensity to self-harm and who feel alienated from other youth cultures are attracted to it (Young, Sweeting, and West, 2006). However, even if a bisexual young person did feel included and supported in a mainstream heterosexual friendship group, these peer groups themselves were also commonly involved in the consumption of alcohol and other substances, as these behaviors were signifiers of one's membership in a "cool" friendship group for many young people regardless of sexuality (Duff, 2003; Martino and Pallotta-Chiarolli, 2003; Pumariega et al., 2005). For example, Victoria in Pallotta-Chiarolli and Martin (2009) started drinking at the early age of thirteen with her heterosexual friends at slumber parties. There were some perceived benefits of drug use among our research participants, which are similar to those expressed by many heterosexual young people (Hatzenbuehler et al., 2008). Like many heterosexual young people, Victoria stated that sometimes she did enjoy "getting pissed," and that drinking was a way to alleviate her shyness with other people in social settings.

Research with same-sex attracted Australian youth in relation to gay/lesbian youth social and support groups found that members of groups were more likely to be exclusively attracted to the same sex and to identify as gay or lesbian (Hillier, 2007). According to Hillier, this could be due to bisexual labels being more acceptable to friends and families and so young people without support groups do not want to risk "further alienation in their choice of a more exclusive label." Thus, their membership in same-sex attracted groups provides the "increase in support and acceptance" that allows young people "to acknowledge their attractions more freely and match their identity to them" (2007: 5). While this may certainly be the case for some young people, another probability is not raised within this report: that bisexual young people may feel coerced to mismatch their attractions to a gay or lesbian identity in order to gain acceptance and support from this group membership. They may only be asked about their same-sex relationships and behaviors and therefore feel reluctant to disclose their heterosexual relationships and behaviors. Thus, "the invisibility and isolation they experience in broader society is mirrored in these youth groups" (Travers and O'Brien 1997: 131).

In relation to specifically bisexual support groups and services, Mike in Martin (2007) mentioned that in the only renowned bisexual support group in his Australian city, the members were older, and young people are more likely to want to participate in a youth-specific service or group.

Other health workers in Martin and Pallotta-Chiarolli (2009) also stated that bisexual networks in Australia were more social groupings of older members, which may indicate a need for more professional support groups for young bisexual people as well as bi-youth-specific social networks. However, there is some debate in regard to whether sexual categorization should be either inclusive or specific in social and support groups, can there be a balance of both, or should umbrella terms like "queer" be used (Gammon and Isgro, 2006). How do we acknowledge the specificity of bisexuality but simultaneously step away from putting young people into exclusionary divisive sexual categories? It may be beneficial for support and education services to put less emphasis on categorizing people with such terms or resorting to such categories, but at the same time, a balance must be achieved in embracing minority-within-minority populations such as the bisexual youth population. This supports the findings of Dobinson (2005) who recommended visible inclusion of bi-specificity in all public health services as well as public health education including a large-scale media and information campaign.

The above overview of the available research highlights the need for much more research, health promotion, and educational interventions and evaluations to increase the health of bisexual young people. As my research will show later in this chapter, there appears to be a strong link between the research reports and findings I have reviewed and the underrepresentation and misrepresentation of bisexuality in school curricula, school cultures, and school communities (Owens, 1998; McLean, 2001, 2003, 2005). Bisexuality "messes up" the binary of heterosexuality and homosexuality that frames and informs antihomophobic policies, programs, and practices in schools such as in health education, sexuality education, and student welfare programs. In doing so, many young people are left feeling like "X-files" at school—alien, isolated, and disconnected—thereby potentially leading to risk-taking and self-harming behaviors. "We're not straight A files or gay B files. . . . But that means they make you feel like you're messed up yourself, as if there's no way their filing system is what's really fucked" (Marita, seventeen, bi student).

As adult researchers, health providers, and educators, we need to ask how school policies and programs reflect the dominant discourses of hierarchical sexual dualisms prevalent within our own formative years, and how these may be increasingly out of step with the shifting contexts and "diverse sexual cultures proliferating around the world" that today's young people are immersed within, engaging with, and negotiating (Herdt, 2001: 280). These social changes are precipitated by the marked decline in heterosexism and homophobia in our society, which is facilitating the emergence, and I would add, visibility, of new sexual minorities, including bisexuality. Herdt refers to the Horizons study of the 1980s, at a time when the "undoing of preconceptions of sinfulness, illness, and self-hatred required resistance to any ambiguity of identities, including opposition to bisexuality." Adolescents would experience intense pressures from peers to stop being "bisexual" and start acting out their "true identities," declaring themselves as gay or lesbian. This "social performance" of reacting to a heteronormative polar extreme with a homonormative polar extreme was not only applauded by the adult gay and lesbian community, including youth workers, but also was regarded as "fundamental in the teenager's own ritual passage into gay culture" (2001: 273). Herdt also points to the fact that the adult advisors in the Horizons project were nearly all lesbian or gay and saw bisexuality as confusion. He concedes that he shared this opinion at the time:

> I sympathised with their plight in wanting to provide a more secure environ-
> ment for the youths. . . . The adult gay and lesbian-identified advisors were
> strongly disposed to think of bisexuality as a "closet defense"—a stage of
> sexual adjustment immaturity—before the "real thing"— being gay or les-
> bian—was accepted by the self and performed on the stage of society. This was
> all the more remarkable because the same cultural truisms and idioms were
> resisted when it came to the hegemonic attribution that being gay or lesbian
> was just a defense against heterosexuality or a "stage of confusion" that would
> pass on the way to being mature. (2001: 274)

Herdt predicts that as the range of variation in sexual behavior increases, "the gay and lesbian movement will become a victim of its own success" (2001: 278). Again, this statement reveals a problematization of sexual diversity, as it may be seen to imply that sexual duality is still the desired outcome. The sociohistorical contextualization of sexual labeling and its connection to adult "advisors" and resource development is highly signifi-cant today as well, as some of my research participants will illustrate. For example, Bonnie, a bisexual young woman, who is a volunteer in a queer youth group, explores what happens there in relation to bisexuality:

> I'm always the one putting in my bit about bi stuff, because the guy who runs it
> is gay and he's very gay. And so he never says anything about bi stuff. . . . If you
> have a support person or counselor who's gay or who's lesbian, I think that
> often can be problematic for bi people too because it's just not represented,
> it's not talked about and they won't say, "Oh, it's fine if you're gay or bi or not
> straight or, you know, not sure." . . . I haven't had anyone in the group say that
> they're bi. . . . And I think about whether it's because they feel like they need
> to conform to this gay image or if there's something they're worried about.
> (Bonnie, bi-poly university student)

Before presenting the findings of my research with "bi kids" in more detail, there is one other area of sparse research that needs to be foregrounded: the schooling experiences of children being raised by bisexual parents (Garner, 2004; Buxton, 2006a; Pallotta-Chiarolli, 2006b; Karlson, 2007; Block, 2008) or being taught by bisexual teachers. The bisexual parents in Dobinson's study expressed concerns about being involved in the gay community as they did not want their children finding out they were bisexual and not accepting them. The implications for health care providers and educators who work with families and parents are clear: needing to "understand the range of ways that bisexuals take on parenting roles . . . as well as the barriers to disclose" (2005: 50). "Exclusion by inclusion" (Martin and Pallotta-Chiarolli, 2009; Pallotta-Chiarolli and Martin, 2009) is very evident in most studies of bisexual parents wherein bisexual and gay/lesbian parents are subsumed into one category (see for example, Morris, Balsam, and Rothblum, 2002). Raymond was a bisexual father in my research who was also a teacher. He called for specifically bisexual-targeted health education:

> That means stuff about bisexual relationships, not just a one-line definition saying "bisexuals are sexually and emotionally attracted to both sexes," which says nothing about bi pride, bi life choices, bi relationships. But bi people will need to actually be the educators. There are GL educators everywhere getting their message out there, so we have to too! (Raymond, bi-poly dad and teacher)

Indeed, there is an absence of research and cultural texts on bisexual teachers and other adults who mentor and work with young people in various capacities.

A recent article in the *New York Times* reported the following: "In Harlem a week ago, a 32-year-old math teacher [Chance Nalley] handed out slips of paper inviting the entire seventh grade of Columbia Secondary School to his upcoming ceremony, where, the names on the invitation made clear, he'd be celebrating his commitment to another man" (Dominus, 2009). The article documents the diversity within the student population in relation to multiculturalism and socioeconomic status, that the school's mission statement "includes a commitment to diversity," and how the principal successfully and confidently resisted the complaints of four parents who were angry that Mr. Nalley had been able to issue these invitations as well as actually be a teacher at the school. Of particular interest in relation to my research is the response the journalist received when she asked some seventh graders the following question: "Were they surprised to learn he was gay?"

> "He's not gay," said Japhet Guzman, 12.
> "No," agreed a lanky 13-year-old . . . "he's not gay. He's bisexual. Why don't you ask him?" (Mr. Nalley confirmed this.) (Dominus, 2009)

In Victoria, Australia, Ken Campagnolo, who came out as bisexual in 1997, is a rural firefighter, forestry worker, and trainer of a local rural youth football club. He took his case to the Victorian Equal Opportunity and Human Rights Commission in 2007 after ten years of tolerating increasing discrimination, harassment, unfair dismissal as a trainer, and subsequent mental health issues. "He has been denied work. He has been spat at on the street. He has been called a paedophile. His reputation, as a person and as a skilled firefighter and forestry worker, has been trashed" (*Mansfield Courier*, 2008). Of particular significance to this research, Campagnolo was sacked as a trainer from the Bonnie Doon Football Club because of his sexuality and is seeking compensation against the club, the Australian Football League, and the Benalla and District Football League in the Victorian Civil and Administrative Tribunal. The sacking was shockingly supported by former state premier Jeff Kennett because

> you had this gentleman there who was obviously close to young men—massaging young men—it ran an unnecessary risk and that's why it [the club] decided it was best that he not perform those duties again. . . . When you are in charge of a group of young boys, as this club was as I understand it, it's got to make sure. . . . It's the same if you have a pedophile there as a masseur, right? (Campbell, 2008)

Not only did the whole situation and Kennett's comments anger many GLBTIQ activists and their heterosexual allies, it was doubly shocking given that Kennett was the founder and chairperson for Beyond Blue, a National Depression Initiative Internet site supporting young people against depression, suicide, and mental health issues that had long stated that many young people who used its services identified as same-sex attracted (www.beyondblue.org.au). Toward the end of 2009, Beyond Blue held a roundtable with over seventy delegates from various GLBTIQ communities, services, and organizations, led by Gabi Rosenstreich of the newly formed National LGBT Health Alliance, to begin the necessary task of addressing GLBTIQ mental health. One of the issues highlighted as being in need of research and implementation was bisexual groups. Indeed, in their publication, *Feeling Queer and Blue*, prepared for Beyond Blue by the Australian Research Centre in Sex, Health and Society (ARCSHS), there is a specific section on the needs of bisexual people. It points to the "pervasive tendency" in research literature "to exclude bisexual people or to obscure them by collapsing bisexual samples into gay, lesbian or same-sex attracted categories" (Corboz et al., 2008: 7).

In relation to schools, the autobiographical reflection by a bisexual mother below specifically addresses concerns with educational systems:

I've become increasingly concerned, as Sam gets older, about education. . . . Difference and dissent in conventional education is rarely encouraged, let alone celebrated, even in enlightened schools committed to equal opportunities. . . . It's so frustrating to see that, despite heterosexism training for staff in Sam's nursery, homophobia (and sexism) in the children's lives doesn't seem to be tackled in the way that racism is, thankfully, starting to be addressed. (Arden, 1996: 253)

Yet, Arden also reflects upon how these bring to the fore her own unresolved childhood and current tensions as she borders social categories and constructions of bisexuality, parenting, and nonmonogamy (see also Iantaffi, 2006; Block, 2008):

Early on I used to worry about how Sam would cope at school with the "burden" of having two out bi parents, whilst feeling relieved we were of opposite genders. I also felt vaguely uncomfortable with the few American children's books Sam's father found about lesbian and gay families—because, I think, they featured such families. I was worried by the idea of Sam seeing my partner or myself with other lovers (of whatever gender), fearing that Sam might see this as a betrayal of the other parent. Now I think that probably these reactions resulted from two very different sources. Firstly, from my own homophobia: homosexuality and non-monogamy may be good enough for me, but they aren't for Sam. And secondly, they resulted from a desire, at whatever cost, to spare Sam any kind of pain—pain I'd endured at home as a young person. Children suffering at the hands of parents who could have done a better job was especially resonant for me. . . . The problem is, of course, not my bisexuality, but society's attitude to it. I realised that children equipped with lots of support and self-esteem, and (probably) more information than their peers, might even *benefit* from a more unconventional home environment . . . exposed to the concept of diversity as positive rather than threatening. (1996: 250–51)

Watching her own child's attractions and relational behaviors makes Arden question how essentialist or "natural" are our social constructs of monogamous marriage and relationships, and yet how education is promoting—indeed insisting on—certain codes regarding marriage:

At present Sam comes home from nursery talking of girlfriends and boyfriends. Sam seems to want to marry a different person every week. This openness to the possibilities of love is inspiring, and I want to encourage that. Yet I hate sometimes having to allude to the restraints of our backward culture. Perhaps Sam needs to know, rather than finding out the hard way, that most people think that you can only have girl/boyfriends of the "opposite sex" (and then just one at a time). . . . My observation of Sam has reinforced my beliefs that cultural norms, such as heterosexuality and marriage, are the result of conditioning, rather than being universal or "natural" behavior. (1996: 252)

Arden also draws attention to how the issue of bisexual parents and their children does not attract much attention in the bisexual movement. Many bisexual events are organized by "youngish people without children" who are not always aware of children's and parents' issues. This results in events not being very child-friendly, especially for older children who are beyond going to day care. "So how about sessions/workshops for young people (where they could meet, have fun, talk)? Most importantly, what about asking kids what *they* want?" (1996: 254). Thus, like Dobinson (2005), Arden calls for more information and research about bisexual parents and their children: "Our children are the next generation, whose attitudes to bisexuality, to the value of themselves and others will be crucial" (1996: 256).

Having presented an overview of the available research and its gaps, I will now present the findings from my own research, and how young people adopt the strategies of passing, bordering, and polluting in order to navigate their way through schooling and minimize harassment and harm.

"IT IS A BIT LIKE A PERFORMANCE IN A WAY": BISEXUALITY AS PASSING

In this section, I will explore the diverse experiences and meanings of passing as articulated by some of the young people in my research. Several young people spoke about passing as not being something one consciously initiated or decided upon. Rather, it was imposed from the outside, externally ascribed and enforced. Passing as a response to external ascription and societal/school forces of normalization is a way of attaining simplification, avoiding complications and harassment, particularly in new or hostile social settings (Fuss, 1991; McDonald, 2001; Kroeger, 2003). Bonnie describes the panopticonic environment many bisexual young people grow up in where the heteronormative gaze leads to self-problematization: "It's like everyone's looking through these glasses or lenses. Everyone's looking through this big screen that just blurs what they're seeing and it's just tainted with this idea; it's a bit wrong" (Bonnie, bi-poly university student). As Bryan says about his peers in his private boys' school, where he felt unable to come out,

> Bi babe porn's everywhere for these guys, on the Net, in the magazines stashed under their beds, but if I was to come out as bi, I'd be dead either from the other guys or from the school who'd never deal with these issues. It makes me feel sort of schizoid. I see it [bisexuality] everywhere, except at school. I'm the real thing but I can't be real about it, although it's what my friends are checking out. So who and where am I? (Bryan, seventeen, bi student)

Benjamin remembers as a child deciding to pass as straight because the external representations of homosexuality were not what he wanted for himself:

I remember early on I think it really hit home . . . when I did actually think I was gay, and I was very worried about it. The way the definition of "gay" meant to me these sorts of things like no family, no children, lonely existence sort of desolation and isolation, and I didn't want that so I was very, very sort of upset. (Benjamin, nineteen, bi university student)

After years of passing as straight in high school, Benjamin found himself adopting the passing strategy as a response to externally ascribed sexual categories within the queer group he had recently joined at his university. Thus, even within a group that represents itself as a "community" or support group of significant others, Benjamin was aware of the machinations of "in-group purification" (Goffman, 1973; see also Adler and Adler, 1994):

Everyone has already assumed that I'm homosexual, so it's the same thing as this assumed heterosexuality within the heterosexual community, . . . I just haven't been able to tell them I'm bi, because I feel somehow, sometimes, they feel that you're not part of it, you're not sort of a full part, you're in a phase, there are all these connotations, and all the stereotypes, and I just have to say, look, fuck it, I'll just be gay. You know, I can be gay, I can be straight, whatever. . . . It is a bit like a performance in a way. Sometimes I feel like I have to perform . . . and definitely lately I've been saying that I've even got like two distinct groups of friends, my gay friends and my straight friends. (Benjamin, nineteen, bi university student)

Thus, passing means performativity (Butler, 1990, 1991), or "haciendo caras" (Anzaldua, 1990), making the "straight face" and the "gay face" in two distinct groups and worlds (see also Cohen and Taylor, 1976). This compartmentalization can be very distressing and emotionally unhealthy for some young bisexual people as their bisexuality is experienced as a conflict between "being gay" and "being straight" (Richardson, 1985; Zinik, 1985; Evans, 2003).

As well as passing being a response to external prescriptions and policing, it was also a strategy or response to external omissions. Many bisexual young people could not recall any education around bisexuality. As Bonnie said, "I just don't have any memories of it." Josie recalls the silence about bisexuality at her school that was interpreted and internalized as one's own abnormality and confusion. Thus, while socially she passed as straight in response to a school setting that provided no discursive framework, definition, or validation of bisexuality, internally she was searching for external definition and affirmation of the "realness" of her bisexuality:

It's just so missing. It's just not there. It's just like it's not a concept that people consider and that's probably why I suppressed it a lot because it's like, well, my god, I don't know who I am, how can I explain it and they don't understand. . . . You've [schools] got to respond to what the [bisexual] kids are feeling and

they're feeling confused and abnormal and concerned and so it's just addressing that need that people have for validation. (Josie, bi-mono)

Passing was also a response to school ignorance, inadequacies, and mis-
information on the topics of sexuality, as Jack points out in the following:

> In our sexual education it was said that it's perfectly all right to be curious. That
> was actually mentioned in grade six. In what was called "Family Life." We were
> told that a period of curiosity about homosexuality or homosexual behavior
> was perfectly natural. But it was when I got to about fourteen or fifteen when
> I wasn't growing out of it, and I was becoming more sexually interested in my
> male friends. And that was when I started to go, well, okay, I'd had girlfriends
> and stuff, but men still attracted me. . . . I knew who I was. But we're so often
> taught that we don't exist unless we exist in someone else's framework. . . . And
> teachers are always so clinical about sexual education that there was no person
> you could trust enough. . . . No information was offered up to us. It would
> have been useful, in my opinion, even if it was just planting the seeds of "there
> are different shades of sexuality, it's not black and white." . . . The insinuation
> was a very classical attitude of people who don't get over this curiosity and
> made it sound like a lifelong curiosity, which is ridiculous. . . . Growing up for
> any young person sexually is very difficult, let alone when you don't fit with
> what they're telling you or "you may be feeling these feelings, but they'll go
> away" was essentially what I was told. And I never admitted it to anyone. (Jack,
> bi-poly university student)

This surface passing and the need to respond to official silence with
personal silence also bred an underlying layer where young people were
having sex with each other, or in the official discourse, "experimenting,"
but rarely talked about this among themselves. Thus, official silence meant
there was a lack of language: an inability to express or articulate what was
being felt when it did not match the surface definitions and ascriptions
(Foucault, 1977; Fuss, 1991; Sedgwick, 1993; Lehmiller, 2009). The reper-
cussions of this are long-lasting, where, even after leaving school, some of
the boys Jack had sex with are unable or unwilling to discuss it:

> Even the ones in high school who I became physically involved in, we never
> talked about that. And I look back on it now and I think God, that's bizarre,
> and I still have friends who I see who I quote, unquote, "experimented" with,
> which is not a term which I particularly like, who, some of which if I brought
> it up, I would expect that they would freak out completely. . . . There were two
> guys in particular that I would refer to, one of which considers himself bi but
> doesn't openly identify as bisexual. He's mainly interested in girls. According
> to him, he would never be in a relationship with a guy, but sexually he is at-
> tracted to men. I was involved with him sexually on and off for three or four
> years. . . . [The other one] I was only involved with around sixteen or fifteen
> and considers himself completely straight and yeah, although he's quite happy

talking to me about who I am, wouldn't like to admit about what happened before, wouldn't like to discuss it. (Jack, bi-poly university student)

Thus, in an educational institution that was meant to be promoting learning and articulation, the exact opposite was happening. As Jack recalls below, the culture of bullying was premised on the basis of targeting anyone who was too interested in education. Thus, students were well trained to not look or behave too interested in learning and self-development. An alignment was made between being a learner and being not normatively masculine, which thus throws into suspicion a boy's heterosexuality (Martino and Pallotta-Chiarolli, 2001, 2003). According to Jack, this panopticonic self-surveillance was not only based on policing by peers, but was framed by the larger institutionalized heteronormativity that prevented any questioning or articulation of bisexuality:

You're taught by your peers at your high school and primary school that if you're too educated, if you absorb too much information or act on it too much, it's a negative. So even if there were these tiny threads, leads you could follow as young queer people, you wouldn't do it. You were trained not to and not encouraged to in any way, shape or form. I don't know what would have happened if I'd walked up to a teacher and asked [about bisexuality]. (Jack, bi-poly university student)

What is also problematic is the way the boys who were homophobic could also be having sex with guys or identifying as gay or bisexual, as Jack recalls below. Thus, the panopticonic system perpetuates and enforces heterosexuality; any transgression is reacted to with shame, and compensated for by greater violence and harassment of others like oneself:

The ironic thing is a really homophobic guy I met had been sexually involved with one of my male partners in the past, which was really an eye-opening experience to walk into a class, having been told by this friend of mine who I had been involved with for years, which no one knew about, he said to me, "Oh, the only other guy I've been with is this guy, he's a family friend of mine," and I walk into a class and there he is. And he's the most red-necked, right-wing, fascist young man I met in high school, and it was really scary! (Jack, bi-poly university student)

Although Rowan chose to come out as bisexual in his school, he was also aware of how others were passing as straight or gay as a response to the omission of bisexuality (Zinik, 1985). He explains how the hierarchical sexual binary left little room for the elaboration of bisexuality:

I don't even think that the word *bisexual* was ever, ever used while I was at school except just to say, like, these are the types of sexualities that there are, but otherwise it was always just an issue of like, yes, you're either gay or you're straight and even homosexuality had so little visibility that bisexuality had nothing. (Rowan, nineteen, bi student)

In schools where bisexuality was named or made unofficial appearances, usually in some derogatory or negative way among students, passing was often a response to the lack of educational legitimation. In the following, Sibyl recalls the offhand and dismissive way bisexuality was mentioned in high school. It was not until she began university that she undertook any serious and educational understanding of the term after the "epiphany" that this kind of discussion had been absent in secondary school:

My only memory of any teacher explicitly mentioning anything to do with bisexuality was an English teacher, who would mutter "ac/dc" whenever he talked about Shakespeare. . . . He would also look directly at my friend, who was gay. Pretty illogical, huh? . . . When I was in first year at uni it suddenly occurred to me that "bisexual" simply meant attracted to both genders. Before then I had associated the term only with ridiculous jokes, in which it sounded exotic, like laughing about "bisexual midgets from obscure African countries" and so forth. It just wasn't on the map at any time before this epiphany. Since that day in first year uni, after reading a stack of books, I realize that it is a much more complex concept than "being attracted to both genders," and that its meaning can change all the time, with situations and people and cultures. (Sibyl, nineteen, bi university student)

Some young people talked about how schools inadvertently or "accidentally" provided access to information about bisexuality, but it was never followed up in an official or legitimizing way, thus undermining its significance and positive possibilities. Benjamin recalls an excursion to the performance of the play *Rent*, which included content that opened up the possibility of bisexuality for him. However, there was no development, endorsement, and analysis of this discourse back at school in the official educational domain of the classroom:

It was year ten and it was theatre studies. . . . And I think that was the real big turning point. . . . It [*Rent*] confronted me with issues. . . . We just went to see it as a school, but we didn't really discuss it afterwards, which would have been good. . . . Like, I mean, there are so many queer movies out there or queer theory movies and I can't believe that this doesn't come up in school. . . . It can be taught. It can be taught in your history class, it can be taught in your English class. . . . I mean, when we studied *Cabaret* . . . there are a lot of issues about the MC and his sexuality, androgynous, bisexual, and with Brian, the love triangle there. She [the teacher] didn't go into it, though, that much, but she could have. You know, the study guide doesn't even have that much of a theme about sexuality. (Benjamin, nineteen, bi university student)

Thus, Benjamin provides strategies for bringing the external world of popular culture and queer culture into the classroom as a way of acknowledging and legitimating his bisexuality. By not doing this, his school and teachers were reinforcing his perception of his "abnormality" or illegitimacy. Bisexuality remained confined to the unreal realm of entertainment, fiction, and theatrical performance, thereby reinforcing his decision to keep passing as straight within the "real" world of school.

In relation to safer sex education and safe school programs, Herdt comments upon the fewer "concerned and supportive caretakers" for bisexually identified youths that offer the sort of positive programs and resources provided by gay and lesbian organizations for schools (2001: 276). Thus, even schools that claimed to be "out" about the need for nonheterosexual inclusion and education were still closeting bisexuality or expecting bi-specific education to pass as gay and lesbian education. Josie's experiences reflected this concern with "exclusion by inclusion" (Pallotta-Chiarolli and Martin, 2009). She spoke about how gay and lesbian youth workers and other members of the gay and lesbian communities who worked and liaised with her school in antihomophobic education were biphobic in silencing her reality:

> I used to think, well, hang on, you guys face oppression and marginalization on a daily basis because of your sexuality. Shouldn't you be a bit more open to the fact that we have eyes on us all? Why do you treat us badly? (Josie, bi-mono)

Her comment, "we have eyes on us all," endeavors to position bisexuality alongside rather than bordering homosexuality: homosexual and bisexual young people are both recipients of the panopticonic and regulatory heteronormative gaze.

Passing as a strategy of protection was adopted by many young people who were bisexual, as well as by young people whose parents were bisexual (Fuss, 1991; Kroeger, 2003). When young people of whatever sexuality talked about their multisexual families or bisexual parents, they talked about negative schooling experiences if they "outed" their families or feeling coerced not to talk about their families due to the biphobia experienced from teachers and peers (Arden, 1996; West, 1996; Easton and Liszt, 1997; Pallotta-Chiarolli, 2002): "My son said to me, 'Mum, the number of times that I'd have loved to have just gone up and talked to one of the teachers about it'" (Brenda, hetero-mono mom with a bi-poly husband).

A young man in my research from a rural area, Trent, refused to apply sexual labels to himself. His father was bisexual and in a loving twenty-year non-monogamous marriage with his mother. Trent felt disillusioned with and resistant to schooling because sexually diverse supportive and nurturing families such as his family had never been discussed at school. Indeed, he was angry that his parents' lives and livelihood could be severely jeopardized if he spoke about them at school within the small rural community. Thus, he passed his family as monogamous and heterosexual while he also believed that his "real education" was occurring outside the school gates:

> Since mum and dad opened this world up to me I've found there's so much more out there. There's a lot more bisexual people out there, and I'm more happy to know that instead of it hidden away from me. . . . [At school] all you hear about is the basic mother, father, and child. You don't hear father and father and mother and child. There's not all varieties, and that's not the way it works. . . . I feel lucky, to tell you the truth, because I'm blessed that I've got such an open family and I look around and see all these people at school who are living with this very small mind, very narrow minded, and I can look around with this wide open view and see the real world and how other people are going about life. (Trent, seventeen, son of bi-poly dad and hetero-mono mom)

A heterosexual woman in her late twenties, Madelaine, who works in the mental health profession, recalls what it was like having a bisexual mother who was in a relationship with a woman and then with a man while she was going through schooling:

> Outside my school, I knew lots of people who were perfectly fine with bisexuality. . . . I did not face discrimination at school, since I only told a few of my friends about my mother. . . . We were all very good students and pretty activist in some ways. . . . I always wanted to speak out but I also wanted to have a so-called normal life, to be a normal teenager, to be liked, to have boyfriends, to be accepted, to be successful. . . . We must educate mental health professionals who work with youth to expect and facilitate disclosure of sexual minority family statuses. (Madelaine, hetero-mono daughter of bi-mono mom)

Thus, passing has led to separate performances and undertakings of learned "cultural gestures" in separate worlds of home and school, for young people like Trent and Madelaine (Meyrowitz, 1985; Evans, 2003).

In the following, Paula talks about the detrimental effects on her sons' education as stemming not from having a bisexual father and the family's arrangements, but from her sons' inability to connect their "multiple life-worlds" of home and school (Cope and Kalantzis, 1995). It appears that attending school imposes a silence on her sons that is removed as soon as they leave school. Indeed, one son cut his education short, thereby dealing with the home/school dissonance by removing school from his life:

> Our sons manage it in different ways. They all say they love their dad and spend time at his boyfriend's house. The youngest is still at school and manages by not talking about it at all, while the older boys talk about it a little now. But when they were at school they were terrified of anybody knowing, but then

both told their friends, one soon after leaving school and one in his last year. Actually, one of them, the one who said nothing, left school halfway through his second-to-last year. He was doing so well, the teachers were whispering that he was a likely school captain the year after, and soon after he finds out his dad's bisexual, he suddenly decides he wants to leave school. His dad's boyfriend lived quite close to us, and his neighbors had kids at the same school. . . . He couldn't bear the stress of thinking word would soon get around school, so he's lost a solid education and the school lost a great student leader. All because having a bi dad in love with a man as well as your mum is not talked about. (Paula, hetero-mono mom with bi-poly husband)

Paula also attributes her sons' differing decisions on whether to talk about their dad at school to the particular kind of school they had chosen to attend before their father came out. External constructions of religiosity and hegemonic heterosexual masculinity act as particularly potent silencing and policing frameworks:

My son who left school early was in a Catholic boys' school which I had always felt had a very homophobic atmosphere. But he said he was happy there, felt really settled there and then leaves halfway through a year. . . . It was a real rugby-, football-playing school and bad luck if you don't fit in. There wasn't even a school counselor there. They had a priest who was supposed to help the boys, but there's no way they'd approach him. . . . They did cadets, military stuff, and they pushed that instead of health and personal development courses. You were a wimp if you didn't join. Even the headmaster would say that the state personal development curriculum was airy-fairy wimpy rubbish. So there was this real push to join cadets and march around and do all this stuff, which I hated, but my son wanted to be like his friends, and like I said, you're not the real man; you don't fit in if you don't join cadets. But it got too much for him. . . . My youngest son wanted to go to a Catholic school too, coeducational, and he says nothing about his dad, but says he likes the school. At least they talk about sexuality with the students there. They have health and personal development there. . . . My other son went to the local high school, . . . had a gay teacher who was just wonderful, and I think really inspired him, and I was really pleased that he had that at the time that he found out about his dad. But, again, he still didn't tell anybody until his final year. A group of them went on a skiing holiday together and shortly after that I said to him "Have you told any of your friends about Dad yet?" and he said, "Oh, yeah, when we were skiing I got drunk and told them all." . . . And I said, "So, how did they handle it?" and he said, "Oh, they were okay," and I thought that was a real sort of turning point for him, particularly as his very, very best friend comes from a fairly fundamentalist Christian family, so that's a big thing. I was just so relieved. He was clearly in an environment where he could be himself, and where everyone could be himself. . . . You could just tell the way he blossomed in that place, it was wonderful, and the sort of friends he had. A lot of the boys from the private schools would come around our house and there'd be a lot of homophobic talk, but I didn't notice that with my son's friends from the new local government school. (Paula, hetero-mono mom with bi-poly husband)

Passing as protection of parents was also a strategy adopted by Rowan. As much as possible he performed the healthy, happy bisexual boy at home in order to protect his lesbian parents from heterosexist blame for his "condition," from hurt if they knew of the harassment he was experiencing, and from any homophobia they might experience themselves when coming into the school institution in support of their son (see Garner, 2004):

> I've sometimes thought that having lesbian parents that I always have to kind of keep up this façade of being able to deal with things and because I feel that if I don't and if I break down and if things go wrong for me, and people see that that's happening, then they will say, "Well, that's why" [because his parents are lesbians] and I just don't want that to happen at all because it's not. . . . I think in ways I was kind of trained to protect them [parents] as well because I don't think there was anything they could do about it and I know that if I was a parent I would be so angry and hurt if I knew that my child was getting victimized all the time, so I kind of wanted to spare them that. (Rowan, nineteen, bi student)

Indeed, several bisexual young people believed the parent community of a school was responsible for the school not addressing sexual diversity. In previous research, a gay young man referred to this as the "Three Parent Syndrome" (Martino and Pallotta-Chiarolli, 2003; see also Pallotta-Chiarolli, 2005b). In other words, a vocal minority of parents could prevent any sexual diversity program from going ahead if they complained. Whether parents would actually complain or not is often not the issue in schools. It is the panopticonic fear or anticipation of parental surveillance and policing that prevents certain programs from even being initiated (Foucault, 1977). As Benjamin and Jack explain,

> It's hard to say that the school can do something when the school is funded by people in the community to a certain extent. It's a private school. People pay to go there. . . . The school's making money. You know it wants to survive. (Benjamin, nineteen, bi university student)

> I had some really wonderful teachers who I look back on now and think, gee, maybe they did want to talk to us, but if one kid in that class had gone back to his parents and said, "It's all right for me to be gay, isn't it, Mummy and Daddy?" you know it would be a terrible thing to do. Which is why the government I think needs to put it in policy. They need to make it what you have to do. That way you're not being a rogue element in the school. (Jack, bi-poly university student)

Often, information about bisexuality was kept with the school counselor. This created another barrier, as it was problematic to be seen going to the school counselor. Jack recalls feeling the panopticonic gaze at the thought of seeking support from the school counseling service:

> I remember they had some information on it, [bisexuality] books, in the counselor's office, and I remember the counselor was a very good man, but the thing is again in that competitive environment, everyone is watching each other. If I went to the counselor's office, because I was a very anxious young man, . . . and had anxiety attacks in class and had to leave all the time, I was watched by everybody. They thought I was bizarre, because I wasn't a stock standard, ordinary tough bloke sort of individual. . . . All this self-referential discipline, you know. (Jack, bi-poly university student)

Those young people who did see their school counselors were mainly dissatisfied with their response, especially at the stage where they were wanting to come out and seeking support for this. It appears counselors would try and dissuade them from this or offer no resources, as was the case for Bonnie:

> Definitely the school counselor could have had more resources, and then educated herself about it. Maybe school counselors need to do some kind of course or something on sexuality because it was just completely inappropriate, yeah. I suppose it's like a bit of a double-edged sword. I mean, at the same time their responsibility is to protect you from getting hurt, which might be the case. I mean if I had come out more I would have got someone saying something about me that I didn't like, and that would have upset me. It is a very vulnerable time of your life when you're doing these things, especially when there is so much pressure from everyone else to perform well. But at the same time, I don't think they should be discouraging you from coming out, because that's the kind of thing that stops you in the future from thinking it's okay. (Bonnie, bi-poly university student)

Certainly, the decision about young people coming out at school is dependent upon issues such as whether they have emotional, social, financial, and other forms of support (Pallotta-Chiarolli, 2005b). However, rather than counselors questioning what it was about their school structures and culture that made it difficult for young people to come out, it appears from my research that bisexual young people were prevented from taking considered, cautious, but significant actions. Thus, counselors and other adults in school settings could enforce "coerced closeting" or passing in young people.

My research also found that bisexual young people adopt passing as strategies of agency and resistance (Aruna, 1994; Fisher, 2003; Kroeger, 2003). Some pretend to the outside world of school, home, and the wider society to live heteronormative or, at the most, homonormative, lives while still at school. The closet, even if it means being closeted among the closeted as in relation to some gay and lesbian peers, represents a possible mode of evading "other more undesirable forms of governance" and a method of "assert[ing] a degree of control" over life (Mason, 1995: 87; see also Richardson, 1985; Sedgwick, 1993). Andrea recalls how a friend of her sister's utilizes the closet in order to queerify the gay and lesbian group on campus:

> My older sister's got this friend, this bi girl who's the sexuality officer at uni, but she's been told not to let people know she has a boyfriend or she won't be taken seriously. But she's slowly making the gay and lesbian group really "queer" not just gay and lesbian focused, but doing all that without outing herself, or else she wouldn't be able to do it. (Andrea, seventeen, bi student)

Benjamin was aware that coming out as bisexual at school would have caused too much harassment and disruption to his ability to study. He would have been unable to attain the grades he needed to go to university where he planned to come out in a more sexually diverse environment:

> You were put into a box definitely during the final year [of high school] and you didn't want to lose anything or fuck anything up because you know that's going to be detrimental to your mark. . . . There is no room also in [final year]. It's very structured. Do your work, get good marks and stuff. (Benjamin, nineteen, bi university student)

Thus, closeting as a temporary, transitional, or contextual strategy was utilized by some students (Lizarraga, 1993). Senior secondary school was a place of structured intellectual and vocational pursuits where one's emotional, sexual, and psychological development was assumed to be heterosexual and/or was given no space or time for exploration and reflection. Even after leaving school, Benjamin was very careful about whom he came out to in order to avoid his younger sister receiving homophobic harassment by association while she was still at the same secondary school:

> I didn't want my sister or my parents to have to face it, because I know how to handle it, but I knew that they wouldn't to a certain extent. . . . I got a phone call from my mum, very angry, saying, "You're so selfish" and all this sort of stuff because supposedly at my school, people were teasing my sister saying that, "Benjamin's come out of the closet, Benjamin's gay," and the first thing I was absolutely sort of shocked that she was blaming me for this. The second thing, my sister was crying, because she didn't know how to handle it and I'm like thinking, I don't understand, this is a school issue, very much a school issue. Like, other things like the fact that it was somehow the Chinese whispers got changed from being bisexual to gay. . . . I would advise my sister things to say. I said "Say whatever you want to say, you can deny it, you can say yes, you can do whatever you want. I don't care." Really, anyway, if people want to label you, then they're going to label you. (Benjamin, nineteen, bi university student)

For some young people, the strategy of passing allowed a certain detachment, or what Richardson (1985) calls "withdrawing," or "cloaking," a shield that deflected any homophobia or allowed the young people to disengage from whatever was happening around them. It also allowed them to excel and participate in the school in other dimensions (see Kroeger, 2003). For example, Sebastian, a young bisexual man, recalls homophobic language and attitudes in his Catholic school but explains:

> It didn't really bother me, because I'm not the type of person that really got bothered by what other people thought or what other people said, and I was always quick on my feet. I always had a mouth on me and if anyone sort of threw a comment on me, then I'd be ready to throw one back, but it never bothered me as such. . . . I was the school captain and I was the class captain and I was everything at that school. . . . I was never a troublemaker. I was one of the more academic type kids, but it's funny because [school captain] was peer voted . . . and, geez, I must have a lot of people who like me, because I thought that the troublemakers didn't want anyone who was slightly academic, but for some silly reason, I got along with all of them. . . . I have a close family and a close knit of friends and a close school community and everyone was different in their own sort of different bizarre way, so I think that what it was was that everything else was so accepted that it [homophobia] just didn't bother me. . . . I just had other things to worry about. Like, I enjoyed being at school and I enjoyed playing tennis and I enjoyed watching television and I enjoyed other stuff. . . . I was a sport captain which was different for me, because I'd never been like a sports person. I'd always been like a fairly big boy so I'd never really played much sport up until year ten and then I was like captain of the tennis team, captain of the soccer team . . . like I wouldn't get home until six o'clock on most nights and I lived like five minutes from my school. (Sebastian, bi university student)

Sebastian also believes that if the school had attempted to discuss sexual diversity in health education rather than its standard reproductive heteronormative education, it would possibly have been more detrimental to any same-sex attracted teachers or students. He believed that any sexual diversity education was not adequately framed by effective pastoral care and classroom management of his particular year level on other issues. Sebastian is also dismissive of the limited curriculum at his school in terms of masculinist norms, which made it even more unthinkable that it would undertake sexual diversity education:

> We were actually the worst to go through that school, and our school had a lot of troubled kids in there. Like, when I think back there was a lot of immature sixteen-year-olds, that wouldn't have been able to sit in the classroom for forty-five minutes and listen to a teacher speak about sexuality without labeling the teacher, without labeling the students and stuff like that. . . . I'm not going to

want to be the person in front of thirty boys going, "This is homosexuality and this is how the term was coined and this is the implications that it could possibly have on someone," that sort of stuff, because I'd not be scared, but I wouldn't know what to expect from the kids. . . . And another thing is that there's not time in the curriculum for that. Like, you have to teach to a curriculum. You can't sit there and go "So in our class today, we're going to talk about sexual diversity. What do you think?" Nah it has to be "This is sport. Now write about your favorite footy player." I said, "I don't like football." "Write about your favorite footy player." I said, "Can I write about a tennis player?" "No. Write about your favorite footy player." (Sebastian, bi university student)

Many young people reported privately seeking out information about bisexuality while still at school, as it was not forthcoming as part of the official curriculum or public school culture. Passing as straight or scripting a straight self for a straight school culture and other strategies of "script manipulation and script evasion" (Cohen and Taylor, 1976) gave students the ability to undertake private individual research and investigations without leaving themselves open to scrutiny and ostracism. Thus, given the "plurality of resistances" available to individuals, passing allowed for a measure of situated agency (Foucault, 1978, 1984). Sometimes, these excursions into knowledge about the self were not always planned or the initial intention, as Benjamin recalls:

Bisexual didn't even come to me until after my own reading and my own sort of finding out about this concept. . . . I was very interested in psychology and I wanted to go into studing psychology [at university] . . . so I thought I'd read up on some psychology so I went to the library and got this book and I remember actually learning a bit about bisexuality. (Benjamin, nineteen, bi university student)

Under the guise of pursuing a "legitimate" educational interest, Benjamin continued to access the "secret" "unspoken" information he personally desired, within the school walls and within a legitimate place of learning, the school library. Benjamin also spoke about education outside the school walls—accessing Internet sites and pornography as a way of "learning" and exploring his desires. It's poignant that he dealt with the initial feelings of shame about accessing the sites and then actually enjoying them on his own, without any official or supportive guidance:

I think I came through definitely due to the Internet and pornography on the Internet, which is not a good thing. It's really like, you know, I got on to a wrong site with naked men on there, and I think we got the Internet maybe when I was about twelve or so, though my parents weren't like those Net Nanny people who bar it, and I don't agree with pornography, I don't like it, but I did just during those years, but I really like blocked it out and it was like thinking, "Oh, I'm actually turned on by that and I'll go back to this." And it wasn't until like year eleven or especially like year twelve that I really felt like I actually enjoyed this and I'm going to look at it, and not feel ashamed that I'm going to look at it. (Benjamin, nineteen, bi university student)

Other young people recalled the effect passing had on relationships with teachers, particularly teachers who themselves may have been GLB-TIQ. Thus, closeting is occurring on both sides of the educational fence in teacher-student relations and preventing healthy mentoring, role modeling, and supportive relationships from developing. Many young people are left piecing together a teacher's queer reality based on "clues from within the closet" as Linda explains:

> You could tell this teacher or that teacher was gay or queer but it was like you might as well have been on opposite sides of the planet 'cause you'd never be able to talk about it openly and get support from them. So you spent your time in their lessons looking for clues from within the closet, from inside your closet and looking inside the cracks or the keyhole in their closet. Weird things like they way they talked or walked or looked at you. I must've looked really scary staring at them all the time like a serial killer. Or you'd try and have a joke that only someone in the know would get, and you'd read any little sign like an eye twitch or the way they smiled to see if they got it. (Linda, seventeen, bi student)

Other young people were left wondering to what extent they were impacted upon by some teachers who were "different," as Bonnie, for example, reflects:

> My fifth grade teacher was a lesbian. Someone told me after [I left] school. . . . And I thought that was really cool. I probably didn't understand it [at the time] but she was a sport teacher and she was very sporty and active and, yeah, didn't wear makeup or anything. . . . It probably influenced me without me thinking about it. Yeah, she had all these posters all around the room like, "Women can do anything" with all these sporty women. Yeah, it was fantastic, and she was part of the women's cricket team or something. (Bonnie, bi-poly university student)

"I'M BOB, A BIT OF BOTH": BISEXUALITY AS BORDERING

> The straight community think we're confused and weak, but the gay community think you don't belong, you have to get your shit together. . . . I fell quite deeply in love with a girl, and I was with her for two and a half years and while I was with her, I was a lesbian, but I knew that even then I didn't fit into being a lesbian. . . . Like, I made two friends in particular who are lesbian separatists and I can't be their friend anymore, they do not want to be my friend.
>
> —Josie, bi-mono

Many young people in my research saw themselves as border dwellers with a "dual marginality" (Rutledge, 2005), residing between and within the worlds of straight and gay. Probyn's term, "outside belonging" (1996: 9) is applicable to the border existences of many bisexual-identifying or bisexual-behaving young people in my research. They are both "outside" heteronormative and homonormative constructs of sexual binaries, and yet "belonging" in the sense that they may "pass" as a "normal" heterosexual or "normal" homosexual (Evans, 2003; Billson, 2005). They are also "outside" the dominant constructs of gay identity and gay community while simultaneously "belonging" due to their same-sex attractions and relationships:

> The big thing that I really have at the moment which is just pissing me off is that assumed homosexuality within the homosexual community and the fact that now they're set up it's almost to a certain extent that it's quite acceptable to be gay. It's almost like there's these polarized corners or boxes and it's like you either fall into one or the other and the bisexual male does not seem to exist to a certain extent, and I'm sick of it—like, lately, there was this guy who sort of said, "You're just confused." (Benjamin, nineteen, bi university student)

In the following, Rowan speaks about his shifting self-ascribed multiple positioning (Trinh, 1990b), while other students at school try to locate and fix him into the heterosexual/homosexual duality:

> Being bisexual, people generally assume that you're heterosexual because that's the way their minds work. . . . I was the only person there who actually identified as bisexual, although there were people who behaved bisexually, but at that stage most identified as gay or straight. At school people who were straight thought of me as straight, and people who were gay thought of me as gay. (Rowan, nineteen, bi student)

In an e-mail interview, twenty-two-year-old bisexual singer/songwriter/ activist Skott Freedman wrote,

> I believe many gay and lesbian people feel threatened by bisexuality; since we're similar to them, they want us to be exactly like them (because they already feel they don't fit in with heterosexual society). Bisexuality is a separate sexuality though. . . . I am neither straight nor gay. Why should I hide under either label because it's easier for someone else? It's my sexuality.

Some bisexual activist groups are reclaiming the border site, or nepantla (Anzaldua and Keating, 2002), as the place of possibility, proactivism, and resistance (Anzaldua, 1987a; hooks, 1990, 1999; Bhabha, 1990a, 1990b; Lugones, 1994). For example, Glenn Vassallo (2002) at the Seventh International Bisexuality Conference in Sydney spoke about how bisexual social spaces are a strong and inclusive border zone between repressed and exclusive polarities of "Homo and Hetero spaces" for bisexual people, their sexually diverse partners, friends, and allies. He provided the following table of the differences:

In Hetero Spaces	In Bi Spaces	In Homo Spaces
must explain and justify	no explanation, no justification	must explain and justify
exclusive	inclusive	exclusive
invisible	visible	invisible
behavior policed	anything goes	behavior policed
monogamous and single	mono, poly, single, with partners	mono, poly, single, with partners
ask to be there	it is ours	ask to be there

Some young people in my research found that the feeling of being on the borders was prevalent when being in a relationship with an opposite-sex partner. For example, Benjamin wondered whether having a girlfriend, who he'd come out to as bisexual and who was very comfortable about it, meant he'd have to live a straight life at the expense of a queer life:

> I told her and she was like, "I'm cool about it." And I had a real battle because I've got these gay friends now and, shit, what happens if I bring them to a straight place on Thursday night? . . . It's really problematic. I'm like, as soon as I get a girlfriend, does that mean I'm not part of the group anymore, and I still want my queer life, it's part of me, and I still want to go to the queer society . . . [and] I still want to have a girlfriend. (Benjamin, nineteen, bi university student)

Sebastian had also thought through the implications of being bisexual on future relationships, and how he would construct and live out his border relationship and family as monogamous:

> If I'm with someone, I'm with someone, and what I've done in the past and what I may do in the future has got nothing to do with the relationship at hand, and yeah, I might say something about it [to my wife], but only because it would be really uncomfortable if, you know what I mean, meeting one of my ex-boyfriends in the future. And it's like what the hell, you're married with kids now, because I've done nothing wrong, and I don't want her to feel uncomfortable about it as well and if she felt that uncomfortable about it, then I'd have to think twice about it [marrying her]. (Sebastian, bi university student)

In an earlier research project into masculinities in schools, Simon, who self-labeled as a "tomgirl," talks about the dilemmas heteronormative and gender-normative schooling structures and practices construct for young people wishing to explore sexual diversity beyond sexual duality (Martino and Pallotta-Chiarolli, 2001a, 2001b, 2003). At the time of the interview, Simon was hoping to find a girlfriend to "find out if I'm gay." Within a normative framework of sexual duality, homosexuality shifts into the zone of "normality" for Simon, as opposed to the "abnormality" of bisexuality:

> Actually I've felt sad about it but, yeah, I thought I might be bisexual. It would be a bit hard to cope with. I want to be myself like every other kid, be normal and not like both guys and girls. It's normal being gay, but it's going to be really hard if I am [bisexual]. (Simon, thirteen, "tomgirl")

Here we see an example of the use of panopticonic silence that prevents any other option for Simon to explore in order to situate himself as gay, heterosexual, or bisexual (Foucault, 1977). The options and strategies are severely limited within the heteronormative context of the school and the homophobia of other students.

Sebastian was another young person who bordered, indeed fluctuated and meandered, between using the labels "gay" and "bisexual," and constructing a gay or bisexual self:

> I don't really like those labels, but the label that I use is gay, even though I do feel that I am bisexual. I don't know why, but it just seems harder to explain and so like I've sort of drifted away from being bisexual a lot in the last few months . . . but I don't like to put myself in a box. Like, I don't want to restrict myself. I feel like if I go, okay, I'm gay, then I can't do what I want to do with females. . . . I probably am using gay as it's an easier way to explain. Like you go, "I'm gay," it's just easier to go than, "I'm bisexual." "What do you mean by bisexual? What's bisexual?" . . . I think the actual notion of being bisexual is problematic because it's like, well, you're either one or the other. You're not both. How can you be both? Like how can you like both and it's like, yeah, I do sort of like both. . . . But like I don't actively seek either [males or females]. Just whatever comes along. (Sebastian, bi university student)

For those young people who hoped to leave the sexual dualist confines of high school to go into sexually diverse GLBTIQ communities, the reality was not often as simple or positive. As Rowan explains,

> My best friend, who is gay, it's become like a lot more of an issue for him because he's now got to the stage where he thinks that if you're bisexual you should choose to be homosexual because by having a heterosexual relationship you're supporting heterosexual privilege and also, as I've left school, I've seen more of the homosexuality culture and I've seen a lot more the invisibility of bisexuality. (Rowan, nineteen, bi student)

Leaving a homophobic school culture to enter into a politicized, visible, and cultural gay community is a significant step for many gay and lesbian young people, such as Rowan's best friend. This may also involve enculturation, the learning of new "group norms" and ideologies of sexuality, being given opportunities to think about and challenge "heterosexual privilege" in ways that were unimaginable at school, and to rethink "boundaries" of belonging and not belonging (Dowsett, 1997; Young, 1990a, 1990b). Thus, postschool experiences of entering sexual minority communities may find the previous unity between gay and bisexual friends is severed as one takes up the central position within the marginal, while the other is relegated to the margins of the marginal (Goffman, 1973; Anzaldua, 1987a; Trinh, 1990b; Bersten, 2008). Benjamin felt that he bordered the gay and straight worlds in not wanting to embody or perform the stereotype of a gay man that he saw being enacted in "the scene," and that he acknowledged as being constructed by the heteronormative world:

> There's a stereotype of gay people, but being in the scene, the stereotype is actually enacted and . . . I think that a lot of people feel that I've got to enact the stereotype to feel more part of the gay community, and they put on the accent, they dress in clothes that they don't want to dress in, and they're letting sexuality define them. I think there are a lot of people who are gay and bisexual who are doing that. I definitely blame heterosexuality for this, entirely, because they create the stereotype in the first place. (Benjamin, nineteen, bi university student)

This feeling of bordering the gay community did leave Benjamin feeling isolated, wondering how he could make friends and engage in sexual encounters to explore his bisexuality without risking his sexual and social health. This isolation and border existence affected his learning in his first year of university, which makes Benjamin glad he did not come out in high school where he would've been even less able to handle the isolation and depression:

> I felt very isolated. I couldn't meet people and I just wanted to meet people and explore. I think it was in some ways to justify am I really bisexual. . . . I don't want to go to a gay club. I don't want to just end up with some sort of unsafe person. I want to meet people and form friendships and that sort of stuff. . . . Towards the end of last year with my exams, I was very depressed and quite upset and it affected the way I was studying. Like, I was sort of very indifferent to study and I was glad that this didn't happen in my final year of high school. And I could feel for people who went through this in year twelve. If I did I would have even been worse. (Benjamin, nineteen, bi university student)

Some young people saw their bisexuality as positioning them on the borders of binary school structures. Jack recalls the fear and anxiety that came from realizing he was bisexual while still in high school. He links the categorization of sexuality into "competing teams" to the broader cultural and structural division of all aspects of society and culture, as manifested in schooling, into groups and teams, which are then pitted against each other:

> [I remember] developing a very strong fear . . . when I turned around to myself and thought well, what am I, who am I, there was no one to talk to, there was no one. . . . It's like there's all these boxes out in the school field and you have to be in one of them. You can't be out in the open air, you can't be yourself, because to be an individual as opposed to part of the group is just too terrifying and traumatic at school, the competition and the pressure that we breed into our children at a very early age. . . . They're put in teams to compete against each other. . . . We wonder why we're having problems [in schools]. . . . I made the mistake of going to a boys' schools for my last year of schooling, which I hated, absolutely hated. Any homophobia which may have been present in my previous school was magnified ten times. They put them in these horrible uniforms and they had cadets . . . where they enforce these military values on adolescent boys, not that they haven't enough aggression. . . . Competition is so strong. They breed it into them in this most rabid way. There is no individuality; you exist as part of whatever faction you're in there. The house that you're in, the group that you're a member of. I could not stand it . . . and I was desperate. I was starting to get into contact with myself, really get into contact with myself, and I just couldn't stand it. (Jack, bi-poly university student)

Again, we see the strong connection between hegemonic constructions of masculinity in the school manifested through the culture of competition and cadets/militarism and the construction of border masculinities such as those of Jack (Martino and Pallotta-Chiarolli, 2003). Jack's analogy of bisexuality being something beyond set either/or categorizations supports Angelides's contention: "I aim, therefore, to situate bisexuality in fragmented and fluid spaces; that is, in subject-positions without rigid borders" (1995: 38; see also Wark, 1997; Angelides, 2001). The inclusion of bisexuality in education and the acknowledgment of some young people's fluid sexual attractions, identities, and behaviors may mean the very disruption and subversion of the dichotomous logics of pedagogical organization and school programming.

Some young people were located within and between "multiple life-worlds" (Cope and Kalantzis, 1995) and multiple interwoven borderings. Layers of multiplacement, in-betweenness, and insider/outsider locations, or having "too much truth" (Derrida, 1981), were experienced and expressed by bisexual young people of diverse ethnic and religious backgrounds (Trinh, 1991; Pallotta-Chiarolli 1995b, 1996, 1999b; Audinet, 2004; Fuji Collins, 2004). These young people were not just sexual border dwellers; they also bordered other forms of community and culture, such as ethnic and religious affiliations. For example, Josie said she grew up referring to herself as "Bob, a Bit of Both," for not only was she bisexual, but her bi-cultural and bi-class border backgrounds also positioned her as a multiple border dweller, as a mestiza:

My father's from a working-class, migrant, Italian family, where the only books in the house were the Bible. My mother's from a French intellectual family, not hugely well off, but an intellectual class, and so I come from quite a strange mix. You know most people are brought up with two working-class parents or two middle-class parents. I've got one of both. . . . I started off very young calling myself "Bob," and that stood for "A bit of both," and that summed up what I felt . . . growing up in New Zealand, which was the other dynamic, there wasn't many wogs around. . . . I was different, in one of many ways, but just probably the food we ate, you know, because Dad did the cooking. I had a very unusual childhood. I suppose I always had the legacy of my big long wog name, so you know you couldn't try and escape it, even though I didn't want to, and I think the ramifications of the policy in the sixties of trying to get rid of your culture has come through with me as well, when my dad wasn't allowed to speak Italian. My mother speaks fluent French, but Dad speaks Italian like a child because when he was six, seven, eight, he wasn't allowed to speak it at school, the nuns used to make him speak only English. And this was in Melbourne, so I think now, he is reverting to the biggest old Italian man you've ever met. (Josie, bi-mono)

Thus, through her father's experiences, Josie has also witnessed the effects of other forms of assimilation and passing—in this case, cultural assimilation.

Benjamin was from a Jewish background and had attended a Jewish secondary school. He talked about the minority status of his Jewish school and Jewish community as a significant reason for the absence of sexual diversity education:

Not because of the religion but more because it is a cultural minority school, and in a minority culture, you have a very strong set of norms of heterosexuality, and because of that there's less of a chance for the school to sort of promote these "others" in terms of sexuality. I think that's the reason, because it wasn't a very religious school . . . but because it's such a small community and there's not many people that come out in the community, it's quite problematic. (Benjamin, nineteen, bi university student)

As discussed earlier, Benjamin's education had included a study of the musical *Cabaret*, based on Christopher Isherwood's short stories of life in Germany at the time Nazism and organized anti-Semitism took hold. Thus, it would seem a pertinent text for a Jewish school, as it addresses Jewish, Nazi, and Holocaust histories. However, the sexual diversity and triad relationship within the musical was not addressed alongside these themes. Such selective analysis and engagement with texts was problematic for young people like Benjamin, who were connecting to both the Jewish and bisexual elements of the play but finding only one was discussed while the other was silenced.

The question of marrying within the Jewish community had also been put to Benjamin, and his response is telling of his bordering the Jewish community, both belonging and not wanting to belong to it:

> One friend brought up one problem about this [being out as bisexual]. He said, "Benjamin, but don't you think that this label is going to stay with you throughout the community? Like, say you decide you want to get married to a girl in the community. You know, they're all going to sort of say, 'Oh he's bisexual, don't marry him,' or people will have these preconceived thoughts." I mean, the way I figure it, I wouldn't want to marry those people anyway. . . . I mean, I'm not one in the community who has to marry someone of the same community. Because I don't believe in the religion, I'm free to marry whoever I like. I open up myself to the world, I don't really care, so I don't see that as an important issue. . . . And I said that whoever I go out with, they're going to have to know, I can't lie to them. (Benjamin, nineteen, bi university student)

For some bisexual young people, being metissage for other reasons made it much easier to add the issue of bisexuality to the list of border dwelling criteria. Indeed, being on the borders became a positive site of being free to explore (Anzaldua, 1987a; McLaren, 1993; Audinet, 2004). As Mateusz writes,

> I'm a bi boy, my Dad's bi, I'm Jewish, Polish-American, dirt-poor background, so I'm already outside 'cause of my religion and culture and class and family. I've never been accepted anyway or bought into mainstream notions and myths, so I always knew I had a weird kind of freedom to explore my sexuality because it'd never be worth it trying to fit in by playing straight. (Mateusz, sixteen, bi son of bi-poly dad)

Likewise, Sam has a physical disability as well as identifying as bisexual:

> I have a physical disability, which has put me way outside the boundary of being a normal male, so not belonging because of my bisexuality is just another reason to find my own spaces and not try to find one group or one space that's going to meet all my needs or accept all of me. I mean, most people, gay or straight, think being in a wheelchair means I shouldn't have a sexuality anyway. Well, I've got one and it's not straight and it's not gay. (Sam, sixteen, bi student)

Some students gained strength and support for their bisexuality and bisexual activism from schools that were inadvertently situated on the borders of the "appropriate to challenge" and "inappropriate to challenge" injustices and discriminations. In other words, even if homosexuality and bisexuality were not publicly listed as the discriminations the school was challenging, Jess, who came out as bisexual when she stood for state elections at nineteen, found that her school provided an environment where the rhetoric of social justice and activism was linked to other issues such as poverty and racism. Thus, the school's discourses of justice and equity, even if not considered "appropriate" to publicly apply to sexual diversity, were viscously leaked into meanings and interpretations that served the purposes of other students situated in the sexual margins (see Douglas, 1966; Zerubavel, 1991). As a Catholic bisexual activist, with a physical disability, who was also her school's captain, the mestiza Jess recalls that

> I went to a Catholic all-girls school that had a real emphasis on social justice, and gave me the chance to sort of further my interests in that area, so we had the Social Justice Club and we had people going out working with the homeless on Friday nights and forums on Indigenous issues and all that sort of thing. There was that real encouragement of all those things. . . . Well, this school was fantastic, so I was really pleased to grow up in that sort of environment. . . . I don't doubt that most of the people at our school were open-minded about the issue [of sexuality]. I think a lot of the teachers, if they'd had the opportunity, probably would have spoken positively or at least, you know, not extremely negatively, and I was aware, while I was going through high school, particularly in the older years, that some teachers were of diverse sexualities. But, only aware on a very sort of secretive level. (Jess, bi university student with lesbian partner)

So, by the time Jess began to experience a crush on a female teacher, the school had inadvertently provided her with a set of values and outlooks: be open-minded, seek information, and be politicized. This provided an affirming framework for her later personal investigations:

> I started to realize that this might be something more than just a single crush on one person. At that stage, I think I started to go and look for my own information. So at first I only sort of admitted to myself that I was trying to find out more about it, so that I could be open-minded. . . . I was a member of all sorts of groups and always involved in political activity, and I just saw this as another political area that needed my attention, you know, needed a bit more education and information. . . . After I told my best friend, my first port of call was the Internet, and I looked a little bit, but I was worried that I wasn't going to find anything that was really suited to my age. I felt that a lot of what was on the Internet—like, you know, I typed in "lesbian" on an engine search and it came up with a whole lot of porn sites made for men, and I couldn't seem to find something that was just talking about coming out, how to do it, what it feels like, but I guess it was good in that it was the first time I was actively going and trying to find something. (Jess, bi university student with lesbian partner)

Three factors—her "nerd" academic and leadership passions; being advanced from the year nine to year eleven level due to being a gifted learner; and her "friendship group of loners"—also had Jess inhabiting the borders as a nepantlera (Anzaldua and Keating, 2002). She now sees this nepantla location as a vantage point (hooks, 1990; 1999):

> I was a nerd. I always have been, and, you know, that's become something that I pride myself on now instead of feeling bad about it. . . . I often got along better with teachers than I did with my peers, until I moved into the different year level and was able to find people who I could relate to and get along with, but I also seemed to attract a large sort of friendship group of loners, people who didn't fit in; they didn't necessarily get along with the other people that I was friends with. I'd developed one-on-one relationships with people who weren't accepted by the mainstream, so, you know, there was one girl who had come from Vietnam, and she still had a very strong accent and couldn't speak English very well and for that reason and that reason alone, she was bullied terribly. . . . And I think spending a lot of time with people who were marginalized and bullied and didn't fit into the mainstream probably helped me to sort of come to terms with my stuff, because I was also part of one of the 'in' groups. . . . I was well liked. It's a funny thing. You know, I was well liked by people but I was never one of the cool people. . . . I was always passionate about those who were forgotten or who weren't accepted by the mainstream, and it was ironic that I eventually slotted myself, not intentionally, into pretty much as many marginalized groups as was possible. You know, I lost my leg and joined the army of disabled. You know, I came out as bisexual, and became a vegetarian. . . . I never had the boyfriends like everyone else. . . . I mean that was always one of the differences with the peers that I didn't get along with. I didn't want to sit there and talk about the boys I'd kissed on the weekend, because, firstly, I hadn't kissed any, and secondly, I found the whole topic of conversation fairly boring, so I would focus on my studies instead, which is how I really got the nerdy sort of tag. . . . So I didn't feel connected to that sort of culture of girls sitting around and talking about boys and [I was] thinking that was really stupid, so I'd just go and find my own thing. (Jess, bi university student with lesbian partner)

Jess also believes she was fortunate having a family with gay friends so that by primary school level, she was aware of nonheterosexual possibilities, thereby bordering the heteronormative silences of her school world and the informed homonormative world of home:

> I was aware that there were gay and lesbian people at that [primary school] stage because my parents had friends who were gay and lesbian. . . . I didn't sort of see them a lot or talk to them a lot, but knowing that they were there, knowing that my parents were friends with them, knowing that my parents were sort of a bit open-minded about that sort of thing I guess had a big influence on me being open-minded about it. . . . So I'm lucky that I had that experience with my parents, because I imagine that people at primary school who didn't have that sort of influence from their families, would not have been exposed to it at all. (Jess, bi university student with lesbian partner)

As mentioned earlier, Jess had also had personal experience of being a border dweller due to her disability, which had implications for her when she moved onto the sexual borders. She found that not only did her school provide only heterosexual reproductive knowledge about sexuality but that it was appallingly ableist:

I had my left leg amputated when I was ten years old, so I guess that disability, if that's what you like to call it, has probably impacted a lot on my personality, my view of myself, my place in the world, and I think it's also had an impact on my sexuality. I had a lot of self-esteem issues, which you know, trying to come to terms with my sexuality, you know, in terms of being bi and trying to figure all that out and at the same time, trying to feel okay about my body. You know, every girl goes through the self-esteem issues, their looks and everything, but having the one leg probably exacerbated a lot of those problems. . . . I had my first same-sex sexual experience with one of my partners along the way, who was also bisexual and just feeling completely inadequate in front of her and being completely terrified about taking the leg off because no one ever tells you. There's a real problem with a lack of information with young people with disabilities about sexuality so you feel like you're not normal, and therefore you can't have normal sex. There's this whole thing about not even knowing whether you're supposed to leave your leg on or take it off when you have sex, and just trying to figure out how I'm supposed to have sex as an amputee and then trying to figure out how you have sex. So my first sexual experience, the first time I actually slept with someone was a girl, so I was terrified, because I had no idea how I was supposed to do things, and then I also had this thing I don't want to take my leg off. Am I attractive? I don't know what to do. Am I going to be able to move okay? . . . So it was really scary, a lot of learning and also just that self-esteem thing of yes, I am attractive, someone actually finds me attractive, no, they're not pretending, no, I don't have to hide it [my disability] as much as possible. (Jess, bi university student with lesbian partner)

Thus, Jess's personal learning and experiences occur on the borders of a school system that does not support her in relation to her interwoven mestiza sexuality and disability:

The only time I'd ever heard anything about amputees and sex was jokes in high school about amputee porn and the only time I'd heard mention of gay sexuality and lesbian sexuality was jokes about guys liking chicks getting together and really negative pictures of sexuality in both cases as a lesbian person having lesbian sex and a person who's disabled having sex. . . . They teach you about reproduction with straight sex and they teach you about falling in love, they talk about that sort of thing, they talk about families and marriage and having children, you know, all those sorts of things, but they don't apply it to any same-sex attraction. . . . The reality is they teach straight kids how to have sex. They show you a banana and a condom. And they explain it. As early as grade one and two, we were being brought into the classrooms, and they talk about the parts of your body as though they're normal and explain in a very straightforward, scientific way, this is how sex works; this is the male part, this is the female part, this is how they fit together, this is normal, this is good. You know, there would be lots of giggles and all that sort of thing, but by the end of it, yeah, you'd have this sense that this is normal, that it's okay. But the idea of this is how (two) women have sex, you know. I had no idea that, you know, you could use your hands, you could use toys, you could use all sorts of things. (Jess, bi university student with lesbian partner)

Sebastian's experiences were also those of metissage. He had not come out to his Italian parents, as he saw his ethnicity as placing him between the world of his parents, where sexual diversity was not known, and the world he is part of in the wider community:

I don't think it was unspoken about. I think it was just not what they knew. . . . Like, my mum grew up with nine brothers and sisters in a village town. Like, I mean a village town, where they just ate off the land and didn't eat well, and my dad was sort of more industrialized city, but still the same sort of understanding, and so like I don't blame them for not understanding, because it's not their fault; it's where they grew up, but it sort of makes it hard for everyone else, for the next, following, generations. (Sebastian, bi university student)

Nevertheless, Sebastian honored his home world and acknowledges his family and lower socioeconomic background as giving him the skills to handle any conflict from others in the wider world he also borders:

They [my parents] started off with nothing when they came here, and I know it's a cliché, but it's true. My dad started with nothing and my mum started with nothing and they worked, like, painting jobs, to sort of get to where they're at now. . . . My mum's really tough and I always say that I take after my mum . . . I just try not to let things bother me. . . . But developing a thick skin, I don't know, I think I've just grown up not caring but sort of going, "Well who are you? Like, who are you to judge me when you're not perfect yourself?" And I just pass it off as ignorance. . . . I don't play the victim. (Sebastian, bi university student)

Thus, being on the borders was both problematic and empowering for Sebastian, as it was for many of our nepantla young people (hooks, 1991; Trinh, 1991).

Another example is Rowan, a mestizaje border dweller or "marginal man" in his bisexuality, his lower-class background, the way he constructed a nonnormative masculinity, and his having lesbian parents, which had already made him the target of harassment in his younger years. Yet, it's from these marginal positions, particularly in regard to his two mothers, that Rowan believed he had gained invaluable perspectives on gender relations that were from the Margins rather than those of a Center dweller such as the white Anglo heterosexual boys he found he was unable to associate with (see hooks, 1990; 1999):

> I think having lesbian parents meant that I grew up in an atmosphere that was relatively unprejudiced. . . . So I always felt that that set me apart straight away, and then being bisexual as well was another issue which gave me a whole different perspective on things generally. . . . Something that I've always noticed about myself is that I don't have any close friends who are straight men, and I was thinking about that and I thought, well, most of the boys, men, that I would have known who were straight would be straight Anglo-Saxon middle-class men, so would never have really been in any position to have any prejudice directed against them, and I think having prejudice of any sort, like, directed against you, especially when you're growing up, is quite a kind of formative experience and, yes, forms your personality quite a lot and the way you react to the world and the way you expect the world to react to you. . . . I kind of started to think about the way men and women were treated, but because that had always been an issue in my life, because it had always been something that my parents would talk about and would kind of bring up, like gender relations is something I've always been taking into consideration. (Rowan, nineteen, bi student)

Indeed, many of the male research participants saw themselves as border dwellers not only because of their bisexuality, but also because of the way they performed non-normative or marginal masculinities. Benjamin believes his attitudes to sport and study had already set him apart as a border dweller in not conforming to dominant masculinist behaviors:

> I wasn't that good at sport, though I did play sport, but I didn't play the, you know, there's the macho sports, the football, the soccer, and then there's the sports that I used to play, like tennis and golf, which you're not going to sort of go into the school playground and just get a tennis racket, so no one would know that you're good at tennis or play tennis. All they'll know is that you don't play football, you don't play soccer and you don't play cricket. So I didn't play sport. . . . And most of my friends were girls. . . . Then I got involved in drama and theatre at school, so it just sort of added to this sort of feminized extracurricular. I fit into that box. "Yeah, he doesn't play sport so he must be therefore gay." And, I also studied a lot and do my homework and that sort of thing. (Benjamin, nineteen, bi university student)

Rowan and Benjamin were also aware of the gendered discrepancy among their male school peers where bisexuality in girls was encouraged while their own bisexuality was rendered invisible or silenced (Russell and Seif, 2002; Simpson, 2006; Fahs, 2009,). Thus, their "not okay" male bisexuality bordered the "okay if male-centered" bisexuality of girls and the "normal" straight sexuality expected of boys:

> I remember things like when I would go to parties and people would play spin the bottle or something and girls were always expected to kiss other girls but

guys never ever would, yes, so I think bisexuality has come to be more accepted among girls probably because it's straight male fantasy. (Rowan, nineteen, bi student)

Jack found the same gender differentiation happening among his peers, although even girls' bisexuality could be trivialized as "trying to be trendy":

> It was my first real girlfriend in year ten, a girl who'd had a lot of issues in her life with drugs and eating disorders at a very young age, and it was in year twelve and she was now with a girl, and I remember the party that I went to. At the party, I met her girlfriend, and everyone was talking about how Audrey was gay now and ranting on about it and I actually said to her, "Do you consider yourself gay? Have you ever been attracted to men?" She said, "I'm still attracted to men," but everyone had pretty much labeled her that way, without her consent, even if she used the term "bi." I even remember a girl saying, "Oh, she's just trying to be trendy. She's probably a dyke." (Jack, bi-poly university student)

The issue of gendered constructions of bisexuality could impact on relationships (Atkins, 2002; Anderlini-D'Onofrio, 2003; Burleson, 2005; Sheff, 2008; Fahs, 2009). For example, when Benjamin told his ex-girlfriend he was bisexual, she responded with "So am I," but he distinctly felt that her construction of bisexuality was the "trendy" connotation. Thus, gendered constructions of bisexuality can mean that while female bisexuality is normalized and objectified, male bisexuality is marginalized, and the gender borders between the two have to be negotiated in relationships:

> I did have one girlfriend during year twelve, and we only went out for maybe two months, around that, but I didn't say anything because while I was going out with her it didn't sort of come up. Afterward, which was about two months after we broke up, I said to her "Oh, actually I want to say to you I'm bisexual," and she said to me, "Well, I am, too." Oh, it was great to know that she was, too, but I kind of felt like she was also a bit like it's getting to the point it's fashionable. . . . I felt really angry that she said this to me. You know, "Why are you sort of doing this?" "Oh, it's just one time, or it's just something that would never happen again" or something like that. (Benjamin, nineteen, bi university student)

Josie was a young bisexual woman who did make strategic use of the dominant stereotype of bisexual people as having "double the options" to allay people's fears. She also used her being a female and adopting "normal" feminine gender fashioning to help others become more comfortable about bisexuality, and indeed think about it in terms of their own sexuality. Thus, she bordered a transgressive sexuality and a normative feminine performance, strategically manipulating her costuming and "cultural gestures"

(Meyrowitz, 1985; Thompson, 2006; Fahs, 2009), and hoping her peers would meet her on that border. However, in acknowledging this strategy, she was also on the borders of whether it was appropriate or problematic to do so:

> People don't find it as threatening, two girls, as two guys. . . . I always joke about how I have double the options and make silly comments like that. . . . I guess I use my bisexuality—ah, see I hate even saying it, but I guess I use the fact that I have been with girls and guys to maybe help other people feel a bit of it, you know. I look fairly normal. I'm not like with really short hair . . . and I'm not one of the girls who are really butch, so I guess I use that to say, hey, it's okay. . . . And I think sometimes you'll find that if you're open to both sides, they try out their own sexuality on you and test out how they feel. (Josie, bi-mono)

Thus, Josie's sexuality becomes a border site of experimentation and "playfulness" (Lugones, 1994; Molina, 1994). She becomes the litmus test with which others can test and explore their own sexuality. Nevertheless, in bordering the "normal" girl and the "'bisexual" girl, Josie also found herself having to carefully straddle the border of the "slut/bad girl" or "sexy/good girl" divide (Thompson, 2006), thereby being policed as a woman in relation to how much sex she was actually having: "Sometimes I do find it hard with friends because they see me going on dates with guys but they also see me being attracted to girls, and it does make it a bit—because you don't want your friends to think that you're a slut" (Josie, bi-mono).

Benjamin also speaks of "crossing the line" between gay and straight friends, his bisexuality also being a kind of permission to his friends to experiment and feel a little more at ease with their sexualities without having to identify as gay:

> I have been sort of mixing some friends in with some straight friends and some gay friends, crossing the line. I've got one friend who would label himself as completely heterosexual, except because of me I guess he would like to experiment and that sort of stuff. I find that of the university friends, my close friends at university, that me being or identifying myself as bisexual has been less confronting than saying that I was gay and the fact that they themselves are trying to be open-minded at times because this guy who looks sort of straight and dating girls can just sort of say, "Well, I just want to try it with guys, and why can't I? And what's so bad about that," because it's sort of still the girl bit. And so although it's harder in a way to actually be bisexual because of the two distinct categories it's also easier because it's much less confrontational than saying you're completely sort of gay. (Benjamin, nineteen, bi university student)

Jack found that while peers began to say they accepted his bisexuality, he was still treated as the "stranger" (Wood, 1934; Simmel, 1971; Kristeva,

1991). He recalls being at a party where his bisexuality becomes a border zone others navigate around and deconstruct:

> I don't know what happened; people at that party started to ask me whether I was bi and it was surreal, it was really odd. . . . I even had a guy that night crack on to me and he was curious to see how I'd react. I was being experimented upon. I remember leaving that party going it was really weird. Like, not only did I meet all these people that say they're really fine with it but who have an odd approach and like to whisper about it and rant about it, but I met these people who were trying to deconstruct me in this really horrible way. (Jack, bi-poly university student)

When he attends university, he does come out about his bisexuality but finds he is still on the borders in relation to his polyamory. Outside the university, he is mixing with bisexual polyamorous groups and communities, while inside the university and as part of the wider society, he needs to select only one of those categories—polyamory is beyond what even those who accept his sexuality would tolerate or understand:

> That's the next barrier that I feel I really need to break. . . . How do I tell my mates at school about my life, when I have to cover it up, when I have to lie to them? . . . It's very bizarre in the sense that like in one circle I feel totally normal and totally clear and wonderful and I know what I'm doing, know where I'm at, but in a wider society I find myself editing my conversation, and that's bizarre. I shouldn't be made to feel that way. . . . I'm getting better at it. I'm talking to people, I'm getting braver. (Jack, bi-poly university student)

Hence, it's as if the university and the wider society are the binary poles that insist on a certain level of closeting of both/either Jack's sexuality and/or relationship style. In the middle, on the borders, in the nepantla or metissage zone, (Anzaldua, 1987a, 1987b; Anzaldua and Keating, 2002) Jack belongs to border groups of polyamorous people.

"I'M A UFO, AN UNIDENTIFIED FUCKING OBJECT": BISEXUALITY AS POLLUTING

> I'd say just enjoy it [being bisexual]. Just be happy with yourself. . . . I don't think I could ever not be out about it. . . . I couldn't imagine staying in the closet about it.
>
> —Bonnie, bi-poly university student

Many bisexual young people speak of self-ascription, personal agency, and noncompliance: implementing polluting strategies of resistance (Douglas, 1966); constructing their own identities despite external hierarchical dualisms, negations, and invalidations at school (Burbules, 1997); and disrupting the neat sexual categories peers and teachers operate within. Duren-Sutherland and associates (1999) present Australian bisexual young people talking about negative schooling experiences based upon biphobia or bisexual invisibility when they did come out and disrupted normative sexual discourses. Emily recalls well-meaning heterosexual peers primed up in antihomophobic discourses at school feeling "confused" and not understanding her specific situation. Sven remembers graffiti in the boys' toilets saying, "Sven, you're straight," while boys would call him "fag" as they rode their bikes past him. Alison recalls coming out to a teacher as bisexual, which was then "invalidated with a comment like 'Oh, seems like everyone is these days.'" She recalls facing harassment and abuse from both heterosexual and gay and lesbian students for not being one or the other (1999: 44).

For some young people, the very power of what is defined as bisexuality is its unclassifiability and multiplicity, its being everywhere and elsewhere and nowhere (Angelides, 1995, 2001; Wark, 1997; see also Derrida, 1981; Bauman, 1988–1989, 1990, 1991; Garber, 1995). These young pollutants want schools to acknowledge and discuss the reality that sexuality can be a fluid and changeable part of being human:

> I'm of the opinion that people change from month to month and week to week, and we're all different people and it all depends on the individual. . . . I would love to just storm into all the schools across Australia and say to them, "Tell them that we change as we grow older." And they might hit forty and decide that they want to change who they are. I mean, it's all about having that freedom. (Jack, bi-poly university student)

Benjamin also discussed the use of fixed dichotomous sexual identity constructs within the school context. He proceeded to simultaneously use and pollute the meanings of socially ascribed sexual labels, as well as the need to have and use these labels at all:

> I feel labeling or categorizing is the core of our sort of problems or prejudices. I think as human beings somehow we've got to classify, label, to put each other into a box and I don't see that as beneficial; I see it as detrimental. However, because we're in a society where I cannot exist without a label, I have to label myself, and so therefore to people, I would say I'm bisexual. . . . And I mean the bisexual construct is a construct in itself too. It implies 50/50, and I don't agree with it at all. . . . I'm my personality, I'm not defined by my sexuality. I'm Benjamin, and I've always been Benjamin before I came out and after I came out. (Benjamin, nineteen, bi university student)

Benjamin was also polluting by readily subverting the negative stereotype of bisexuality as a phase. Rather than being problematic, he considered phasing as polluting, as a positive possibility of bisexuality. He also refused to define as gay or straight based on the relationship he was currently in. Benjamin's desires, whether acted upon or not, were bisexual:

> It's like these girls, I'll date them and they'll be like, "But what are you?" . . . And the gay guys would be like, "Oh, you're so gay, aren't you. It's just a phase. I was like you, I liked girls but then afterwards I didn't like them anymore." I'm like, "Okay." . . . And I still don't think that if I were to go through a phase and then end up my whole time with a guy, I still wouldn't consider myself to be gay, then it implies if I'm dating a girl, I'll be straight, but I wouldn't be ever bisexual. (Benjamin, nineteen, bi university student)

Andrea came out as bisexual in a school that was proud of its reputation for having clear antihomophobic student welfare policies and health education resources. Even in that environment, she found that her refusal to label her sexuality or cooperate with school procedures regarding same-sex attracted students made her feel alien. Nevertheless, she reveled in being unclassifiable (Schutz, 1944; Bauman, 1990; Marotta, 2002) and disrupting/polluting the categories and classifications of sexuality that were predominant in her school's antihomophobic policies, resources, and programs.

> It's like they can only do all this good stuff for you if you fit into the boxes. So okay, they've got more boxes than most schools, but they're still boxes. Like they act as if they can't help you unless they have a label for you, a name tag for your sexuality. Like instead of, "hi, I'm Andrea," your name tag has to read, "hi, I'm gay" or "hi, I'm lesbian," so they can go to their sex kits and pull out the words, the program, and all that school stuff that are for people like you. . . . I did crack it one day when the counselor kept pushing me to say what I was, and I went, "Look, if I have to wear a sticky label, I'm a UFO, an unidentified fucking object." I got detention for that and all these warnings about being promiscuous, STDs, the lot. They kinda went into a panic. . . . The thing is, I wasn't even having full-on sex with anyone, but I was feeling shitty about their boxy ways, and I let them have it with the UFO thing. I was quite proud of my creative imagery. You'd think my English teacher would be pleased, but he said I was disrespectful. That's what he called it. Well, how about respecting me in letting me tell you what my sexuality is or isn't? (Andrea, seventeen, bi student)

Like Andrea, several young bisexual people in the research made themselves very visible, thereby polluting through visibility. They showed enormous personal agency in rejoicing over their bisexuality despite institutional repression or lack of information. The following is a discussion with seventeen-year-old Jason who fashions his bisexuality and masculinity from the available options, all with minimal engagement and support from school. He is aware of how he needs to "work with people" to gain their respect, and thus positions himself as a border agent within a heteronormative and sexually dualistic society. Indeed, like Benjamin, he remains unconcerned by external assumptions, such as "bisexuality is a phase." Whether it is or isn't, whether his sexuality is fixed or not, is of no concern to him, as he is an "undecidable," beyond such beliefs and deliberately polluting them (Derrida, 1981; Bauman, 1990):

> Jason: A lot of people know that I'm bi, and I haven't copped much for it but I know that I've earned their respect a bit, yeah, pretty much everyone. . . . I took the time out for everyone; it's not hard.
>
> Maria: And when did you first come to the decision of being bisexual?
>
> Jason: A couple of years ago, I was probably on the fence; one day I'd be gay, one day I would be straight, one day I'd start on one side and then during the day switch teams, so now it doesn't bother me. . . . Bisexuality in society is really considered on the bench; you make a decision sooner or later, you don't be bi forever. Who knows, maybe that's the case for me but right now I'm content. (Jason, seventeen, bi student)

Jason also disrupts/pollutes normative stereotypes of closeted bisexual young men who have sex with men while going out with women. In the following, he talks about how he discusses his bisexuality with his sexual partners and negotiates the boundaries of the relationship with them, including the need to disrupt mainstream stereotypes of bisexual men as promiscuous or wanting threesomes:

> When I first met her [girlfriend], we were chatting and she was saying, "I don't know how this person goes out with this other girl because she's bi. How would you put up with it?" I said, "Maybe it's not the time and place to tell you, but yes [I'm bisexual]," and I think that sort of changed her, spending time with someone who is bisexual. . . . I've actually told most of my girlfriends that I'm bi, and most of them have been cool, a lot of others have been cheeky and said, "Oh, let's have a threesome." It's not that easy. . . . I haven't really had a boyfriend. I've fooled around with guys. . . . I've knocked back heaps of girls for sex. I've only ever slept with one girl. . . . I will only have sex with the condom. . . . I didn't start having sex until this year; it was something that I got paid out a lot about that, why are you still a virgin, blah, blah. (Jason, seventeen, bi student)

Jason is also very skillful in avoiding confrontation, deconstructing and disrupting any biphobic challenge put to him. Communication, collaboration, negotiation, and maneuvering are his strengths as a visible bisexual adolescent at school (Cohen, 1987). Even when challenged or harassed, he explains he does not get distressed but maintains a caring but cool assertive demeanor. He also makes students aware that he will take action against any violence or harassment. Thus, he is informed about antihomophobic policies and laws and ready to act upon them. Jason also believes that his weekend activity as a football umpire, an interesting position he thought was quite symbolic of his bisexuality, has taught him skills for dealing with biphobia and homophobia. Again, the school is not referenced as the place where this skill-learning has occurred. Rather, it is a major site where he needs to utilize these skills in order to protect himself by engaging with, standing confidently against, and earning the respect of other students:

> *Jason:*   Because I do professional football umpiring, I've learned how to handle situations; I work with people. . . . A lot of people, I'm not big loading myself here, think with a closed mind. You should be able to look at both sides of the story, reassess the situation. . . . There's these really homophobic guys here who will talk about how they really hate poofs and they'll put on the really deep male accent and they'll talk about how they kick the shit out of everyone and it's like, I say to everyone, "You can kick the shit out of me but I'll win in the long run because I'll go to the police, I'll have you up on charges, that'll create a criminal record which will always be there, which will make it harder for you to find a job and blah, blah, and one thing leads to another and you're up shit creek, while I'm happy and content."
>
> *Maria:*   Have you been threatened physically?
>
> *Jason:*   Yeah. But as an umpire, like I said, I've been taught how to handle situations and I'm quite good at it. I can usually talk myself out of a situation; that's why I'm hardly ever in a fight. I'm educating people more. I tell them it's a proven psychological fact the most homophobic people are confused about their sexuality. (Jason, seventeen, bi student)

Jason also makes strategic use of his class background in a school where many of his peers would be constructed as inferior due to their lower socioeconomic status. Thus, as a border dweller pollutant, visible as both bisexual and of a higher class status than most students at his school, Jason is aware that his inferiorization and targeting due to his sexuality can be compensated and minimized by his giving money away to his peers:

> I've been called the rich kid because we own our own house, I live with both my parents, we holiday around the world all the time, you know, that type of stuff. . . . . I help out a lot, I feel I should give a lot of money away, I don't expect it back, you know. I just count myself as one of the fortunate ones. . . . People go, "Oh, can I pinch some money," and they'll do the whole puppy dog eyes thing, and it's like, "It's not working with me, but I just give the money so you can quit hassling me." . . . Of course you're very popular. Of course they're going to be nice; you never bite the hand that feeds you. (Jason, seventeen, bi student)

Like many of the young bisexual people in my research who wanted to be visible, Jason fashions a visual self that symbolizes his bisexuality, his pollution of normative binary markers of embodied and adorned gender (Butler, 1990; 1991). On the day of the interview, he had bright pink shoulder-length hair and was wearing one red shoe and one blue shoe.

> You get a few smart arses and then you'll get a lot who say, "Oh, I love your shoes." A lot of times I walk on the train, when my hair, the first time it's done, it's bright, bright pink, and they start chatting away and that's cool because I'm able to take the time out for people. (Jason, seventeen, bi student)

Indeed, Jason had been asked to leave a previous single-sex private boys' school due to his gender disruptions and fashioning of a non-normative masculinity. Thus, he was the stranger, challenging the "taken-for-grantedness" and "questioning the unquestionable": "I was too much unwanted politics" (Wood, 1934; Schutz, 1944; Simmel, 1971; Bauman, 1990):

> I was asked to leave because I wasn't fulfilling their expectations. . . . I mean I used to go to class with different color hair and they would send me home to shave it off. I'd come to class with piercings and they would send me home, so, yes, they pretty much didn't want me, I was too much unwanted politics to handle. . . . They know that I can get just as good a score as anyone else except the only thing that matters is the reputation at schools. (Jason, seventeen, bi student)

Although he does experience some harassment at his new public community coeducational school, Jason believed the school's emphasis on and affirmation of diversity, indeed the bringing into the school the real world of diversity outside the school gates, framed his ability to feel safe, to belong, to handle any harassment before it got out of hand, and get on with his learning:

> Look at everyone; everyone's different in so many ways and so you're more accepting. . . . You know how you see someone out on the street who is dressed differently, like a head turner, when they walk past you, you just go, ah, yeah, type of thing, and all these people you see out on the street are in this school. . . . If you don't stamp on something that is wrong it gets bigger and bigger, like it starts off with the classroom names; if you can stop the classroom names, it doesn't lead to schoolyard names and that doesn't lead to the fights. . . . I get hassles all the time, I come in with my pink hair, two different color shoes, people have a go at me, you have a smile, have a laugh, and that's it. . . . It ain't fun [to fight], . . . and I'm here for a long time . . . just want to do my work and go home. (Jason, seventeen, bi student)

Rowan also fashioned a visual self with deliberate signifiers of his bisexuality. He wore traditional young men's clothing such as black T-shirts and black jeans, but also wore black or purple nail polish and black eyeliner. Despite receiving harassment and ostracism, he also showed much agency in refusing to conform to gender normative constructions of masculinity in style, behavior, and attitudes:

> I wasn't traditionally masculine at all and at that school a lot of people around me were, and that made life quite difficult for me, but I would think to myself that I didn't want to be like that anyway. . . . I used to do things like wear nail polish or wear eyeliner, not that anyone would be nasty to me about it, but they would comment on it and make an issue of it. . . . I remember teachers treating me in the same way. Like at one point I think I had a purple streak in my hair and my deputy said to me, "What's that thing that you've got there?" and this kind of attitude [from teachers]. (Rowan, nineteen, bi student)

Simon saw himself as transgendered, and indeed performed a different femininity or masculinity each day as an "undecideable" (Derrida, 1981; Martino and Pallotta-Chiarolli, 2001b). His clothing ranged from surfie male wear to feminine dresses and makeup to military uniforms to dance party gear. Andrea kept her head closely shaved, with a few spiky strands, two-toned purple and blue, while wearing Goth femme corsetry, long velvet, ankle-length gowns, lace tops, and ample jewelry and makeup. Josie wore masculinist jeans and T-shirts while keeping her blond waist-length hair soft and curly, minus facial makeup, but keeping her nails long and painted red. Bonnie often wore khaki and masculinist jeans and tops, while keeping her red hair long and straight. She recalls:

> I didn't ever consider myself to be anything weird. . . . I went through this little stage in high school where I'd be like army pants and khaki jacket. And I was just playing around with it. Like, I wasn't taking myself that seriously, but I was like, "Yeah, I can dress up really dykey if I want. That's cool." Oh, I suppose when I was wearing the army pants, I was still conscious of looking attractive to other people, so I didn't shave all my hair off and wear a dirty jacket. It's like I still would try and look pretty, I suppose, at the same time. But, yeah, no one really reacted that much to it. A guy that I knew at high school that I suspected was gay, and he was really camp, I remember he came out to me. He's going, "Wow, you're looking butch today," and I just thought "Oh, cool." You know, it was really nice just to have that recognition from someone who knew what it was like. (Bonnie, bi-poly student)

In response to such visibility, and its resultant targeting by some of the other students, the young people in my research would have liked to have seen schools intervene in the harassment rather than ignore or deny its occurrences or demand that the student comply with gender-conformist attire and adornment. Instead, teachers and schools appear to be very reluctant to pollute their own veneer of heteronormativity by even acknowledging the presence of nonheterosexual students, let alone that they are being harassed. It was left to the student experiencing the harassment to initiate any intervention, rather than antiharassment strategies and interventions being part of the structural and cultural work of the school. As Rowan remembers,

> In earlier years I think a lot of the time teachers just ignored it really, unless I would make an issue of it, like unless I would say to someone, "Look, I'm having a problem," which I did once or twice but unless you actually brought it up, it would just really be ignored. . . . There was one time I was really upset and this was about my parents, not about my own sexuality. . . . I think everyone had just been teasing me as usual and it all just got to be too much and I went to the sick bay and I said, "Look, I'm feeling sick, I want to go home" and my principal actually came up to me and said to me, "Look, Rowan, are you really feeling sick or are you having problems?" and I said, "Yes, I'm having problems," and he said, "What has happened?" and I told him the people who have been persecuting me and that was quite good. In that case my principal actually spoke to all of the people. . . . I don't know what he said to them but they were a bit better about it after that, which I find quite surprising, like I wouldn't expect that to be the case. . . . I just don't place very much faith in institutions and especially what I would see as justice, especially at school. (Rowan, nineteen, bi student)

One of Rowan's strategies was to mix with other students who were a "strange mixture," pollutants or nonconformists of various sorts. This group included gay students and anyone else who was antiauthority. Thus, having a nonheterosexual sexuality was aligned in the hierarchical system of peer groupings with challenging normative authority:

> Well, it was quite a strange group that I hung around with because it was mainly the people that didn't fit in with the kind of accepted groups like the intellectuals and the jocks. . . . On the one hand it was people like me and my friends who were gay, who didn't fit in for those reasons, and on the other hand it was people whose attitudes were I think really bad but who didn't fit in because of a general kind of resistance to authority and this kind of thing, so it was a really strange mixture. (Rowan, nineteen, bi student)

Another kind of pollution/intervention young bisexual people called for was role models in schools or bisexual visibility in the school curricula when discussing historical or contemporary individuals. This is seen as reflecting increasing positive representations in adolescent popular culture. For example, Missy Higgins is a twenty-five-year-old Australian singer-songwriter who has become a household name for young Australians after releasing several hit albums and winning numerous ARIA awards, as well as performing in large concerts in Australia and abroad. Her songs have often been broadcast on mainstream Australian radio stations in recent years, and she has become an idol for young people through her ability to write and produce heartfelt music. In late 2007 she talked about her sexuality to the Australian media, describing how sexuality is fluid and how it's important to be comfortable with oneself, as she herself was "definitely" comfortable with being identified as a "not-so-straight" girl (see, for example, Kroenert, 2007; Moran, 2007; Purdon, 2007): "Sexuality is a fluid thing and it's becoming increasingly more acceptable to admit that you're that way" (Higgins in Kroenert, 2007). This positive publicity and promotion of bisexuality and sexual fluidity via an Australian who is idolized by many teens reflects the experiences and feelings of an increasing number of adolescents and young people.

In 2008, popular U.S. young adult actor Lindsay Lohan, who had constantly been in the tabloid press for excessive drinking and drug taking, and who had starred in *Mean Girls*, a film that dealt strongly with bullying and harassment in girl cliques at school, came out as bisexual in her relationship with DJ Samantha Ronson. She attributed her efforts to address her substance abuse to the relationship with Ronson as well as stating that her sexuality had never been an issue with her family: "They're supportive of me whether I'm with a guy or a girl. They're just supportive of me as a person" (News.com, 2008). Unfortunately, the tabloid press still created a frenzy around Ronson's androgynous appearance as well as presenting paparazzi shots of arguments and kisses between the women. But significantly, the media treatment of their relationship dramatics was no different to the way a heterosexual relationship of a "naughty" celebrity girl such as Paris Hilton would have been dramatized and portrayed for the tabloid teen market.

British artists such as Lebanon-born Mika and Patrick Wolf, and from the United States, Antony Hegarty of Antony and the Johnsons, are also leading a new pop pansexuality in teen music culture. We are also finally seeing a positive representation of a bisexual man, Captain Jack Harkness, on a television series avidly watched by young people. His popularity in the *Doctor Who* 2005 series led to his being the central character in *Torchwood*, the adult-themed spin-off series (Burrell, 2005). As an ongoing depiction of bisexuality in mainstream television, as well as featured in *Doctor Who* and *Torchwood* books, and having children's action figures created in his likeness, Captain Jack has become a role model for bisexual young people (Ryan, 2007). Time-traveling Jack, played by John Barrowman, first appears in *Doctor Who* as a con man and matures into a hero. In the final episode, he kisses both the Doctor and Rose, the Doctor's assistant, when he leaves. Indeed, in his first appearance in the episode, "The Empty Child" (2005), the Doctor suggests that Jack's orientation is more common in the fifty-first century, when humanity will deal with multiple alien species and become more sexually flexible. The labels "pansexual" and "omnisexual" are also frequently applied to him. In *Torchwood*, Captain Jack battles alien threats, is romantically interested in his team's policewoman, Gwen, as well as having a long-term loving and sexual relationship with his employee Ianto Jones. One episode also recalls his marriage in a different era (Itzkoff, 2006). Thus, his sexuality is a given, "matter-of-fact," not to be problematized or interrogated. Indeed, Captain Jack refers to the sexual orientation classifications of the twentieth and twenty-first centuries as "quaint" (Jensen, 2007; Channel4.com's LGB Teens Health Site, 2007).

The History Boys, a recent film based on Alan Bennett's play, introduces a queer or bisexual young man, Dakin, as one of the major student characters in a 1980s class of A-grade boys from an English boys' school. Although being presented as manipulative and seductive, and able to charm his way to getting whatever and whoever he wants, Dakin is also charismatic, bright, worldly, and likeable. Indeed, his open, ambiguous sexuality becomes a catalyst or pivotal point that holds a scrutinizing mirror up to other characters struggling with the silences, insecurities, and hypocrisies regarding their own sexualities. For example, he enjoys being adored by a Jewish gay student, Posner, who is seeking a way of reconciling his sexuality, spirituality, and short physical stature. Secondly, he is also the only student with any heterosexual experience, seen in sexual situations with the headmaster's young secretary, Fiona, who is dealing with the unwanted sexual advances of the headmaster. When the headmaster intends to expel the aging teacher, Hector, for inappropriately touching boys as he gives them rides home on his motor scooter, it is Dakin, Hector's favorite motor-scooter partner, who intercedes by threatening to reveal the headmaster's inappropriate behavior with Fiona. Third, he challenges another student, Scripps, about his lack of masturbation and sexual exploration due to his strong Christianity.

Of major significance in the film is the contrast between Dakin's openness and ease with his own sexuality and its borderland positioning between the polar opposite sexualities of the aging teacher Hector, a married homosexual or bisexual with a passion for learning and camaraderie with the boys that compensates for the loneliness and sexual repression in his personal life, and Irwin, a young go-getter teacher who sees education as being a performance, a means to an end, and who Dakin propositions in order to make Irwin reveal his homosexuality. As Talburt writes, "The boys, and Dakin in particular, demonstrate more confidence regarding sexuality and desire and more awareness of the hypocrisies of institutional discourses than do their teachers" (2010: 59). Indeed, within the homophobic environment of a boys' school, the sexual expressions of the two gay teachers are distorted and suppressed. Hector's is manifested in touching the boys on his scooter and Irwin's is subsumed beneath a demeanor of cynicism about truth, and a pragmatic approach to success and survival. Indeed, when Posner approaches him for some advice and solace in regard to his own homosexuality, he is told by Irwin, "It will pass." Significantly, in contrast to the repressions, deceptions, and insecurities of their male teachers, Hector, Irwin, and the principal, the boys "do not express the sexual and gender phobias 'expected' of males of their age: they comfortably 'act' like women in class, openly enact queer desires, and take turns on Hector's motorbike" despite his "inappropriate touching" (Talburt, 2010: 61).

The significance of making such media examples and cultural texts available for discussion in schools is evident in Josie's words below. She calls for role models and bisexual people being presented in schools, and her inability to list bisexual figures in history is telling of the absence of such knowledge in her own education:

I'm very aware of the need for role models, for kids to know that they're not alone. . . . When you don't see anyone, you think, fuck, it's true, if no one else is, it must be abnormal and I've got to work out whether I'm A or B . . . Drew Barrymore, I think, she's an obvious one. I know that she's got a good following with young kids, especially young girls because she's not picture perfect, she's not weight perfect, and she's kind of alive and a bit hippyish and has got that alternative bent, and I think she'd be a good role model because she's off the drugs. But I don't know. I mean, who are some good bisexual role models? There are a couple of people around Oscar Wilde's time I think. . . . Just having lessons about it and holding just constructive discussions . . . using people, celebrities to make a difference. (Josie, bi-mono)

Rowan calls for "alternative sexualities" to be incorporated into the mainstream curricula of the school, rather than being presented within an additive model: as something additional or extra to the normal daily learning and workings of the school (Pallotta-Chiarolli, 2005b):

It would just be good for alternative sexualities to have a lot more visibility in school. . . . It would be better to have some kind of education specifically about sexualities, which I never had through school at all, on a kind of regular basis. (Rowan, nineteen, bi student)

Bonnie also calls for greater visibility of bisexuality in schools and she has seen the effectiveness of visibility in other schools (McLean, 2005; Nathanson, 2009):

They could include material from nonheterosexual lifestyles and sexuality in the sex ed and have more than like two weeks or whatever it is. . . . I think earlier on in high school it should be talked about as well. I mean, like the difficult thing is finding a context for it, because to just sit all your students down and say, "Okay, you know, in whatever class it is, we're going to talk about queer stuff,"

I think teachers might find that difficult because if you're an English teacher you're going to say, "Well, what's that got to do with my curriculum? I've got to teach kids how to write stuff. I don't need to talk about sexuality in my class." But at the same time, you'll be reading books and studying texts that are about straight kids having crushes on other straight kids and maybe they could include it more in the material. . . . They definitely could be just putting materials around the school because at the moment I'm helping out at Family Planning, helping run the youth program, which is all high school–aged kids. And I've got one of the guys from a group and he's great and we took a whole bunch of pamphlets about a support group and posted them all over his school. And he said there's so many people that are so interested in coming. And I'm sure there's so many kids at school who just don't have any contacts or any exposure to anything that's available. (Bonnie, bi-poly student)

Although bisexual young people like Bonnie are calling for texts to be available in schools, there have been few books written for adolescents and young adults that include positive representations of bisexuality and bisexual characters (Bryant, 2005a). *Pink* is a recent Australian novel about adolescent Ava who is on a quest to find out whether she is gay or straight by moving in and out of various youth and school subcultures, including various performances of femininity, only to find that sometimes sexuality cannot be known or chosen from an either/or selection (Wilkinson, 2009). My own novel for young adults, *Love You Two*, is an attempt to address this absence with its multicultural, multisexual, and multipartnered characters, based on people in my research over fifteen years, who disrupt, subvert, and agentically construct their own sexual identities and families according to their own needs (Pallotta-Chiarolli, 2008). For example, Zi Don is sixteen-year-old Pina's bisexual Italian-Australian uncle with a Vietnamese-Australian partner, Wei Lee. After being outed to Pina by an ex-boyfriend who wonders if Don "still likes girls," Zi Don explains to Pina,

"You can't fit the straight box? Okay, there's the gay box over here that comes with a whole lot more dents, shredded wrapping and graffiti from having to survive bashings from the straight box. Then along comes this intelligent, beautiful, passionate strong woman"—he gestures to Wei Lee—"and my box begins to split at the seams. But I can't jump out of the gay box and knock on the straight box and say, 'Let me in, I belong in there,' because that's not true either. And Wei Lee wouldn't live with my illusion." (2008: 164)

I will now outline four books that young people referred me to as being useful and empowering, although these were usually accessed in queer bookshops, queer groups, and at home rather than being readily found in school libraries.

Postcards from No Man's Land

Written by Aidan Chambers, this novel received international acclaim after its 1999 publication in Europe. The story itself plays with binaries and borders in its narrative and temporal structure, and its border dweller bisexual character Daan. The book has the same cover on both sides so there's no back cover, but one is green and one is pink. The title of the book, *Postcards from No Man's Land*, is also a motif of that border zone between warring either/or camps. The book is made up of two narratives, one set in the mid-1990s and the other in 1944. The inevitable but surprising ways in which these two tales connect form the novel's border. Intense and self-conscious, Jacob Todd, seventeen, leaves his English home to spend a few days in the Netherlands paying homage to the soldier grandfather he never knew and visiting Geertrui, the Dutch woman who took care of his grandfather after he was wounded in battle. He also meets her strong and freethinking grandson, Daan. The second story, set in occupied Holland at the time of the battle to liberate Oosterbeck, and narrated by Geertrui, chronicles her long-ago relationship with Jacob's grandfather. As each narrative unwinds and interweaves, parallels, crossings, and differences between the two eras emerge. Bisexuality is not constructed as a problem to be solved. It just is. Jacob is intrigued and excited by new ideas engendered by initially bewildering experiences with Daan, Ton, and Simone, who are crossing gender lines. Daan, the bisexual polyamorous character, speaks about how he loves both Ton, who is gay, and Simone, who is monogamous to Daan. He explains that love "is not finite," nor in "limited supply," nor should it be based on gender and sexuality labels. What does matter is being open and honest in negotiating relationships with partners (1999: 298–99).

By the end of the book, there's a feeling that Jacob has learned that he can live with and use ambiguity to understand himself and the world around him.

Lucky

Eddie De Oliveira's (2004) novel has the narrator, nineteen-year-old Sam, living in London and being attracted to both boys and girls. He finds himself sitting in a park leafing through the dictionary to find a term that describes him, only to find that, as Derrida (1981) would define as "undecidable" or "in excess of," there is no term that he can fit or confine/constrain himself within. He explains feeling under pressure to "identify" his feelings and reflects upon definitions of terms such as "friend," "bisexual," "multisexual," and "unstraight." After all, he stresses, if he is not in the dictionary, how can he exist? "And yet love is in the dictionary, even though no one knows how to describe it" (2004: 14).

Sam acknowledges that the wider society has prevented him from know-ing and being himself: "I'd been conditioned by those around me, and even by things like TV shows and pop songs, to think straight all the time" (De Oliveira, 2004: 68). By the end of the novel, after exploring his attractions, friendships, and relationships, Sam can conclude that the "facts" are he is at-tracted to boys and girls and he's "ready to love and be loved" (2004: 210).

Geography Club

Written by Brent Hartinger (2003), this novel includes a positive repre-sentation of a bisexual girl in high school who does not comply with mas-culinist constructions of "hot bi babe." The story centers around a group of gay and lesbian students who want to set up a secret club and meeting place at school. In order not to draw attention to themselves and provoke harass-ment, and yet having to follow school policy that all student clubs have to be publicized and open to any student, they settle on calling it the "Geogra-phy Club," a club that sounds so boring nobody will want to join it. One of the most level-headed, calm, and considerate members of the club is Min, a Chinese-American young woman who identifies as bisexual. When she tells her best friend, the narrator, Russel, that she is bisexual, not gay, he reflects on how that explains "her general braininess" and "ridiculous perfection-ism," as if being bisexual is beyond the human limitations imposed upon those who can only be attracted to one gender (2003: 31). Finally, after a series of events in the novel, both funny and sad, the Geography Club is renamed the "Goodkind High School Gay-Straight Alliance," which Min promptly corrects to "Gay-Straight-Bisexual Alliance" (2003: 223).

Boy Meets Boy

The fourth young adult novel, which I would define as queer in its multi-sexual, multigendered friendship groups and love interests taking place in a very queer school and community, is written by David Leviathan (2003). In-deed, one of the central characters who is able to confidently transcend many dichotomies is the transgendered queer Infinite Darlene, who is the school's best/toughest footballer as well as central to any social event such as decorat-ing the school hall for the prom. Infinite Darlene dresses in hyperfeminine clothing, heels, and full makeup when not on the football field, although s/he also plays football with some makeup and other "bits" of femininity. What is also of importance is how Infinite Darlene's performativities go unremarked by the school authorities, and even her "rivals" are frustrated and envious of her prowess and multiple abilities, while she dismisses them as ignorant of the sex-gender permutations around them. The novel begins with an explicit affirming declaration of queerness among the town's young people by the narrator, Paul, who explains there isn't a "gay scene" or a "straight scene," as they "all got mixed up a while back" (2003: 9).

A major subplot in the novel is Paul's interest in both a new boy and also his ex-boyfriend, Kyle, who has been seen out with girls. As part of re-establishing a strong friendship with Kyle, there is much discussion around bisexuality as not being the issue of conflict between the two. When Kyle explains to Paul that he is "confused" because he still likes girls, Paul replies that Kyle is "bisexual," not "confused." When Kyle says he hates that label as it makes him sound "divided," they try other labels such as "ambisexual" and "duosexual." Finally, Kyle decides he wants no word for his sexuality, but to let it "just be what it is." Paul agrees, although he worries that the "bigger world" loves "stupid labels" (2003: 107–8).

꙳

In my research, several parents in multisexual relationships also called for texts and other resources to be made available to their children in schools in order to affirm their families. They support Bryant's wish and my attempt in *Love You Two* (Pallotta-Chiarolli, 2008) at creating everyday characters who happen to live in mixed orientation families:

> [On TV and film] I would like to see bisexual parents who are honest and open with each other and their children. I would like to see monogamous bisexuals and polyamorous bisexuals. I would like to see bisexual people of color, . . . bisexual health service providers, teachers, cab-drivers, fire-fighters, athletes, activists and software developers. . . . I'd like to see what I see in my everyday life. (Bryant in Alexander, 2007: 123)

In my novel, *Love You Two* (Pallotta-Chiarolli, 2008), Pina, a sixteen-year-old third-generation Italian-Australian teen discovers, through an e-mail accidentally left on the family computer, that her mother has a male lover besides her dad. Shortly after this discovery, she is pressured into sex by her insensitive boyfriend. At the same time, Pina's long-haired younger brother, who "may turn out in the future to be gay, bi, or not, is beaten up at school for it anyway" (Lambert, 2009). In her review of my novel, Lambert comments:

> Refreshingly, in this novel, it's the straight characters who are poly and the bi character is monogamous . . . often true in real life but rarely represented that way in fiction. (2009)

Another novel that features a seventeen-year-old bisexual girl as the protagonist is *The Suicide Year* by Lena Prodan (2008). She lives on a military base with her dysfunctional family, obsesses about suicide, and, as Lambert describes, "is all over the map when it comes to attractions. She fools around with Sean, the sexy bad boy she wishes she wasn't attracted to" and "has a fierce crush on Amanda, a girl in her gym class" (Lambert, 2009). Lambert also points out that her suicidal feelings "aren't caused by anguish over being bisexual, she is fairly self-accepting about that, even when confused about her feelings—as most teens are of any sexual orientation" (2009).

One text that a few parents referred to as being pivotal in their own understanding of multisexuality and multipartnering is *Bingo* by Rita Mae Brown. Nickie, the female narrator who identifies as gay, is in love with Jackson, who is married to her best friend, Regina. They know Nickie is a lesbian, and Jackson relies on her understanding of marginality to point out his dilemma: "I'm in love with two women at the same time. In our society there's no more room for me than there is for the gay person" (1988: 173). When she finds out she is pregnant by Jackson, Nickie makes the painful choice of ending their relationship, only to find that Mr. Pierre, the town's gay hairdresser who is still mourning the death of his long-term partner Bob, wants to marry her. He explains that he loves her and indeed will make a "better wife" than Nickie (1988: 255).

Just before the wedding, Regina tells Nickie she knows about her relationship and love for Jackson and that the baby is his. What hurts is not the relationship between her husband and her best friend, but that they didn't tell her about it: "We could have worked it out." She explains that she doesn't believe love is "a controlled substance" to be outlawed or confined within marriage, and that she doesn't "own" her husband (1988: 279–80).

The friendship between the two women becomes even stronger. When the twins are born, Jackson and Regina visit daily and take their turn in caring for the babies, while equal coparenting is set up between Nickie's newspaper office and Mr. Pierre's hairdressing salon. Mr. Pierre also tells Nickie about a woman who has a crush on her. What Nickie will do about this isn't decided in the novel, for it really doesn't matter within this new construction of an extended poly-bi family that allows an expansion rather than subtraction of love, and a "win/win situation" for everyone (Anderlini-D'Onofrio, 2009a; 2009b).

A student counselor in my research whose husband had come out as bisexual called for the insertion of family diversity studies in schools:

> School libraries could stock a lot of interesting books which I don't believe they are at the moment. Curricula materials and then with pastoral care, I think that school counselors should have a role or if they don't have a school counselor, whoever takes that, should have a role to give regular talks to invite people in to talk about their family, to encourage children to talk about their family and to celebrate that. I mean, at the moment they have these cultural

awareness weeks where you bring in the food, you know. It's a start but it's so simplistic. I mean, "Let's talk about families today. Does anyone have a family that's different from just a mum or a dad and so what is a family anyway?" All these sort of things. There's just so much that could be done. . . . You can make it compulsory reading, you know, story-time reading, that sort of thing, just to make these kids feel included. Because I imagine they must get the message very early on. Even a little five-year-old going to school, you know, who knows that daddy lives with his boyfriend or mummy lives with her girlfriend. All they get presented with is stories of a nice little nuclear family with a mummy and a daddy and two children and a dog. They must get the message very, very quickly that "Oh, my family's different and it's something we shouldn't talk about." (Paula, hetero-mono mom with bi-poly husband)

The importance of pastoral care programs and school counselors was highlighted by many young people in my research. Bonnie explains how her visit to a school counselor for study reasons touched upon her sexuality, and despite the counselor not providing Bonnie with any immediate resources or direction, the very discussion with the counselor solidified Bonnie's understanding and self-affirmation of her bisexuality. Bonnie came out as bisexual soon afterward to her close friends at school, their families, and her family, and thus received support of peers and parents without any framing institutional support from the "school counselor":

I was seeing a school counselor because I was really stressed and my teacher said, "You better go and see a counselor because you're going to burn out." So, I ended up talking to this counselor about the fact that I had a crush on a girl and I said to her, "Are there any support groups or anything that I can go to, anyone I can talk to about this stuff?" And all she said to me was, "Just wait until you're at uni. It will be fine then. You'll meet lots of queer people there." And to this day, I'm just shocked by that because it was so irresponsible. . . . I mean, maybe she didn't have any resources on it, which was also awful. . . . I remember thinking to myself when I was talking to her, "Oh, I've got a crush on a girl. That means I like girls and guys. That means I'm bi. Wow, that's really awesome." . . . I was so happy for myself. I remember just running around the school yard, just like I couldn't tell anyone and I was so excited. So I was just running, running, running around. . . . I think later on that year I told most of my close friends about it. And they were great, too. A couple of them were really religious but they didn't have a problem with it. I don't think they fully understood, but they were still my friends. I had this one really close friend who is sort of like my best friend all through high school and she was really great and she said, "Oh, my mum's got friends like that and they're really nice." . . . I was really scared that she'd think I was going to crack on to her or something, but she was great. And, she sat me down and plaited my hair and talked to me. . . . Maybe school counselors need to do some kind of course or something on sexuality because it was just completely inappropriate, yeah. (Bonnie, bi-poly university student)

Bonnie's words provide a vivid image of celebration and self-affirmation when she describes how she ran around the schoolyard with joy. There is also such intimacy and connection in her description of how she and her best friend talked about her sexuality while her best friend plaited her hair. What is also pertinent is that Bonnie and her friend had been raised in "polluted" or queer-friendly and pro-feminist households of significant others and thus were already aware of nonheterosexual sexualities as a positive reality. At home, without recrimination, she was able to access films and other popular cultural depictions of bisexuality:

> I remember talking to my parents about my uncle being gay and I didn't know what that was, and my mum just explained to me it's two men who love each other and that was great. I was probably about maybe eight, eight or nine. Yeah, yeah, they [my parents] were great about it. He's my favorite uncle. . . . I think I came out to him before I came out to my parents. Yeah, he was fine. He just told me to be careful, because he is HIV positive, so is a little wary about some things. . . . When I was about fourteen . . . I went with my best friend to get a video from the video shops and it was called *Threesome*. And so I'm thinking "Oh, yeah, that looks like a nice movie about some friends" and I ended up watching it with her [my best friend], and my mum watched it too. I think my mum was saying "I've got to watch this with you just to make sure it's okay" but she really just wanted to watch it. That was a great movie. I mean, that was like really positive depiction—except for the fact that they ended up sort of breaking up in the end. . . . They [parents and best friend] didn't say, "Oh, that's really weird" or anything. I think we all just watched it and thought "Yeah, cool." . . . Because I was raised in such an open-minded family, I really all along hated it when people just discriminated against people and I really have such strong beliefs about racism, about sexism and I suppose homophobia, too, when I was young, and that probably comes from being raised in a household which wasn't racist, sexist, which my dad was always encouraging me and helping me build stuff with power tools. And my nanna was a cricketer. . . . She played footy [soccer]. She met her husband at the footy. I suppose she was a really good role model, too. (Bonnie, bi-poly university student)

Rita was another "polluted" noncompliant bisexual young woman in high school who had grown up within a queer family:

> My dad is bisexual and when I first came out bi he was so excited, and so was my mom, and they congratulated me like I'd won some major school prize, and then they took me shopping for cool queer clothes. I wore them the first chance I got to some school function and I'm sure my eyes said, "fuck you" to any cloney Barbie and Kens from dysfunctional fake Brady Bunch setups who dared to stare at me as if I had the problem. (Rita, seventeen, bi student with bi-poly dad)

Other young people also spoke about how the realities of their polluted home lives and their locations at school as "foreigners," "strangers," and the "excess" (Schutz, 1944; Kamuf, 1991; Kristeva, 1991) led them to question the one monolithic and monosexual Reality presented at school (Derrida, 1981). Mateusz recalls the events that led to his coming out as bisexual:

> My dad and I went on a holiday interstate as part of a father-son bonding session, just the two of us. One day I went off by myself to do some sight-seeing with a younger group, and Dad said he wanted to laze around. When I got back that evening to the hotel, Dad wasn't there. I didn't think anything of it 'cause we'd talked about doing our own thing that night. So I thought I'd take the chance to explore the "gay" side of the town, since Dad wasn't around. I found the address of a gay sauna in the newspaper and went to check it out. Well, there I am stripping down in the change-room, and there's my dad getting dressed on his way out! Talk about mega-awkwardness. The strange thing is that we carried on as normal afterwards for the rest of the holiday and didn't talk about it all. It's like we pretended it never happened. I mean, what do you say anyway? It didn't affect our close relationship—he is my dad and we love each other heaps and all that, but it left me confused about who's really in the closet here. About six months later, and totally out of the blue, Mum sat me down for a deep and meaningful talk to tell me that Dad was bisexual and that she'd known this when she married him and that it was nothing to worry about and I wasn't to let Dad know she'd told me. Well, what do you do? I told her her son is one of those too. Anyway, we're still a real close family and Mum and Dad have accepted me, and we joke that it's "in the genes" or "you men's pants" as Mum says. It's just so weird how this stuff can be in your family but you're all too scared to talk about it. It made being at school a lot easier knowing my family are 100 percent with me. My father is happily bisexual and married, and one day I hope to be too, with a guy or girl or both! I hope the both can happen in my lifetime. (Mateusz, eighteen, bi son of bi-poly dad)

In the following, Madelaine is also confident about her mother's bisexuality. Indeed, she experiences normative kinds of concerns about a parent's attire and demeanor as being possible points of embarrassment with her peers at school. However, if her peers find her mother's sexuality a problem, then it's their problem:

> I kind of took the attitude—to hell with it, this is my mother and I love her. She's still a mother, she's no different. She still tells me off like she's my mother, she still teaches me like she's my mother, she still annoys me like she's my mother. And because she's been so open, I think we're closer. . . . I told my friends [when Mum went on TV]. I was so afraid that she'd wear really dicky clothes. I was worried that she'd slip up and do something really dorky. I mean, there actually is nothing to hide. I feel that I know more than a lot of people my age because of my mum. I've experienced more, I feel like my mind's way so much more open because of her. It's somebody else's problem if they're uncomfortable with it. (Madelaine, hetero daughter of bi-mono mom)

What is so poignant about the above examples is that some young people receive so much learning and support from home that is not actually reinforced or affirmed at school. And, of course, the question arises, What happens to children and young people who do not have that family context that gives them the strength to become "pollutants" at school, to effectively deal with the negativity and ostracism from peers? Some bisexual young people do not come in to school with positive messages about themselves, and then, in dealing with the school institution and its silences and negativities, their sense of isolation and alienation is reinforced. Jess explains the need for schools to positively pollute students with information because students will pollute themselves anyway in potentially negative and harmful ways:

> They don't have to talk about anything in extreme detail . . . just saying this is normal, this is okay, this is how you do it, this is what happens, you know. . . . Even at ten, you have a very complex understanding of the world around you. It's not an adult understanding but it incorporates a whole lot of adult ideas, and to say that it's too early to start talking to kids about this thing, they're already figuring out things about the world, they're already making their own ideas and figuring things out for themselves. . . . Having information that is visible, that says if you want to initiate something, this is where you can go . . . something that specifically says if you are going through sexuality or gender issues you can talk to somebody, or you go to this website or ring this information hot line or the phone number for the gay and lesbian switchboard or something like that. The access to information, because as a kid when you do go to the Internet, you're going to find a whole lot of things that are completely inappropriate to your age. You know, people say we don't want to talk about it in the classroom because it's inappropriate, but the fact is that kids are going to find out their own information anyway, and if you don't provide appropriate material or what might be termed appropriate material and provide access to information that's specific to that age, then they're going to go and find information that isn't appropriate and isn't specific to their age group. You know, porn and all that sort of thing. . . . When you're just trying to find out a little bit about the community or a little bit about how to come out or that sort of thing, the last thing you need is being blasted by lesbian porno to straight men. (Jess, bi university student with lesbian partner)

Several multisexual families in my research, although being constructed by schools as polluting their children and in turn polluting the school if the children speak out about their families, saw the damage and pollution of their children coming from the schools, which did not support and continue the good work done at home. Helen found that after her daughter told her school friends that her dad was bisexual, one of her daughter's friends also came out as bisexual and would talk to Helen, as she had no one at school or at home to talk to: "She was spending a lot of time with me and talking to me, but that was okay." She and her husband, Michael, also found that having been raised in a home where sexual diversity was named and discussed from an early age caused problems for one daughter at primary school when she used the word "lesbian":

Helen: Because they've grown up with such tolerance for everybody, regardless of who they are, she was under the impression that if you kiss a woman, which she kisses her mum, she kisses her sister and if you sleep with another woman, which she's slept with me and she's slept with her sister, that she'd be a lesbian. So when this came up at school when she was in year three, what are you going to be when you grow up, she turned around and she said, "I'm going to be a lesbian." . . . And the teacher said, "Well, that's not really a career choice." But anyway, I got called up to the school over this, because the principal asked, "What are you teaching your children at home?" And I had quite a discussion with the female principal about this particular matter.

Michael: Just the, "What are you teaching your children at home?" It's like, "Well, we teach our children that they could be purple with green spots and we don't care."

Helen: I only remember snippets of it, because I was so furious that I virtually blocked out the entire thing. This principal I didn't have much luck with, because she was bending over backwards to help minority groups, but at the same token, . . . when it came to this, obviously she was really against it. Anyway, so I remember saying something along the lines of, "We've taught our children tolerance. Did you bother to discuss it with our daughter to find out what her understanding of 'lesbian' was?" And they hadn't. . . . And I said, "Well, how about we call her up now?" So she was called up and I said, "You had an incident in class today. What do you understand a lesbian being?" And she described it as I've said, a woman who sleeps with another woman "and I've slept with you and I've slept with my sister, haven't I, Mummy. And a girl who kisses another girl and I've kissed you, Mummy, I've kissed my sister" and it was like she didn't understand the sexual part of it. It was just a very innocent comment and they turned it into something, and after she left I said that. I said, "You've taken a very innocent comment from a child. You haven't even bothered to question the child further. You've dragged me up here and really, was it worth it?"

Michael: And they set up a horrible thing in our daughter's head now. Now it's not the right thing to be a lesbian.

Helen: Yeah, so school has done more damage than we've done. (Helen, hetero-mono mom, and Michael, bi-poly dad)

Many bisexual young people in my research believed education about sexual diversity needed to begin in primary schooling (see also Curran, Chiarolli, and Pallotta-Chiarolli, 2009). Jack believes this "pollution" or "gentle background buzz" needs to begin in childhood rather than at secondary school, across the curriculum, and enforced via policy as other issues have been, particularly in relation to health:

> Start as early as possible, probably grade five or six, with ideas, a very gentle introduction to the concept, nothing too aggressive or scary because the fact is we need to start slowly. For me it would have been great to just have, "Okay, today we're going to talk about the fact that straight isn't just the way to go." . . . Then in high school there needs to be a much more in-depth and direct thing and it's not to be, "Today we're going to talk about gay things." It needs to be every lesson that we're talking about sexuality and health. . . . If you keep that exposure, that visibility, just that gentle background buzz of information, people will get used to it and they need to watch out for the fact that they need to turn around to kids and say, "Hey, stop it, don't use that word, don't say those things, that's really bad." . . . The [primary school] kids are like sponges. We're all sponges at all points of our lives, really, but particularly at that point. It's really easy to intervene but it needs to be done quickly and it needs to then be done at high school at such a level where they say, "Okay, how can you make it better?" . . . Why can't they just say, "Well, what are you going to do when you see this happen?" Proactive, you know, teach your kids. (Jack, bi-poly university student)

Brad was a young bisexual man training to be a junior primary school teacher. He spoke about his observations and experiences when he was out on teacher training in schools:

> Kids play these bisexual games, like I must've done, and then as they grow they get repressed by middle primary. The kids think I'm a straight man, and staff think I'm gay. My bisexuality is not considered at all by students and parents and dismissed and ignored by staff. I say I'm bi, they still come back and talk to me about being gay. (Brad, bi teacher trainee)

His view that children play bisexual games is supported by Susanna, another bisexual teacher trainee:

> I remember when my friends and I used to play getting married, I'd always imagine having a husband on one arm and also being in love with a maid of honor and she's on my other arm. We'd walk down an aisle and all say "we do," but it stopped there, it was like we didn't know what to do after that because we never saw anything like that in real life or in TV shows. What then? Then I learned the word "gay," then a few years later the word "lesbian," but never the word "bisexual." It's like you never learn resources and skills about what to do. (Susanna, bi teacher trainee)

Jack calls for out gay and bisexual teachers in schools to support students, and is aware of the heterosexist and pedophilic constructions that would be an obstacle to this: "I would have loved to have had a gay or bisexual teacher who I could talk to, but of course for that to happen that would have raised all sorts of suspicions and feeling uncomfortable and weird" (Jack, bi-poly university student).

Despite the absence of such support in his own schooling, Jack has shown much agency and activism on his university campus, although he was reluctant at first to come out in student residences where he lived:

> Student residences are a haven for the middle-class white country kids with money. . . . They are a very sort of straight community. Two hundred kids, all living in close proximity, all about drinking and scoring. And it was terrifying for me. . . . I couldn't find any sign of any queer collective or queer officers or anything on campus. I'd been promised by friends of my pre-university days, "Oh, don't worry, it'll be great. You'll get there and you'll meet all these people and finally fit with your own age to talk to." . . . I really wanted to meet people my own age. And yeah, I got to this place and it was so disappointing. . . . It's supposed to be a place where you go, after you leave school, a buffer zone, after you leave home, where you learn about life. (Jack, bi-poly university student)

Jack finally found a leaflet about the queer collective: "I e-mailed the first one three times and they never responded and I was thinking, well, shit, where am I or what is this place? It's horrible." By this stage, he was also "letting my guard down" on student residences, "being a person who moved in very I suppose the term is 'fringe' scenes with openly bisexual and polyamorous people" outside of university and drawing strength from that. He also discovered a few other nonheterosexual people living in student residences, and together with an incident involving his gay friend, he found enough encouraging support to come out on student residence:

> One bi girl and one bi (now identifying as gay) guy, who lived on res, who I couldn't stand, this guy. He was just very, very offensive. He ended up dating my gay friend, and had a horrible break-up. It was all very big. And, that was the first gay scandal that occurred on res. . . . And I found out there were some people who I was really surprised by who were really supportive and didn't bat an eyelid and there were some people who were really uncomfortable, who I was shocked with. So I learned not to evaluate people on face value and in the last half of the year, I learnt just to say, "I'm bisexual" where I could. And, by doing that, it made them think about what that meant. (Jack, bi-poly university student)

This combination of factors—personal agency and a community of significant others—found Jack becoming even more outspoken and taking on the leadership position of queer officer, being not only the university's first queer officer but openly identifying as bisexual and polyamorous rather than the expected gay. In this position, he is now able to lobby student residence coordinators "about making it a more queer-friendly environment and about vetting for homophobia." In the following, Jack describes how he found himself running for queer officer and what it has meant to him:

> There was one guy in my classes who I know he was gay, who knew me particularly, and he said, "You'd make a great queer officer. You're a great student leader." . . . And I went, "Oh, my God, how do you do this?" And apparently it had to go to the Heads three or four times before they'd approve it. That was pushed through and next thing you know, I was part of this queer collective. . . . And, I just sat there staring and was spaced out and thought, "Oh, my God, I've just become the most out man out of thirty thousand," because I was the only queer officer that ran out of all four campuses. Out of 33,000 students, I was suddenly the most out man. . . . Induction, walking around with this badge, "Queer Officer" you know, everyone was just like, "Oh my God, you're the first queer officer. It must be so exciting and so fantastic." . . . And I'm like, "Oh my God, this is fantastic." (Jack, bi-poly university student)

Josie strongly called for pollution through normalization in any educational setting, from primary to tertiary level. She believed young bisexual people needed to be validated by being told that whatever they were feeling was "normal." In this way, they would get to the point of self-affirmation and self-validation:

> Say to kids, "As long as you don't hurt anyone it's okay to be, to express who you are," and that's the simple concept. . . . Just being told it's okay, just the validation that your feelings are okay and it's normal. . . . It's the normal thing to feel confused and then it's a normal thing to feel attraction to the same sex and the opposite sex, even though it feels confusing, but it's normal. (Josie, bi-mono)

⌒

As the many voices, experiences, and individuals in this chapter have shown, and whether they be constructing, negotiating, and living their bisexuality by passing, bordering, and/or polluting, the need to focus on bisexuality in schools is actually a part of a journey to ultimately positioning bisexuality within a broader framework, acknowledging the diversity of love, intimacy, family, and relationship. The participants in this research have also pointed out numerous ways of achieving this in schools through pastoral care, programming, and policy.

However, as we will discuss further in the concluding chapter, this research raises the debate in regard to whether sexual categorization should be either inclusive or specific. Can there be a balance of both, or should umbrella terms like "queer" be used when addressing young people in health and education settings (Gammon and Isgro, 2006)? How do we acknowledge the specificity of bisexuality but simultaneously step away from putting young people into sexual categories? It may be beneficial for educational and support services to put less emphasis on categorizing people with such terms or resorting to such categories, but at the same time a balance must be achieved in embracing minority populations such as the bisexual population within our schools. It would be useful for all educational institutions, from early childhood to tertiary, and their supportive health and family services, to have bi-specific policies, programs, and practices, as well as inclusive resources and programs so that the particular requirements and requests of individual bisexual young people and young people with bisexual parents can be catered to (Martin and Pallotta-Chiarolli, 2009; Pallotta-Chiarolli and Martin, 2009).

In conclusion, Josie's words below exemplify the level of self-affirmation and self-validation that all bisexual young people should be able to achieve instead of feeling like "social puppets" with minimal or problematic methods of agency (Boden, 1990). This appears to occur without hesitation when bisexual young people, and their adult gatekeepers, censors, and mentors such as teachers and school counselors, construct "communities of commitment" (Ancess, 2003) wherein bisexuality is perceived as being part of the bigger picture of learning, school community and culture, interpersonal connection, and love:

> When I was with my girlfriend, I didn't deconstruct it. When I was with my guy, I didn't deconstruct it. I fell in love, and when you fall in love, you fall in love. And if it's reciprocated, that's beautiful and you've got something magical and you've got to treasure it and as long as you're not hurting anyone, it's okay. I guess the message is it's okay, and when you fall in love, you fall in love, that's it. (Josie, bi-mono)

Indeed, toward the end of the interview, and quite fitting as the final voice for this chapter and as an apt introduction into the next chapter, Josie had wanted to speak less about her specific sexuality and more about the commonalities of human love and relationships.

4

"Messing Up the Couples Cabinet"

Multisexual and Polyamorous Families in Schools

> Steph has crushes on two boys. Getting out of the car one afternoon with a friend who's come to play, she looks at the houses across the street and declares, "I wish Peter lived there and Anthony lived there. Then I could see both of them."
>
> Her friend looks scornfully at her. "You can only love one person."
>
> "Who says?"
>
> "That's the way it is. Unless you're a lesbian."
>
> "If I was a lesbian, I'd want Peter and Anthony to be girls. Anyway, maybe I'll love no one. Maybe I'll love girls or boys, or both. Maybe lots of both!" And she laughs cheekily as her friend remonstrates.
>
> —Pallotta-Chiarolli (1999c: 79)

I remember this exchange. I watched and wondered while the two preadolescent girls had this conversation and gazed at the houses across the street. What do children know about relationships, love, and sexuality before they are taught what they are "supposed" to know? How and when do they learn "that's the way it is"? What processes and machinations get deployed into turning what seems matter-of-fact and a matter of choice to children such as Steph into thought processes, feelings, and behaviors that require complicated, contained, and corrective regulation and surveillance?

I remember being raised as a shared child by my mother and father, and by an uncle and auntie who could not have children of their own. My mother had not wanted to be a full-time stay-at-home mother and welcomed my auntie, who had come to Australia wanting to be a middle-class stay-at-home mother, to share in the raising of preschool me. I have documented my upbringing in *Tapestry* (Pallotta-Chiarolli, 1999d). It was an exciting, love-filled, nurtured childhood despite the poverty and marginalization of being part of a migrant community. There were at least four adults, as well as several others in the Italian-Australian community, who cared for me and loved me unconditionally, and with whom I got to attend all sorts of events and festivities. Watching these adults work out child-minding schedules and discuss the various aspects of raising a child, such as handling her injuries and naughtiness, taught me valuable skills of communication and negotiation. Having two bedrooms, two homes, two sets of friends, two examples of family and parenting (such as having a working mother and a housewife auntie-mother; a book-reading uncle with a car who loved weekend drives and adventures; and a storytelling, cooking, and cleaning father who made swings, tents, and other toys in the backyard), and shopping for Mother's Day and Father's Day gifts as well as lots of Christmas and birthday gifts with some adults for the other adults, was pure deliciousness.

And then I went to school and acquired the "knowledge" that children could only have one mother and one father in one home; that migrants were raising their children in negligent or inappropriate ways; that migrant mothers were going out to work rather than staying at home and raising their children in orderly nuclear households; and that you could make only one Father's Day and one Mother's Day card. So I learned to edit what the outside world of school could know about my home. Indeed, as a child I became an expert in what Thorson (2009) calls "communication privacy management" (CPM). I would go home with the one piece of paper my Irish-Australian working-class school had given me with which to make a card, tear it into two for two cards, but take only one back to school as the official card. I pretended I had made a mistake on the rest of the paper and had to throw it away, risking disapproval and scorn from the teacher and my peers. Meanwhile, the card was safely at home being readied to be given with a gift to the other parent-adult in my life.

I remember the time I was brought to hospital by my auntie and uncle. I required surgery and stitching on my badly bleeding foot after a childhood accident that had happened while on one of the numerous weekend outings with them. I recall the frustration and anger on my auntie and uncle's faces when confronted with forms and paperwork that were not only far too difficult to understand for migrants with limited English, but required the signature of a parent before my wound could be seen to. It was only after what seemed an interminable time to a child in strong pain and bleeding profusely, and only after repeated explanations in broken English by my auntie and uncle that my parents did not have a phone, did not have a car, had been told I was going to the hospital with my auntie and uncle and had no qualms with that, and that they would catch the bus later to come to the hospital and sign the forms, that I was actually operated on. On that day, I learned that for health services, forms and regulations were more important than my health, and that wherever I went in the outside world, my family would never quite fit in because of their poverty; lack of English; and the very fact that they were, all of them, defining themselves and being defined by me as my family.

So when I began to meet polyfamilies in the course of previous research projects, and I listened to their stories and observed the relational dynamics with their children, it didn't require a huge leap across a chasm to find points of connection and understanding. Indeed, in some ways it was like being on a bridge between, at one end, the past of my childhood and the childhood of many of us who were raised in migrant extended families and working-class communities rather than in nuclear middle-class households, and at the other end, the realities of family diversity that would become more visible and vocal in the future, such as GLBTIQ families and the polygamous families of newly arrived migrants and refugees from Africa and the Middle East.

ON THE BORDERS OF FAMILY RESEARCH: INTRODUCING "THE POLY X-FILES"

A good friend of mine had always tried to piece together what was going on with two Aboriginal teenage students in the South Australian school where she taught. These students always kept to themselves, particularly avoiding contact with white children. They also seemed very reluctant and afraid to talk about their family to teachers and other school authorities. After finally gaining the parents' trust, being allowed into their home, and watching the confidence and joy in the children when they were away from the school, my friend understood.

The two students were not "cousins" as they labeled themselves at school: that was the word they used for whites to prevent suspicion. Their mothers were not blood-sisters but certainly sisters. They shared the same husband; the children shared the same father. They all lived happily in one house. At school, the children kept to themselves in order to discourage any intimacy with other children that could lead to discovery and a further reason to harass them, as they were already experiencing ongoing racist harassment. They had also been warned by their parents not to let white teachers know or else they'd be taken away from their family, a theme that was all too real for this family, whose own childhoods had been mostly spent in mission homes as part of the "Stolen Generation": being forcibly removed from their families as part of Australia's racist and assimilationist policies.

My friend found the teenagers came from a home and community where there was so much love and warmth. The same students lurking in school corridors and playground corners took centre stage: they became forthright, animated, and cheerful. They spoke enthusiastically about family visits to Point Pearce, community celebrations both in the bush and in the suburbs, where they were the centre of their Aboriginal worlds: not needing to explain, not needing to lie, not needing to feel ashamed according to white man's laws.

—from my research notes

The above example regarding two Indigenous Australian children illustrates the borderland positioning of children from polyamorous, multipartnered, or multisexual families as they challenge the limited and limiting Anglocentric, Western, normative nuclear constructions of family. Jackie Huggins, the widely published Aboriginal feminist writer/activist in Australia, wrote about her being "the other wife":

> I fell in love with, horror of horrors, a married man who was all I ever hoped to meet in my life. . . . His wife and half the Murries [a particular language-group of Aboriginal people] in Australia knew who he was. The full emotional intensity of my love for Reg [pseudonym] lasted for thirteen years. To this day I remain firm friends with him, his wife Margie [pseudonym] and family. In fact Margie and I became close allies. Polygamy rules and I will always be known as "his other wife." (Huggins, 1994: 332)

In conversation with Jackie Huggins, she told me it was about time she acknowledged this part of her history and its significance in terms of how Aboriginal peoples had differing notions of relationships that have been disrupted and viewed negatively by Western, Judeo-Christian colonizers. Other feminists are also examining the impact of colonial values and economic systems on precolonial relationship structures and disrupting Eurocentric and androcentric anthropological interpretations of such models, such as the work of Ralston (1988) with polyandry, or women with more than one husband, in Polynesian communities.

As well as upholding Western or white middle-class constructions of family, and while there is increasing scope for gay and lesbian parents in school policies and communities, the definition of family still remains first, heteronormative in its espousal of heterosexual coupledom and to a lesser extent, heterosexual single parenthood; and second, constructed within a paradigm of sexual duality, with both parents being defined as gay or straight. The much-needed growing discourse supporting gay and lesbian parenting and families is coming from within sectors of the gay community, health organizations, scientific discourses such as those of reproductive technologies, and socio-psychological discourses whose research exposes the fallacy of maladjustment and trauma for children being raised in gay and lesbian households. Meanwhile, bisexual or polyamorous parents are still facing a great deal of resistance or ignorance from both the wider heteronormative society and from within the gay and lesbian community. As Garner points out,

So much of the conversation about LGBT parents is really about "same-sex parents." Bisexual parents who are married to someone of the opposite sex are often overlooked for the very reason that their sexual orientation is not as obvious—they are mistaken for heterosexual couples. . . . . They [the children] will need you [bisexual parents] to help them find the words to be able to understand their family. (2003)

The realities of multipartnered and "queerly mixed" families have been and are currently invisible, causing major social and mental health concerns for families and their children within school communities. Weber (2002) found that 38 percent of a sample of polyamorous people who had participated in counseling or therapy had not revealed their polyamory to their health service providers, and 10 percent of those who did reveal it experienced a negative response. Even if the health service providers were open-minded and willing to learn about polyamory, clients had to use some of their paid session time to educate the professional.

The 1970s saw some initial attempts at researching and documenting the experiences and well-being of children from group marriages (Francouer, 1972; Constantine and Constantine, 1972, 1973, 1976). A pioneering study of forty children from twelve group marriage families by Constantine and Constantine found that children enjoyed a "permissive environment," extending to their schooling, which was generally in a community-run school or cooperative with other communes (1976: 11). Their findings supported those of two previous studies: Johnson and Deisher (1973) found that the majority of children from polyamorous families displayed a high degree of maturity, self-confidence, and self-reliance, and they were "confident in interpersonal relations and lacked fear of unfamiliar people" (in Constantine and Constantine 1976: 25); and Hunt (1972) found that half the children had a preference for independent behaviors ("takes initiative, desires to attack and solve problems, self-directed, little or no guidance needed"). Another 24 percent were judged to have evolved to fully interdependent styles. Hunt concluded,

Collectively, the results are skewed toward leadership, self-motivation, and acceptance of responsibility. . . . They saw themselves as valuable people and accepted and valued differences in themselves and others. Only 7 children were regarded as having significantly negative self-images. (in Constantine and Constantine, 1976: 26–27)

Another study conducted by Eiduson (1973) found that polyparents placed great emphasis on nonsexist practices, particularly encouraging girls to reject a passive stereotype and to be assertive in resolving interpersonal relationships (in Constantine and Constantine, 1976). Constantine and Constantine concluded that any difficulty children faced in adapting to polyparenting was exacerbated by the lack of positive and supportive services, and the prevalence of prejudice:

> Participants in alternative lifestyles sought professional help and received instead heavily pejorative, punitive, or paternalistic responses. The belief is widespread within the counterculture that the helping professions are inseparably allied to the establishment, committed to the isolation and excision of "deviance" and to the maintenance of the status quo. (1976: 34)

More recent studies support the above findings regarding the pathologization and problematization of polyfamilies, multisexual parents, and their children by therapists (Strassberg, 2003; Weitzman, 2006). Although children are found to generally benefit from having "multiple loving parents" who can offer "more quality time" and "a greater range of interests and energy levels," polyparents are extremely reluctant to disclose their family structure to outsiders (Strassberg, 2003: 464). Since the 1970s, issues related to the disclosure of polyamory to children still require research and action (Davidson, 2002; Weitzman, 2007). The few studies that have been conducted indicate that the lack of disclosure can be problematic for children as they are deprived of a "positive moral and emotional framework for their reconfigured family" (Strassberg, 2003: 514). A study in the 1980s by Watson and Watson (1982) found that while 75 percent of polyamorous survey respondents wanted their children to know of their lifestyle, only 21 percent had actually informed their children of the full extent of their involvement with other partners. A major barrier to disclosure was the fear of legal interventions, social stigmatization, and disapproval of themselves and their children. And yet, in its blatant policing and panopticonic surveillance, society has previously responded similarly with other types of families. In the following, Brianna, a heterosexual mother with two male partners, points out the levels of stigmatization polyparents and their children may experience as well as referring to the stigmatization experienced by black families earlier in history:

> To be poly you are dead opposite of everything your contemporaries are taught from the day of their very birth. You instantly become part of the perverted and sick clan that already encompasses killers, pedophiles and pornographers. You will be distrusted by all and likely a legal target of the government. After all, sick people, of which us polys are often included, cannot raise normal, healthy children. Right? Your neighbors will band together to show their dislike of you. Their kids will not be allowed at your house, not allowed to play with your kids. After all, kids of sick people grow up to be sickos themselves. Right? Once you are poly, you can never have anything to do with children in any normal capacity—that is, being a boy/girl scout leader, a big brother/sister, sports coach, or a camp counselor. See, if any child ever makes a complaint against you, you lose. . . . Who can blame people for bowing to such incredible

peer pressure? That's how strong the social conditioning is to prevent people from daring to step away from the norm. . . . None of this sort of pressure is new. Ask any black family who dared move into a white neighborhood how it all works. Their kids coming home from school with bloody noses because the white family across the street taught their kids to hate blacks so much that the kids are willing to attack to show solidarity with their mum and dad. (Brianna, hetero-poly mom with two hetero-mono partners)

It must be stated here that discrimination experienced by polyparents cannot be equated to the discrimination experienced by black families earlier in history. As we shall see later in this chapter, there is some privilege in being white and thus being able to "pass" that was not and is not available to black people. As discussed in the introduction to this book, the predominant whiteness and middle-class status of polygroups needs to be addressed as indicative of internal hierarchies of acceptance and inclusion, as well as indicative of what can be called the "perversions as privilege" that can only be "afforded" by a certain class and color that already provides a foundation of normativity (Noel, 2006; Sheff, 2008). However, Brianna's point that at different times in history different kinds of families have been targeted as inferior, abnormal, or to be discriminated against is warranted. Indeed, being polyamorous may shift otherwise "normative," otherwise privileged white middle-class families and individuals from the sociopolitical Center to the Margins:

Being poly will be the white person's first real experience with stereotyping and bigotry. And a trial by fire it will be, I assure you. . . . There are actual laws against and banning you. . . . The very second you go poly, you leave the safety of the majority and become an unprotected and hunted member of the minority. (Brianna, hetero-poly mom with two hetero-mono partners)

In education and other social institutions, sensationalized stereotypes about nonmonogamous relationships conspire with silence about diverse partnering realities to perpetuate ignorance, self-and-other doubt and self-and-other hatred. What are the negotiations and silences around multipartnered families within school communities? What are the schooling experiences of children from multipartnered families? These questions remain unasked in the majority of more recent research with polyamorous families. For example, a study by Hill (1997) of 2,750 survey responses found that 52 percent of polyamorists had children but no data was collected regarding the schooling experiences of the children and their families. A more recent study by Walston of 430 survey respondents from various polyamory e-mail lists found that the participants were of higher than average education, of a wide range of ages with a large concentration in their thirties, not "from traditional Judeo-Christian religion," and included a "high incidence of bisexuality among both men and women" (2001: 11). Also, 27 percent reported having children living in the house full or part time, and 6 percent had children that did not live at home. Four percent of those with children said polyamory had affected their child custody to some degree, while 32 percent of those with children expressed concern that polyamory would affect child custody in the future. Interestingly, over two-thirds who have children (71 percent) were out to all or some of them. Although there was such a strong interest in parenting issues in the survey, no data on the family's feelings and experiences of schooling was collected.

There have been a few personal accounts, biographical writings, and opinion pieces describing polyparenting (see Iantaffi, 2006; Trask, 2007). For example, Easton and Liszt (1997) devote a chapter to child rearing for "ethical sluts" or "slutty parenthood," showing the "creative options" for raising children in polyamorous households. Although the chapter raises issues about "how to prepare them for difficult questions in the outside world," it does not explore this to any significant extent (1997: 222). It does raise the issue that "living in a nontraditional sexual lifestyle is considered a justification for legally removing your children from your custody," which supports the need for silence when dealing with government-linked educational institutions (1997: 224). One of the writers talks about having "willingly agreed to maintain a discreet closet" when her daughter's junior high school friends came to visit; her daughter got to "come out to her friends about her mom at her own pace" (1997: 226). As with most personal writings on children in "queerly mixed" and multipartnered families, the focus is on the positives these children experience growing up in such homes: "children equipped with lots of support and self-esteem, and (probably) more information than their peers, [who] might even *benefit* from a more unconventional home environment" (Arden, 1996: 251; see also Nearing, 1996b; Halpern, 1999; Newitz, 2006).

There have also been some opinion pieces that argue that children being raised in polyamorous households experience many difficulties. For example, Kaye does not believe in bisexuality and constructs a label, "Limbo men," for any men who are having sex with men but are not coming out as gay. She does not provide any research to support her opinions, but writes,

> Our children are the real victims of these circumstances. . . . Many of these fathers expect their children to not only accept their homosexuality, but to stand up against the tide of ignorance and homophobia of their peers in their defense. . . . They are sacrificing their children like lambs to the wolves. These men are adults who can pick and choose where they go and whom they socialize with. Their children don't have that luxury when they have to face their schoolmates on a daily basis in a small confined schoolyard. (2003)

The lack of research into polyparenting and its implications on children within families and within schools means we may need to draw on pioneers such as Buxton (1999) on parents coming out as gay or lesbian and consider what would be the similarities and differences for children within polyamorous and multisexual families, given that there is even less cultural knowledge or acceptance of bisexual and polyamorous parents than gay or lesbian parents. Buxton found that children who are "sensitive to their parents' tension (or upset by the disclosure if they have been told) may act out in home or school" and that the reactions of children to the parent's disclosure reflects "their age and development stage." She found that preschool youngsters "usually take the announcement as a matter of fact" while school-age children "tend to feel embarrassed but not seriously upset," although they may feel "conflicted" when hearing outsiders' discriminatory remarks about their parents. Adolescents, "facing puberty issues of sexuality and identity and feeling increased sensitivity to peer attitudes against homosexuality, sometimes feel confused about their own sexual identity" and will often keep their parent's sexuality secret. Older teenagers, "having worked out their own identity and sexuality issues and formed a personal value system, are typically less disturbed" but may judge the parents according to dominant moral, political, or social discourses (1999: 323). Even if told when young, adolescents have to "reprocess the information as they begin to understand sexuality, adult gender roles, intimate relationships, and life choices" (1999: 344). However, contrary to the parent's fear of rejection, "most children accept the information when it is first communicated," although their reaction may not "always match their inner feelings, then or in the following months" (1999: 337; see also Buxton, 2006a, 2006b, 2007).

What is largely absent from all the research projects and writings discussed above are children and adults who have grown up in polyfamilies relating their own experiences, insights, and perspectives about being raised in polyamorous and/or multisexual households and its impact on their well-being and education. Researchers such as Strassberg (2003) consider this absence to be a major hindrance to initiating and implementing legal and educational policies and practices that support these children and their families. One group of young people from a particular type of polyamorous family, Mormon polygamy, have begun to speak out against dominant media constructions of child physical, mental, and sexual abuse in these "cults" (Dobner, 2006; Winslow, 2006). On August 19, 2006, a rally was held in Salt Lake City, Utah, where children and young adults from polygamist Mormon families "praised their parents and families and said their lives were absent of the abuse, neglect, forced marriages, and other 'horror stories' sometimes associated with polygamist communities" (Dobner, 2006). They reported being harassed at school such as being called "plyg" or being afraid to tell their peers about their families (Winslow, 2006).

"Queerspawn" is a term used by some offspring of LGBT parents who claim and celebrate their identity, acknowledging that, regardless of their sexual orientation, their upbringing has "queered" them (Garner, 2001). The term was invented by Stefan Lynch, the son of a lesbian mother and a gay dad, and the first director of Children of Lesbians and Gays Everywhere (COLAGE). However, it could easily be applied to children being raised in polyamorous families, some of which are multisexual. Most studies of children whose parents are coming out as gay or lesbian find that children's stress stems "primarily from hearing negative remarks of friends and schoolmates," and that "problems for children arise more from anticipated or actual negativity outside the home than from factors inside" (Buxton, 1999: 340; see also Buntzly, 1993). Buxton advises that parents use "discretion, communication, and guidance" to support their children (1999: 340), for the major negative impact comes from fears that teasing and ostracism might occur at school and "the secrecy or isolation many children impose upon themselves to avoid this. . . . The problem is then self-imposed isolation to maintain peer approval" (1999: 346; see also Buxton, 2006a, 2006b). Buxton qualifies this by saying that all studies on stigmatization show how

> through such coping with painful discrimination, children learn social sensitivity and ways to detect trustworthiness. . . . In retrospective interviews, a number of children report more benefits than problems dealing with social negativity. . . . [They] have a greater understanding of prejudice, feel free to change and have choices, and are more tolerant of differences and intolerant of discrimination. (1999: 346)

Indeed, no study has shown

> a deleterious effect on their ability to form relationships with peers. . . . The strain of not feeling "normal" does not appear to last. . . . By the time children end their teen years, knowing their own identities and values, separated psychologically from their parents, and possibly out of the house, they feel free to tell others that they have a gay or lesbian parent without regard to social reactions. (1999: 347; see also Buxton, 2007)

Several bisexual polyamorous mothers have written about their children in relation to school. West (1996) draws upon her interview research and provides sound advice on discussing polyfidelitous relationships with children. However, her only reference to schooling is that

> polyfidelity rarely comes up with teachers or casual acquaintances or strangers, by name, anyway, it's still too radical a form. Usually, just being bisexual takes

all the heat. So I let sleeping dogs, and multi-gender lovers, lie, especially when it comes to people I'm not even going to know in a year. The kids are pretty savvy about this, but they talk about poly with best friends and can get hurt by negative opinions. (1996: 274)

Arden (1996) suggests schools hold sessions/workshops for children from queer families and provide information and children's books about bisexual parents and bisexuality. Anapol (1992) also considers strategies such as home schooling or private schooling in a school that acknowledges and celebrates queer family diversity. She believes that children could be much better educated in polyamorous families, because with a larger number of adults "pooling their resources and their expertise, children would have direct access to a diverse group of tutors as well as educational software, videos, and databases" (Anapol, 2003: 4). This would make home schooling or private schooling a viable option, as well as making adequate funds for college more available.

A few mothers who are not bisexual have also written briefly about their children at school. Bear (1998), who is in a polyandrous relationship, talks about how well their son does in school and how he is complimented for being "well-behaved, intelligent and mature" (1998: 28). One of the interviewees in Nearing's book discusses the positive impact on her daughter of living in a polyamorous family, although sometimes other children at school give her a hard time about her "different family":

> But so many kids have step-parents that it's not that unusual having more than one Mum or Dad. I think the benefits of our kind of family life really outweigh having to deal with the lack of acceptance by people who are ignorant and prejudiced. We can't live our lives to meet their limits. . . . It's hard knowing that our lifestyle could be used against us as parents. (1992: 75)

The most recent study into polyfamilies did ask questions regarding raising children and schooling. This was the Polyamory Survey conducted by *Loving More* in 2001 to 2002 which elicited over 5,000 responses. The sections on children and schooling that I analyzed (Pallotta-Chiarolli, 2002, 2006b) revealed that approximately 29 percent of respondents were biological parents of children under eighteen; approximately 16 percent were legal guardians of children under eighteen; and approximately 26 percent had children under eighteen living with them. The survey also showed that some polyfamilies had children over the age of eighteen of whom they were biological parents (approximately 18 percent) and legal guardians (approximately 4 percent). Approximately 5 percent of the respondents also had children over the age of eighteen living with them. In response to another question on having children, approximately 69 percent said they would have children or had children within a poly relationship. In regard to adopting children, out of the approximately 61 percent who considered adoption in their families, approximately 3 percent had already adopted while approximately 97 percent would be open to it.

Interestingly, despite the percentages above illustrating that many poly-families in the Polyamory Survey had children or wanted children, only approximately 30 percent of survey respondents had told their children about their poly relationships or their desire to be in one, while approximately 45 percent had not done so. Of those polyparents who had told their children, approximately 45 percent had received positive responses, while approximately 15 percent had received negative responses, and approximately 40 percent of the responses from children had been neutral (Pallotta-Chiarolli, 2002, 2006b). Brosnan writes that we must try "pulling the family out of the closet" in schools and popular culture (1996: 53). This was very much supported by the families in the Polyamory Survey. Approximately 98 percent of the survey respondents supported "the creation of positive images on TV, in books and movies of people living in poly relationships." In relation to educational issues, when asked, "How strongly do you support the creation of positive images in high school curriculum of people living in poly relationships?" approximately 94 percent of the respondents to the Polyamory Survey supported this. These survey findings raise the question, To what extent is a low degree of disclosure to one's children and outside social institutions such as schools due to the lack of positive images in popular culture that would provide a discourse that affirms polyfamilies and thereby the emotional and social health and well-being of their children?

Other issues that arose in the survey responses included the concern that "living in a nontraditional sexual lifestyle is considered a justification for legally removing your children from your custody," which supports the need for silence that polyparents feel when dealing with government-linked educational institutions (Easton and Liszt, 1997). Approximately 98.5 percent supported child custody rights for people in poly relationships while approximately 13 percent of respondents had experienced discrimination or knew someone who had experienced discrimination when coming into "contact with Child Protective Services." These Polyamory Survey results raise the question, To what extent is the low rate of actual experienced discrimination due to the low degree of disclosure to outside structures regarding one's polyfamily?

Issues of disclosure will be explored further in the rest of this chapter as we consider how polyfamilies pass (normalize), border (negotiate), or pollute (challenge) in their children's schools.

"THE SIGNS ARE THERE BUT THEY DON'T KNOW HOW TO READ THEM": POLYFAMILIES AS PASSING

Naomi's smiling wistfully as we sit on a low brick fence of her old university. "I'm polyamorous, have two male partners and two children at school. My children pass as kids from a monogamous family because even though the signs are there, the teachers, the school, the system doesn't know how to read them. But then when I was at school, the signs had always been there, but I didn't know how to read them. Why wasn't I able to have one best friend at school? I always had at least three best friends and a range of other close friends, which drove them all crazy. You know what little girls can be like in this culture of exclusivity and possessiveness."

She laughs and waves a hand around, her eyes taking in the campus. "Then I get here, the place of knowledge, radicalism, and freedom! Yeah, right! I fall in love with two guys while an undergrad. One becomes my husband, the other I've never seen again. It was so ironic, so prophetic that they both asked me out for the first time on the same day, just minutes apart. I only chose my husband because he asked first, but it could easily have been the other. . . . And then years later when I fall in love again but don't fall out of love with my husband, I realize it could easily have been both."

Naomi points to the brick fence we're sitting on and shifts around on it. "You know, later that day, I sat on this very spot looking up to the library where they'd both asked me for a date. I just sat here confused, exhilarated, troubled, realizing that my destiny had been molded into a groove by the making of that decision. I remember wondering how it would've turned out if I had said "No," or "I'll let you know," and then got asked out by the other guy. Because I could've just as easily decided the other way. But it's like the possibility of deciding both ways just wasn't there in my consciousness. But it was there deep inside my heart. So here I sat, really happy about who I was going out with, knowing I'd been in love with him for over a year and knowing this was going to be a lifetime kinda love. But I was also really sad, like an empty space had just opened up, but I couldn't find words to describe what was going on."

Naomi sighs. "I spent a lot of time here learning all sorts of stuff, researching in the library, attending lectures. But there was nothing about polyamory, nothing that could help me decipher the signs of my own polyamorousness, 'cause I had no words, no labels, no skills to do that. Now I still keep passing as mono for the sake of my children at school, even though my children now know polyfamilies exist through us. So much for institutions of learning."

—from my research notes and interview with Naomi

As Naomi discusses above, for the sake of making it possible for their children to have a safer, easier, and successful time at school, a place that many parents saw as filled with harassment and inequities over many more known or commonplace diversity issues, most polyfamilies in my research chose to pass as monogamous heterosexual couples:

> My son goes to public school in a small, unwealthy community. He's had a top-notch education thus far, and has the most amazing teachers, and the most understanding principal. The school has a very strong anti-bullying program. He is also in the gifted ed program. So why don't I come out? Because I don't want to jeopardize my son's success and good time at school, and also because even though the anti-bullying and caring policies and atmosphere in the school are amazing, I don't have any guarantee that it would be applied to us. So I don't tell my son, so he doesn't go to school already worried about being found out. (Kathy, bi-poly mom)

Many polyparents expressed their panopticonic fears based on known and surmised external surveillance and punishment (Foucault, 1977):

> I am sick of looking over my shoulder. I am sick of being afraid to call an ambulance or talk to a policeman or anything like that for fear of coming under the public eye. I am sick of worrying whether or not the parents of my children's playmates know the score. Certainly it's none of their business, but if it became obvious, will we have to cope with our children having friends taken away without understanding why? (Nina, bi-poly mom)

Thus, as Kentlyn (2008) explains, their family lives were lived within their "queer" homes as a "safe space" and simultaneously a "scrutinized space":

> [The] private space of the queer home can be seen to embody the tension between safe space to be queer in, but also a place where the subversive performance of gender, sexuality and family comes under scrutiny (Kentlyn, 2008: 327–28).

Brianna, a heterosexual woman in a relationship with two heterosexual men, explains why she closets her family even though her children are fully aware of the relationships she has. Her descriptions of her home reveal it to be the "safe space" Kentlyn (2008) discusses, not only for her own children but for many of their peers as well. Simultaneously, she is strongly aware that it is a "scrutinized space," and while currently being categorized as "normal," should the scrutiny reveal the polyamory within the home, this categorization would immediately become its polar opposite, "abnormal," and thus render the home "unsafe" for all children:

> How do you then get on with sleepovers, children's parties, coaching school sports, etc., etc.? All of that would be nonexistent in my home and I can't do that to my children. I mean, the irony is that we're known as the neighborhood kid hangout. We're the ones with a pool, a trampoline, basketball hoop, pool

table, Playstation, a TV and DVD player in every kid's bedroom, tons of toys, etc. Yes, you could say we run a youth center! And other families are so relieved their kids have somewhere safe and normal to go to so they can get away from their own hassles at home. They think our family is normal in that we are actually a happy loving family. Well, my kids think our family is normal too in that definition and in being a polyfamily. But others wouldn't. That worry is with me every day. (Brianna, hetero-poly mom with two hetero-mono partners)

For many parents, passing was easy due to the similarities between their families and monogamous families, particularly in the realm of the public images and actions of normative families, and whereby the only differences were in the private domain of sexual and intimate relationships. Thus, they believed that normative terms such as "family values" and "family life" applied to them:

I'm very much into those great "family values" the conservatives are always going on about. I want a nice, quiet family life. I don't want my partners for wild, sexual, all-night clubbing hedonism. I don't have the energy when you're raising three children! I want my partners for chicken soup when I'm sick, foot rubs, TV nights, road trips, hugs, school schedules, and homework schedules . . . just the mundane, wonderful, magical stuff of family life. (Nina, bi-poly mom)

I own a home, have a responsible professional job, am a loving parent to a happy, well-adjusted, straight-A-earning eight-year-old. I'm a member of the parent association and I donate my time and efforts to the various community clubs I'm a part of. (Andrew, in hetero group marriage of two men and two women)

Families will give existing known normative labels to family members in order to pass in schools (see Kroeger, 2003):

We use terms like stepdad and stepmum and the teachers then don't find it too odd that we all live together. We say it's for the kids, and they seem to be able to deal with that. It's probably a nice change for them [the school] to have amicable stepfamilies rather than dealing with stepfamilies, divorced families who hate each other and use the kids as pawns. Also, our kids like those terms as well because they can use them with friends and teachers at school; it's terms they know well themselves from their friends. I'm astonished at how well he [our son] handles our line: "We believe or practice this, but don't say it at school." Still, sometimes I feel like I'm teaching hypocrisy because of a school system that teaches honesty but doesn't really let you practice it. (Cate, bi-poly mom)

Thus, closeting (Aruna, 1994), "cloaking" (Richardson, 1985), and "scripting" (Cohen and Taylor, 1976; Meyrowitz, 1985) of one's family according to normative and taken-for-granted labels is a form of agency that allows for protection and the ability to live out one's realities with the minimum of external surveillance and interference (Fuss, 1991; Kroeger, 2003). Indeed, some parents encouraged the use of the school's official structures and procedures to assist in the passing of their families:

> At the beginning of the school year, normally "emergency cards" are sent home with the children. You fill out all the info, and there is usually a space for "people allowed to pick up the child" and "people to contact in an emergency." I have always had three or more people listed here and I have never had an issue with the school about it . . . and I would think that sending a letter to the school authorizing a coparent would be enough. (Andrew, in hetero group marriage of two men and two women)

In the following, Tania, a heterosexual polyamorous teacher, discusses how easy and beneficial it is for a school to not question the performativity or surface image of a multipartnered family. The school operates on shared knowledges and discourses rather than questioning what may lie beyond or in excess of the known and normative (Derrida, 1981; Kamuf, 1981). Indeed, many schools are so grateful to have family involvement that they do not problematize or interrogate the structures that families present themselves within. Thus, today's increasingly diverse forms of heterosexual families, the outcomes of acceptable processes of serial monogamy, provide a cover or closet for polyamory. However, as Tania cautions, the nonscrutinizing approach by schools is only maintained if the family presents as functional and the child as healthy and happy. Any problem, even if it is not connected to family structure, would be seen as sufficient cause to problematize and pathologize the family:

> As a high school teacher in a very large suburban school, I can say that any adult who has signed permission forms with the school is allowed to pick up, drop off, and sign kids out of school without stares, question, or judgment. With so many working parents, most parents list three to four other people as "emergency contacts." No one questions who these adults are or what their family/biological relationship to the child is. Most are neighbors, friends, or family members who are available during the day when the parent isn't. Also, many of our kids live in homes with other families and, again, unless there's a problem of some kind, a multifamily house would be assumed to be just that type of situation unless something happened or was said to suggest otherwise. . . . I think I can also say, with more than a fair degree of certainty, that most teachers have so much trouble contacting or getting involvement from so many parents in "traditional" family setups, that to have any adult who is involved with the kid's life actually become involved in their schooling is welcome! . . . If there were serious problems with the child, or if the relationship between the school and home were in conflict, I am sure that most schools would tend to look closer at and question the "family" setup or blame a nontraditional setup as being at fault, but as a matter of routine, I don't think that most schools would even bother to question a setup that was working. (Tania, hetero-poly teacher)

Hence, due to the lack of discursive knowledge about polyamory, it appears that passing was generally a very easy thing to do with schools. Some kind of pleasure and power was gained by polyparents from this agentic use of the closet (Davies, 1991; Davis, 1991; Aruna, 1994; Mason, 1995; Fisher, 2003; Kroeger, 2003):

> We selected two adults to be the parents in all public situations for our kids even though they weren't even the biological parents, but the school just classified them into what they know—"Oh yes, a blended family, stepparents" and went into automatic pilot. Well, we are blended, just sexually blended as well, something that wouldn't even enter their brains. (Rina, in hetero group marriage of two men and two women)

> I currently volunteer once a week in our kid's classroom and her teacher knows that I am the kid's "other mom." But she doesn't know about "the rest of our life." Up until now, it hasn't been relevant. The principals and office staff and teachers at both kids' schools know that I am the kids' godmother, and that all of us are working. They consider the kids lucky to have so many concerned adults around and say so regularly. (Sally, lesbian-mono partner of bi-poly woman who has a hetero-mono husband)

> Since we didn't say anything, and just went about raising them, with all three of us showing up at school functions, it was normal for them. And their friends were heard to say things like, "How come Shane has two daddies and I don't have any?" So, it turned out that there was no such thing as normal, and the kids just grew up like the rest of their friends. (Renee, hetero-poly mom with two bi-poly male partners)

One parent even recommended utilizing existing legal procedures for divorce in order to more easily pass as a stepfamily or blended family, as well as gaining legal protection. John's recommendation below of parodying or mimicking normalized legal divorce proceedings is an example of Butler's (1991) theory of performativity:

> Go through a mock divorce. Odd, but in hindsight I think it would be the best thing any couple/group who wants to marry or even seriously live together should do. Modify it to fit your group, even if you can't legally marry, but do the mock divorce. (John, hetero-poly dad with two hetero-mono partners)

The normative discourses or "taken-for-granted," "unquestioned and unquestionable" (Schutz, 1944) discourses within schools also prevent a child's "outing" of his or her family from being taken seriously. Children may hang out their queer understandings of family on the clothesline, but the school may unintentionally closet this disclosure by dismissing the child's discussions of family as inconceivable childish fantasy or error:

> My daughter has said at school that she wants to marry both a little girl and a little boy, but I think the school dismissed it as a typical comment made by

kids who have no idea. The thing is, my daughter has a better idea than her own teachers but passes as this naïve child. (Cate, bi-poly mom)

The power of external ascription and community acknowledgment were discussed by many parents of adolescents. For example, even if their children had been raised in a multipartnered and/or multisexual family, some parents of adolescents believed the school social cultures perpetuated and enforced the construction of monogamy, which gave young people minimal opportunity to consider any other option:

> At the moment, my teenage daughter is quite monogamous. . . . She's clear that she doesn't respect my choice to be married and polyamorous. On the other hand, my daughter shows many traits that indicate to me that the only reason she's really monogamous is that she has convinced herself it's required of her. . . . As the mum of two teens I can honestly say that this generation's peer group places enormous pressure to conform to monogamy from well before they even start dating. Indeed, the idea that you can even go on just a "date" with someone and then another "date" with someone else seems foreign. That's scary. (Nora, hetero-poly mom)

> Kids are incredibly peer driven and they are often really, truly terrified of losing that peer acceptance by having "weird parents." Sadly, many parents undervalue the importance of those peer relationships and thus put a wedge between themselves and their children. When our son was in middle school it was really important to him that we be discreet. This wasn't always easy, because we live in a relatively small area. . . . We simply didn't hold hands at school functions or "flaunt" it in front of his friends. Interestingly enough, as he's gotten older, he has gotten more comfortable being "out." (Rina, in hetero group marriage of two men and two women)

> One of the reasons why I held off talking to the kids about it is because I think that they're going through major and very demanding issues to do with sexual identity and sexual development and they don't need in a sense their parents' issues with those same things imposed upon them in a dramatic way as well. (Peter, hetero-poly with one bi-poly woman and one hetero-mono woman partner)

Many polyparents such as Peter above worried about the effects of disclosing their poly relationships to their children because the invisibility of their families, the feeling that the outside world has no knowledge or discursive framework of their kind of family, can create "a sense of unreality" for children, "as if one is seeing something that others cannot see." This realization of "invisibility and unacceptance" can "plant the seed of fear in the child's heart" (Wright, 2001: 288; see also Buxton, 2007). Thus, in order to protect children from this cognitive and emotional dissonance, and to protect themselves as parent members of local communities, many polyfamilies will pass as monogamous to their own children, as Summermoon writes to her adult children:

> It must have been lonely, sensing this truth about our lives and that we did not want to talk about it. I wanted to tell you, but your dad thought I might cause confusion during your teenage years, the years of your sexual development. . . . I feel vulnerable as a community leader and role model. (1998: 33)

> The need to keep things secret would be a huge burden on the children. One of us is in a professional position that makes staying closeted essential and we're not in an environment where poly life would be well accepted. So the feeling is that the kids should not know something they can't talk about to anyone. (Conrad, bi-poly dad)

Some parents decided not to disclose to their children, as they acknowledged that their children may "slip up" one day at school in their performances of passing and keeping up pretensions. Thus, it was rationalized that the less their children know, the less likely that "outing" will happen:

> If they slip up, you'll have to be prepared to cover for them and yourselves. . . . Mostly all kids need to know is that you have friends you care for very much. You might even leave off the "very much" part until the parrot-phase in little kids passes. . . . If it's a pretty "normal" situation, then they may never see fit to talk about it to anyone else. (Paul, bi-poly dad)

Brianna was a married heterosexual mother of four who began a relationship with another man when her youngest two children were still at school. She did not come out to them but recalls how her children had soon worked out that their family was "different" and chose not to out it at school:

> Our youngest figured out pretty early on if she said anything that differed from what was considered the normal, she would get a really hard time. . . . And one of my sons said to me when he was still at high school, "You don't realize, Mum, how different our family is to other families and other kids don't have the freedom to think, but we do." It disturbed me because I was so sad and disturbed for other families, but I was so proud and he was not saying it as criticism, he was saying it with a sense of gratitude. (Brianna, hetero-poly mom with two hetero-mono partners)

The following woman in Nearing's study recalls the stresses and confusions of growing up in a polyfamily:

> Too much information, too much exposure, too soon to an alternative sexual lifestyle can lead to confusion for a child and their developing sexuality. I was fearful of following in my parents' footsteps. I was not comfortable with their lifestyle for my own future. To protect myself from the interest of men, both

my own peers and adults I feared, I gained weight. I didn't send out "signals" that I was interested in dating in high school and college and that protection worked well. (2001: 11)

She proceeds to describe the panopticonic burden of passing and closeting for children as living with the "pink elephant in the lounge room" and yet acknowledges the difficulty of the either/or decision parents had to consider: either tell the children to not keep a secret and expose them to external damage; or risk damaging the children by expecting them to keep a secret:

I understand why they didn't tell us [more openly] . . . to protect us from our friends and our friends' parents who wouldn't understand if we told them. But that stance left us wondering, fearful and very much alone. I didn't dare talk to my sister and she didn't talk to me. It's the proverbial pink elephant in the middle of the living room. . . . It's there, but no one talks about it. . . . The most damaging thing to children is having to keep adult secrets. The second most damaging thing is to have to defend their parents' lifestyle to other children. . . . Now that I'm older, more mature, I can understand that people can love, even be in love, with more than one person at a time. . . . I have learned that I can love more than one man at a time. (in Nearing, 2001: 12)

This woman believes parents need to discuss and resolve the following questions: "How will we explain the structure of this family to the child and when is the best time to do that?" . . . "What do we do about other children coming over? How do we instruct our child to explain it to their peers?" (in Nearing, 2001: 13). Thorson's work on communication privacy management (CPM) in relation to adult children who grew up knowing about their parents' infidelities offers some insight and strategies in the negotiation of these dilemmas. CPM involves parents and children negotiating "information ownership" and "privacy rules," and enacting "protection and access rules" for any processes of disclosure (2009: 34).

Thus, my research shows that polyfamilies need to consider and negotiate which forms of passing and CPM may be the most useful in their specific contexts: *withdrawing* from the world of school as much as possible; *compartmentalizing* and segregating the worlds of home and school; *cloaking* certain realities so that they are invisible or pass as normative; or *fictionalizing* certain aspects of one's life and family (Richardson, 1985). In the following, Robin describes the decisions she and her partners have made in regard to when, what, and how to tell their children:

We asked the kids if they wanted to know about our relationship and they firmly said "No, thanks!" So if the situation isn't causing the children any confusion and you don't have a group of poly folk around for the kids to see it's truly normal for some people . . . then I'd let it be. Our philosophy has always been "Don't burden the children with your adult issues." Which basically means if they don't show any interest in knowing, then we keep it to ourselves and live life as we are. If they question or show signs of being confused or distressed, then we fix it! (Robin, bi-poly mom with two hetero-mono male partners)

Some parents in my research believed that children could be taught to lie at school and be told why this was necessary. They advocated teaching their children the skills of "haciendo caras" (Anzaldua, 1990), parody, and mimicry (Bordo, 1992) in order to minimize external disruption and maximize internal familial function:

> Regarding children and school, teach them to lie. Make sure that they understand why. Those who will hurt you or your children do not deserve the truth. . . . Your children are vulnerable and honest. Teach your children to keep family business private. Teach the older ones to police the younger. (Carl, hetero-poly dad)

Other parents found that their children redefined their home relationships in ways that might gain them some kind of "coolness" at school, thereby constructing and passing their parents' relationships and sexualities in normative sensationalist ways that appeared to gain some kind of peer acknowledgment and discursive fit. For example, having a "heterokinky" father may be a known "cool" category among adolescent boys aspiring to hegemonic heterosexual masculinity as meaning access to lots of sex with women—"hetero" and "kinky":

> I'm a bi man with two women partners raising a fourteen-year-old son. We've always been absolutely honest with him but always been aware he couldn't discuss this at school. Recently, some of his friends have worked it out, so he's now telling them his dad has two women partners and that he accepts that as kinky, and I think it's because it's heterokinky. It's like he gains points for his dad's a stud, like in the porn they watch. (Conrad, bi-poly dad)

> Interestingly enough, as our fifteen-year-old son has gotten older he has become much more open about his family life with his peers. . . . But then, when you're a teen, having parents who live an alternative lifestyle is "sort of cool." . . . When I asked him about this, he informed me that (a) he's comfortable enough with who he is now that he isn't afraid of rejection from people that "I wouldn't want to hang around with anyway," and (b) "Mom, you guys are weird, but ALL my friends' families are weird, you guys are just more honest about it." (Margherita, hetero-poly mom)

Parents with preadolescent children found that "kids" were less interested in family dynamics and had their own criteria of what constituted a "cool" or "passable" family:

> It seems to me that my kids' friends are a lot more interested in the parent who can make the funny-looking pancakes or is willing to play squirt guns with them than the social dynamic of the adult stuff. (Robin, bi-poly mom with two hetero-mono partners)

The adults in the research who had grown up in polyfamilies and who had learned to lie at school believed that the positives they had gained from being raised in such closeted families far outweighed any negatives such as lying (McDonald, 2001). Indeed, it provided the vantage point of being raised in the Margins and able to interrogate the "taken-for-grantedness" of the Center (see hooks, 1990; Kroeger, 2003):

> It hasn't always been an easy road but in the long run I think it's made me more open-minded and mature than a lot of my peers. I've had a lot of life experiences that a lot of my friends haven't had, and also so many of my friends have dysfunctional families that even though mine might not be "normal" by most standards, we're happy and functional and our parents have been together going on fifty years this summer. I always knew my life was different, . . . so by the time I was thrust into the public education system I knew enough to keep my mouth shut or people were going to think I was weird. (Marianne, hetero-mono daughter of hetero group marriage)

A major reason parents gave for not outing their family was the fear of being accused of child abuse or having to battle child custody issues. Many parents stressed the need for families to collect documentation and legal papers in order to protect themselves should any situation arise at school:

> I'm scared to death of anything being misinterpreted. What if someone at the school objects to our family and decides to get nasty? A common tactic is to accuse someone living with the child of some sort of abuse—especially sexual. Schools are more vigilant about all that, and that's a good thing, but prejudice and ignorance about our family could mean they use that kind of knowledge and policy against us. I don't want to drag my kids through all that. . . . I recommend parents document, document, document! . . . See a poly-friendly lawyer *before* everything hits the fan. (Robin, bi-poly mom with two hetero-mono partners)

> Little minds who don't like alternative lifestyles only have to make the claim that your child is being "emotionally neglected/abused" by the family living situation in order to start something that could have tragic consequences. . . . You should familiarize yourself with the laws in your state and with your rights as parents. . . . The children are very likely to be interviewed in school without

the parents' knowledge or consent. The children, depending on the allegation, might be removed from school and strip searched and physically examined by a doctor for signs of abuse or neglect, *without* the parents' knowledge or consent. The caseworker may talk to the school guidance counselor, teachers, the principal about the child's behavior, appearance, and well-being, *without* the parents' knowledge or consent. The caseworker then *might* contact the parents and let them know that an investigation is being conducted. Dealing with these agencies is a dangerous proposition for families. (Carl, hetero-poly dad)

Another strategy of passing utilized by some polyfamilies is the opting out of or withdrawing from public schooling altogether. Although extremely uncommon in Australia, many parents in the United States talk about homeschooling as an option because it removes polyfamilies from any kind of panopticonic and external surveillance:

> Most of those that choose to homeschool do so to shield their children. . . . I hate the idea that my children have to listen to people call their mother a whore and a tramp because their mother chooses an other-than-"normal" lifestyle. (Charmaine, hetero-poly mom)

Some parents, however, felt that this kind of passive passing could also draw unwanted and problematic attention:

> We chose the homeschool option for awhile, but it has its danger too. If you keep your kid out of the school system, it can look suspicious. What's not so normal in your family that you can't have your kids attend a normal school? (Nina, bi-poly mom)

A few of the parents in this research were also teachers, thus bordering and negotiating their positions within the school as "insider/outsider" (Trinh, 1990a, 1990b) or claiming an "outside belonging" (Probyn, 1996). In order to maintain their professional positions of responsibility, and because of their insider/outsider locations within the school whereby they could see what happened to anyone who was "different," polyamorous teachers passed off their own families as monogamous:

> Schools are places of fear and conformity. I'm a teacher, so I know. . . . There was a time when a female teacher couldn't even be married. She had to be a spinster or leave the profession. My grandmother married my grandfather secretly so she could keep her job. But once she was "outed," she was forced to resign. Now female and male teachers can be married, but it has to be a monogamous marriage 'cause if we're openly poly, we'll be forced to resign. (Raymond, bi-poly dad and teacher)

Jai Lin, a Chinese heterosexual woman in a relationship with two heterosexual men, works in a Catholic child care center, which she loves and within which she's loved. She acknowledges that "if news got around about my polyamorous relationships, I'd get fired, no matter all the good work I've done and the good reputation I've established." Thus, several teachers passed as "normal" monogamous members of their local communities and schools and were unwilling to risk these normative positionings:

> I am a primary school teacher and I don't think the school board members would be so open to me being poly! My second partner is the chief of the local fire station. It's his passion and he's concerned about the reaction this would cause. His wife is a teacher in the local high school, which is also a position that, since children are involved, people would be "up in arms." I'm also concerned about "gossip" for the kids' sake—it could be vicious and I'd hate to put them through that. (Martina, bi-poly teacher)

Several polyamorous teachers also commented on the impact that being polyamorous and passing as monogamous had on their peer relations with other teachers in the school community:

> It really sucks but I stay away from work-related social things like picnics and dinners. I don't want to go without my partners, but I can't take them and either lose my job or have us all trying to act like something we're not. I think the other teachers think I'm elitist or aloof because I avoid answering questions about my personal life, so I miss out on the close personal relationships you can have with other teachers outside of the school that make working in a school environment so much less stressful and more like a community. (Tania, hetero-poly teacher)

The effective workings of panopticonic systems of policing and regulating are evident in the above examples from teachers. For fear of the consequences to their employment and their own families, polyamorous teachers do not "come out." This, in turn, only sustains the fears of disclosure in any polyfamilies of children they might teach, as there are no role models within the school community, and they fear the reactions of teachers, whom they assume are all monogamists.

"YOU'RE HANGING OVER THE FENCES OF WHAT FAMILIES ARE MEANT TO BE": POLYFAMILIES AS BORDERING

> Nora and Gayle are sisters, and they live next door to each other in a lower-middle-class outer suburb, so when I visit them, we sit outside in Nora's backyard munching on nachos while their four kids go backward and forward through an adjoining gate made of chicken-wire, as is the fence. "We'd take the fence down," Gayle says, "but Nora's dog tends to roam, and I don't want my flowers destroyed." I look through to Gayle's yard: a neatly manicured lawn and garden. Nora's yard houses a dismantled car for the children to play in, and a large wooden dog kennel.

With the soundtrack of crunching nachos and kids running around, they talk to me about sharing men as if they're talking about the weather and shop sales. "Nora walked off with my hubby, Peter, eight years ago. I was so angry and bitter for ages. And then she got pissed off because Peter still spent so much time with me and the kids, and eventually he realized he was in big trouble!"

The sisters laugh. Nora continues the story: "The poor thing realized he still loved her and me but by now I was pregnant and there he was caught like a mouse in a maze. Gayle was demanding I have an abortion, so his decision of going back to her could be easier!"

"But once we got past all that 'do this or else' kind of stuff, we realized that we had a simpler solution right there in front of us," Gayle says with a smile. "We could be an extended family. So we worked it out in a realistic way. We could have the good things that we wanted, like Peter and our closeness as sisters, negotiate the problems like finances and timetables, and ensure that the children, who are all very close, weren't destroyed by the whole thing. Indeed, they could stay cousins and be siblings as well. They thought that was pretty good. Especially when we bought these two houses next to each other."

"The kids' schools and some of the kids' friends' families don't know what to make of us. On the one hand, we're the family they knew eight years ago, Mum and Dad and Auntie. But we're also this new shape that they don't know what to do about. So they're on the fence about us 'cause we're on the fence of what families are supposed to be," says Gayle. "We had a bit of trouble at first because the school and the parents had originally taken sides, and then when we worked it out, they were confused or pitied us, and some just tried to ignore us. But once we just got on with our lives and continued to turn up to school events, cook hot dogs at sports carnivals, and invite them over to kids' birthday parties and sleepovers as usual, they realized we expected them to be civilized toward all of us, so it has sort of settled down."

—from my research notes and interview with Nora and Gayle

As Nora and Gayle discuss above, many participants in this research spoke of feeling as if they and their children bordered two worlds (Moore and Norris, 2005), or were on a fence between the private world of home wherein family was defined and constructed in a positive and functional way, and the public world of school and community, wherein their family was defined and constructed problematically, whether they were out or passing (Trinh, 1990a, 1990b; see also Nearing, 1992; Bear, 1998). These parents spoke about their border families as being places of education, learning, and well-being that were not always understood or affirmed in schools:

There are four of us to take them to practice, play computer games with them, go over homework, praise, love and be there for them. This creates a tremendously stable environment for them. At one point last year A had special schooling that meant he couldn't take the bus home three days a week. My work situation was such that if I wanted to keep my job I couldn't leave early, period. Even if one of the kids was sick, I couldn't get to them. J, R, or B were always there for us and would pick the child up and look after them at their home until I got off of work so I wouldn't have to worry about the boys being sick and/or unsupervised. (Morgan, 2001)

Thus, border polyparents explained their "sitting on the fence" position of their children and themselves as being due to the benefits their children were gaining at home that far outweighed any negatives due to passing at school (Anzaldua, 1987a; hooks, 1990, 1999). As discussed in the previous section, border polyfamilies were often "out" to their children at home while instructing their children to pass the family as "mono" at school:

Our girls think they're the luckiest kids in the whole world—except when they're in trouble. There is almost always someone available to help them with homework, to answer their questions, to give them a hug, to talk to them, etc. . . . The kids get to experience and observe positive (and occasionally not-so-positive . . .) examples from four good, intelligent, loving parents—who have a wide variety of skills, talents, methods, and abilities. . . . They are personally exposed to a greater variety of life choices. . . . From the point that we first decided to pursue this relationship, we wanted to be up front with the kids. We explained to them that we all loved each other (and them). We told them that it was unusual for four people to love each other and live together, but that there was nothing wrong with it. We also told them that some people might tease them if they knew about it, but that there was no reason for them to be ashamed. They asked a few questions, heard our explanations, and were all set. (Janette, in a bi group marriage of three women and two men)

Being on the border is also seen as necessitating the need to think about labels for family members that feel appropriate within the home but may need to be altered for use in the wider world's normative discourses of family. Thus, mestizaje polyparenting may involve working with one's children to redefine, reconstruct and/or fictionalize the family for the outside world (Richardson, 1985):

One of the hardest issues for us in the beginning was what the kids should call us. The girls wanted to call me their "other mother," but we thought that would necessitate more explanations at school. For a while, they called us Aunt and Uncle, but that didn't feel right. Eventually we just had them call us by our names, but both of them occasionally call me "Mama" and their biological Mum is "Mum." This usually only happens at home. (Janette, in a bi group marriage of three women and two men)

Border polyparents may also see their role as providing an education about "the real world" or filling in the gaps in relation to sexual and familial diversity, which they do not believe their children will obtain from school:

> I recognize that we live in the real world. Even worse, we happen to live in a town where security clearances are common and necessary for our continued employment. So my children have had to learn that (a) we aren't ashamed of our lives, and that we do not believe that what we are doing is wrong, but (b) we have to be discreet about what we share with "outsiders" because it can have negative consequences for our family. I have had people tell me that this is "too tough" for kids to understand, but I think that my kids have done very well with it. Honestly, I think that sometimes people don't give children credit for being able to understand the real world. In my opinion, I want my children to understand how the world works, and to give them the tools to deal with that. . . . About sexuality and relationships, my children have been given this information in a manner that (a) expresses our values and educates them about the real world and the amazing variety and diversity of the human race and (b) recognizes their developmental skills. . . . I think that it is especially important for those of us outside of the mainstream box to actively educate our children about our values and how they are expressed because if we don't . . . mainstream culture will do that education, and I don't believe that's what I want. Personally, I do not believe that "protecting" our children from knowledge is doing them any favors, neither is inundating them with more information than they can handle. Part of being a parent, in my humble opinion, is to provide that balance for our children. I am not afraid of my children knowing that there are other definitions of poly other than mine. I am not afraid of my children knowing about bisexuality, or seeing people of varying or similar genders being affectionate with one another. I am pretty confident in my ability to put things into context for my kids so that they will be able to understand and cope with the diversity of our community. (Margherita, hetero-poly mom)

> Children can understand public and private at an early age. After all, we teach them things like some parts of our bodies are OK to leave bare in public and some are not. This does not mean that we are ashamed of any part of our bodies, but we don't go around without trousers in public. I've had the conversation with our daughter that addresses the shared assumptions of society and how we do work within that construct for many things in order to all live together peacefully. She gets it and she is five years old. It's not too tough to understand. . . . We give her the information she needs, and it's usually quite clear to us when she has reached information overload and it's time for us to quit. . . . We have stressed that families come in all shapes and sizes and as long as they love each other and are kind to each other, it all works. We work actively to promote tolerance and diversity. (Kaye, bi-poly mom with bi woman partner and two hetero male partners)

Many border polyparents spoke as Kaye does above about living on the nepantla or border zone (Anzaldua and Keating, 2002) between "public and private" (Evans, 2003; Rutledge, 2005). This necessitated the very negotiation and construction of what that border site would look like, and how it was to be straddled in ways that would be comfortable and supportive for all members of the family:

> Teach them to differentiate between "private family business" and things that are public domain. That's an issue in any family, poly or not. It isn't an issue of hiding anything, or being dishonest or ashamed, thus giving the impression we feel there is something wrong with what we do. . . . Again, you don't want to impart a sense of secrecy or hiding things. You just have to teach children what is appropriate to discuss with people outside the family and what isn't. (Demetrio, hetero-mono partner of hetero-poly woman who has a bi-poly male partner)

Wright believes the children of border families, such as children from GLBTIQ families, may not understand this form of "situational ethics" (see Fletcher and Wassmer, 1970) and may feel "particularly torn by this strategy's similarity to lying. . . . 'I don't tell, but I don't lie cos they don't ask'" (Wright 2001: 283; see also Garner, 2002). They may devise strategies such as waiting till other children at school get to know them before they tell these children about their families: "after they start to know that I'm not different or I'm not mean or I'm not different just because I have three mums, they realize it's OK to have me as a friend" (Wright, 2001: 283). Wright also talks about the "ongoing tension" these children may experience between their selves within their families, "which feels 'normal' and safe and nurturing," and their experience outside their families, "in which they often feel invisible or vilified. These children must uphold the value of difference and uniqueness in the face of a society that enforces conformity" (2001: 288). These tensions of bordering home and school for children of border polyfamilies are evident in the following mother's account:

> I tried my best to explain to our twelve-year-old daughter about our family. She finally seemed to understand but cried over the fact that her family was so different and the fear of getting made fun of by her peers. I told her I would help her anyway I could, short of pretending to be someone I am not. I reassured her that we wouldn't broadcast our family makeup but we wouldn't lie about it either. Our children reap the rewards of having more adults to love and support them, but I also can't forget that our family also has the potential to cause them stress and pain when it comes to the outside world's views. I think we should take the "if they don't ask, we won't tell them" stance. . . . She has told me that most of her friends think gay and bi people are "gross and nasty." While I am very saddened that her friends are not more accepting, I cannot ignore their attitudes and how they might view our family. It is so tragic that the love our family shares is a possible source of ridicule and embarrassment for her. . . . She is a popular girl and just wants to fit in. I hope as she ages that she will become more of her own person and not try so hard to be like everyone else. (Kathy, bi-poly mom)

Another very important border that families inhabit is the temporal one, the preschool and after-starting-school border (Buxton, 2006a, 2006b, 2007). Preschool children may come from a happy family where polyamory is accepted and "normal." However, after starting school and becoming more aware of the larger world's dominant discourses of family, these children may begin to redefine their family in negative ways or experience confusion:

> My preschool daughters are often confused by TV and movies when they portray situations involving sexual jealousy or marital troubles caused by affairs. Since they have positive examples of polyamory all around them, they cannot grasp the concepts of "jealousy" and hurt caused by "adulterous infidelity." . . . But my eldest daughter, who also used to be like that, is now starting to question how we cannot feel jealousy and hurt, as everything she hears and reads at school, as well as what some of her friends' parents are going through, now tells her we are wrong. So I worry about what will happen to my younger ones in a few years. . . . The hardest part about being poly and having children is explaining to them why society thinks differently than we do, first when they're little and question society and then later when they're at school and they question their family. (Nina, bi-poly mom)

Another transition seems to occur at the post-teen young adult stage, when offspring have gained a certain degree of independence from their family and greater control over how they wish to live their own lives. At this stage, they may reflect back upon their upbringing in multipartnered and/or multisexual families and perhaps come to terms, as in the following example, with living on a new border in regard to how they judge their families: being both and in-between problematic and positive (Trinh, 1991; Buxton, 2006a, 2006b, 2007):

> When the eldest son wanted to move out of the house a couple of years ago, he actually sat us all down (four parents and our girlfriend) and outlined his reasons. In the midst of this conversation he told us that he was angry at us for choosing this lifestyle because he felt that it had been forced upon him and he wasn't consulted. He went on to say that in the formative time when he was discovering his own sexuality, our choices had been difficult and confusing for him, setting up conflict between our reality and the rest of the world. It was a very hard discussion, and these were things that were painful for all of us to hear. However, we heard him out and he said his piece, and then he went on to say that he loved us all and hoped that we would continue to love him. We felt, in hindsight, that his ability to actually have this conversation with us was a testament to our successful parenting. He's home for the summer now and is entirely at ease with the family. (Miguel, hetero-poly dad)

Some mestizaje families not only found themselves on the borders as polyfamilies or multisexual families, but also inhabited cultural borders as multicultural families (Anzaldua, 1987a; Yoshizaki, 1992). Karlson, who describes herself as a "Bisexual–Pagan–Philosophical–Political–Forth-right–Free Spirited–Community Developer" who married a man and had a family, writes,

> Way before I am a parent, I am a daughter of two "Turkish–Christian–Straight–Homophobic–Racist–Completely Intolerant of Anything Different From Them parents." In spite of this I do love them dearly—family values, love and cohe-sion are important to me. . . . These parents of mine live down the road, and can see our house from their front lounge-room window. This limits any extra sexual activity (besides that which I have with my husband) and dating to other venues. (2007: 1)

Karlson describes how she established a bi-parenting group so that she can raise her daughter "to know that her mother and father are not weird or deviant" and to counteract questions such as "Why am I able to call three women my mums and the kids at school only have one or none?" (2007: 3). Thus, bordering cultures, spiritualities, sexualities, and families, Karlson sees herself as being "half in and half out of the closet. . . . I can't hide my ethnicity, or pagan ways. . . . I wish I didn't have to hide any part of my life [from anyone]" (2007: 4).

As well as seeing themselves as cultural/sexual border dwellers like Karlson above, some participants in my research described their whole families as being on the cultural/religious borders of metissage: "We're a polyfamily with diversity; our adults are black from a traditional African American upbringing, white hippie, white Bible background, and me, the old school punk. Our kids range from 100 percent black to 100 percent white" (Onetta, bi-poly mom).

In the following, a father and daughter talk about their "multiple life-worlds" (Cope and Kalantzis, 1995), multiple marginalities, or multiple borders experienced in their nepantla lives as a multiracial polyfamily liv-ing "alternative lifestyles" in communes in Japan and then in Australia, and the strengths and insights such a metissage existence provides (McLaren, 1993):

> *Yuki:*   I think because we had so many people coming in and out of our lives and we always had visitors staying with us, that sort of line [between normal and abnormal family] is pretty blurred, but I guess in sort of early to mid–primary school was the first time I think I really became conscious of how my family was different. . . .
>
> *Tim:*   . . . We were living in Japan. The house was basically bilingual, English and Japanese were spoken equally, openly, and the house was an off-shoot of the [alternative] community. . . . Up to age five, she [Yuki] grew up in basically a house that would sometimes have three or four people

in it, sometimes would have ten or twelve people in it. It was seasonal, rice harvesting, rice planting. So she grew up in many ways with almost like multiple parents. . . .

Yuki: It was fantastic for me. I think I was lucky that in the places that we lived in Japan and in Australia we were children at the right age when there were a lot of parents or a lot of adults that were interested in children and so we had a lot of adult playmates. As well as being half Japanese, which made us completely different to all of the other kids in Australia. So it wasn't unusual for me just to say goodbye to my parents in the morning and go off for a whole day with somebody I'd only just met and become best friends with them. . . . I think it's certainly given me a lot of independence, and it's made it easier to relate to any age group of people. (Yuki, hetero-mono daughter of Tim, hetero-poly dad)

Kaye described her family as "normality in suburbia in the guise of what others would construct as abnormality," being a multicultural, multisexual, multigenerational "family tribe":

My family is racially diverse, which also became interesting at school upon occasion. One of my partners is Japanese and American and one of my partners is English, and my sons, one is white and one is black [foster son]. It's never been an issue within the family. It has brought some interesting questions from other people, and it ranges from "No way, you can't be brothers" to "Oh, wow, look, he has your eyes." They'll either assume that it can't possibly be correct and then they'll operate out of that base or they'll assume that they should see some connection there and they'll make it happen. (Kaye, bi-poly mom with bi woman and two hetero male partners)

The either/or thinking described above as a reaction to Kaye's family from outsiders in trying to draw blood links between all members also occurs within school and community multicultural events, where the blurring and intermixtures beyond binary cultural boundaries is not considered (Root, 1992). Interestingly, her border-dwelling sons challenge this externally prescriptive dichotomous framing of cultural identity, as their membership in a multisexual, multicultural, polyamorous family has provided them with a lived knowledge of mestizaje realities (Anzaldua, 1987a; Root, 1992; Lugones, 1994; Audinet, 2004):

They do these things [hold parent events] by racial profiling and they assume that the race of the child is going to mirror the race of the parents. You know, they do their multicultural crap, and what multicultural means is everyone but white, interestingly enough. So Benji and Nathan and a bunch of their friends were walking into the football stands [to attend a school multicultural event] and there were these signs, Koreans here and Japanese here and black there, so Benji says, "Well, [as a white boy] where am I supposed to go?" And it was a complete reversal of the whole civil rights situation, and the person there I think completely unconsciously said, "Oh, you can sit up in the back." And then his friend says, "Well, where am I supposed to sit? I'm half Korean and half black." So, yeah, it was completely ridiculous, and of course they made a huge scene and were wildly unpopular with the organizers. But they did make the scene, yeah, they didn't go quietly by. (Kaye, bi-poly mom with bi woman and two hetero male partners)

Thus, school and community events may establish rigid boundaries within which all members of a mestizaje family cannot situate themselves (Anzaldua, 1987a; Trinh, 1990).What is also significant in the following is how Kaye's sons resisted and subverted binary normative constructions of gender and sexuality within the security of a mestizaje family. This appeared to give them the confidence and agency to take their resistances, disruptions, and subversions to school. Thus, having access to "other" knowledges and ways of being, and participating in the interrogation of Central constructions of culture, sexuality, gender, and family may place children of polyfamilies permanently on the borders of society with their "edge identities" (Bersten, 2008; see also hooks, 1990, 1999):

While my boys were very social and had tons of friends, they were also very, very alternative. They both worked with the local Safer Sex teen peer counseling group, and the older one was in a punk rock band, while the younger one was and still is a drag queen. So you can imagine my house, in the front room, Benji and three bandmates with some girls and seventies punk on the CD player just hanging out—and in the back bedroom and bathroom, Nate with four other young men who are half dressed with mini-skirts and bras on, mostly made up, but wigs not on yet, for a lip-sync contest, with Patti LaBelle on the CD player. (Kaye, bi-poly mom with bi woman and two hetero male partners)

As well as interrogating normative societal constructions of gender and sexuality, some parents find that by growing up in a polyfamily and being part of polycommunities on societal margins, their children will also have difficulty accepting monogamy as the only and correct way of having relationships:

We handled the monogamy questions the same way we've handled everything where our personal philosophies clash with the dominant culture: "At school they teach you this and that, but we think/do/believe this and that is also right/viable/moral/honorable/wiser." Our fourteen-year-old concluded that poly is a saner and healthier choice than monogamy is—she watches her friends the same age go through their two-week-long serial-monogamy soap operas (the average teen "relationship" seems to have a life cycle no longer than that), and shakes her head over the folly of it all. She enjoys her guy friends far too much to limit herself to just seeing one of them at a time, not sexually, though—she decided on her own against becoming sexually active before, at least, the end of her middle years of high school, and she may not then. (Steve, bi-poly dad)

Thus, poly border dwelling means the child is a stranger/foreigner "questioning the unquestioned and unquestionable" (Schutz, 1944; Bauman, 1990; Kristeva, 1991) of the Center. It requires children to make decisions about how they will define and construct their sexual and intimate relationships with peers within the normative social space of a school, as well as deal with the realization that they will most likely experience some degree of marginalization and harassment. It also may lead to self-interrogation and problematization for parents who are border dwellers between a parental philosophy of raising their children with a broader understanding of sexuality, family, and relationships, and a parental protective concern that their children will experience ostracism and stigmatization because of this philosophy:

> My nine-year-old announced to me that she's poly. This came during a discussion about how she wants her toy horse to marry her friend's toy pig, but the pig already had a spouse, I believe it was a toy puppy, and her friend didn't understand that people could marry more than one person and anyway, "I'm *poly*," she says. . . . I suggested to her that just because she lives in a polyfamily doesn't mean that she's necessarily a poly person herself and that that was okay too. . . . "Nope," she said. "I'm poly." "That's a mighty strong statement to be making," I said. "Monogamous culture, that being the dominant paradigm and all, it's not really accepting of polyamory in general. You've got to be pretty firm in your convictions to be openly out about stuff like this and really believe that it's the best thing for you, because you'll get flak." "Still poly," she insisted. "My best friend knows I'm poly and she doesn't mind." . . . So I wonder: are we doing her a favor here? I mean, sure, she's being raised in an openly polyfamily and a large tribe of folks who are all very much on the same line. It's what she sees, it's what she's having modeled—so it makes sense. But I feel like she's a little young to be identifying that way. And, I worry that she will discover herself not accepted by people—and trust me, this kid is already being bullied mercilessly by the dominant cliques in her school. She does not need one more glaring difference and huge shiny thing above her head that reads "GIVE ME A HARD TIME!" Then again, I was thirteen when I had my first boyfriend and *that* was a triad, and I've identified as nonmonogamous in that sense since I was old enough to like boys. The whole "I am a polyamorous person" thing came about after years of struggle and angst, and it's not been easy, so it's a little strange to me to be seeing my kid just . . . be there in her head. (Renee, hetero-poly mom with two bi-poly partners)

Many parents concluded that they needed to compensate for the lack of resources and knowledge about family and relationships diversity at school, indeed challenge the dichotomous simplistic teaching of the school, by providing these perspectives and opportunities at home or in polycommunities:

> We've decided that a good way to answer questions, bring ideas and discussion out in the open with our children, who are preteen and young teen, is to have a family reading time. We read any poly books like *Stranger in a Strange Land* and try to watch anything that's poly on video. While we have to be careful about any violence or pornography, we know that we're going to have to give our children words and discussion time, while providing a type of bonding and activity that they enjoy, because this is so missing from school. (Rina, hetero-poly mom in hetero group of two men and two women)

In the following conversation between Yuki and her father, Tim, the absences of polyfamilies at school are discussed as well as what schools could provide. Both agree that it was fortunate that the home and home community environment provided opportunities for learning as a form of collective agency (Sewell, 1992) that allowed a border perspective to be made available:

> Yuki: If it was in the media and was sort of more discussed at school, it would've been easier for us to sort of understand the situation. As it is now, we've just had to sort of learn through experience, and it takes time to become comfortable with a situation and to understand it, whereas if it was more openly discussed and shown to you, it would be easier to say, "Okay, so that's what he [Dad] does." You know this is sort of the scope of what a life is like in this situation, whereas a sort of a normal family is spelled out everywhere. And in every TV show it is presented.
>
> Tim: . . . As a parent, what I would find most useful in the schools, yes, a life skills class that clearly gives the kids a sociology, the psychology and the art of relationship and living and how multivaried it is and how important it is to understand that most of the stuff that's put across from the television has been very carefully crafted to extract the maximum amount of money out of people . . . (Yuki, hetero-mono daughter of Tim, hetero-poly dad)

Indeed, Yuki could claim the vantage point of critiquing the Center from the Margins (hooks, 1990; Trinh, 1990), or as a stranger/foreigner "questioning the unquestioned and unquestionable" (Schutz, 1944; Bauman, 1990; Kristeva, 1991). She was in a monogamous long-term heterosexual relationship herself, but this was a consciously arrived at choice, knowing that she could choose otherwise (Davies, 1991; Davis, 1991; Chambers, 1994). Her partner and his family were aware of her family's polyamory history. In the following, Yuki is thankful that she was raised with parents who, together with learning critical literacy skills at school, taught her how to deconstruct normative romance narratives and scripts:

Yuki: I did a subject on Mills and Boons novels, and that was very fascinating to learn how constructed they are. I mean, there's a formula, and to see how addicted some people can be to that formula. . . . I think having parents that are very self-analytical, and have always discussed this sort of stuff [really helped]. . . . So many other people that I've met have never, ever considered any of these things.

Tim: I look back on all of that [raising his children to deconstruct normative relationship scripts] and I think thank God I did all of that stuff. Thank God I was in a situation where I was forced to look at that stuff. How awful it must be for some families that never do the self-discovery, they never come to the self-awareness and the self-actualization that I've come to as a result of doing that. And I just look at it and think, God, why can't schools see that by embracing this stuff, by being clever and clear about this stuff, that they could make such an incredible reputation for themselves as a school. Why can't they see the advantages of this? . . . They're actually going to get their kids to reach out into the families and draw the families into a situation where they can start looking at themselves more rationally. (Yuki, hetero-mono daughter of Tim, hetero-poly dad)

In the above, Tim refers to another facet of raising border-dwelling children who can then make their nepantla locations a site of agency and change, particularly at school. If the school encourages, validates, and affirms the kinds of insights and perspectives these children bring with them, these children can be the bridges between polyamorous homes and broader communities for the betterment of all (Moore and Norris, 2005). The role polyfamilies can play in schools as polluters will be explored in the next section.

"IT'S LIKE WE MIGHT CONTAMINATE THE SCHOOL WITH SOME POLYVIRUS": POLYAMORY AS POLLUTING

For fourteen years, Catherine has been what she labels, with a smile, the "illegal wife" of Paul. For most of those fourteen years, Paul lived with his "legal wife" in order to coparent but saw Catherine one day on weekends and three nights a week. This suited them fine and the arrangements were always open to negotiation. About three years ago, Paul began to want his own home, as he had never lived alone. He purchased a house geographically located equally distant from Lucy and Catherine. His children are able to stay with him as well as at their mother's and Catherine's and attend school. As Catherine explains, "This suits Lucy really well because she now has the freedom to pursue the weird working hours of her career and have her own time. It also suits me, as I've never wanted to share my home with a lover and I enjoy the freedom of visiting Paul. You know,

I've never wanted to be a full-time mother, but I'm loving being a part-time second mother to the children."

Catherine feels the relationship has worked for years because the various needs of the three seem to mesh well. All three are willing to negotiate issues and work out arrangements such as time, finances, child-rearing and career demands, both regularly and with flexibility. "The hardest parts of the relationship have been the lack of understanding by family and friends, but we're adults, we can handle that. But it's really hard when the schools treat our kids as if we might contaminate the school with some kind of polyvirus. Meanwhile, some kids at that school come from families where drug addictions, domestic violence, and child abuse are rife but they're treated as "normal" while our kids come under extra scrutiny from student welfare and the counselor because of our setup. Our kids have been asked not to talk about their family in case other kids "get ideas" or other parents take their kids out of a school that has deviant families like ours there. Our kids have been asked questions about what they see going on at home. As if we have sex in front of the kids, or don't do what other families do: pay bills, check homework, go to work, clean the toilet, prepare costumes for school events, buy raffle tickets for school fundraisers. We're not aliens from some other planet launching a major invasion and contamination of earth families! We're just part of the diversity of families on earth!

—from my research notes and interview with Catherine

Some polyfamilies decide that rather than pass as monogamous or negotiate border-dwelling positions between two worlds, they will be poly pollutants in their children's schools:

> We always attend the Parent's Night at the beginning of the school year and explain to the teachers that we are a family and that we all live together. We let them know that any one of us can be responsible for the kids and that any one of us may be contacting them for P/T conferences and so forth. One teacher said she'd had a family like ours the year before. She didn't seem at all fussed by it. (Onetta, bi-poly mom)

> We get the "Who is the mom?" or "Whose daughter is she?" question a lot—to which we normally answer "We are" or "Ours" and leave it at that. (Cate, bi-poly mom)

These families resisted panopticonic fears and policing, deliberately polluting the normative family discursive frameworks within which schools operate:

> I sometimes suspect that we in multiple households or other poly lifestyles sometimes imagine more grief for ourselves than we need to. Sure we need to be cautious, but unless we have some reason to be on guard, we should be-

have toward others and talk to them as if our lifestyle were a perfectly normal, obvious thing—which of course it is; but my point is that if we act as if it's normal, that'll hasten the day when mainstream society really does embrace multiple households and other forms of polyamory as normal, because if anyone thinks what we do is wrong, our acting as if it's normal will put them on the defensive; conversely, the longer we are selective of who we're out to, or tell half-truths and sound defensive ourselves, the longer the mainstream will feel that we have something to hide, something to be guilty about. It has worked for gays and lesbians; it works for us polys too. (Miguel, hetero-poly dad)

All our kids' friends know about our family. They come over on a regular basis, hang out, spend the night. The kids tell their friends that we all love each other and that has been it. In our experience, kids, teens especially, are much more open and accepting. They grow up on *Will and Grace*, *Degrassi High*, etc., which prepare them for things that their own parents or schools might not teach. When kids have problems, need help with homework, or just want to eat chips and watch TV, they come to our house. It makes for a loud, fun house. (Steve, bi-poly dad)

Pollutant polyfamilies are forging new relationships with schools. By presenting their relationships as legitimate and worthy of official record, polyfamilies not only claim public space but compel institutions to adapt to new and expanding definitions of family:

Earlier this spring, for the second time, a child of ours graduated from high school, with two flowers for the moms and two dads to hug. . . . It was a culmination of the united front we had represented to the school over the years. The school conferences we all attended as a family were something to see: four adults, all cramming into the guidance office, all intent on getting the best education for our son. . . . When we first started going to school functions as a whole family, they did not know what to make of us. Most of the dealings they had with divorced and remarried parents were not as harmonious as our situation. But over time, they became used to having all of us show up for school conferences, concerts, sporting events and awards ceremonies, sitting together as one family. Cheering on our kids as they played soccer was a particular favorite. . . . At one time we had a 6, 7, 9, 11 and 13 year old all playing for the same team. Almost a whole team with just our clan. (C., 1997–1998: 22)

Our daughter just entered preschool. The director of the school asked us to write a letter to them to explain our family life just so that there would be no confusion about the variety of last names and the number of people that could (a) pick her up, (b) would be attending conferences, and (c) could make decisions for her. . . . I explained that the three adults in her life are committed to each other and to the well-being of our children, that it was important to us that as her teachers, they were aware of her family life in order to better understand her. We said we were absolutely comfortable answering any questions that the teachers might have. I also said that one of the things that this relationship style has given to all three of us is excellent communication skills. We are consistent and good at keeping each other informed of decisions that we have made regarding the children. Okay, so what I got in return was a wonderful phone call from the teacher who said after her first day, "What a delightful little girl!" She then said that "it is obvious from her confidence that she is very loved. Thank you for sharing about your family, I'm hoping that the extra adult means that you will be available to volunteer in the classroom?" (Margherita, hetero-poly mom)

Some parents defied the power of panopticonic surveillance, refusing to comply and self-police in reaction to some possible external policing. Indeed, polyparents like Kaye below deliberately and confidently drew attention to themselves, "standing underneath the light," while simultaneously turning the discomfiting gaze back onto those who were questioning the polyfamily (Wood, 1934; Schutz, 1944; Douglas, 1966) and challenging them as to why they are doing the questioning in the first place and as to what they actually can handle knowing:

The way in which we go about being open is, "This is who we are and you don't have to know any more than what you want to know, but this is what you have to know here. . . . I don't need to prove to you that my family is as good as yours. I already know that." And so that confidence in who you are and how you behave tends to put people a little off guard in the sense that even if they think there's something weird about you, they don't necessarily feel comfortable saying that they think there's something weird about you, because clearly you don't think there's anything weird about you. You know, the way that you're presenting yourself is perfectly happy, confident, and normal. . . . There's just something about you that says, "I am not a victim. Do not mess with me. It's not worth your effort." . . . And I have been known to say to people, when they've asked me a question, "Are you really sure you want to know that? I'll tell you. I don't have an issue, but make sure you want to know what you're asking." . . . I have never felt at any risk of legal action. I strongly believe that this is the best argument for being out and proud of being poly. It's like standing underneath the light in the parking lot. You are less likely to get attacked. (Kaye, bi-poly mom with bi female and two hetero male partners)

Kaye also points to how polyfamilies can use the shifting discourses of family diversity in schools and subvert/pollute the school's increasing awareness of the importance of establishing strong links with the home in order to foster a more effective education of the child:

The school's primary outlook was that if they could engage the family of a child, then they had a hope of educating that child. . . . They understood that they were dealing with a lot of economically disadvantaged children and that their families were not going to look like mum and dad and two kids and a dog. That however they managed to come together as a family, if it worked, it was a good thing. So, that general attitude was a huge way in [for us as a polyfamily]. . . . If there is a family that's engaged, that's the important thing. (Kaye, bi-poly mom with bi female and two hetero male partners)

A strategic form of pollution discussed by many polyparents was inserting oneself or "leaking viscously" (Zerubavel, 1991) into the school community as a proactive parent undertaking what "good" normative parents do. This gaining of validation, or "insurance policy," appeared to prevent any legal action or investigation being undertaken by the school and child welfare systems:

> In our community we are the parents who regularly volunteer at the children's preschool and school. . . . We are known in a variety of volunteer situations, and we have made an effort to be good neighbors. The point? Well, if anyone decided to pursue us legally, we would not only have a good standing legally, we would be able to provide numerous credible affidavits as to our parenting ability, accountability, etc. . . . I consider that an essential part of our "insurance policy." (Margherita, hetero-poly mom)

Unlike some parents who tried to pass as nonpoly in order to avoid legal attention, some pollutant polyparents were prepared to take legal action themselves if their children were harassed at school:

> I would have to say that if my kid is being persecuted on a daily basis, I'm going to war. Especially if the battle ground is a public school that my tax dollars are paying for. My kid has to go to school, and the school has an obligation to sustain an environment where learning can occur. If that isn't happening, the school is not doing its job and is wasting my tax dollars, not to mention the fact that it's making my child unhappy. . . . Starting a paper trail of documentation on the school and getting a lawyer involved can really drive change. Say your kids get assaulted at school for being gay or poly or fat or whatever. He/she knows who did it and reports it to the teacher, and then the administration. If they don't act and do something, if it happens again or is even threatened, you can legally call it a conspiracy. Failure to act makes them part of a cover-up. Big time lawsuit. And as much as I hate the system, that is how change is driven. It's called working the system. I don't have to like it, but it does work. (Demetrio, hetero-mono partner of hetero-poly woman with bi-poly partner)

Thus, while some parents were prepared to take legal action to address any discrimination they and their children might experience for being a polluting deviant minority in the school's range of family structures, others became "engaged" and "committed, participating" parents in ways that would make others in the community get to know them and thus reduce discrimination based on fear or ignorance, an "insurance policy," as Margherita said in the earlier quote. This kind of parenting is itself considered a positive minority form of parenting in a society where parents have decreasing time and decreasing inclination to volunteer their services to schools. This increasing disengagement of parents from schools is occurring at a time when schools are being told by educational researchers that they need to become "communities of commitment" if they wish to improve the learning and well-being of their students (Ancess, 2003). Of course, if we recall the way that many polyparents considered having multiple adults to share in the raising, resourcing, and education of children to be extremely advantageous, it stands to reason that there would be more adults, resources, and time available to participate in a school community:

> The things that helped us enormously are primarily that we are very engaged in our daughter's educational process. We also volunteered last year as parents for field trips, lent the teacher books and other random teaching materials for particular segments, and we ran the recycling program last year. The new director has asked us to run it again this year. We talk regularly to Ruth's teachers and get to know the teaching assistants and the after-care providers. . . . We found that being committed, participating parents often overrides other things. There are not many of us involved parents left. . . . One of my husbands has offered to work on the yearbook committee, as he is a fine amateur photographer. My wife and I have offered to work in the gardening program, and my wife has offered to be part of the regular clerical support team. The other husband handles most of the afterschool activities. (Kaye, bi-poly mom with bi female and two hetero male partners)

Proactive polyparents also spoke of a "plurality of resistances" (Foucault, 1978) including subversive strategies of infiltration such as getting into positions of parent power and decision making in the school and/or establishing solid working relationships and friendships with those in power in the school. These strategies consolidated their security, provided access to policy making, community thinking, and action, as well as made it possible to forge strong trusting bonds with other "deviant" minority persons in the school community:

> I was the president of our school PTA. I was in charge of fundraising and very active at the school. In fact, later one teacher even came out to me about being a lesbian, which not many of the staff knew. (Felicia, bi-poly mom)

> Having one or more parents volunteering in the classroom on a weekly basis or at school events is a good way to keep you in the loop. The more you help out, the more "voice" you have in what goes on. The more the PTA parents, staff, and other folks recognize your face and know you from your work around the school, the more pull you get and the more you hear about problems the school might be having with resources, with other families, with you. Office ladies are prone to cut you a little more slack if you're one of the helpful moms

or dads. Principals work with you a little more smoothly. The teachers are grateful and glad for any help you can offer. (Renee, hetero-poly mom with two bi-poly partners)

As Wright states in relation to children from GLBTIQ families, parents can work toward making the school more inclusive through their presence and advocacy in relation to the school curriculum and school community: "It is crucial that our children see themselves and their parents reflected positively in a school setting. This inclusiveness will ease the fears born of erasure" (2001: 289). The following mother provides an example of encouraging her children to interrogate the "taken-for-grantedness" framework of families (Schutz, 1944) that schools may be operating within:

The twins were asked to draw a picture of their family before parent-teacher night. We noticed that they had drawn just the two parents and three girls. When we asked them about it, they said that the teacher had told them that Peter was not part of the family. We told them that it is up to us, the members of the family, to decide who is part of our family, and we say Peter is family. . . . We said that if anyone ever tells them that Peter is not part of the family to tell that person to phone Mummy or Daddy. The model of "family" which is assumed is something to be addressed before children of nontraditional parents can feel safe and included at school. (Joanna, bi-poly mom with two bi-poly male partners)

The following parents, part of a triad with another woman, discuss particular qualities they believe a school and teachers need to have, and that they have found in their children's school, in order for polyfamilies to feel able to come out:

Shane: They're a fairly progressive school. They work more on the community atmosphere of a school. It's a very small school. . . . The teachers are friendly. Welcoming.

Nadia: Oh, she's [the teacher's] got a lot of experience of different families and ways of thinking. . . . I think a lot of it is nonverbal, too, their stance, whether they appear to be listening to you or not. . . . I think it has to do with the suburb, too. There are a great many different family structures here.

Shane: I reckon it would be good if schools had some sort of program that someone went in and gave them a talk about different family structures. . . . Again it comes back to that awareness. They need someone down there in the system that's changing the system. (Shane and Nadia, hetero-poly parents)

Many parents called for more resources on family diversity in schools, including the inclusion of popular cultural texts such as film and television programs. I have discussed some of the available texts earlier in this book such as the movie *French Twist.* A polyparent wrote the following as part of her review of the movie in the magazine *Loving More:*

> To most people, this movie will be considered a complete fantasy. To my lovers and I, it was totally real. The three major characters looked and acted like people we have known and loved. The arguments of the couple were not unlike our own. . . . It's wonderfully empowering to see the beauty of poly love on the big screen. (Bonobo, 1996: 34)

HBO's *Big Love*, albeit set within a Mormon religious context, explores the positives and challenges of polygamy, particularly in relation to external stigmatization, children's mixed responses to polyparents, how children handle peer-group curiosity at school, and the internal differences within Mormon polygamy, ranging from cultlike rural fundamentalism to urban, modern socioeconomic settings. It would be very useful to have such texts about Muslim and African polygamous families, which show the range of ways these relationships are lived in both positive and problematic ways. This is particularly needed given the number of children in Australian, American, and British schools who come from polygamous African and/or Muslim families that often conceal or edit the structure of their families for external systems and organizations. Likewise, an increasing number of articles in magazines (see Newitz, 2006, for example), documentaries, and talk show appearances are elements of mainstream popular culture and media that can be utilized in the classroom to give young people opportunities to initiate and facilitate discussions and further projects:

> It's important for it [polyamory] to be part of a young person's education in the sense of saying you need to be able to look at all these different options and you need to be able to accept people who have these lifestyles. . . . I think there's always a place in school for books about polyamory. . . . One thing which is very, very interesting is the number of films that have come out recently with very strong and positive poly content in them. One of the two notable ones, unfortunately they all have criminals as heroes, but *Ordinary Decent Criminal* has got a poly relationship of a guy who just has this very matter-of-fact, very loving relationship with two sisters who live in separate places. . . . There's another one called *Bandits,* which stars Bruce Willis and Cate Blanchet and Billy Bob Thornton, and there is a very strongly written polyamorous element in that film. . . . In fact it ends up with a conclusion which says that it doesn't have to be a choice between this man or that man, she can have both men, and that's okay. . . . I think the fact that it's [polyamory] appearing in films makes me think that it's on the agenda for young people. . . . And novels, I think for kids are really good and school counselors who understand those issues and who are well trained and well understand sexuality both in adolescents and in adults including polyamory would be really helpful so that

they [students] can have informed responses to some of these issues when they come up. (Peter, hetero-poly dad with bi-poly and hetero-mono partners)

As Peter points out above, it is important to have representations of poly-amory, particularly polyamorous parents and families, which are positive and not linked to crime or pathology as discussed previously in relation to *Dallas Doll*. Nor should film scripts resolve the dilemma of multiple loves through death, thereby using what I call the "poly potential" as a romantic narrative device with which to "up" the drama/trauma quotient and elicit more heart-rending and gut-wrenching responses from the audience. This occurs toward the end of *Pearl Harbor*, *Marie-Jo and Her Two Loves*, and *2012*.

In *Pearl Harbor*, two Air Force pilots, Rafe and Danny, who have been the best of friends since childhood, find themselves in love with the same woman after Rafe, who was presumed dead, returns to Hawaii. After a fight in a bar, the two wake up the next morning, which happens to be the morning of the bombing of Pearl Harbor, and discuss the situation. Danny tells Rafe that he's the only family he has, and that he knows there has to be a way to "work things out." The perfect plot device that prevents us see-ing how the three of them will work out their polyfamily is, of course, the Japanese air raid. Before they leave to fight, Evelyn promises Danny she will be true to him and then tells Rafe she will wait for Danny as she is pregnant by him. However, not a sunset will go by in her life that she will not be thinking of Rafe, she says. Unbeknownst to Danny is the fact that Evelyn is pregnant by him. The convenient "resolution" comes in the form of Danny's death, and absolution comes in the form of Rafe raising Danny's son as his own.

Death also provides an unsatisfactory resolution in the French film *Marie-Jo and Her Two Loves*. Raw and real in its representation of a woman in love with her husband and a lover, the compromises, pains, and plea-sures each undertakes in order to love and be loved are explored. It also depicts the anger and ostracism Marie-Jo experiences from her teenage daughter, as does her husband, Daniel, for even contemplating sharing her mother. The themes of what is choice and what choices do people have in such situations are presented. Her daughter asks that Marie-Jo choose be-tween her lover and her daughter. Her husband tries to share Marie-Jo and decides he can't, so she will have to choose between them. Marie-Jo travels between her marital home and her lover's home, being unable to choose where to reside. Choosing not to choose remains the impossible option for all. Finally, soon after Marie-Jo has chastised herself for contemplating how much easier the "choice" would be if her husband died, we see her husband taking her out on a boat that he has repaired and named after her. He hits his head and falls overboard. She dives in to save him. They both drown and are found washed up on the shore with their fingers entwined.

The film *2012* is an end-of-the-world disaster movie that follows an ensemble of characters who narrowly escape multiple catastrophes and the eventual flooding of the planet due to a tsunami. They make their way to a modern-day Noah's Ark in the Himalayas to wait for the waters to recede before they embark on the task of beginning a brand-new world. But it seems polyfamilies are not part of the plan for the new world, just as the animals supposedly entered the biblical Noah's Ark two-by-two in the making of the old couple-family world. The characters that have the "poly potential" are Jackson, his ex-wife Kate, their two children, and her new boyfriend Gordon who the children dearly love as much as their Dad. By the movie's final scenes, the two men have gained an understanding, affection, and appreciation of each other through the various near-deaths they have saved each other, their children, and Kate from. In turn, Kate's love for her ex-husband has been rekindled while her love for her new partner hasn't wavered. The two men are even scripted a short conversation about this situation, particularly in relation to how they both treasure their relationship with the children, before the boyfriend is conveniently killed, thereby reinstating a nuclear couple family alongside all the other couple-families on the Ark.

Another film involving death as a plot contrivance is the dark comedy *Eulogy*. A dysfunctional family gathers to bury the family patriarch, a supposed traveling salesman who is constructed as negligent, narcissistic, and chaotic in traumatic, endearing, and humorous ways. It is at the screening of his video as part of the reading of his will that he reveals his secret polyamory—his "three full lives"—and the existence of two other families, which has left him in financial debt. It becomes the granddaughter's task to find these families and deliver the news of his death. Before setting off to do so, she is also given the task of delivering the eulogy at his offbeat cremation and begins to cynically describe him as certainly a "family man" even when he wasn't always around. Such quips elicit laughter until her grandmother, who had previously wanted to end her life and had erupted in anger at the video-screening, intervenes, saying that although he wasn't the man they all thought he was, he is the reason for their being together as a family, and that he always made her laugh. This is the first time in the film that a look of peace, resolution, and love appears on her face. What is also poignant about this film is that most of the characters are living some form of self-deception or deception of others, and so the patriarch is positioned within these human flaws. Again, as Hart (2005) theorizes, what may be comedic or "trash" may simultaneously be the vehicle for dominant cultural values and constructions to be explored and interrogated.

Some films have ventured beyond the death-as-resolution device, or at least depict polyparents as "good parents," regardless of whatever other situations they may be in. For example, in *Ordinary Decent Criminal*, the thief Michael is depicted as a devoted father in various scenes: motorcycling to the homes of his two very confident, independent, and sassy partners, the sisters Lisa and Catherine, to read his children bedtime stories before tucking them in; helping organize a lavish Holy Communion party for one of his daughters; picking them up from school and other events, even as the police follow him; and playing and chatting with his children, indeed imparting traditional values about loyalty, love, and family to his children. Interestingly, there is a death in this film. Michael stages his own death to escape the police. At the very traditional Catholic pseudo-funeral, both partners and all the children (the actual number is difficult to determine but in good Catholic breeding tradition, there appear to be at least six!) are there in dignified, albeit staged, mourning.

Films like *Splendor*, *French Twist*, and *December Bride* incorporate pregnancy and having babies in a polyfamily structure, with the fathers having to grow and adjust to responsible poly relations and polyparenting while the women are already comfortably and confidently in that space. Indeed, *December Bride*, set in rural Ireland at the turn of the twentieth century, follows the relationship between a woman and two brothers into the young adulthood of their two children. Throughout the years, she has defied religious authority by refusing to marry one of the brothers in order to legitimate her children in the eyes of the Catholic Church by giving them a surname. However, when her own daughter wants to marry in the Church and finds she cannot unless she has "a father," her mother agrees to marry the older brother. Nevertheless, it is significant that the relationship between mother and daughter is constructed as strong and loving, and the resignation to marry is presented as an example of the older generation needing to sometimes relinquish its own ideals and values in order to serve the differing needs and ideals of the younger generation. Also of significance is the presence of the younger brother/partner at the wedding: he stands next to her in the position traditionally assumed by a maid of honor. Thereby, even as she undergoes the Catholic marriage ritual with one partner, she is standing between both partners.

A final film of note in its efforts to portray polyamory is from Brazil and entitled *Me You Them*. Based on the true story of a woman with three male partners and four children, it explores the economic hardships in a drought-ridden rural area that require the whole family to work together in order to survive. What is particularly powerful about this film is its stripping away of any Hollywood glamorization, sensationalism, and airbrushing of these characters and their relationships. The film is raw, real, and multidimensional in its presentation of complexity, love, sensuality, and negotiation.

Thus, as I have shown above and in previous chapters, we are beginning to see filmic and television representations of polyamory, albeit most of them using death, devastation, and dark humor, rather than positively presenting polyamory for polyparents and their children. What we also require are novels for young adults that explore living in a polyfamily, as I have attempted to do in my novel, *Love You Two*:

> I take a deep breath, feel like I'm going to faint. But the words that could follow, that I have scripted and rehearsed all morning, that I deliberately came here with my best friends to declare, . . . just can't get said: "My Dad knows they're more than friends. He loves her. So does Nathan. And my Mum loves them both." (Pina in Pallotta-Chiarolli, 2008: 285)

Pina is a sixteen-year-old protagonist in my novel who discovers her mother is in a polyamorous relationship with her father and a "family friend," Nathan. One of the many dilemmas that arise is what to tell her school friends and teachers. The novel explores her emotional and physical journeys as she comes to understand her polyamorous family, as well as the various permutations of love, family, and sexuality in the worlds around her. As Lambert (2009) writes in her review,

> While in Melbourne, Pina meets many friends of Zi Don whose lives have taken non-traditional paths. And she bonds with a bi-racial boy who is Italian-Aboriginal and a boy who has a gay grandfather. As her horizons expand and she gets a taste of what it could be like to fall in love with two people at once, she begins to forgive her parents.
>
> *Love You Two* tackles polyamory, bisexuality, interracial relationships, AIDS, late-in-life same-sex couples and their blended families, gay grandparents, teen sexuality issues and Italian immigrant culture and its impact on three generations of an Italian-Australian family.

Two other recent teen/young adult novels have also touched upon polyamory in young people. Prodan's (2008) *The Suicide Year* has the bisexual girl protagonist getting sexually aroused when she finds herself in the middle of a three-way kiss as her best friend Eric and boy crush Sean begin to hook up. Later, she fantasizes about living in a cabin in the wilderness away from the "world . . . the way we wanted to, our own little family" with Eric and Sean, and the girl she has a huge crush on, Amanda (2008: 135).

The second book, *A Queer Circle of Friends* (Lees, 2006) is a sequel to *Fool for Love*, (Lees, 2005) that continues to explore the relationship, families, schooling, and social worlds of two eighteen-year-olds, intersexed Jami and self-identified "genderqueer" Carys. In the sequel, Jami and Carys have set up their own apartment and are pursuing their post–high school studies, creative ambitions, and queer activism. Carys finds herself kissing transgender Tam, experiences guilt and confusion, although also acknowledging that it felt so "natural" to "hold hir and kiss hir" (2006: 34). She rushes home to tell Jami and through conversation and negotiation, realizes that despite internalized mononormative thinking, Tam does not pose a threat to their relationship, and indeed, Jami is interested in developing a relationship with her too.

Through further conversation, the three characters, who are already between, beyond, and on the borders of gender and sexual binaries, decide to meet on the relationship borders and construct a polyamorous relationship based on honesty. Jami comments on how because they don't fit any gender or sexuality boxes and are "outlaws" who aren't allowed to have any legal relationships anyway, they will do whatever they feel like doing.

Throughout the book, and as the plot around the death of a friend is developed, their polyrelationship is a secure and sexually and emotionally satisfying given, which occasionally requires affirmation between themselves as well as explanation to friends, families, and others, with a range of responses. Two things in particular highlight Lees's pioneering portrayal of an unproblematic polyrelationship for a young adult and teenage readership: first, the book's cover depicts the three of them happily and comfortably walking down a street touching each other, while a male/female pair who appear to be aloof with each other are united in their looks of doubt, fear, and anger at the threesome. Second, the sexual relationship between the three is described as negotiated and pleasurable.

Two children's picture books that can be used to introduce and discuss polyfamiles are *Six-Dinner Sid* (Moore, 1991) and *Else-Marie and Her Seven Little Daddies* (Lindenbaum, 1991). "Six-Dinner Sid" could easily be defined as a polyamorous cat that lives on Aristotle Street, where the residents do not talk to one another. Thus, a polycat finds himself living his "polyness" in secret, as it's simple for him to make six different people think he belongs only to them. He works hard for his suppers, with six different names and six types of behavior. But when a cough precipitates six visits to the animal hospital by the six different owners, he is found out by the vet. His owners agree to make sure he receives only one meal a day, perhaps symbolic of imposing a monogamist lifestyle on him, but since Sid is a six-dinner cat, he moves to Pythagoras Place, where the neighbors do talk to one another about him and don't mind sharing their dinners with him. Moore's large, colored-pencil illustrations portray the six different households and individualized characters in the multiethnic neighborhood where Sid lives, as well as the different wonderful lives Sid has in those households and the joy he brings to all those households.

Lindenbaum's (1991) book is about Else-Marie's family, which comprises one normal-size mother and seven tiny, identical daddies who, apart from their size, behave like daddies everywhere, and whom she loves. They do all the regular things associated with fathers: go to work, come home on the bus, eat supper, and read the paper. Indeed, their life is so normal that Else-Marie does not in the least regard her situation as peculiar. However, when her mother announces that she has to work overtime and that Else-Marie's daddies will pick her up at playgroup, thereby "outing" her family's structure and her fathers' stature, the child begins to worry that her playmates may find it strange that she has several little daddies instead of one big one. Although the girl spends an anxious day imagining all the dreadful things that could happen when her school friends discover how unusual her family is, her fears prove ungrounded. Her daddies are a big hit as they show the students and teacher their skills in bird-watching and imitating birdcalls, and their expertise in making birdhouses. The book ends with Else-Marie's relief at the end of the day when, after her mother comes home from work and they eat the dinner her daddies cook, they all curl up in her mom's lap to look at their family photo album and Else-Marie declares she wouldn't trade her seven little daddies. Lindenbaum's muted watercolors are filled with amusing details, such as a wedding picture on the living room wall with the bride towering over her seven diminutive grooms.

Some polyparents in my research constructed their own resources, or reinscribed/extended the resources they have, to compensate for the enormous deficits within the school system:

> Every child gets their models for how families look from the stories that they read, and it has been an incredible challenge to us to find things that show families in all their diversity. Now at least you can get some stuff that talks about same-sex parents. You can get stuff that talks about single parenting, about grandparents who are the primary caregivers, and so on, although there is still nothing for polyparents. So, I have two stories I tell her that have poly characters. The first one is "Princess Valentine," who has two husbands and who are named Paul and Percy. And I actually wrote up one of the stories . . . and I've now sent it off to Sand's sister to draw pictures for it, and once she actually draws the pictures for it then I'll reformat it around the pictures and see if I can actually get it into shape where I am willing to submit it to a publisher. (Kaye, bi-poly mom with bi female and two hetero male partners)

> There is a wonderful book we have called *Blue Dads* [Valentine, 2004], and it's about a kid who has two blue (in color, what a shade!) dads. It goes on to ask why the dads are blue (did they eat too many blueberries, etc.) but answers again and again that, "No, they are just blue. They were born blue." At the end of the book we get some different-colored moms. We were laughing and talking it up, "And this little girl has three orange moms and a purple dad and a bright blue dad," etc. Then we went playing with the idea of *Heather Has Two Mommies* [Newman, 2000] and came up with "Heather Has Two Mommies and Two Daddies and Someone That Is an Uncle or an Aunt Depending on Who the Mini-Dress Looks Good on That Morning." It was a hoot! (Janette, in bi-poly group marriage of three women and two men)

These types of preschool experiences mean children of polyfamilies are entering school systems with certain discourses, language, and understandings already in place, which may construct them as the "foreigner" or "stranger" or "third element" to the school (Bauman, 1990; Bhabha, 1990b; Kristeva, 1991). In the following, sixteen-year-old James, with a bisexual father and heterosexual mother, wants to use school as a site where he can further research and learn about the multisexuality in his family and feel comfortable about his own multiple-within "undecidable" self (Derrida, 1981; Marotta, 2002):

> I'm not going to change my values to avoid teasing! Like should I change that I'm a vegetarian sometimes vegan, not Christian, supportive of gay rights, etc., etc.—all those things that may or may not be popular in my neighborhood? I wanted to do a paper on polyamory for school. It was only then that I saw dad's lifestyle was so much more than a three-way relationship. It's more connected with the mind and soul and how you really feel about your love for others and the way you want to live in a relationship. . . . From the days our whole family has spent together there has been a great sensation of fun and a real family atmosphere. It really feels quite natural and as if it was meant to be. . . . In the long run, not only are my parents learning about their own thoughts and feelings but so am I and my siblings. (James, sixteen, hetero son of bi-poly dad and hetero-mono mom)

The one concern and sadness that many polluting polyparents talked about was the fear that their being out would lead to the harassment and stress of their children. Many tried to prepare their children for the consequences of their pollution, their being constructed as "the stranger," and to provide them with verbal, mental, and emotional strategies to counteract or deflect any negativity at school so that they would be active agents rather than "social puppets" in the hands of educational institutions (Boden, 1990; Buxton, 2007):

> I hated the idea that my choices would cause pain to my child. One of the things that we did with him was to work on giving him a large variety of ways to handle questions and issues. . . . I think that it is critical to give them something that they can say to diffuse a situation that they may not have the tools to cope with. "Yeah, my parents are weird . . . all parents are weird. Sometimes I think they must have come from another galaxy. . . ." "Wow, that's a totally rude question. I'm blown away that you would ask something so personal about my family." These responses were basically meant to give our son a way to change the subject . . . something that at times he really felt like he needed to do. We also told him that it was totally acceptable for him to tell his friends, "Hey, this is something that my parents do and it pisses me off." Primarily, he needed to know that we weren't expecting him to be a poly activist. We also helped him come up with a list of things that he really liked about our family. This had two purposes. First,

it gave him some ammunition to deal with people who were being negative. He once told an obnoxious kid, "Look, your father doesn't make any time for you, I've got two fathers who *both* want to spend time with me, and you think that *my* family is *sick*. . . . You're an idiot." However, more importantly than giving him debate material, this list really seemed to help him stay centered when things got tough. He could walk away frustrated and upset, and it gave him a place to look at his family and feel like there were some positive things for him in our lifestyle despite the things that were difficult. (Margherita, hetero-poly mom)

They know that we are not what is considered socially "normal," but then again, we have taught them that if someone says that we are odd, strange, or in some other way "not normal," we say "Thank you." It works. If they don't make a big deal out of it, neither will their peers. (Demetrio, hetero-mono partner of hetero-poly woman with bi-poly male partner)

When our daughter is asked why she has more than the usual number of parents, we've taught her to say, "Cos I'm lucky!" Kids and most teachers don't want a treatise on polyamory, they want a quick answer. (Kaye, bi-poly mom with bi female and two hetero male partners)

I can't believe that teaching children to hide in the crowd is the wisest course, and I want them to be more accepting of others than children reared in homes where hate seems to be the only family value. Dr. Martin Luther King Jr. probably heard the same thing from his peers—don't make waves, think of your kids, etc.—but he made a difference in his short life that his kids and many, many more still thank him for. I feel that my beliefs are worth standing up for, and I want to pass that on to my children. Refer them to the struggle that parents of young black men face every day, the prejudice they must teach their children to handle. And what about gay couples who adopt or choose to have children? And those who immigrate to this country and get teased for having different beliefs, customs, etc. . . . Seems to me the fear isn't what your kids will face but rather what they themselves will have to face within. (Cate, bi-poly mom)

Young polyamorous students also called for a broader education around family diversity, and indeed sometimes performed their polyamory at school as a form of resistance, albeit risking harassment and ostracism (Foucault, 1978, 1984). Chihara writes about "a new breed of polyamorist" that is springing up who are teenagers or in their twenties who may come across polyamory via other "alternative lifestyles," or want to find a way of "doing" relationships that avoids the "traditional cycle of dating-cheating-marrying-and-divorcing" and who, having "grown up under the shadow of AIDS" and other STDs, are "interested in experimenting with commitment as much as—if not more than—sex" (2006; see also Larsen, 1998):

People at school think that because I'm young that I will grow out of it. We get dirty looks from teachers and kids, not only because we're all holding hands but because my gf and I don't have any problems with affection in public. Then I get, "Look at that! Not only are those two girls kissing but they are holding hands with that guy too!" Now I truly understand the value of good friends who just want me to be happy and tolerate my relationships without the lectures and comments. Plus, I'm a show-off, and when I hear people comment it just makes me more affectionate or even do that dreaded three-way kiss in the schoolyard that just grosses everyone out! (Evette, seventeen, bi-poly student)

I was poly in all my teen relationships, even without the word available to me. I know a triad that started when they were in high school who are still together almost twenty years later. I have a seventeen-year-old stepdaughter who is openly poly, and many of her friends are in, have been in, or are seriously considering poly relationships. I worry that there are young polys lurking in our schools who feel rejected. (Rina, in hetero group marriage of two men and two women)

In high school my car was covered in animal shit by some local bigots because I was different in various ways, including being poly and out. (Rowland, hetero-poly university student)

As stated throughout this book, it is important that popular cultural texts be made available for young people to see representations of polyamorous possibilities. A recent film marketed for teenagers and young adults via its New York urban school setting and soundtrack, *Take the Lead*, is based on the real-life story of a dance teacher, Pierre Dulain, who gives a group of "problem kids" a second chance by exploring their dance skills and entering them into a city competition. One of the subplots in this film is the rivalry between two boys, Ramos and Danjou, over the affections of Sasha. When the rivalry flares into a physical skirmish one too many times during rehearsals, Dulain intervenes and states that they will both partner Sasha, and that they will have to work out who dances what with her.

This is followed by various scenes that show the threesome that develops between them. Sasha is seen rehearsing with each one separately in her bedroom, culminating in sensual/sexual intimacy. She enters the competition dance floor on the arms of both of them, and chooses who she will dance each number with. When they make it to the final round of the tango competition, the boys plan to stage a dance performance of rivalry over her affection, thereby melodramatically and theatrically reenacting their past rivalry in the present state of choreographed cooperation and collaboration as a threesome. The dance ends with both boys wrapped around Sasha. Although the audience erupts into stunned applause at the power and originality of the dance, they are unable to score as, with apt symbolism, the rules state that the dance is for couples only. A plot resolution is arrived at when the major dance rival, who has a reputation of winning past competitions, hands over her trophy to the threesome and calls it a tie for the evening. She recognizes the power and expertise of their dance despite the rules and does comment that she has never seen a performance like theirs in her life. The boys are seen as definite friends after that scene, and the film ends with an eruption of frenetic exuberant dancing by audience and dancers, with Sasha dancing with both Ramos and Danjou.

Indeed, one of the other themes of the film has been the tension and opposition between traditional ballroom dancing and urban Latino/black dancing, often symbolized by white/black, affluent/poor polarities. Gradually, Dulain's students interweave the two forms of dance to their advantage, culminating in the exuberance of interwoven "urban black ballroom dance" that allows white/black rich/poor audiences and dancers to meet, share, and celebrate on the borders.

YouTube has allowed the wide dissemination of a short film for young adults called *Boyfriends*, produced by Robert Anthony Hubbell, a film-maker who says on his website that he "creates digital media that evokes critical thinking and encourages people to explore new ideas" (www.robert anthonyhubbell.com). He has also made films about body image, gender, and 9/11. *Boyfriends* is the story of a sixteen-year-old boy, Will, whose girl-friend tells him she loves him but is in love with someone else as well, their friend Brian. She introduces the idea of polyamory to him and the audience via Deborah Anapol's (1992) book, *Love without Limits*. The film shows the two boys having a conversation, with Will demanding an explanation from Brian. The ending shows a happy resolution, with Will giving his girlfriend a card from him and Brian. The end credits are accompanied by the "Poly-amory Song" sung by David Roves which explains how the world will see them as mad and bad. However, the music is whimsical and flippant, indi-cating that the young people will ably deal with such marginalization.

Some polyamorous young adults who came out to their parents found themselves initiating situations where their parents finally disclosed their own poly relationships. In the following, Nadine, in her early twenties, refers to this "second-generation poly" situation she uncovers when, as her "tummy is flipping, I'm looking up references and reviewing my motiva-tions in my head so I can make a rational case," she comes out to her father, and then her mother:

> I started to mumble about Heinlein, then TV shows, and finally polylists, then that I'm sad I'm polyamorous. . . . He [father] asks me to clarify . . . [then] asks me if I knew about his marriage to my mom. . . . He said to ask her and to say it was okay to get details. So that was that. . . . I'm quite bouncy, as a load has been taken off my shoulders. . . . Now that I think about it, little details fit in place and I can see it, but wow. . . . The things you don't know about your parents. . . . So I'm skating on air, everyone knows and it's all okay and I'm in love! (Nadine, hetero-poly with hetero-mono male partner)

Indeed, some young people who had grown up in polyfamilies polluting their schools were grateful for this experience of handling marginality with openness and confidence, being situated at a critical vantage point as a "stranger" learning how to deconstruct and question the "unquestioned and unquestionable" (Schutz, 1944); and having the skills and confidence to tackle other forms of conformity, ignorance, and discrimination in their own acts of pollution and noncompliance (McLaren, 1993; Audinet, 2004). Ruth, eleven, is the daughter of Kaye (in a group marriage with another bi female and two hetero partners), who participated in my research when Ruth was just about to start school. In a recent media article, Ruth said, "People ask which is your real mum and dad. I always say if I pinch them and they say 'ouch,' aren't they real?" (Antonowicz, 2008). This is similar to the way young people from gay and lesbian families come to feel:

> Discovering that my otherwise unremarkable family was by societal standards abhorrent made me suspicious of values that the mainstream touted as ideal. I learned that I needed to critically analyze any assumption that broader society presented to me in absolute terms. Phrases like "because that's just how it is" or "because that's how it's done" have never satisfied me. They only provoked me to ask more questions. Filtering through societal assumptions and pressures was a skill I developed for enduring prejudice against my family. (Garner, 2004: 33)

> My parents are quite prominently involved in social issues; then when I grew into my teens, I also got involved in black civil rights (although I'm white), and feminist causes (although I'm male), etc., etc. My parents taught us about the importance of standing up for what you believe in and bucking the status quo. And here I am today, protesting darn near everything and refusing to live my life on other people's terms. (Kyle, twenty, bi-poly son of polyparents)

> Their teacher was doing the back-to-school thing, you know, like a third week in school trying to connect with all the parents. So she gave them five extra-credit points for every parent they brought in, and of course our son brought the lot of us in. Fair is fair, so she gave him his twenty extra-credit points. . . . He's very bright, which tends to be disconcerting to a lot of teachers. He'd never let things pass if he thought they were wrong or stupid. He got in a huge argument with a teacher about whether or not monogamy was a component of true, mature love. He was sixteen, and it was a classroom exercise in the qualifications of infatuation, lust, and mature love. . . . Oh, he got beat up a number of times. The times he got beat up were typically one of two things: either he was taking some political stance that was very unpopular or he was getting called a fag and getting beat up because he was perceived to be gay. He had a spate of wearing skirts. He wanted to see if they were comfortable. He eventually gave them up because they didn't have enough pockets, but the period of time that he wore skirts he came home beat up a couple of times because, you know, the little gangster boys were completely threatened by a guy

in a skirt, and I know he gave as good as he got, and, he would always kind of brush it off, but you know, that's kind of an ugly thing to go through. . . . The only time I really dealt with the school was about when they were both safer sex peer counselors. They kept driving it in to be able to distribute literature and condoms on campus and the administration of the school was really bitter about the whole thing and did not want any safer sex education going on in their campus because it would promote promiscuity, blah, blah, blah, and the usual crap, so we went toe to toe a couple of times on that, and the net result was that they ended up standing in the gutter next to the pavement outside the whole of campus, passing out their stuff. You know I totally supported them, making sure that they had supplies and a space and all those things. (Kaye, bi-poly mom with bi female and two hetero male partners)

Another significant paradox for pollutant polyfamilies was their intersection with passing as, or parodying (Butler, 1990, 1991; Bordo, 1992), a "perfect family." We have already seen how polyparents became committed and engaged members of the school community in order to prevent prejudice or gain some bargaining power or a vantage point should any issues of discrimination arise. This strategy of parodying or mimicking "perfect parenting" was also utilized by many polyfamilies in order to prevent any perceived deficit or dysfunction in their family being used to justify, explain, or exaggerate their child's learning difficulties or other concerns at school. Thus, even as they "came out," or clotheslined themselves as "not normal," risking a great loss of control over how they would be constructed or related to (Fuss, 1991; Sedgwick, 1993; McDonald, 2001), they ensured that they would appear not only "normal," as that would entail the usual complexities/dysfunctions of "normal" families, but beyond normal or beyond fault. Sheff (2008) discusses the way polyfamilies may idealize potentially positive outcomes and deemphasize actual or potential negatives as strategies of what I would call hypernormalization and stigma management. In other words, many polyparents strive to present themselves as perfect parents because

being a polyparent can put you in the spotlight, and anything about my kids at school, like if they're playing up, or not learning well, or have a grumble about their family like most kids do, would be made bigger or worse than it really is and be blamed on us instead of being handled in a normal way like you do with other kids. Whatever's a problem with the kids at school, it's because they come from this bad family of ours. So you find yourself trying extra hard to come across like this impossibly perfect family who never argue, who never make mistakes, who are raising inhumanly perfect children. (Cate, bi-poly mom)

Indeed, their children may also need to pollute/pass as perfect in order to signify the success of the family. This is also found in same-sex families, a process that Garner describes as "straightening up for the public" (2004: 179) and that could be termed "monogamizing for the public" in relation to polyfamilies:

> Our families currently lack the "luxury" to be as openly complicated, confusing, or dysfunctional as straight families. . . . [The] sense of being in a fishbowl has as much to do with how these children "turn out" as does the sexual orientation of their parents. . . . Issues surrounding a parent's sexuality [/relationships] become confused with issues that could well be unrelated. Is a child falling behind in school because both of her parents are women, or is it because she has an undiagnosed learning disability? Is a teen skipping school because of problems with his gay family, or is it just because he hates algebra? (Garner, 2004: 6, 23)

Panopticonic self-monitoring by pollutant "queerly mixed" families in order to pass as perfect for the outside world may also mean that some children will pass as perfect to their own families to avoid distressing their loved ones:

> Children can be so successful at covering up the realities of teasing, harassment, or their own internalized homophobia that parents are oblivious to them. . . . Grown children frequently say that their LGBT parents underestimated the effects and the pressures of navigating through a homophobic world. The issues that arise are not always blatant threats or harassment, but general ongoing discomfort about how people are going to react. (Garner, 2004: 29, 97–98)

Thus, because their parents openly pollute the schools or have "clotheslined" their families, the children may feel the pressure to "closet" (Sedgwick, 1993) any facets that may be constructed as flaws emanating directly from polyparenting. They may feel compelled to display how "normal" and unpolluted they themselves are, or they develop what Garner calls the "poster-child mentality" (2004: 29):

> We fear normal won't be good enough. So instead, we strive for perfect. Anything less leaves weak spots for critics to poke holes though our argument that our families are worthy of social acceptance as straight families. I was one of those children who pushed myself to become an overachiever, striving to build an airtight case for my family's success. That way, when people found out my dad was gay, no one could use an imperfection of mine as bogus evidence that gay men would make lousy parents. . . . They [children] grow tired of having to constantly watch what they do or say. They experience anxiety about getting caught with their guard down and fear it could result in someone exploiting their families' vulnerabilities. All these consequences take their toll on children's self-esteem and self-worth. Somewhere along our path to equality, the GLBT-family community started believing that perfectionism was our trip to mainstream acceptance and freedom from oppression. . . . Our

families deserve nothing less than to gain full equality, not because we are flawless, but because we are human. (Garner 2004: 2–3)

I try to be perfect at school so that'll like please my family so they can see that their lifestyle isn't causing problems for me at school. I'm also trying to be perfect at school so that the school doesn't think that my family's bad. It's like I'm always trying to prove something to everyone. I can't have a bad day, like I can't stuff up, because everyone's looking for the sign that my family's the cause of everything wrong. Like I'm even too scared to say we had an argument at home, or that my parents really annoyed me, but all the other kids can come to school and whinge all they like about their families, but like that's okay, they have a normal family, and normal families argue and normal families have parents who annoy their kids. My parents are so abnormal they have to be perfect. They have to be fake families. (Annie, fifteen, hetero-daughter of bi-poly parents)

Thus, panopticonic surveillance leads to self-regulation and assimilation in children from polluting families as well as children from passing families, and indeed, passing and polluting become interwoven, blurred constructs that meet, mesh, and conflict on the borders of normalization and noncompliance (Trinh, 1991):

[They] internalize a paradox: to be accepted for being different, they first have to prove that they are "just like" everyone else. . . . Many children in queer families grow up with the sense that their lives are not their own—they are *symbols* of something much bigger. They figure out that they are being observed, and that because of their parents, their otherwise normal lives are interesting or even exotic to outsiders . . . that we are some kind of zoo people. (Garner, 2004: 15–16, 19; see also Fuss, 1991; Sedgwick, 1993)

Like the children from same-sex families that Garner is writing about, children from polyfamilies also "have to make daily choices about if and how to come out" to their schools about their families, and thereby risk having their families blamed for any harassment they receive, and if and how to come out to their families about what is happening to them at school (2004: 105). Nevertheless, most offspring from out polyfamilies and most out polyparents concluded that despite these problems and potential dilemmas, the positives generally outweighed the negatives:

I don't think my emotional or social growth was stunted at all by my loving, multiparent family, when compared to the depressing norm in my school of broken families, cheating families, or various forms of abuse that my peers went through at home. (Rowland, twenty, hetero-poly university student)

I was introduced to poly relationships when I was about eleven. My mum was in an FFM for many years. It taught me that honesty and communication can lead to very fulfilling relationships. (Abigail, twenty-one, bi-poly)

I think that the majority of consequences for my children have been positive in nature. They have learned, through my example, to seek their own path. They have learned that doing so may bring social disapproval and even pain, but that integrity and being true to yourself is more important than adhering rigidly to society's mores. They have learned how to communicate in an honest and healthy manner about difficult and emotionally charged issues. All three of my children score high on development tests. My children have learned how to deal with people that don't agree with our lifestyle in a positive manner. I am confident that this skill will transfer to many areas of their adult lives. (Rina, in hetero group marriage of two men and two women)

We are an FMM (full-triangle) family with a nine-year-old son. We enjoy a large social network of polyfamilies with children. The kids in this network have benefited not only from the love of additional parents, but from a support system of other polyfamilies and their kids. Many of the kids have trouble understanding the mainstream culture's attitudes toward love. They are used to an ideal where having lots of kinds of love and friendship is considered healthy. There is a high value placed on sharing, caring for each other, and accepting differences among them. We are talking about a couple dozen kids ages four to fifteen who regularly socialize together. The kids were actually the ones to point out the many ways in which they have benefited from polyamory, but they wanted more resources, including material, emotional, and educational. They say they always have people to turn to for emotional support. They compared themselves with kids they knew from nuclear families who didn't have the kinds of support they do. (Debra, bi-poly mom with two bi-poly male partners)

Growing up in a polyamorous household did not mean the children would automatically seek polyamorous relationships themselves. Rather, it gave them the opportunity to witness, experience, and consciously reflect upon the kinds of relationship options available to them:

Growing up as the eldest son of a polyfamily has been an interesting and occasionally trying process. . . . I have not strongly considered living in a polyfamily myself, although it is not because I am opposed to it at all, just that I don't think it would work for me. I think the stability that can be achieved by a long-term poly relationship like my family is very healthy for raising kids. (Zlatko, eighteen, hetero-mono son of a bi-poly family)

Benji went through that whole period of figuring out whether he liked boys better or girls better or whether he wanted to be poly or whether he wanted to be mono and spent some time multiple dating and doing all those kinds of things and in the end decided that what he really wanted to be was be monogamous and relatively straight, and so he's now married and he has a lovely two-year-old daughter. (Kaye, bi-poly mom with bi female and two hetero male partners)

Thus, pollutant polyfamilies want schools to know that their children, whether they are polyamorous or not, are turning out well-adjusted because they come from queer families, not despite them:

> Many times one or the other household provided the quiet spot to finish a school project. . . . If they need help creating a map of Civil War territories, or figuring out their algebra assignment or dealing with the complexities of siblings, they see multiple sources for help within the family. . . . Our children are happy, doing well in school and better adjusted than many of their peers. (C., 1997–1998: 22–23)

In the following, Kaye talks about the positive impacts on her foster son's learning, well-being, and social connectedness by joining her mestizaje family. Although her family was not officially recognized by the fostering systems, it has provided the strong base of diversity, nurturing, and love within which Nathan could agree to attend and complete school, explore his African-American heritage and queer sexuality, and see individuality and independent decision making rather than conforming and passing being modeled:

> He was fourteen. And he was a runaway. . . . He was on the streets, and Benji brought him home and said, "Can he stay over the holidays because he has nowhere to go, he's on the street," and I said, "Of course." . . . I told him [about our family]. I just said this is how it is, you know. . . . His mother is in and out of jail, a drug addict and dealer. . . . And she gave Nathan all kinds of crap that we were a rich white family and disconnecting him from his culture and his roots. Although interestingly enough, he learnt more about black history and about Africa as a continent in my house than he ever learned in her house. Just discussions and books and when they did various things at school or when things came up and we talked about it. . . . He finished high school and he's the first person in his birth family in three generations to finish high school, and his grandma actually came to his high school graduation and she was just so proud of him. . . . Schools are hard because there is such an enormous amount of peer pressure to conform. . . . It was really tough initially for Nathan to kind of come to grips with that personally. Because he did a lot of his growing up in the social services system, and he was in group homes and hostels and foster homes and so on, he learned very early on that one of his survival mechanisms was to tell people what he thought they wanted to hear, and he lied horribly, and it was very difficult to teach him that the truth mattered and that it wasn't tied to how I thought about him or whether or not I loved him, and I think that was really tough for him to understand and learn that he was an individual, that he had his own ability to make judgments for himself, make choices for himself, and that who he was and how he acted was not going to withdraw our family's affection for him. . . . We told him he couldn't stay with us unless he went to school and that was like the one hard and fast rule. . . . We did have a go at going through the foster system and

actually becoming licensed foster parents, but they were not prepared for our family. . . . So, we finally gave it up and sort of had an informal arrangement, but his worker kind of kept an eye on school, and she kind of poked around a little bit and figured out that he was staying with us and that he was in school regularly and that he was thriving, and so she actually called him and told him that she had done whatever the appropriate paperwork was to make sure that he was no longer listed as a runaway. (Kaye, bi-poly mom with bi female and two hetero male partners)

There were also a few polyamorous teachers in this research who were "out" and who also used being a "perfect" teacher as a strategy preventing the problematization of their poly pollutant selves:

I'm a teacher . . . public high school, for nine to ten years. . . . My job is one of my greatest passions, but I am also not going to live a lie so that I can keep it. I am queer, kinky, and poly, as well as a Jewish Buddhist with definite pagan lean-ings, so frankly, if they want to look at my life and find something to complain about, it won't be hard. . . . I did once suggest that a student read *The Ethical Slut*. . . . That seemed very risky, but she really needed to read it, and I swore her to strictest secrecy. My defense against trouble—and so far I have found it 100 percent effective, even as an out, trouble-making, queer Jewgirl at a conservative suburban school in an area with much right-wing Christian influence—is to be the best damn teacher I can be. I make sure they need me much more than I need them. I make sure they know that I am smart and confident and will ac-tively stand up for what I believe in. (Serena, bi-poly teacher)

Via the voices, experiences, and narratives of polyfamilies and their chil-dren, and poly teachers, this chapter has shown that much work needs to be done in schools to bridge the chasm between the diversity of "queerly mixed" families in communities and the way they are redefined or under-mined in schools. As Garner writes in relation to same-sex families,

The reality of my family and the common assumptions about families like mine were vastly different. When queer families remain hidden and mysteri-ous, curious people tend to make up answers to their own questions with worst-case scenarios—scenarios fueled by prejudice and homophobia. I discovered that each time I mentioned the mundane details of my everyday life—going to the movies with my father and his partner, or washing the dishes together—I challenged people's stereotypes about gay parents, and gay people in general. (2004: 3)

I will conclude this chapter with the words and work of Valerie White, a lawyer specializing in the area of domestic violence and substance abuse treatment. She is also a member of Family Tree in Boston, a poly support and discussion group, and often supports polyfamilies in legal situations. She questions why children being raised in a stable polyclan are considered to be in a worse situation than children raised in modern "blended" families—with stepparents, absent parents, stepsiblings, half-siblings—who may have to deal with much chaos and change:

> As more and more polyamorous people find each other and establish intentional families . . . they will produce a cohort of young people who are confident, ethical, self-actualizing, open-minded and secure. Two of them live at my house. (2007: 13)

5

From Difference to Diversity

"X-Files" to "whY-Files?"

I'm an anonymous random. I like being a random, but it's being anonymous that's crap. I want someone to explain to me WHY randoms are such a problem, and WHY it's so hard for schools to get real and say, yes, there's lots of randoms in our students and there's lots of random families, and it's our job to take care of everyone, to educate everyone. But no one deals with the Why question, like Why are you pretending randoms don't exist? or Why is it so bad being a random? because there's no answer that makes sense.

—Marita, seventeen, bi student

This chapter will summarize the research findings and the recommendations that research participants have made for the further recognition and inclusion of diverse sexualities and families in schools. The metaphors of passing, bordering, and polluting within a mestizaje theoretical framework have been used to interrogate sociocultural boundaries, hierarchies, and categorizations in relation to bisexual students and multisexual and multi-partnered families. The reader has been taken into the borderlands inhabited by border families and border sexualities to explore lives lived on the multiple-within nepantla (Anzaldua and Keating, 2002). It is critical that the realities of mestizaje persons, "anonymous randoms," "X-files," or what Bauman (1991) and Derrida (1981, 1982) call "undecidables," are explored and addressed in educational research and in school policy, pedagogy, and pastoral care in order to challenge the hegemonic dominant discourses that render them invisible or safely distanced by neat binary classification. The potential consequences of personal and relationship concealment (Lehmiller, 2009) on personal, relational, and familial health and well-being, as well as professional well-being for bisexual and/or polyamorous teachers, have been documented throughout this book.

Ironically, my very constructions of "border family" and "border sexuality" are a reflection of hierarchical dualisms and models of difference and dichotomy that uphold the Center and perpetuate panopticonic fear and regulation for those in the Margins (hooks, 1991). There needs to be a discursive shift to models of diversity and multiplicity that erase constructs of Center and Margin and that incorporate all families and sexualities. Instead of problematizing and pathologizing certain families and sexualities, there is a need to problematize their problematization and pathologization and ask, Why is this occurring, by whom, and for whose purposes? In this way, the real concerns that may be impeding student learning, student welfare, and family/school connectedness can be foregrounded and addressed. As Firestein writes in relation to bisexuality and polyamory in the health sector:

> Our clients are no longer coming to us because they want to be "normal." They are coming to us because they want to be *whole*. . . . This mythical norm of a single trajectory of psychological health is an ideal that never really existed. The false gods of heteronormativity have been shattering at our feet for decades now. (2007: preface; see also Weitzman, 2007)

BORDERING THE "RESIDUAL" AND THE "EMERGENT"

> The social and cultural worlds will always be shaped by combinations of the residual and the new and by competition between the emergent and what has always been. . . . As educators, we must acknowledge and incorporate these new forms of subjectivity and family into our planning and pedagogy.
>
> —Carrington (2001: 195)

The discourses of sexual diversity and polypartnering have demonstrated that the reality of contemporary social relations and identifications for many children and their families in our schools are not dichotomous, but rather fluid and multiple. This process of exploring the "queerly mixed" realities of our schools and their familial communities has unveiled and un-silenced some of the complexities of mestizaje lives lived on borders, within the gaps, in order to interrogate singular notions of Identity, Reality, and Truth. As Anzaldua explains,

> It's easier to remain in entrenched systems and erect defenses to keep out new ideas. Or we can learn to navigate through the whirlwinds. Intelligence is the ability to make adaptive responses in new and old situations. . . . The ideological filters fall away; we realize that the walls are porous and that we can "see"

through them. Having become aware of the fictions and fissures in our belief systems, we perceive the cracks between the different worlds, the holes in reality. . . . Living in the midst of different vortexes makes it hard for us to make sense of the chaos and put the pieces together. But it is in the cracks between worlds and realities where changes and consciousness can occur. In this shifting place of transitions, we morph, adapt to new cultural realities. (in Keating, 2000: 279–80)

This research has demonstrated the limitations, oppressions, and silencing of realities inherent in the ways both powerful mainstream "residualist," heteronormative, and monogamist groups and power-challenging marginal homonormative groups have utilized bifurcating strategies to homogenize, categorize, and scissor the lives of so many "emergent" children and their families in our school communities. The pathway through these discourses lies in the constitution of multiplaced persons, or mestizaje persons, and in the acknowledgment and understanding of "emergent" sexualities and families:

Subversion of the past, emergence of the future; two sides of the same undertaking. On one side, ideas, values and institutions that become outdated and constantly have to be readjusted and reformulated. On the other side, lifestyles, relationship modes, expressions and languages ceaselessly appearing and which must be given a place . . . the "something new" constantly, indefinitely recreating itself. Unpredictable, just like the continuous flow of humans commingling . . . with the resulting emergence . . . of a wide variety of societies and cultures. (Audinet, 2004: 140, 147)

The experiences and negotiations of polyfamilies, multisexual families, and bisexual young people in our schools have illustrated the significance of three interwoven forces of sociopolitical structure and power, which are

- social ascription: being the labels and categories (both affirming and negating) imposed on one by the sites of panopticonic power in the wider society, such as an educational institution;
- community acknowledgment: being the labels and categories one's significant others affirm or disapprove, such as a school community, a poly community, a bisexual community, and a gay and lesbian community;
- personal agency: being the individual young person or family selecting and determining necessary or desired labels from the constructions available, and attempting to devise a model of living for oneself that claims the agentic power to bypass, disrupt, and subvert existing discursive frameworks of sexuality, family, and education.

Three strategic modes have been found to connect mestizaje or "random" persons to personal agency, the wider society, and the community of significant others:

- experiencing conflict and dissonance between the heteronormative and homonormative polarities, resulting in an either/or antagonism or coerced location that mainly engenders the adoption of strategies of passing, closeting, and normative performativity;
- negotiating and synthesizing elements of both polarities, resulting in a both/and intersecting border, or nepantla location, between the two binaries that mainly adopts strategies of bordering and negotiation;
- resisting, subverting, and disrupting the polarities to interweave a mestizaje identity that is multiple, fluid, and "in excess of" binaries and dualities, even as it acknowledges the realities of the binaries in these very acts of noncompliance, mainly resulting in the adoption of strategies of polluting, noncooperation, and what I have called "clotheslining."

The research participants in this study, the "X-files," are creating and locating space beyond the prescribed normative orders, beyond the economy of closets, beyond binary conflicts and syntheses in both form and content. Their experiences, behaviors and self-ascribed identities illustrate that mestizaje and shifting, flexible boundaries are real and not necessarily problematic. Indeed, they are increasingly asking *why* their sexualities and families are problematized by institutions such as schools. To be able to serve socially diverse local communities, and to embrace all children within a duty of care and of fostering their well-being and learning, educational policies, programs, and pastoral care are needed that "question the unquestionable," the "taken-for-grantedness" of family and sexuality. They need to encompass diversity and metissage within a framework of common social justice and equity principles.

The adolescents, young adults, and families whom I have worked with are calling for a deconstructive recognition and analysis of "residual" sociocultural and sexual boundaries, their strategic usefulness, as well as their potential destructiveness. They want to know *why* the knots and tangles on the underside of the social tapestry are not displayed, *why* the illusory and damaging "mainstream" societal and educational discourses in relation to sexuality and family in schools are not being challenged in order "to undo the logic and the clarity" of such constructs (Lionnet, 1989: 14). Discursive strategies in education are required that interrogate and disrupt the constraints of these traditional paradigms as well as expand current paradigms in relation to same-sex families and gay and lesbian students, which may also be blocking the "emergent": "Like schooling itself, however, lesbian and gay school reform is neither neutral nor inconsequential. Such efforts must also be scrutinized, since ideology inheres in the various strategies of implementation" (Irvine, 2001: 251; see also Pallotta-Chiarolli, 2005b).

My research was based on Pettman's queries in her work on Indigeneity, ethnicity, class, and gender in Australia: what happens when "who I say I am may not coincide with the views of the group I claim, nor with the [external] others' views of me" (Pettman, 1986: 6). The response in most schools to this insider/outsider border position is the prohibition and disavowal of what others within the group consider "taboo" and "unreal." Heteronormativity has functioned for far too long because of the silencing of nonheterosexual "others." In the challenging of heteronormativity, there appears to be another attempt in schools at neatening the boundary, maintaining the dichotomy, which I call "homonormativity." We need to ask,

- Why has the model of "difference" been sustained in this shift, rather than an encompassing of "diversity"?
- Why are schools beginning to cater to gay and lesbian families and gay and lesbian young people while still ignoring, problematizing, or denying the existence of bisexual young people and multisexual/multipartnered families?
- Why do the recognition of gay and lesbian realities and the establishing of some power and leverage within the wider hegemonic sociopolitical and educational framework have to be at the expense of "queerly mixed" realities or a replication of and assimilation to hegemonic constructions of the sexual binary and monogamist constructions of heteronormative family?

As Atkinson writes,

> We do not teach about diversity in a multisexual society: diversity of preference, practice, orientation and choice. . . . While policy-makers might wish this absence of explicit reference to non-heterosexual lifestyles to be seen as an openness to all possibilities . . . social theorists have long recognised the power of silence as a dominant force, and the possibility of the construction of norms through the absence of the Other. (2002: 126)

Nathanson offers a "bisexual pedagogy" that "centers on what a theoretical focus on bisexuality and other hybrid identities can offer our students," such as making bisexuality "an open object of academic inquiry," fostering in students a "necessary acceptance of discord" and a "willingness" and ability to engage in "critical thinking and questioning" of identities, dichotomies, and possibilities as part of a multicultural, interdisciplinary approach that is "at the heart of our teaching as critical and feminist educators" (2009: 83).

Instead of meaning being taught and discussed as deriving from dualistic difference, meaning is seen as deriving from multiple differences or diversity

(Burbules, 1997). *Why* can't schools allow for difference to not just mean "difference between" or "difference from," although these dualisms are certainly acknowledged as significant to address? How do we encourage schools to work with the "difference beyond" that challenges the very framework of differentiation by attempting to describe

- "difference as excess" or "queerly mixed" young people and families beyond a point which "language and explanation cannot proceed";
- "difference within" that shows the differences within groups of "queerly mixed" young people and families such as in relation to gender, ethnicity, Indigeneity, disability, and socioeconomic status; and
- "difference against," whereby conventional norms and dominant discourses are questioned and their gaps revealed by "queerly mixed" young people and their families (Burbules, 1997: 106–8; see also Derrida, 1981)?

The realities of bisexuality and nonmonogamy in youth cultures and in families, in all their positive and problematic possibilities, need to be articulated and included within school policy, curriculum, pedagogy, and student-welfare programs, given their increasing visibility in adult and popular cultures:

> All sides of the issue need to be considered in the media, research, social theory, and religious thought [and education]. . . . We need: social realists to affirm society's need for stability by exploring alternative marriage and family arrangements and sexual realists to point out the diversity of sexual orientations as part of the natural order and but one aspect of the individuals who make up society. (Buxton, 1991: 275)

For example, as discussed earlier in this book, in Australia there has been an emergence of increasingly vocal and visible national and state social and political groups such as Biversity, Bi Pride Australia, the Australian Bisexual Network, PolyOz, and PolyamoryAustralia. These groups are taking their place alongside an increasing number of international groups, listed and accessible via a multitude of websites, such as Loving More, UKPoly, Bifempoly, Polyde (Germany), Sacred Space Institute, Polyamory Society, BiPolyamoryOttawa, NZPolyamory (see Anderlini-D'Onofrio, 2004). Researchers and activists such as Fox (see 2004 for a comprehensive bibliography on research and literature regarding bisexuality), Anderlini-D'Onofrio (2004, 2009a), Barker (2004), McLean (2004), Sheff (2008), and Barker and Langdridge (2010) are continuing to develop the work of pioneers such as Kinsey and associates (1948, 1953), Klein (1993), Anapol (1992, 2010), Nearing (1992), and Lano and Parry (1995). Listservs such as Polyfamilies, Polyparents, CPN-Polys with Mono Partners, PolyResearchers, and Academic-Bi are providing vibrant supportive international communities of individuals, families, activists, media makers, writers, and researchers that explore and share experiences about the living of the everyday; share and critique media, literary, popular culture, and educational resources; and (for researchers) share and critique findings, methods, and concerns.

The Unitarian Universalists for Polyamorous Awareness (2004) is a prime pioneering example of a religious community opening up discussions around polyamory and spirituality. In their workbook for high school students, they have a workshop handout that includes an activity asking young people to write "a word or phrase that expresses how you feel in each case" listed there: celibacy, heterosexual marriage, interracial relationships, polygamy/polyandry, monogamy, cohabitation, singlehood, and multiple serial relationships. The next section then repeats this example of an "inclusion with specificity" exercise with the above list but in relation to the following questions: "If my best friend expressed his/her sexuality in this way, I would feel . . ."; "If one or both of my parents expressed their sexuality in this way, I would feel . . ."; "If my child expressed his/her sexuality in this way, I would feel . . ."; and "When I hear about people I don't know expressing their sexuality in this way, I would feel . . ." (Goldfarb and Casparian, 2000: 149–51).

As we have explored in earlier chapters, visual texts such as *French Twist*, *Bandits*, *Splendor*, *Take the Lead*, *The History Boys*, and *Torchwood* are part of an increasing popular culture engaging with these issues. Media personalities such as Dolly Parton (1994), Angelina Jolie, Michael Stipe, Drew Barrymore, Will and Jada Pinkett Smith, Tilda Swinton, and Mika are "coming out" as nonmonogamous and/or bisexual (see also Evans, 2001, for an example of a newspaper article). In 2005, on the adolescent favorite show, *The O.C.*, Alex Kelly was a high-visibility bisexual character, forming relationships with two of the show's main characters. Unfortunately, as with most social diversity issues in the past, schools are lagging behind in engaging with these shifts in the media and popular culture: "Schools are so mono, so unreal, like the world's so non-mono, . . . schools need to get real" (Andrea, seventeen, bi student).

In earlier chapters, we have also explored a growing range of young adult fictions, including *A Queer Circle of Friends* and my own *Love You Two*, and even a few children's picture books, that could be used in schools so they can "get real."

From within the GLBTIQ communities, some queer activists and theorists such as Tatchell are challenging the hetero-assimilationist "residualism" of gay and lesbian incorporation and participation into hetero-dominated structures and institutions such as marriage and school:

> We have now reached a situation where the dominant gay agenda is equal rights and law reform, rather than queer emancipation and the transformation

of society. . . . Equal rights for lesbians and gay men inevitably means parity on straight terms, within a pre-existing framework of values, laws and institutions. These have been devised by and for the heterosexual majority. Equality within their system involves conformity to their rules. This is a formula for submission and incorporation, not liberation. . . . The end result is gay cooption and invisibilisation. . . . The "good gays" are rewarded with equal treatment. . . . This nouveau gay reformism involves the abandonment of any critical perspective on straight culture. In place of a healthy skepticism towards the heterosexual consensus, it substitutes naïve acquiescence. Discernment is abandoned in favor of compliance. . . . The advocates of gay equality never question the status quo. They are straight minds trapped in queer bodies. Accepting society as it is, these hetero homos want nothing more than their cosy place in the straight sun. (Tatchell, 2002: 9)

As Melinda Paras, the executive director of the United States National Gay and Lesbian Task Force (NGLTF), says, "By the time equality finally gets won universally, we will be in a whole other place about the definition of family, and gay marriage may become almost irrelevant" (in Findlen, 1995: 23; see also Valverde, 2006).

It is important to reiterate here that my research and this book are not positioned against gay and lesbian marriage or in opposition to equal rights and law reform for gay and lesbian individuals and relationships. My concerns are the new forms of exclusion and hierarchy that occur within queer communities while the difficult work for marriage, parity, and equality is undertaken and the extent to which queer emancipation is determined and defined by hetero-assimilationist discourses and parameters.

Thus, the interrogation in this research can be situated within the call for the queerification of education (Letts and Sears, 1999) rather than the assimilation to traditional heteronormative scripts, which many straights are also eager to transform. Undoubtedly, the inclusion of bisexuality, multisexual families, and polyamory into education will be initially disruptive. After all, the "emergent" pollute with their "too many truths" and realities that "mess up the filing cabinet" of school structures, curriculum, and cultures:

Fashioning teaching in the place of metissage is a subversive act; it is also an act of caring, a willingness to go into the unknown, a move toward social justice. . . . A place of metissage arises out of dissonance, creates dissonance, and is itself dissonant. Will teachers harness the movement that dissonance generates for educative means and ends, or leave it to chance, to act upon students however it will? (Worley, 2006: 529)

This dissonant engagement with sexual multiplicity and making bisexuality visible rather than submerging everything into heterosexual or homosexual categories will ultimately be transformative in creating healthy individual, social, and institutional systems and cultures. As Epstein and Johnson write, "It may be that certain elements of sexual life or discourse . . . constitute such a 'pre-emergence' or 'that dangerous supplement' which has the potential to transform the whole field" (1998: 192).

"QUEER COYOTES":
BORDER RESEARCH AND RESEARCHERS ON THE BORDERS

The long-term impact of a growing population of people with fluid ideas of gender and sexuality involves asking questions that defenders of so-called family values don't want to consider.

—Garner (2004: 147)

As one of the first pieces of empirical research and theoretical engagement with bisexuality and polyamory in schools, with all the limitations, flaws, and problematics that this entails such as the absence of transgendered research participants and the lack of a greater range of culturally, religiously, and socioeconomically diverse participants, this book has addressed the following specific components of border research:

- It has described experiences that have hitherto not had a voice or a known label in a specific sociopolitical site such as a school, apart from imposed labels that sustain the negative images required by dominant groups for their own purposes of exclusion, silencing, and perpetuation of power.
- It has utilized qualitative research methods and standpoint epistemology to uncover, describe, and articulate issues, experiences, and values from the perspectives of the participants.

It is hoped that this book and research invite further critical interrogation and act as catalysts for further exploration, research, and implementation in education, for there are certainly areas that have yet to be explored (see Noel, 2006; Sheff, 2008). Thus, this research is an attempt to provide preliminary maps and draw attention to the gaps in educational research that require further journeys of queerification in the border zones in order to more fully understand the whole terrain: "Desire is multi-faceted, contradictory, subversive: its inevitable social organization requires that we are engaged in a continuous conversation about both its possibilities and limits" (Weeks, 1995: 50).

This book is calling for educational researchers to become "queer coyotes" in "assisting and mediating queer border crossings in schools" (Valadez and Elsbree, 2005: 176). As presented in chapter 1, Valadez and Elsbree outline four strategies that are important to "queer coyote" educational researchers and that will, in turn, encourage educational policy makers and teachers to become "queer coyote" educators. These are

- operating in "secreto" (secrecy): being trustworthy in the way we provide a safe space for bisexual and polyamorous students and families to tell their stories so that their realities can be heard by schools;
- knowing "los codigos" (codes): becoming aware of and informed about bisexuality and polyamory through our research so that we are able to convey and explain these terms and ways of being to the wider world;
- having "la facultad" (knowledge): becoming knowledgeable about border sexualities and families so that we can direct educators and their school communities "to resources, queer literature, the law and support services"; and
- expressing "compromiso" (commitment): undertaking our research and encouraging educators to work with us in its dissemination and implementation with a sincere commitment "toward educational transformation and border pedagogy" that situates bisexual students and polyamorous families within a broader framework of "social justice for all groups" (2005: 176–77).

In the boundary-pushing analysis of border subjectivities, the methodology question that framed this research and that requires ongoing attention is, How do we utilize and perhaps invent "new methodologies for research and new forms of expression while at the same time being academically rigorous and respectable?" (Brew, 1998: 29). For "queer coyotes" seeking new knowledges about marginal groups and emerging groups, and accessing these often-hidden groups, are the established methods satisfactory, or may we need to consider new methods? As the methods available to us for conveying knowledge open up, such as the possibilities opened up for me and my research participants through Internet technologies, how do we continue to seek research methods and ways of conveying knowledge that cater to diversity, innovation, and accessibility? As Britzman writes, we need to make our research accessible because "difficult knowledge may be refused" by those in positions of power and gatekeeping in education (1998: 118). For many educators, there appears to be a "passion for ignorance," as Silin states: "Such passion is made when the knowledge offered provokes a crisis within the self and when the knowledge is felt as interference or as a critique of the self's coherence or view of itself in the world" (in Britzman, 1998: 118).

As researchers, we need to interrogate why we may harbor some reluctance to opening up our theoretical and empirical frameworks to the knowledge that comes with the new generations. For instance, is it because "today's young people are harbingers of a time in which sexual identity will have no importance, thus thrusting past research into the garbage heap of antiquated science?" (Savin-Williams, 2005: 221).

In other words, understandably, explorations of family and sexuality in education cannot be comfortably positioned "over the borders" as something pertaining only to the researched, the educated, the students, and their families, and not to the researchers, the educators, and the adults in positions of educational authority. "Queer coyote" interrogation asks and assists educators to move onto the borders and be "the educated" as well. It also strikes deeply into the core of issues that are not just in the realm of the professional but also the personal. Love and family, sexuality and relationships are not just relevant to the Other: marginal students and marginal families. They are inherently about the Center: dominant families and dominant students, teachers and educational policy makers. The questions asked of the Other may be questions the dominant groups have been trying to avoid about themselves. Thus, resistance, evasion, and aggressive reaction are to be expected. However, these responses were also the case, and unfortunately still are in some places, in the research and implementation of multicultural education and gender equity in education (Martino and Pallotta-Chiarolli, 2005). As passionate sociologists (see Game and Metcalfe, 1996), particularly in the fields of sexuality studies, family studies, and education, we need to position ourselves on the borders between what is constructed as "crisis" and "interference" in education, and what is ultimately about an increasing affirmation and dialogue with the socially diverse students and families in our school communities, as others have done before us:

> Postmodern living arrangements are diverse, fluid and unresolved, constantly chosen and rechosen. . . . We are experiencing the queering of the family. . . . An exploration of networks and flows of intimacy and care, the extent and patterns of such networks, the viscosity and velocity of such flows, and the implications of their absence, is likely to prove much more fruitful for future research than attempts to interpret contemporary personal lives through redefinitions of the concept of "family.". . . [We need to] bring to light practices of care and intimacy . . . that have rarely been studied by sociologists. (Roseneil and Budgeon, 2004: 141, 153–54)

BEYOND "HYPERVIGILANT SURVIVAL MODE": STRATEGIES FOR SCHOOLS IN RELATION TO BORDER SEXUALITIES AND BORDER FAMILIES

For thirteen years children will be spending as much, if not more, time with their teachers and peers as their parents. By virtue of the sheer amount of time children spend at school, the climate of acceptance or hostility is a primary influence on their feelings about their families and themselves. . . . It is hard to learn while functioning under the stress of a hypervigilant survival mode. Over time, consistent stress hormones can harm the brain's ability to store and process information.

—Garner (2004: 109, 111)

Throughout this book, research participants have discussed strategies that schools may use to address and incorporate bisexuality and polyamory in policy, pedagogy, and pastoral care. I am aware that none of these suggestions are new, or alien, or problematic pollutants. They have been undertaken before in relation to gender, Indigeneity, ethnicity, disability, and other issues of diversity. Indeed, as a bisexual polyamorous student in my research, Jack, stated, "It's an educational institution, for God's sake; why don't they already know?" Indeed, since multicultural curricula and border pedagogy are the primary means by which children learn about people who are "different," it is "a practical and logical vehicle in which to insert lesbian, gay, and bisexual [and polyamorous] lives," thereby rather than ghettoizing or pathologizing, these issues of sexual and family diversity are normalized (Irvine, 2001: 253).

In other publications in relation to health services, I have proposed an "inclusion with specificity" model whereby specific acknowledgment and understanding of bisexuality and polyamory take place, but at the same time, the external imposition of categories and labels is limited and the individual's self-ascription and agency in how they see and label themselves, and the kinds of specific and/or inclusive services they wish to use, are available (Martin and Pallotta-Chiarolli, 2009; Pallotta-Chiarolli and Martin, 2009). In relation to education, the following strategies exemplify inclusion specifically of bisexual and polyamorous issues:

- Teachers can validate the existence of familial and sexual diversity by incorporating books, visual resources, and prominent historical bisexual and polyamorous figures. Information such as this would be of great interest to adolescents and young adults and is accessible and easily incorporated into a range of curriculum areas.
- Programs such as a Diversity Awareness Week can include discussions dealing with the complexity and diversity of sexual orientation and family. "Speakers bureaus" can include speakers addressing issues from a bisexual and multisexual/multipartnered family perspective.
- Professional development for staff can include sessions about the needs and special issues faced by bisexual students and multisexual/polyamorous families, the resources and resource persons that are available, and how to construct new and deconstruct existing resources.

- Effective antiharassment and antidiscrimination policies, training, and training materials need to include sexual diversity and family diversity, rather than focusing on the binary model of heterosexuality and homosexuality and opposite-sex-couple families and same-sex-couple families.

The implementation of strategies such as those above means that bisexual and/or polyamorous students and children from multisexual and multi-partnered families are supported through curriculum, pastoral care, peer support, mentoring, and policy so that our schools are sites of assured safety rather than hypervigilant survival, and "communities of commitment" to well-being, equity, justice, and learning (Ancess, 2003).

We have now arrived at a point where educational constructions of sexuality and family are increasingly being proven to be inadequate and problematic. The "boundaries" of social ascription appear to be loosening while the "closets" in which persons hide due to negative social and community acknowledgment are opening. Personal agency, whether it be in the form of passing, bordering, or polluting, is a running "against the grain" in pursuit of a sexuality and family negotiated from constantly shifting options and within constantly shifting boundaries (Boden, 1990; Trinh, 1991). Indeed, we need to keep drawing attention to the similarities and connections between various forms of marginalization and oppression and their framing beneath the same patriarchal, heteornormative, ethnocentric, and classed umbrella. Constructing coalitions, creating inclusive social and educational movements, and building bridges are required "at the crossroads of various social justice issues that affect people across the range of nationality, race, class, (dis)ability, age, gender and sexual identities" and must include the "questioning and reconceptualizing [of] relationship and families" and "engage all of us in creating sustainable relationships, families and communities" (Noel, 2006: 616–17; see also Anderlini-D'Onofrio, 2009a; Anapol, 2010). It is hoped that the words of research participant Jack are not prophetic regarding the ways that the experiences and suggested strategies of research participants will be received by those reading this book:

> They'll read the study and go "Oh, that's interesting. We might consider that later." Why not now? Why not say, "Well, let's stand up." . . . You know, there is so much pain and heartache coming out of waiting. We've got the education system. We've got the resources and the information, the Internet. For god's sake, it's the first chance we've got. Let's use it, not miss it. (Jack, bi-poly university student)

I would like to end this book by going back into the past in order to make some sense of the present and envisage a future. I will do this by presenting two examples of the interweaving of the residual and the emergent. First,

I will discuss a short story from the residual, "Felipa," written in 1876, and explore its interweaving with the emergent. Second, I will discuss an example from the present, indeed unfolding as I complete this book, of the emergent interweaving with the residual. This is President Barack Obama's appointment of Chai Feldblum, a signatory to *Beyond Same-Sex Marriage* (BeyondMarriage.org, 2006), as one of his five Equal Employment Opportunity Commissioners (EEOC).

In 1876, Constance Fenimore Woolson's short story "Felipa" (in Koppelman, 1994) introduced an eleven-year-old mestiza: culturally, religiously, sexually, relationally, and in gender performance, who says "I know a great deal," particularly in relation to the natural rhythms of the landscape and animals. She is of Minorcan and Spanish heritage, part pagan, part Catholic, dresses in both girls' and boys' clothes, and is in love with two white wealthy Americans, Christine and Edward, who love each other. When she learns that the Americans are leaving, and sees Edward "devouring Christine" with his eyes and Christine's enjoyment of this attention, she interjects: "Look at *me* so, . . . me too; do not look at him. He has forgotten poor Felipa; he does not love her anymore. But *you* do not forget, senora; *you* love me" (Woolson, 1876/1994: 75).

Interestingly, her grandparents acknowledge, understand, and affirm Felipa's self-awareness and uncategorized sexuality, even as the Americans such as the narrator, Catherine, in the following, try to dismiss or trivialize her suicidal feelings of lost love as infantile, ignorant, and transient. Indeed, the fact that she was in love with both Christine and Edward is seen as evidence of its insignificance, and her age is deployed to deny her a sexuality (see Curran, Chiarolli, and Pallotta-Chiarolli, 2009):

> To the silent old grandfather I said: "It will pass; she is but a child."
>   "She is nearly twelve, senora. Her mother was married at thirteen."
>   "But she loved them both alike, Bartolo. It is nothing; she does not know."
>   "You are right, lady; she does not know," replied the old man slowly; "but I know. It was two loves." (Woolson, 1876/1994: 76)

What does Felipa not know? Does the child who says she knows "a great deal" not know that the adult Western world of hierarchical dichotomous categorization—such as heterosexual/homosexual; white/black; man/woman; Christian/pagan; knowledgeable adult/ignorant child; sexual adult/asexual child—has no place for her mestiza multiple-within sexual childhood self? Koppelman speculates on Woolson's deliberate ambiguities in this story, concluding that in not giving the reader an "unambiguous storyline," the writer has forced the reader to acknowledge that "our natural desire to understand what really happened makes us consider possibilities that aren't supposed to be possible, aren't supposed to happen" (Koppelman, 1994: 56).

Hence, in this short story, a "residual" of over 140 years ago, we find what we today are still calling "emergent" constructions of childhood sexuality, bisexuality, polyamory, mixed gender performance, and cultural/religious metissage.

On September 14, 2009, President Obama, himself an embodiment of cultural, religious, and socioeconomic border-dwelling mestizaje, as he details in his autobiography (Obama, 2004), nominated Chai Feldblum to serve as one of the five EEOC Commissioners. A Georgetown University law professor, Feldblum has repeatedly demonstrated her mestiza sensibilities and experiences as she has been at the forefront of LGBT, HIV, and disabilities equality and antidiscrimination. Her nomination is leading to particular concern and consternation among the religious right because on July 26, 2006, she was a signatory for the manifesto "Beyond Same-Sex Marriage: A New Strategic Vision for All Our Families and Relationships" (BeyondMarriage.org, 2006). This document proposes governmental, systemic, and sociocultural recognition of "diverse kinds" of partnerships, households, and families. They included "committed loving households in which there is more than one conjugal partner" and a "menu of choices that people have about the way they construct their lives." Indeed, there should be "freedom from a narrow definition of our sexual lives, and gender choices, identities, and expressions" (BeyondMarriage.org, 2006). Since her nomination, Feldblum has publicly affirmed her signatory status to the document and stated that polyamorous families and relationships should be considered viable social, legal, political, and economic entities. Thus, into the residual structures and strictures of the current national and international political and religious arena come two emergent personas of mestizaje, Obama and Feldblum. They and the many who follow are finding ways to take us into a future where the Felipas in our classrooms today and tomorrow will find their multiplaces and spaces.

"The time of mestizaje is today" (Audinet, 2004: 147).

References

Acker, Joan, Kate Barry, and Joke Esseveld. 1983. "Objectivity and Truth: Problems in Doing Feminist Research." *Women's Studies International Forum* 6(4): 423–35.

Adam, Barry D. 1978. *The Survival of Domination: Inferiorization and Everyday Life.* New York: Elsevier.

Adams, Mary Louise. 1989. "There's No Place Like Home: On the Place of Identity in Feminist Politics." *Feminist Review* 31: 22–23.

Adler, Patricia A., and Peter Adler, eds. 1994. *Constructions of Deviance: Social Power, Context, and Interaction.* Belmont, CA: Wadsworth.

Alexander, Jonathan. 2007. "Bisexuality in the Media: A Digital Roundtable." *Journal of Bisexuality* 7(1/2): 114–24.

Altork, Kate. 1995. "Walking the Fire Line: The Erotic Dimension of the Fieldwork Experience." In *Taboo: Sex, Identity and Erotic Subjectivity in Anthropological Fieldwork,* ed. D. Kulick and M. Willson. London: Routledge.

Anapol, Deborah. 1992. *Love without Limits: The Quest for Sustainable Intimate Relationships.* San Rafael, CA: Intinet Resource Center.

———. 2003. *The Future of the Family and the Fate of Our Children.* www.lovewithout limits.com/futre_family.html (retrieved 15 June 2003).

———. 2010. *Polyamory in the 21st Century: Love and Intimacy with Multiple Partners.* Lanham, MD: Rowman & Littlefield.

Ancess, Jacqueline. 2003. *Beating the Odds: High Schools as Communities of Commitment.* New York and London: Teachers College Press.

Anderlini-D'Onofrio, Serena, ed. 2003. *Women and Bisexuality: A Global Perspective.* New York: Harrington Park Press.

———. 2004. *Plural Loves: Designs for Bi and Poly Living.* New York: Harrington Park Press.

———. 2009a. *Gaia and the New Politics of Love: Notes from a PolyPlanet.* Berkeley, CA: North Atlantic Books.

———. 2009b. "Plural Happiness: Bi and Poly Triangulations in Balasko's *French Twist.*" *Journal of Bisexuality* 9(3): 343–61.

Angelides, Steven. 1994. "The Queer Intervention: Sexuality, Identity, and Cultural Politics." *Melbourne Journal of Politics* 22: 66–88.

———. 2001. *A History of Bisexuality.* Chicago: University of Chicago Press.

———. 2006. "Historicizing (Bi)Sexuality: A Rejoinder for Gay/Lesbian Studies, Feminism, and Queer Theory." In *LGBT Studies and Queer Theory: New Conflicts, Collaborations, and Contested Terrain*, ed. Karen E. Lovaas, John P. Elia, and Gust A. Yep. New York: Harrington Park Press.

Angelides, Steven, and Craig Bird. 1995. "Feeling Queer: It's Not Who You Are, It's Where You're At." *Critical InQueeries* 1(1): 1–14.

Antonowicz, Anton. 2008. "Four Friends 'Married' for 15 Years Sharing a Daughter and Bedroom," Mirror.co.uk, www.mirror.co.uk/news/top-stories/tm-headline+four-friends (retrieved 21 August 2008).

Anzaldua, Gloria. 1987a. *Borderlands/La Frontera: The New Mestiza.* San Francisco, CA: Spinsters/Aunt Lute.

———. 1987b. "Del Otro Lado." In *Companeras: Latina Lesbians*, ed. J. Ramos. New York: Latina Lesbian History Project.

———. 1989. "The Homeland, Aztlan/El Otro Mexico." In *Aztlan: Essays on the Chicano Homeland*, ed. R. A. Anaya and F. A. Lomeli. Albuquerque: University of New Mexico Press.

———, ed. 1990. *Making Face, Making Soul: Haciendo Caras.* San Francisco, CA: Aunt Lute.

Anzaldua, Gloria, and Analouise Keating. 2002. *This Bridge We Call Home: Radical Visions for Transformation.* New York: Routledge.

Arden, Karen. 1996. "Dwelling in the House of Tomorrow: Children, Young People and Their Bisexual Parents." In *Bisexual Horizons: Politics, Histories, Lives*, ed. S. Rose, C. Stevens, et al. London: Lawrence & Wishart.

Aruna, V. K. 1994. "The Myth of One Closet." In *The Very Inside: An Anthology of Writing by Asian and Pacific Islander Lesbian and Bisexual Women*, ed. S. Lim-Hing. Toronto, ON: SisterVision.

Atkins, Dawn, ed. 2002. *Bisexual Women in the Twenty-first Century.* New York: Harrington Park Press.

Atkinson, Elizabeth. 2002. "Education for Diversity in a Multisexual Society: Negotiating the Contradictions of Contemporary Discourse." *Sex Education* 2(2): 119–32.

Attali, Jacques. 2005. "Monogamy: Here Today, Gone Tomorrow." *Foreign Policy*, www.foreignpolicy.com/story/cms.php?story_id=317&fpsrc=ealert050906 (retrieved 10 October 2005).

Audinet, Jacque. 2004. *The Human Face of Globalization: From Multiculturalism to Mestizaje.* Lanham, MD: Rowman & Littlefield.

Australian Medical Association. 2002. "Sexual Diversity and Gender Identity." Position Statement. www.ama.com.au/web.nsf/doc/WEEN-5HS7D3 (retrieved 30 April 2008).

Babcock, Barbara, ed. 1978. *The Reversible World: Symbolic Inversion in Art and Society.* Ithaca, NY: Cornell University Press.

Baird, Barbara. 2007. "'Gay Marriage,' Lesbian Wedding." *Gay and Lesbian Issues and Psychology Review* 3(3): 161–70.

Balsam, K. F., and J. J. Mohr. 2007. "Adaptation to Sexual Orientation Stigma: A Comparison of Bisexual and Lesbian/Gay Adults." *Journal of Counseling Psychology* 54(3): 306–19.

Barker, Meg. 2004. "This Is My Partner, and This Is My . . . Partner's Partner: Constructing a Polyamorous Identity in a Monogamous World." *International Journal of Constructivist Psychology* 18: 75–88.

Barker, Meg, and Darren Langdridge, eds. 2010. *Understanding Non-monogamies.* London: Routledge.

Bashford, Kerry. 1993. "Fanning the Flames." In *Kink*, ed. K. Bashford, J. Laybutt, A. Munster, and K. O'Sullivan. Sydney: Wicked Women Publications.

Bauman, Zygmunt. 1973. *Culture and Praxis.* London: Routledge & Kegan Paul.

———. 1988–1989. "Strangers: The Social Construction of Universality and Particularity." *Telos* 28: 7–42.

———. 1990. "Modernity and Ambivalence." In *Global Culture: Nationalism, Globalisation and Modernity*, ed. M. Featherstone. London: Sage.

———. 1991. *Modernity and Ambivalence.* Cambridge: Polity Press.

———. 1997. *Postmodernity and Its Discontents.* Cambridge: Polity Press.

Bear, Poohzen Dragon. 1998. "Our Children," *Loving More* 14: 28–29.

Beauchamp, Diane L. 2004. *Sexual Orientation and Victimization.* Ottawa, ON: Canadian Centre for Justice Statistics.

Becker, Howard S. 1973. *Outsiders: Studies in the Sociology of Deviance.* New York: The Free Press.

Bennett, Kathleen. 1992. "Feminist Bisexuality: A Both/And Option for an Either/Or World." In *Closer to Home: Bisexuality and Feminism*, ed. E. R. Weise. Seattle, WA: Seal Press.

Bersten, Rosanne. 2008. "Marginalia: Living on the Edge." *Gay and Lesbian Issues and Psychology Review* 4(1): 9–18.

Bettinger, Michael. 2005. "Polyamory and Gay Men: A Family Systems Approach." *Journal of GLBT Family Studies* 1(1): 97–116.

BeyondMarriage.org. 2006. *Beyond Same-Sex Marriage: A New Strategic Vision for All Our Families & Relationships.* www.beyondmarriage.org/full_statement.html (retrieved 26 October 2009).

Bhabha, Homi K. 1990a. "The Other Question: Difference, Discrimination and the Discourse of Colonialism." In *Out There: Marginalization and Contemporary Cultures*, ed. R. Ferguson, M. Gever, M. T. Trinh, and C. West. Cambridge, MA: MIT Press.

———. 1990b. "The Third Space." In *Identity: Community, Culture, Difference*, ed. J. Rutherford. London: Lawrence & Wishart.

———. 1994. *The Location of Culture.* London: Routledge.

Billson, Janet Mancini. 2005. "No Owner of Soil: Redefining the Concept of Marginality." In *Marginality, Power, and Social Structure: Issues in Race, Class and Gender Analysis*, ed. D. M. Rutledge. Amsterdam: Elsevier.

Block, Jenny. 2008. *Open: Love, Sex and Life in an Open Marriage.* Berkeley, CA: Seal Press.

Blumstein, Philip, and Pepper Schwartz. 1983. *American Couples: Money, Work, Sex.* New York: William Morrow & Co.

Boden, Deirdre. 1990. "The World as It Happens: Ethnomethodology and Conversation Analysis." In *Frontiers of Social Theory: the New Syntheses,* ed. G. Ritzer. New York: Columbia University Press.

Bonobo, Angel. 1996. *"French Twist:* Review." *Loving More* 2(2): 34.

Bordo, Susan. 1992. "Postmodern Subjects, Postmodern Bodies." *Feminist Studies* 18(1): 159–75.

Bottomley, Gill. 1992. *From Another Place: Migration and the Politics of Culture.* Melbourne, Australia: Cambridge University Press.

Botwin, Carol. 1994. *Tempted Women.* London: Vermilion.

Boulton, Mary, and Ray Fitzpatrick. 1993. "The Public and Personal Meanings of Bisexuality in AIDS." *Advances in Medical Sociology* 3: 77–100.

———. 1996. "Bisexual Men in Britain." In *Bisexualities and AIDS: International Perspectives,* ed. Peter Aggleton. Bristol, UK: Taylor & Francis.

Bourdieu, Pierre. 1977. *Outline of a Theory of Practice.* Cambridge: Cambridge University Press.

Bradford, Mary. 2004. "The Bisexual Experience: Living in a Dichotomous Culture." In *Current Research on Bisexuality,* ed. Ronald C. Fox. New York: Harrington Park Press.

Brew, Angela. 1998. "Moving Beyond Paradigm Boundaries." In *Writing Qualitative Research,* ed. J. Higgs. Sydney: Centre for Professional Education Advancement, University of Sydney and Hampden Press.

Britzman, Deborah P. 1998. *Lost Subjects, Contested Objects: Toward a Psychoanalytic Inquiry of Learning.* Albany: State University of New York Press.

Brosnan, Julia. 1996. *Lesbians Talk: Detonating the Nuclear Family.* London: Scarlet Press.

Brown, M. 2006. "A Geographer Reads *Geography Club*: Spatial Metaphor and Metonym in Textual/Sexual Space." *Cultural Geographies* 13: 313–39.

Brown, Rita Mae. 1988. *Bingo.* New York: Bantam.

Brownfain, John F. 1985. "A Study of the Married Bisexual Male: Paradox and Resolution." *Journal of Homosexuality* 11(1/2): 173–88.

Bryant, Wayne. 1996. *Bisexual Characters in Film: From Anais to Zee.* New York: Haworth Press.

———. 2005a. "The Bisexual Biopic." *Journal of Bisexuality* 5(1): 114–18.

———. 2005b. "Is That Me Up There?" *Journal of Bisexuality* 5(2): 305–12.

———. 2009. "Bi the Way." *Journal of Bisexuality* 9(3): 457–59.

Buntzly, Gerd. 1993. "Gay Fathers in Straight Marriages." In *If You Seduce a Straight Person, Can You Make Them Gay? Issues in Biological Essentialism versus Social Constructionism in Gay and Lesbian Identities,* ed. John P. De Cecco and John P. Elia. New York: Haworth Press.

Burbules, Nicholas C. 1997. "A Grammar of Difference: Some Ways of Rethinking Difference and Diversity as Educational Topics." *Australian Educational Researcher* 24(1): 97–116.

Burleson, William E. 2005. *Bi America: Myths, Truths, and Struggles of an Invisible Community.* New York: Harrington Park Press.

Burrell, Ian. 2005. "BBC to Screen: 'Dr Who for Adults' as a New Spin-Off Show." *Independent*, 16 August, http://news.independent.co.uk/media/article320110.ece (retrieved 27 May 2006).

Butler, Judith. 1990. *Gender Trouble: Feminism and the Subversion of Identity*. New York: Routledge.

———. 1991. "Imitation and Gender Insubordination." In *Inside/Out: Lesbian Theories, Gay Theories*, ed. D. Fuss. New York: Routledge.

———. 1993. *Bodies That Matter: On the Discursive Limits of "Sex."* New York: Routledge.

———. 2004a. *Precarious Life: The Powers of Mourning and Violence*. New York: Verso.

———. 2004b. *Undoing Gender*. New York: Routledge.

Buxton, Amity Pierce. 1991. *The Other Side of the Closet: The Coming Out Crisis for Straight Spouses*. Santa Monica, CA: IBS Press.

———. 1999. "The Best Interest of Children of Lesbian and Gay Parents." In *The Scientific Basis of Child Custody Decisions*, ed. Robert M. Galatzer-Levy and Louis Kraus. New York: John Wiley & Sons.

———. 2001. "Writing Our Own Script: How Bisexual Men and Their Heterosexual Wives Maintain Their Marriages after Disclosure." In *Bisexuality in the Lives of Men: Facts and Fiction*, ed. Brett Beemyn and Erich Steinman. New York: Harrington Park Press.

———. 2004. "Works in Progress: How Mixed-Orientation Couples Maintain Their Marriages after the Wives Come Out." In *Current Research on Bisexuality*, ed. Ron Fox. New York: Harrington Park Press.

———. 2006a. "A Family Matter: When a Spouse Comes Out as Gay, Lesbian, or Bisexual." In *An Introduction to GLBT Family Studies*, ed. J. Bigner. New York: Haworth Press.

———. 2006b. "Healing an Invisible Minority: How the Straight Spouse Network Has Become the Prime Source of Support for Those in Mixed-Orientation Marriages." In *Interventions with Families of Gay, Lesbian, Bisexual and Transgender People: From the Inside Out*, ed. J. Bigner and A. R. Gottlieb. New York: Harrington Park Press.

———. 2007. "Counseling Heterosexual Spouses of Bisexual or Transgender Partners." In *Becoming Visible: Counseling Bisexuals Across the Lifespan*, ed. B. Firestein. New York: Columbia University Press.

C., Natalie. 1997–1998. "Everywhere You Look There's a Hand to Hold." *Loving More* 12: 22–23.

Cabaj, R. P. 2005. "Other Populations: Gays, Lesbians and Bisexuals." In *Substance Abuse: A Comprehensive Textbook*, ed. J. H. Lowinson, P. Ruiz, R. B. Millman, and J. G. Langrod. Philadelphia: Lippincott Williams & Wilkins.

Campbell, James. 2008. "Jeff Kennett Gay Storm." *Herald Sun*, 27 July, www.news .com.au/heraldsun/story/0,21985,24083078-11088,00.html (retrieved 23 April, 2009).

Carrington, Victoria. 2001. "Globalization, Family and Nation State: Reframing 'Family' in New Times." *Discourse: Studies in the Cultural Politics of Education* 22(2): 185–96.

Ceres, Dan. 2005. *The Future of Family Law: Law and the Marriage Crisis in North America*. Report from the Council on Family Law. New York: Institute for American Values.

Chambers, Aidan. 1999. *Postcards from No Man's Land*. London: Random House.

Chambers, Iain. 1994. *Migrancy, Culture, Identity*. London: Routledge.

Channel 4.com's LGB Teens Health Site. 2007. "Am I Gay or Bisexual?" www .channel4.com/health/microsites/L/lgb_teens/boys/are-you-gay (retrieved 13 September 2007).

Chihara, Michelle. 2006. "Multi-Player Option: Young Polyamorists Are Rewriting the Laws of Desire." Nerve.com, http://.nerve.com/dispatches/multiplayeroption/ (retrieved 13 August 2006).

Cicioni, Mirna. 1998. "Male Pair Bonds and Female Desire in Fan Slash Writing." In *Theorizing Fandom: Fans, Subculture and Identity*, ed. C. Harris and A. Alexander. Cresskill, NJ: Hampton.

Clarke, Patsy. 2001. *The Internet as a Medium for Qualitative Research*. National Research Foundation, www.nrf.ac.za/yenza/vista/nrf_11feb/index.htm (retrieved 30 April 2008).

Cochran, S. D., and V. M. Mays. 1996. "Prevalence of HIV-Related Sexual Risk Behaviors among Young 18- to 24-Year-Old Lesbian and Bisexual Women." *Women's Health: Research on Gender, Behavior and Policy* 2(1/2): 75–89.

Cohen, Ira J. 1987. "Structuration Theory and Social Praxis." In *Social Theory Today*, ed. A. Giddens and J. H. Turner. Oxford: Polity Press.

Cohen, Stanley, and Laurie Taylor. 1976. *Escape Attempts: The Theory and Practice of Resistance to Everyday Life*. London: Allen Lane.

Colker, Ruth. 1996. *Hybrid: Bisexuals, Multiracials and Other Misfits under American Law*. New York: New York University Press.

Connelly, F. M., and D. J. Clandinin. 1990. "Stories of Experience and Narrative Inquiry." *Teacher Education Quarterly* 21(1): 145–58.

Constantine, Larry, and Joan Constantine. 1972. "Where Is Marriage Going?" In *Intimate Lifestyles: Marriage and Its Alternatives*, ed. J. S. DeLora and J. R. DeLora. Pacific Palisades, CA: Goodyear Publishing Company.

———. 1973. *Group Marriage: A Study of Contemporary Multilateral Marriage*. New York: MacMillan.

———. 1976. *Treasures of the Island: Children in Alternative Families*. Beverley Hills, CA: Sage.

Cook, Blanche Wiesen. 1993. *Eleanor Roosevelt*. Vol. 1, *1884–1933*. New York: Viking Press.

———. 1999. *Eleanor Roosevelt*. Vol. 2, *1933–1938*. New York: Viking Press.

Coomber, R. 1997. "Using the Internet for Survey Research." *Sociological Research Online*, 2(2), www.socresonline.org.uk/socresonline/2/2/2 (retrieved 5 June 2000).

Cope, Bill, and Mary Kalantzis. 1995. "Why Literacy Pedagogy Has to Change." *Education Australia* 30: 8–11.

Corboz, Julienne, Gary Dowsett, Anne Mitchell, Murray Couch, Paul Agius, and Marian Pitts. 2008. *Feeling Queer and Blue: A Review of the Literature on Depression and Related Issues among Gay, Lesbian, Bisexual and Other Homosexually Active People*. A report from the Australian Research Centre in Sex, Health and Society prepared for BeyondBlue: the National Depression Initiative. Melbourne, Australia: La Trobe University, ARCSHS.

Cotterell, J. L. 1994. "Analysing the Strength of Supportive Ties in Adolescent Social Supports." In *Social Networks and Social Support in Childhood and Adolescence*, ed. F. Nestmann and K. Hurrelmann. Berlin: Walter de Gruyter.

Culler, Jonathan. 1982. *On Deconstruction: Theory and Criticism after Structuralism.* Ithaca, NY: Cornell University Press.

Cunningham, Michael. 1990. *A Home at the End of the World.* New York: Picador.

Curran, Greg, Stephanie Chiarolli, and Maria Pallotta-Chiarolli. 2009. "'The C Words': Clitorises, Childhood and Challenging Compulsory Heterosexuality Discourses with Pre-service Primary Teachers." *Sex Education: Sexuality, Society and Learning* 9: 155–68.

Daniels, Les. 2004. *Wonder Woman: The Complete History.* San Francisco, CA: Chronicle Books.

D'Augelli, Anthony R. 2003. "Lesbian and Bisexual Female Youths Aged 14–21: Developmental Challenges and Victimization Experiences." *Journal of Lesbian Studies* 7(4): 9–29.

D'Augelli, A. R., S. L. Hershberger, and N. W. Pilkington. 1998. "Lesbian, Gay and Bisexual Youth and Their Families: Disclosure of Sexual Orientation and Its Consequences." *American Journal of Orthopsychiatry* 68: 361–71.

Davidson, Joy. 2002. "Working with Polyamorous Clients in the Clinical Setting." *Electronic Journal of Human Sexuality* 5, www.ejhs.org/volume5/polyoutline.html (retrieved 16 April 2008).

Davies, Bronwyn. 1991. "The Concept of Agency: A Feminist Poststructuralist Analysis." *Social Analysis* 30: 42–53.

Davies, Raven. 2005. "The Slash Fanfiction Connection to Bi Men." *Journal of Bisexuality* 5(2): 195–202.

Davis, Stephen A. 1991. *Future Sex.* Armadale, Australia: Awareness Through Education Publishing.

De Certeau, Michel. 1986. *Heterologies: Discourse on the Other.* Minneapolis: University of Minnesota Press.

Deleuze, Gilles. 1989. "Michel Tournier and the World without Others." In *Ideological Representation and Power in Social Relations: Literary and Social Theory*, ed. M. Gane. London: Routledge.

De Munck, Victor C. 1992. "The Fallacy of the Misplaced Self: Gender Relations and the Construction of Multiple Selves among Sri Lankan Muslims." *Ethos* 20(2): 167–90.

Denzin, N. 1989. *Interpretive Biography.* Newbury Park, CA: Sage.

———. 1997. *Interpretative Ethnography: Ethnographic Practices for the Twenty-first Century.* London: Sage.

———. 1999. "Cybertalk and the Method of Instances." In *Doing Internet Research*, ed. S. Jones. London: Sage.

De Oliveira, Eddie. 2004. *Lucky.* New York: PUSH

Derrida, Jacques. 1978. *Writing and Difference.* Chicago: University of Chicago Press.

———. 1981. *Positions.* Chicago: University of Chicago Press.

———. 1982. *Dissemination.* Chicago: University of Chicago Press.

Diamond, Lisa M. 2008. "Female Bisexuality from Adolescence to Adulthood: Results from a 10-Year Longitudinal Study." *Developmental Psychology* 44(1): 5–14.

———. 2009. *Sexual Fluidity: Understanding Women's Love and Desire.* Cambridge, MA: Harvard University Press.

Dirlik, Arif. 1987. "Culturalism as Hegemonic Ideology and Liberating Practice." *Cultural Critique* 6: 13–50.

Dobinson, Cheryl. 2003. "Improving the Access and Quality of Public Health Services for Bisexuals." Ontario Public Health Association, www.opha.on.ca/ppres/2003-04_pp.pdf (retrieved 30 April 2008).

———. 2005. "Improving the Access and Quality of Public Health Services for Bisexuals." *Journal of Bisexuality* 5(1): 39–77.

Dobner, Jennifer. 2006. *Teens Defend Polygamy at Utah Rally.* Foxnews.com, 20 August 2006, www.foxnews.com/wires/2006Aug20/0,4670,PolygamyRally,00.html (retrieved 30 April 2008).

Dodge, Brian, and Theo G. M. Sandfort. 2007. "A Review of Mental Health Research on Bisexual Individuals When Compared to Homosexual and Heterosexual Individuals." In *Becoming Visible: Counseling Bisexuals across the Lifespan,* ed. Beth A. Firestein. New York: Columbia University Press.

Dominus, Susan. 2009. "Most of the Seventh Grade Will Be at the Commitment Ceremony." *New York Times,* www.nytimes.com/2009/03/23/nyregion/23bigcity.html (retrieved 30 March 2009).

Douglas, Mary. 1966. *Purity and Danger: An Analysis of Concepts of Pollution and Taboo.* New York: Ark.

Dowsett, Gary. 1997. *Practicing Desire: Homosexual Sex in the Era of AIDS.* Stanford, CA: Stanford University Press.

Drabble, Laurie, and Karen Trocki. 2005. "Alcohol Consumption, Alcohol-Related Problems, and Other Substance Use among Lesbian and Bisexual Women." *Journal of Lesbian Studies* 9(3): 19–30.

Du Bois, Barbara. 1983. "Passionate Scholarship: Notes on Values, Knowing and Method in Feminist Social Science." In *Theories of Women's Studies,* ed. G. Bowles and R. D. Klein. London: Routledge & Kegan Paul.

Duff, Cameron. 2003. "The Importance of Culture and Context: Rethinking Risk and Risk Management in Young Drug Using Populations." *Health, Risk and Society* 5(3): 285–99.

Duncombe, Jean, and Dennis Marsden. 2004. "'From Here to Epiphany . . .': Power and Identity in the Narrative of an Affair." In *The State of Affairs: Explorations in Infidelity and Commitmen,* ed. J. Duncombe, K. Harrison, G. Allan, and D. Marsden. Mahwah, NJ: Lawrence Erlbaum Associates, Inc.

Duren-Sutherland, A., E. Sangrey, B. Tomison, et al. 1999. "Dealing with Responses from the Gay and Lesbian Worlds and the Straight World: Young People's Experiences." *Dulwich Centre Journal: Bisexuality* 1: 44–45.

Easton, Dossie, and Catherine A. Liszt. 1997. *The Ethical Slut.* San Francisco, CA: Greenery Press.

Edwards, Anne R. 1988. *Regulation and Repression: the Study of Social Control.* Sydney: Allen & Unwin.

Eisenberg, M., and H. Wechsler. 2003. "Substance Use Behaviours among College Students with Same-Sex and Opposite-Sex Experience: Results from a National Study." *Addictive Behaviours* 28: 899–913.

Eliason, M. 1997. "The Prevalence and Nature of Biphobia in Heterosexual Undergraduate Students." *Archives of Sexual Behaviour* 26(3): 3–17.

Eliason, Mickey. 2001. "Bi-Negativity: the Stigma Facing Bisexual Men." In *Bisexuality in the Lives of Men: Facts and Fictions*, ed. B. Beemyn and E. Steinman. New York: Haworth Press.

Ely, Margot, Margaret Anzul, Maryann Downing, and Ruth Vinz. 1997. *On Writing Qualitative Research: Living by Words*. London: Falmer Press.

Emens, Elizabeth F. 2004. "Monogamy's Law: Compulsory Monogamy and Polyamorous Existence." Public Law Working Paper No. 58, University of Chicago.

Entrup, Luke, and Beth A. Firestein. 2007. "Developmental and Spiritual Issues of Young People and Bisexuals of the Next Generation." In *Becoming Visible: Counseling Bisexuals across the Lifespan*, ed. Beth A. Firestein. New York: Columbia University Press.

Epstein, Debbie, and Richard Johnson. 1998. *Schooling Sexualities*. Buckingham, UK: Open University Press.

Epstein, Steven. 1987. "Gay Politics, Ethnic Identity: The Limits of Social Constructionism." *Socialist Review* 17(3/4): 9–54.

Erera, Pauline Irit. 2002. *Family Diversity: Continuity and Change in the Contemporary Family*. Thousand Oaks, CA: Sage.

Eribon, D. 2004. *Insult and the Making of a Gay Self*. Durham, NC: Duke University Press.

Evans, Terry. 2003. "Bisexuality: Negotiating Lives between Two Cultures." *Journal of Bisexuality* 3(2): 93–108.

Eysenbach, Gunther, and James E. Till. 2001. "Ethical Issues in Qualitative Research on Internet Communities." *British Medical Journal* 323(7321): 1103–5.

Fahs, Breanne. 2009. "Compulsory Bisexuality? The Challenges of Modern Sexual Fluidity." *Journal of Bisexuality* 9(3): 431–49.

Findlen, Barbara. 1995. "Is Marriage the Answer?" *Lesbians on the Loose*, July, pp. 22–23.

Firestein, Beth A., ed. 2007. *Becoming Visible: Counseling Bisexuals across the Lifespan*. New York: Columbia University Press.

Fisher, Diana. 2003. "Immigrant Closets: Tactical-Micro-Practices-in-the-Hyphen." In *Queer Theory and Communication: From Disciplining Queers to Queering the Discipline(s)*, ed. Gust A. Yep, Karen E. Lovaas, and John P. Elia. New York: Harrington Park Press.

Fletcher, Joseph, and Thomas Wassmer. 1970. *Hello Lovers! An Introduction to Situation Ethics*. Washington, DC: Corpus Books.

Ford, J. A., and J. L. Jasinski. 2006. "Sexual Orientation and Substance Use among College Students." *Addictive Behaviours* 31: 404–13.

Foster, Barbara, Michael Foster, and Letha Hadady. 1997. *Three in Love: Ménages à Trois from Ancient to Modern Times*. San Francisco, CA: Harper.

Foucault, Michel. 1977. *Discipline and Punish: The Birth of the Prison*. New York: Vintage Books.

———. 1978. *The History of Sexuality*. Vol. 1, *An Introduction*. New York: Pantheon.

———. 1984. "What Is Enlightenment?" and "On the Genealogy of Ethics: an Over-view of Work in Progress." In *The Foucault Reader*, ed. P. Rabinow. New York: Random House.

———. 1985. "Truth, Power and Sexuality." In *Subjectivity and Social Relations*, ed. V. Beechey and J. Donald. Philadelphia: Open University Press.

———. 1986. "Of Other Spaces." *Diacritics* 16: 22–27.

Fox, Ron, ed. 2004. *Current Research on Bisexuality*. New York: Harrington Park Press.

Francoeur, Robert T. 1972. *Eve's New Rib: Twenty Faces of Sex, Marriage and Family*. New York: Harcourt, Brace, Jovanovich.

Freire, Paolo. 1972. *Pedagogy of the Oppressed*. Harmondsworth, UK: Penguin.

Fuji Collins, J. 2004. "The Intersection of Race and Bisexuality: A Critical Overview of the Literature and Past, Present, and Future Directions of the 'Borderlands.'" In *Current Research on Bisexuality*, ed. Ron Fox. New York: Harrington Park Press.

Fuss, Diana, ed. 1991. *Inside/Out: Lesbian Theories, Gay Theories*. New York: Routledge.

Galupo, M. Paz. 2006. "Sexism, Heterosexism, and Biphobia: The Framing of Bisex-ual Women's Friendships." In *Bisexual Women: Friendship and Social Organization*, ed. M. Paz Galupo. New York: Harrington Park Press.

Galupo, M. Paz, Carin A. Sailer, and Sarah Causey St. John. 2004. "Friendships across Sexual Orientations: Experiences of Bisexual Women in Early Adulthood." In *Current Research on Bisexuality*, ed. Ron Fox. New York: Harrington Park Press.

Game, Ann, and Andrew Metcalfe. 1996. *Passionate Sociology*. London: Sage Publica-tions.

Gammon, M. A., and K. L. Isgro. 2006. "Troubling the Canon: Bisexuality and Queer Theory." *Journal of Homosexuality* 52(1–2): 159–84.

Garber, Marjorie. 1995. *Vice Versa: Bisexuality and the Eroticism of Everyday Life*. New York: Simon & Schuster.

Garner, Abigail. 2001. "Queered by Family, Queerspawn by Choice." Families Like Mine, www.familieslikemine.com/insight/queerspawn.html (retrieved 30 April 2008).

———. 2002. "My Turn: Don't 'Protect' Me; Give Me Your Respect." *Newsweek*, www.mnsbc.com/news/698891.asp?cp1=1 (retrieved 1 December 2002).

———. 2003. "Advice Column." Families Like Mine, www.familieslikemine.com/advice/0312.php (retrieved 24 June 2003).

———. 2004. *Families Like Mine: Children of Gay Parents Tell It Like It Is*. New York: HarperCollins.

Garofalo, R., R. C. Wolf, S. Kessel, J. Palfrey, and R. H. DuRant. 1998. "The Associa-tion between Health Risk Behaviours and Sexual Orientation among a School-Based Sample of Adolescents." *Pediatrics* 101(5): 895–902.

George, Sue. 1992. *Women and Bisexuality*. London: Scarlet Press.

Gibbs, Jack P. 1981. *Norms, Deviance and Social Control: Conceptual Matters*. New York: Elsevier.

Gibian, Ruth. 1992. "Refusing Certainty: Toward a Bisexuality of Wholeness." In *Closer to Home: Bisexuality and Feminism*, ed. E. R. Weise. Seattle, WA: Seal Press.

Giroux, Henry A. 1993. "Living Dangerously: Identity Politics and the New Cultural Racism: Towards a Critical Pedagogy of Representation." *Cultural Studies* 7(1): 1–27.

Glendinning, Victoria. 1983. *Vita: The Life of V. Sackville-West*. London: Penguin.

Gochros, Jean Schaar. 1989. *When Husbands Come Out of the Closet*. New York: Haworth Press.

Goetstouwers, Leo. 2006. "Affirmative Psychotherapy with Bisexual Men." *Journal of Bisexuality* 6(1/2): 27–49.

Goffman, Erving. 1973. *Stigma: Notes on the Management of Spoiled Identity*. Harmondsworth, UK: Penguin.

Goldfarb, Eva S., and Elizabeth M. Casparian. 2000. *Our Whole Lives: Sexuality Education for Grades 10–12*. Boston: Unitarian Universalist Association, United Church Board for Homeland Ministries.

Golovensky, David I. 1952. "The Marginal Man Concept: An Analysis and Critique." *Social Forces* 30(3): 333–39.

Goodenow, C., J. Netherland, and L. Szalacha. 2002. "AIDS-Related Risk among Adolescent Males Who Have Sex with Males, Females or Both: Evidence from a Statewide Survey." *American Journal of Public Health* 92(2): 203–10.

Goodfellow, Joy. 1997. "Narrative Inquiry: Musings, Methodology and Merits." In *Qualitative Research: Discourse on Methodology*, ed. J. Higgs. Sydney: Centre for Professional Education Advancement, University of Sydney and Hampden Press.

———. 1998a. "Analysing Data in Narrative Inquiry Research." In *Writing Qualitative Research*, ed. J. Higgs. Sydney: Centre for Professional Education Advancement, University of Sydney and Hampden Press.

———. 1998b. "Constructing a Narrative." In *Writing Qualitative Research*, ed. J. Higgs. Sydney: Centre for Professional Education Advancement, University of Sydney and Hampden Press.

Goss, Robert E. 1997. "Queering Procreative Privilege: Coming Out as Families." In *Our Families, Our Values: Snapshots of Queer Kinship*, ed. Robert E. Goss and A. Adams Squire Stronghart. New York: Harrington Park Press.

Goss, Robert E., and A. Adams Squire Stronghart. 1997. *Our Families, Our Values: Snapshots of Queer Kinship*. New York: Harrington Park Press.

Gross, Jane. 1992. "Does She Speak for Today's Women?" *New York Times Magazine*, March 1, pp. 16–19, 38, 54.

Grosz, Elizabeth. 1993. "Experimental Desire: Bodies and Pleasure in Queer Theory." Working Paper given at the Forces of Desire Conference, Humanities Research Centre, Australian National University, August 13–15.

Gunew, Sneja. 1994. *Framing Marginality: Multicultural Literary Studies*. Melbourne, Australia: Melbourne University Press.

Hagen, Whitney B. 2008. "Exploring Female Bisexuality in *April's Shower* and *Imagine Me & You*." *Journal of Bisexuality* 7(3): 345–51.

Halperin, David. 2009. "Thirteen Ways of Looking at a Bisexual." *Journal of Bisexuality* 9(3): 451–55.

Halpern, Ellen L. 1999. "If Love Is So Wonderful, What's So Scary about MORE?" In *The Lesbian Polyamory Reader: Open Relationships, Non-monogamy and Casual Sex*, ed. Marcia Munson and Judith P. Stelboum. New York: Harrington Park Press.

Haritaworn, Jin, Chin-ju Lin, and Christian Klesse. 2006. "Poly/logue: A Critical Introduction to Polyamory." *Sexualities* 9(5): 515–29.

Hart, Kylo-Patrick, R. 2005. "Cinematic Trash or Cultural Treasure? Conflicting Viewer Reactions to the Extremely Violent World of Bisexual Men in Gregg Araki's 'Heterosexual Movie' *The Doom Generation.*" *Journal of Bisexuality* 7(1/2): 52–69.

Hartinger, Brent. 2003. *Geography Club.* New York: Harper Collins.

Hashimoto, Miyuki. 2007. "Visual Kei Otaku Identity: An Intercultural Analysis." *Intercultural Communication Studies* 16(1): 87–99.

Hastings, Elizabeth. 1995. "From Margin to Text: The Work of Transition." In *Voices of a Margin: Speaking for Ourselves*, ed. L. Rowan and J. McNamee. Rockhampton, Australia: Central Queensland University Press.

Hatzenbuehler, Mark L., William R. Corbin, and Kim Fromme. 2008. "Trajectories and Determinants of Alcohol Use among LGB Young Adults and their Heterosexual Peers: Results from a Prospective Study." *Developmental Psychology* 44(1): 81–90.

Hawkins, J. D. 2002. "Risk and Protective Factors and Their Implications for Preventative Interventions for the Health Care Professional." In *Substance Abuse: A Guide for Health Professionals*, ed. M. Schydlower. Elk Grove Village, IL: American Academy of Pediatrics.

Heath, Mary. 2005. "Pronouncing the Silent 'B' (in GLBTTIQ)." Paper given at the Health in Difference 5 Conference, Melbourne, Australia, January 20–22.

Heckert, Jamie. 2005. "Resisting Orientation: On the Complexities of Desire and the Limits of Identity Politics." PhD diss., Sociology, University of Edinburgh.

Herdt, Gilbert. 2001. "Social Change, Sexual Diversity, and Tolerance for Bisexuality in the United States." In *Lesbian, Gay, and Bisexual Identities and Youth*, ed. Anthony D'Augelli and Charlotte J. Patterson. New York: Oxford University Press.

Herdt, Gilbert, and Andrew Boxer. 1995. "Bisexuality: Toward a Comparative Theory of Identities and Culture." In *Conceiving Sexuality: Approaches to Sex Research in a Postmodern World*, ed. Richard G. Parker and John H. Gagnon. New York: Routledge.

Herek, Gregory M. 2002. "Heterosexuals' Attitudes toward Bisexual Men and Women in the United States." *Journal of Sex Research* 39(4): 264–74.

Hershberger, S. L., N. W. Pilkington, and A. R. D'Augelli. 1997. "Predictors of Suicide Attempts among Gay, Lesbian and Bisexual Youths." *Journal of Adolescent Research* 12: 477–97.

Hewson, C., P. Yule, D. Laurent, and C. Vogel. 2003. *Internet Research Methods: A Practical Guide for the Social and Behavioural Sciences.* London: Sage.

Heyn, Dalma. 1992. *The Erotic Silence of the Married Woman.* London: Bloomsbury.

Hidalgo, Danielle Antoinette, Kristen Barker, and Erica Hunter. 2008. "The Dyadic Imaginary: Troubling the Perception of Love as Dyadic." *Journal of Bisexuality* 7(3): 171–89.

Hill, Brett. 1997. "An Unscientific . . . Yet Highly Significant . . . Survey of Polydom . . . Via the Net . . ." *Loving More* 11: 22–25.

Hillier, Lynne. 2007. *"This Group Gave Me a Family": An Evaluation of the Impact of Social Support Groups on the Health and Wellbeing of Same Sex Attracted Young People.* Melbourne, Australia: Australian Research Centre in Sex, Health and Society, La Trobe University.

Hillier, Lynne, Chyloe Kurdas, and Philomena Horsley. 2001. *"It's Just Easier": The Internet as a Safety-Net for Same-Sex Attracted Young People.* Melbourne, Australia: Australian Research Centre in Sex, Health and Society, La Trobe University.

Hine, C., ed. 2005. *Virtual Methods: Issues in Social Research on the Internet.* Oxford: Berg.

Hochschild, Arlie Russell. 1983. *The Managed Heart: Commercialization of Human Feeling.* Berkeley: University of California Press.

Homfray, Mike. 2008. "Standpoint, Objectivity, and Social Construction: Reflections from the Study of Gay and Lesbian Communities." *Sociological Research Online* 13(1), www.socrsonline.org.uk/13/1/7.html (retrieved 30 April 2008).

hooks, bell. 1990. *Yearning: Race, Gender, and Cultural Politics.* Boston: South End Press.

———. 1994a. *Outlaw Culture: Resisting Representations.* New York: Routledge.

———. 1994b. *Teaching to Transgress: Education as the Practice of Freedom.* New York: Routledge.

———. 1999. "Marginality as Site of Resistance." In *Out There: Marginalization and Contemporary Cultures*, ed. Russell Ferguson, Martha Gever, Trinh T. Minh-ha, and Cornel West. Cambridge, MA: MIT Press.

Howard, J., and A. Arcuri. 2006. "Drug Use among Same-Sex Attracted Young People." In *Sex, Drugs and Young People*, ed. P. Aggleton, A. Ball, and P. Mane. London: Routledge.

Huggins, Jackie. 1994. "Alone Again . . . Naturally." in *Weddings and Wives*, ed. D. Spender. Melbourne, Australia: Penguin.

Hughes, T. L., and M. Eliason. 2002. "Substance Use and Abuse in Lesbian, Gay, Bisexual and Transgender Populations." *Journal of Primary Prevention* 22(3): 263–98.

Hunn, D. 2002. "Australian Film," *GLBTQ: An Encyclopaedia of Gay, Lesbian, Bisexual, Transgender and Queer Culture*, www.glbtq.com/arts/bisex-film.html (retrieved 15 November 2002).

Hunter, J. 1996. "Emerging from the Shadows: Lesbian, Gay and Bisexual Adolescents: Personal Identity Achievement, Coming Out, and Sexual Risk Behaviours." PhD diss., City University of New York.

Hutchins, Loraine, and Lani Ka'ahumanu, eds. 1991. *Bi Any Other Name: Bisexual People Speak Out.* Boston: Alyson.

Iantaffi, Alessandre. 2006. "Polyamory and Parenting: Some Personal Reflections." *Lesbian and Gay Psychology Review* 7(1): 70–72.

Irvine, Janice M. 2001. "Educational Reform and Sexual Identity: Conflicts and Challenges." In *Lesbian, Gay, and Bisexual Identities and Youth: Psychological Perspectives*, ed. Anthony R. D'Augelli and Charlotte J. Patterson. New York: Oxford University Press.

Ito, M. 1996. "Theory, Method, and Design in Anthropologies of the Internet." *Social Science Computer Review*, 14(1): 24–26.

Itzkoff, Dave. 2006. "Sexed-Up British Intelligence." *New York Times*, 25 May, http://select.nytimes.com/gst/abstract.html?res=F6091EF63D550C768CDDAA0894DE404482 (retrieved 27 May 2006).

Jackson, Bruce. 1978. "Deviance as Success: The Double Inversion of Stigmatized Roles." In *The Reversible World: Symbolic Inversion in Art and Society*, ed. B. Babcock. Ithaca, NY: Cornell University Press.

Jackson, Stevi, and Sue Scott. 2003. "Whatever Happened to Feminist Critiques of Monogamy?" In *The Feminist Seventies*, ed. Helen Graham, Ann Kaloski, Ali Neilson, and Emma Robertson. York, UK: Raw Nerve Books.

James, Susan Donaldson. 2009. "Calvin Klein Ad Taps Foursome Sex." ABCNews. com, http://polyinthemedia.blogspot.com/2009/06/calvin-klein-foursome-ad -and-its.html (retrieved 1 November 2009).

Jamieson, Lynn. 2004. "Intimacy, Negotiated Nonomonogamy, and the Limits of the Couple." In *The State of Affairs: Explorations in Infidelity and Commitment*, ed. J. Duncombe, K. Harrison, G. Allen, and D. Marsden. London: Lawrence Erlbaum Associates.

Jeffreys, Sheila. 1999. "Bisexual Politics: A Superior Form of Feminism?" *Women's Studies International Forum* 22(3): 273–85.

Jenkins, Henry, Cynthia Jenkins, and Shoshanna Green. 1998. "'The Normal Female Interest in Men Bonking': Selections from Terra Nostra Underground and Strange Bedfellows." In *Theorizing Fandom: Fans, Subculture, and Identity*, ed. Cheryl Harris and Alison Alexander. Cresskill, NJ: Hampton Press.

Jensen, Michael. 2007. "Readers' Choice: The Top 25 Gay TV Characters Revealed." AfterElton.com, www/afterelton.com/people/2007/11/top25gayTVcharacters?pa ge=0 (retrieved 20 December 2007).

Johnson, Sonia. 1991. *The Ship That Sailed into the Living Room*. Estancia, NM: Wildfire Books.

Jones, R. A. 1994. "The Ethics of Research in Cyberspace." *Internet Research* 4(3): 30–35.

Jorm, Anthony F., Ailsa E. Korten, Bryan Rodgers, Patricia A. Jacomb, and Helen Christensen. 2002. "Sexual Orientation and Mental Health: Results from a Community Survey of Young and Middle-Aged Adults." *The British Journal of Psychiatry* 180: 423–27.

Joseph, Sue. 1997. *She's My Wife, He's Just Sex*. Sydney: Australian Centre for Independent Journalism, University of Technology.

Julz. 2005. "Magic Man." *Journal of Bisexuality* 5(2): 213–20.

Kamuf, Peggy, ed. 1991. *A Derrida Reader: Between the Blinds*. New York: Harvester Wheatsheaf.

Karlson, Marylou. 2007. "Bisexuals Exist—and So Do Bisexual Parents." *Bi-Victoria Newsletter*, August/September, pp. 1–4.

Kaye, Bonnie. 2003. "A Tribute to Children." *Bonnie Kaye's Straight Talk Newsletter* 3(25), www.Gayhusbands.com (retrieved 20 September 2003).

Kazmi, Yedullah. 1993. "Panopticon: A World Order Through Education or Education's Encounter with the Other/Difference." *Philosophy and Social Criticism* 19(2): 195–213.

Keating, AnaLouise, ed. 2000. *Gloria Anzaldua: Interviews/Entrevistas*. New York: Routledge.

Keith, Michael, and Steve Pile, eds. 1993. *Place and the Politics of Identity*. London: Routledge.

Kentlyn, Sue. 2008. "The Radically Subversive Space of the Queer Home: 'Safety House' and 'Neighbourhood Watch.'" *Australian Geographer* 39(3): 327–37.

Kieffer, Carolynne. 1977. "New Depths in Intimacy." In *Marriage and Alternatives: Exploring Intimate Relationships*, ed. R. W. Libby and R. N. Whitehurst. Glenview, IL: Scott, Foresman & Co.

King, Michael, and Eamonn McKeown. 2003. *Mental Health and Social Wellbeing of Gay Men, Lesbians and Bisexuals in England and Wales*. London: Mind (National Association for Mental Health).

King, S. A. 1996. "Researching Internet Communities: Proposed Ethical Guidelines for the Reporting of Results." *The Information Society* 12: 119–27.

Kinsey, Alfred C., Clyde E. Martin, and Paul H. Gebhard. 1953. *Sexual Behavior in the Human Female.* Bloomington: Indiana University Press.

Kinsey, Alfred C., Wardell P. Pomeroy, and Clyde E. Martin. 1948. *Sexual Behavior in the Human Male.* Bloomington: Indiana University Press.

Klein, Fritz. 1993. *The Bisexual Option.* New York: Harrington Park Press.

Klein, Fritz, and Tom Schwartz. 2001. *Bisexual and Gay Husbands: Their Stories, Their Words.* New York: Harrington Park Press.

Klesse, Christian. 2007. *The Spectre of Promiscuity: Gay Male and Bisexual Nonmonogamies.* Hampshire, UK: Ashgate.

Koh, Audrey S., and Leslie K. Ross. 2006. "Mental Health Issues: A Comparison of Lesbian, Bisexual and Heterosexual Women." *Journal of Homosexuality* 51(1): 33–57.

Koppelman, Susan, ed. 1994. *"Two Friends" and Other Nineteenth-Century Lesbian Stories by American Women Writers.* New York: Meridian

Kowalewski, Mark R. 1988. "Double Stigma and Boundary Maintenance: How Gay Men Deal With AIDS." *Journal of Contemporary Ethnography* 17(2): 211–28.

Kristeva, Julia. 1991. *Strangers to Ourselves.* New York: Columbia University Press.

Kroeger, Brooke. 2003. *Passing: When People Can't Be Who They Are.* New York: Public Affairs.

Kroenert, Tim. 2007. "Higgins' Honesty Deserves a Sporting Glance." ABC News, www.abc.net.au/news/stories/2007/12/20/2123616.htm (retrieved 24 December 2007).

Kurtz, Stanley. 2000. "What Is Wrong with Gay Marriage." *Commentary Magazine*, www.findarticles.com/cf_0/m1061/2_110/65014588/p1/article.jhtml?term (retrieved 13 March 2003).

———. 2003a. "Beyond Gay Marriage." *Weekly Standard*, www.weeklystandard.com/Utilities/printer_preview.asp?idArticle=2938&R=9DE61 (retrieved 16 June 2003).

———. 2003b. "Heather Has 3 Parents: On the Brink of the Abolition of Marriage and the Family." *National Review Online*, www.nationalreview.com/kurtz/kurtz031203.asp (retrieved 13 March 2003).

———. 2006. "Divorced from Reality." *Weekend Australian*, 21–22 January, pp. 19.

Lambert, Sheela. 2009. "Bisexuality Emerges in Teen/Young Adult Fiction." *Examiner*, www.examiner.com/examiner/x-17829-Bisexual-Examiner~y2009m9d12-Bisexuality-emerges-in-teenyoung-adult-fiction-Love-You-Two (retrieved 23 October 2009).

Lamey, Andy. 2003. "Why Everyone Should Be Able to Marry Anyone: The Case for Polygamy Is Similar to the Case for Gay Marriage." *National Post*, www.nationalpost.com/home/story.html?id=A05E507E-01B1-43E8-88EC-859591991D7F (retrieved 30 July 2003).

Lamont, Ani. 2008. "Drag Icon Prepares to Hang Her Heels in the Closet for the Last Time." *Sydney Star Observer*, 28 February, p. 5.

Lano, Kevin, and Clare Parry, eds. 1995. *Breaking the Barriers to Desire: New Approaches to Multiple Relationships.* Nottingham, UK: Five Leaves Publications.

Larsen, E. 1998. "Poly Sex for Beginners." *Utne Reader* 90: 20–21.

Le Compte, Margaret D. 1993. "A Framework for Hearing Silence: What Does Telling Stories Mean When We Are Supposed to be Doing Science?" In *Naming Silenced Lives: Personal Narratives and Processes of Educational Change,* ed. D. McLaughlin and W. G. Tierney. New York: Routledge.

Lees, Lisa. 2005. *Fool for Love*. East Lansing, MI: LisaLees.com.

———. 2006. *A Queer Circle of Friends*. East Lansing, MI: LisaLees.com.

Lehmiller, Justin J. 2009. "Secret Romantic Relationships: Consequences for Personal and Relational Well-Being." *Personality and Social Psychology Bulletin* 35(11): 1452–66.

Letts, Will, and James T. Sears, eds. 1999. *Queering Elementary Education: Advancing the Dialogue about Sexualities and Schooling*. Lanham, MD: Rowman & Littlefield.

Leviathan, David. 2003. *Boy Meets Boy*. London: HarperCollins.

Lewis, Marilyn Jaye. 2006. *Zowie! It's Yaoi! Western Girls Write Hot Stories of Boys' Love*. Philadelphia: Running Press.

Ley, David J. 2009. *Insatiable Wives: Women Who Stray and the Men Who Love Them*. Lanham, MD: Rowman & Littlefield.

Lincoln, Yvonna S. 1993. "I and Thou: Method, Voice, and Roles in Research with the Silenced." In *Naming Silenced Lives: Personal Narratives and Processes of Educational Change*, ed. D. McLaughlin and W. G. Tierney. New York: Routledge.

Lindenbaum, Pija. 1991. *Else-Marie and Her Seven Little Daddies*. New York: Henry Holt and Co.

Lionnet, Francoise. 1989. *Autobiographical Voices: Race, Gender, Self-Portraiture*. Ithaca, NY: Cornell University Press.

Lizarraga, Sylvia S. 1993. "The Gift?" In *Infinite Divisions: An Anthology of Chicana Literature*, ed. T. D. Rebolledo and E. S. Rivero. Tucson: University of Arizona Press.

Lugones, Maria. 1990. "Playfulness, 'World'-Traveling, and Loving Perception." In *Making Face, Making Soul: Haciendo Caras*, ed. G. Anzaldua. San Francisco, CA: Aunt Lute Books.

———. 1994. "Purity, Impurity, and Separation." In *Signs: Journal of Women in Culture and Society* 19(2): 458–79.

Madison, D. Soyini. 2007. "Co-performative Witnessing." *Cultural Studies* 21(6): 826–31.

Malinsky, Kathleen P. 1997. "Learning to be Invisible: Female Sexual Minority Students in America's Public High Schools." In *School Experiences of Gay and Lesbian Youth*, ed. Mary B. Harris. New York: Harrington Park Press.

Mann, Chris, and Fiona Stewart. 2000. *Internet Communication and Qualitative Research*. London: Sage.

Mansfield Courier. 2008. "Justice for Ken." http://justiceforken.blogspot.com/2008/04/who-is-ken-campagnolo.html (retrieved 23 April 2009).

Marotta, Vince. 2002. "Zygmunt Bauman: Order, Strangerhood and Freedom." *Thesis Eleven* 70: 36–54.

Martin, Erik. 2007. "Exploring Mental Health in Relation to Substance Use and Abuse amongst Bisexual Youth." Honours thesis, School of Health and Social Development, Deakin University, Melbourne, Australia.

Martin, Erik, and Maria Pallotta-Chiarolli. 2009. "'Exclusion by Inclusion': Bisexual Young People, Marginalisation and Mental Health in Relation to Substance Abuse." In *Theorising Social Connectedness and Social Exclusion*, ed. Ann Taket, Beth R. Crisp, Annemarie Nevill, Greer Lamaro, Melissa Graham, and Sarah Barter-Godfrey. London: Routledge.

Martino, Wayne, and Maria Pallotta-Chiarolli. 2001a. *Boys Stuff: Boys Talking about What Matters*. Sydney: Allen & Unwin.

———. 2001b. "Gender Performativity and Normalizing Practices." In *Unseen Genders: Beyond the Binaries*, ed. Felicity Haynes and Tarquam McKenna. New York: Peter Lang.

———. 2003. *So What's a Boy? Addressing Issues of Masculinity in Education*. London: Open University Press.

———. 2005. *"Being Normal Is the Only Way to Be": Adolescents' Perspectives on Gender and School*. Sydney: University of New South Wales Press.

Mason, Gail. 1995. "(Out)Laws: Acts of Proscription in the Sexual Order." In *Public and Private: Feminist Legal Debates*, ed. M. Thornton. London: Oxford University Press.

McCaffery, Larry, Sinda Gregory, Mari Kotani, and Tatsumi Takayuki. 2002. "The Twister of Imagination: An Interview with Mariko Ohara." Center for Book Culture.org, http://web.archive.org/web/20080209112923/http://www.centerfor bookculture.org/review/02_2_inter/interview_Ohara.html (retrieved 27 October 2009).

McDonald, Jan. 2001. "Connecting with the Lesbian Label: A Personal and Professional Evolution." In *Labeling: Pedagogy and Politics*, ed. Glenn M. Hudak and Paul Kihn. London: RoutledgeFalmer.

McGregor, Fiona. 1996. "I Am Not a Lesbian." *Meanjin* 55(1): 31–46.

McLaren, Peter. 1993. "Multiculturalism and the Postmodern Critique: Towards a Pedagogy of Resistance and Transformation."*Cultural Studies* 1: 118–43.

McLean, Kirsten. 2001. "Living Life in the Double Closet: Young Bisexuals Speak Out." *Hecate* 27(1): 109–18.

———. 2003. "Identifying as Bisexual: Life Stories of Australian Bisexual Men and Women." PhD diss., School of Political and Social Inquiry, Monash University.

———. 2004. "Negotiating (Non)Monogamy: Bisexuality and Intimate Relationships." In *Current Research on Bisexuality*, ed. Ron Fox. New York: Harrington Park Press.

———. 2005. "Out of the Shadows: Talking Bisexuality in the Classroom." In *When Our Children Come Out: How to Support Gay, Lesbian, Bisexual and Transgender Young People*, ed. Maria Pallotta-Chiarolli. Sydney: Finch Publishing.

———. 2008. "'Coming Out, Again': Boundaries, Identities and Spaces of Belonging." *Australian Geographer* 39(3): 303–13.

McLelland, Mark. 2000. *Male Homosexuality in Modern Japan: Cultural Myths and Social Realities*. Richmond, UK: Curzon Press.

———. 2005. "The World of 'Yaoi': The Internet, Censorship and the Global 'Boys' Love' Fandom." *Australian Feminist Law Journal* 23: 61–77.

———. 2006. "Why Are Japanese Girls' Comics Full of Boys Bonking?" *Refractory*, http://blogs.arts.unimelb.edu.au/refractory/2006/12/04/why-are-japanese -girls%E2%80%99-comics-full-of-boys-bonking1-mark-mclelland/ (retrieved 1 November 2009).

McLennen, Joan C. 2003. "Researching Gay and Lesbian Domestic Violence: The Journey of the Non-LGBT Researcher." In *Research Methods with Gay, Lesbian, Bisexual, and Transgender Populations*, ed. W. Meezan and J. I. Martin. New York: Harrington Park Press.

McNair, Ruth, Anne Kavanagh, Paul Agius, and Bin Tong. 2005. "The Mental Health Status of Young Adult and Mid-life Non-heterosexual Australian Women." *Australia and New Zealand Journal of Public Health* 29(3): 265–71.

McQuarrie, Vanessa. 1999. "Bisexuals Take Case to ADB Meeting." *Sydney Star Observer*, Thursday, 25 March, p. 4.

Meigs, Mary. 1983. *The Medusa Head*. Vancouver, BC: Talonbooks.

Meyrowitz, Joshua. 1985. *No Sense of Place: The Impact of the Electronic Media on Social Behavior*. New York: Oxford University Press.

Midanik, Lorraine T., Laurie Drabble, Karen Trocki, and Randall L. Sell. 2007. "Sexual Orientation and Alcohol Use: Identity versus Behavior Measures." *Journal of LGBT Health Research* 3(1): 25–35.

Miller, Marshall, Amy Andre, Julie Ebin, and Leona Bessonova, eds. 2007. *Bisexual Health: An Introduction and Model Practices for HIV/STI Prevention Programming*. New York: National Gay and Lesbian Task Force Policy Institute, Fenway Community Health, and BiNet, USA.

Ministerial Advisory Committee on Gay and Lesbian Health. 2003. *What's the Difference? Health Issues of Major Concern to Gay, Lesbian, Bisexual, Transgender and Intersex (GLBTI) Victorians*. Melbourne, Australia: Rural and Regional Health and Aged Care Services Division, Victorian Government Dept of Human Services.

Ministerial Advisory Committee on Gay, Lesbian, Bisexual, Transgender and Intersex Health and Wellbeing. 2009. *Well Proud: A Guide to Gay, Lesbian, Bisexual, Transgender and Intersex Inclusive Practice for Health and Human Services*. Melbourne, Australia: Department of Health.

Mizoguchi, Akiko. 2003. "Male-Male Romance by and for Women in Japan: A History and the Subgenres of Yaoi Fictions." *U.S.-Japan Women's Journal* 25: 49.

Molina, Maria Luisa "Papusa." 1994. "Fragmentations: Meditations on Separatism." *Signs: Journal of Women in Culture and Society* 19(2): 449–57.

Moore, Debra L., and Fran H. Norris. 2005. "Empirical Investigation of the Conflict and Flexibility Models of Bisexuality." *Journal of Bisexuality* 5(1): 5–25.

Moore, Inga. 1991. *Six-Dinner Sid*. New York: Simon and Schuster.

Moraga, Cherrie. 1981. "The Welder." In *This Bridge Called My Back: Writings By Radical Women of Color*, ed. C. Moraga and G. Anzaldua. Watertown, MA: Persephone Press.

Moran, Jonathon. 2007. "Higgins Outs Herself." *Daily Telegraph*, www.news.com .au/daily telegraph/story/0,22049, 22775273-5001021.html (retrieved 18 November 2007).

Morgan, Anne. 2001. "The Effect of Polyrays on Small Susceptible Children." *Alternative Lives*, www.alternativelives.org/theeffectofpolyrays.htm (retrieved 1 November 2001).

Morris, Jessica F., Kimbery F. Balsam, and Esther D. Rothblum. 2002. "Lesbian and Bisexual Mothers and Nonmothers: Demographics and the Coming-Out Process." *Journal of Family Psychology* 16(2): 144–56.

Mosher, William D., Anjani Chandra, and Jo Jones. 2005. "Sexual Behavior and Selected Health Measures: Men and Women 15–44 Years of Age, United States, 2002." *Advance Data from Vital and Health Statistics*, no. 362, www.cdc.gov/nchs/ data/ad/ad362.pdf (retrieved 18 November 12005).

Mroczek, Ken. 1994. "Women Who Love More Than One: A Qualitative Study." *Floodtide* 5(3): 10.

Murphy, Marilyn. 1990. "Thinking about Bisexuality." *Resources for Feminist Research* 19(3/4): 87–88.

Nagaike, Kazumi. 2003. "Perverse Sexualities, Perverse Desires: Representations of Female Fantasies and Yaoi Manga as Pornography Directed at Women." *U.S.-Japan Women's Journal* 25: 76.

Nahas, Rebecca, and Myra Turley. 1979. *The New Couple: Women and Gay Men*. New York: Seaview Books.

Naples, N. 2004. "The Outsider Phenomenon." In *Feminist Perspectives on Social Research*, ed. S. N. Hesse-Biber and M. L. Yaiser. Oxford: Oxford University Press.

Nardi, B. A. 1996. "Cyberspace, Anthropological Theory, and the Training of Anthropologists." *Social Science Computer Review*, 14(1): 34–35.

Nathanson, Jessica. 2009. "Bisexual Pedagogy: Bringing Bisexuality into the Classroom." *Journal of Bisexuality* 9(1): 71–86.

Nearing, Ryam. 1992. *Loving More: The Polyfidelity Primer*. Hawaii: PEP Publishing.

———. 1995. "Viewpoint." *Loving More* 1(2): 28–29.

———. 1996a. "Can Love Last?" *Loving More* 2(1): 4–5.

———. 1996b. "Poly Political Animals Speak." *Loving More* 8: 22–23.

———. 2001. "But What about the Kids: An Interview with Glorianna." *Loving More* 24: 10–13.

Newitz, Annalee. 2006. "Love Unlimited." *New Scientist* 2559, 7 July, pp. 44–47.

News.com, "Lindsay Lohan Says She's Bisexual, Not a Lesbian." www.news.com.au/entertainment/story/0,26278,24634157-7 (retrieved 14 January 2008).

Newman, Leslea. 2000. *Heather Has Two Mommies*. Los Angeles, CA: Alyson Books.

Nicholson, Linda J., ed. 1990. *Feminism/Postmodernism*. New York: Routledge.

Nicolson, Nigel. 1973. *Portrait of a Marriage*. London: Weidenfeld and Nicolson.

Nielsen, J. 1997. "Community Is Dead; Long Live Mega-Collaboration." Alertbox, August 15, 1997, www.useit.com/alertbox/9708b.html (retrieved 4 July 2000).

Noel, Melita J. 2006. "Progressive Polyamory: Considering Issues of Diversity." *Sexualities* 9(5): 602–620.

Obama, Barack. 2004. *Dreams from My Father: A Story of Race and Inheritance*. New York: Three Rivers Press.

O'Brien, Jodi. 2007. "Queer Tensions: The Cultural Politics of Belonging and Exclusion in Same Gender Marriage Debates." In *Sexual Politics of Desire and Belonging*, ed. N. Rumens and A. Cervantes-Carson. Amsterdam: Rodopi.

Ocean, Mia. 2008. "Bisexuals Are Bad for the Same Sex Marriage Business." *Journal of Bisexuality* 7(3): 303–11.

Orlando, Lisa. 1991. "Loving Whom We Choose." In *Bi Any Other Name: Bisexual People Speak Out*, ed. L. Hutchins and L. Ka'ahumanu. Boston: Alyson Publications.

Owens, Robert E. 1998. *Queer Kids: The Challenges and Promises for Lesbian, Gay, and Bisexual Youth*. New York: Harrington Park Press.

Page, E. H. 2004. "Mental Health Services Experiences of Bisexual Women and Bisexual Men: An Empirical Study." *Journal of Bisexuality* 3(3/4): 137–60.

Page, Emily. 2007. "Bisexual Women's and Men's Experiences of Psychotherapy." In *Becoming Visible: Counseling Bisexuals across the Lifespan*, ed. Beth A. Firestein. New York: Columbia University Press.

Pallotta-Chiarolli, Maria. 1995a. "Choosing Not to Choose: Beyond Monogamy, Beyond Duality." In *Breaking the Barriers of Desire: New Approaches to Multiple Relationships*, ed. K. Lano and C. Parry. London: Five Leaves Publications.

———. 1995b. "'A Rainbow in My Heart': Negotiating Sexuality and Ethnicity." In *Ethnic Minority Youth in Australia: Challenges and Myths*, ed. C. Guerra and R. White. Hobart, Australia: National Clearinghouse on Youth Studies.

———. 1996. "Only Your Labels Split the Confusion: Of Impurity and Unclassifiability." *Critical InQueeries* 1(2): 97–118.

———. 1999a. "Diary Entries from the 'Teachers' Professional Development Playground': Multiculturalism Meets Multisexualities in Education." In *Multicultural Queer: Australian Narratives*, ed. Gerard Sullivan and Peter Jackson. New York: Haworth Press.

———. 1999b. "'Multicultural Does Not Mean Multisexual': Social Justice and the Interweaving of Ethnicity and Sexuality in Australian Schooling." In *A Dangerous Knowing: Sexual Pedagogies and the Master Narrative*, ed. Debbie Epstein and James T. Sears. London: Cassell.

———. 1999c. "'My Moving Days': A Child's Negotiation of Multiple Lifeworlds in Relation to Gender, Ethnicity and Sexuality." In *Queering Elementary Education: Advancing the Dialogue about Sexualities and Schooling*, ed. Will Letts and James T. Sears. Lanham, MD: Rowman & Littlefield.

———. 1999d. *Tapestry*. Sydney: Random House.

———. 2002. "Polyparents Having Children, Raising Children, Schooling Children." *Loving More* 31: 2002: 8–12.

———. 2004. "'Take Four Pioneering Poly Women': A Review of Three Classical Texts on Polyamory." In *Plural Loves: Designs for Bi and Poly Living*, ed. Serena Anderlini-D'Onofrio. New York: Harrington Park Press.

———. 2005a. "We're the X-Files": Bisexual Students "Messing Up Tidy Sex Files." In *Sexuality, Sport and the Culture of Risk*, ed. Keith Gilbert. Oxford: Meyer and Meyer.

———. 2005b. *When Our Children Come Out: How to Support Gay, Lesbian, Bisexual and Transgender Young People*. Sydney: Finch Publishing.

———. 2006a. "On the Borders of Sexuality Research: Young People Who Have Sex with Both Males and Females." *Journal of Gay and Lesbian Issues in Education* 3(2–3): 79–86.

———. 2006b. "Polyparents Having Children, Raising Children, Schooling Children." *Lesbian and Gay Psychology Review* 7(1): 48–53.

———. 2006c. "The Someone I Got to Know." In *Gals with Gay Pals*, ed. Tanja Lee Jones. Melbourne, Australia: Tanjable Press.

———. 2008. *Love You Two*. Sydney: Random House.

———. Forthcoming. *Outside Belonging: Women in Relationships with Bisexual Men*. New York: Lexington Books.

Pallotta-Chiarolli, Maria, and Sara Lubowitz. 2003. "Outside Belonging: Multi-Sexual Relationships as Border Existence." In *Women and Bisexuality: A Global Perspective*, ed. Serena Anderlini-D'Onofrio. New York: Haworth Press.

Pallotta-Chiarolli, Maria, and Erik Martin. 2009. "Which Sexuality? Which Service?" Bisexual Young People's Experiences with Youth, Queer and Mental Health Services." *Journal of LGBT Youth* 6: 199–222.

Parsons, J. T., B. C. Kelly, and B. C. Wells. 2006. "Differences in Club Drug Use between Heterosexual and Lesbian/Bisexual Females." *Addictive Behaviours* 31: 2344–49.

Parton, Dolly. 1994. *Dolly: My Life and Other Unfinished Business.* New York: Harper Collins.

Paul, Jay P., Joseph Catania, Lance Pollack, Judith Moskowitz, Jesse Canchola, Thomas Mills, Diane Binson, and Ron Stall. 2002. "Suicide Attempts among Gay and Bisexual Men: Lifetime Prevalence and Antecedents." *American Journal of Public Health* 92(8): 1338–45.

Persson, Ashe, and Wendy Richards. 2008. "From Closet to Heterotopia: A Conceptual Exploration of Disclosure and 'Passing' among Heterosexuals Living with HIV." *Culture, Health and Sexuality* 10(1): 73–86.

Peterson, Larry W. 2001. "The Married Man On-Line." *Journal of Bisexuality* 1(2/3): 191–209.

Petrella, Serena. 2007. "Ethical Sluts and Closet Polyamorists: Dissident Eroticism, Abject Subjects and the Normative Cycle in Self Help Books on Free Love." In *Sexual Politics of Desire and Belonging*, ed. N. Rumens and A. Cervantes-Carson. Amsterdam: Rodopi.

Pettman, Jan. 1986. "Race and Ethnicity in Contemporary Australia." Working Paper No. 7. Centre for Multicultural Education, University of London Institute of Education and Australian Studies Centre, Institute of Commonwealth Studies.

———. 1992. *Living in the Margins.* Sydney: Allen & Unwin.

Phelan, Shane. 1994. *Getting Specific: Postmodern Lesbian Politics.* Minneapolis: University of Minnesota Press.

Pieper, Marianne, and Robin Bauer. 2005. "Mono-Normativity and Polyamory." Paper delivered at the International Conference on Polyamory and Mono-Normativity, November 4–6. Research Centre for Feminist, Gender and Queer Studies, University of Hamburg.

Pitt, R., Jr. 2006. "Downlow Mountain? De/stigmatizing Bisexuality through Pitying and Pejorative Discourses in the Media." *Journal of Men's Studies* 14(20): 254–58.

Plummer, Kenneth. 1975. *Sexual Stigma: An Interactionist Account.* London: Routledge & Kegan Paul.

Polyamory.org. 2006. www.polyamory.org (retrieved 28 January 2010).

Prineas, Eleni. 1995. "The State of the Date." *Lesbians on the Loose*, April, pp. 22–23.

Probyn, Elspeth. 1996. *Outside Belongings.* New York: Routledge.

Prodan, Lena. 2008. *The Suicide Year.* Round Rock, TX: Prizm Books.

Pumariega, A. J., M. D. Kilgus, and L. Rodriguez. 2005. "Adolescents" in *Substance Abuse: A Comprehensive Textbook*, ed. J. H. Lowinson, P. Ruiz, R. B. Millman, and J. G. T. Langrod. Philadelphia: Lippincott, Williams and Wilkins.

Purdon, Fiona. 2007. "Age of 'Fluid Sexuality.'" *Courier Mail*, www.news.com.au/couriermail/story/0,23739,22822577-23272,99.html (retrieved 24 December 2007).

Rabinow, Paul. 1984. *The Foucault Reader.* London: Penguin.

Rafaeli, S., F. Sudweeks, J. Knostan, and E. Mabry. 1994. *Project H Overview: A Quantitative Study of Computer-Mediated Communication*, www.arch.usyd.edu.au/~fay/projecth.html (retrieved 8 January 2000).

Ralston, Caroline. 1988. "Polyandry, 'Pollution,' 'Prostitution': The Problems of Eurocentrism and Androcentrism in Polynesian Studies." In *Crossing Boundaries:*

Feminism and the Critique of Knowledges, ed. B. Caine, E. A. Grosz and M. de Leper-vanche. Sydney: Allen and Unwin.

Rambukkana, Nathan Patrick. 2004. "Uncomfortable Bridges: The Bisexual Politics of Outing Polyamory." In *Plural Loves: Designs for Bi and Poly Living*, ed. S. Anderlini-D'Onofrio. New York: Haworth Press.

Rasmussen, Mary Lou. 2004. "Wounded Identities, Sex and Pleasure: 'Doing It' at School. NOT!" *Discourse: Studies in the Cultural Politics of Education* 25(4): 445–58.

———. 2006. "Play School, Melancholia, and the Politics of Recognition." *British Journal of Sociology of Education* 27(4): 473–87.

Rasmussen, Mary Lou, and Vicki Crowley. 2004. "Wounded Identities and the Promise of Pleasure." *Discourse: Studies in the Cultural Politics of Education* 25(4): 427–30.

Rehaag, Sean. 2009. "Bisexuals Need Not Apply: A Comparative Appraisal of Refugee Law and Policy in Canada, the United States, and Australia." *The International Journal of Human Rights* 13(2): 415–36.

Richardson, Laurel. 1985. *The New Other Woman*. New York: The Free Press.

Richters, Juliet. 1997. "Bisexuals." In *Health in Difference: Proceedings of the First National Lesbian, Gay, Transgender and Bisexual Health Conference*, Sydney, 3–5 October 1996, ed. Juliet Richters, Ross Duffin, Janet Gilmour, Jude Irwin, Richard Roberts, and Anthony Smith. Sydney: Australian Centre for Lesbian and Gay Research.

Riggs, Damien W. 2007. "Psychology, Liberalism, and Activism: Challenging Discourses of 'Equality With' in the Same-Sex Marriage Debate." *Gay and Lesbian Issues in Psychology Review* 3(3): 185–94.

Ritchie, Ani, and Meg Barker. 2006. "'There Aren't Words for What We Do or How We Feel So We Have to Make Them Up': Constructing Polyamorous Languages in a Culture of Compulsory Monogamy." *Sexualities* 9(5): 584–601.

Robin, Leah, Nancy D. Brener, Shaun F. Donahue, Tim Hack, Kelly Hale, and Carol Goodenow. 2002. "Association between Health Risk Behaviors and Opposite-, Same-, and Both-Sex Sexual Partners in Representative Samples of Vermont and Massachusetts High School Students." *Archives of Pediatrics and Adolescent Medicine* 156(4): 349–56.

Robson, R. 1992. "Mother: The Legal Domestication of Lesbian Existence." *Hypatia* 7: 172–85.

Rofes, Eric. 1997. "Dancing Bears, Performing Husbands, and the Tyranny of the Family." In *Our Families, Our Values: Snapshots of Queer Kinship*, ed. R. E. Goss and A. Adams Squire Stronghart. New York: Haworth Press.

Roiphe, Katie. 2007. *Uncommon Arrangements: Seven Literary Marriages*. New York: Dial Press.

Root, Maria P. P., ed. 1992. *Racially Mixed People in America*. Newbury Park, CA: Sage.

Roseneil, Sasha, and Shelley Budgeon. 2004. "Cultures of Intimacy and Care beyond 'The Family': Personal Life and Social Change in the Early 21st Century." *Current Sociology* 52(2): 135–59.

Rothblum, E. D., and R. Factor. 2001. "Lesbians and Their Sisters as a Control Group Demographic and Mental Health Factors." *Psychological Science* 12(1): 63–69.

Rubin, Gayle. 1984. "Thinking Sex: Notes for a Radical Theory of the Politics of Sexuality." In *Pleasure and Danger: Exploring Female Sexuality*, ed. C. S. Vance. Boston: Routledge & Kegan Paul.

Rubin, Roger H. 2001. "Alternative Lifestyles Revisited, or Whatever Happened to Swingers, Group Marriages, and Communes?" *Journal of Family Issues* 22(6): 711–26.

Rudy, Kathy. 1997. "'Where Two or More Are Gathered': Using Gay Communities as a Model for Christian Sexual Ethics." In *Our Families, Our Values: Snapshots of Queer Kinship*, ed. R. Goss and A. Adams Squire Stronghart. New York: Harrington Park Press.

Russell, Stephen T., Brian T. Franz, and Anne K. Driscoll. 2001. "Same-Sex Romantic Attraction and Experiences of Violence in Adolescence." *American Journal of Public Health* 91(6): 903–6.

Russell, Stephen T., and Hinda Seif. 2002. "Bisexual Female Adolescents: A Critical Analysis of Past Research and Results from a National Survey." *Journal of Bisexuality* 2(2/3): 73–94.

Russell, Stephen T., Hinda Seif, and Nhan L. Truong. 2001. "School Outcomes of Sexual Minority Youth in the United States: Evidence from a National Study." *Journal of Adolescence* 24: 111–27.

Russo, Vito. 1987. *The Celluloid Closet: Homosexuality in the Movies.* New York: Harper & Row.

Rust, Paula C. 1992. "Who Are We and Where Do We Go from Here? Conceptualising Bisexuality." In *Closer to Home: Bisexuality and Feminism*, ed. E. R. Weise. Seattle, WA: Seal Press.

Rutledge, Dennis M. 2005. "The Age of Marginality." In *Marginality, Power, and Social Structure: Issues in Race, Class and Gender Analysis*, ed. D. M. Rutledge. Amsterdam: Elsevier.

Ryan, Caitlin, and Ian Rivers. 2003. "Lesbian, Gay, Bisexual and Transgender Youth: Victimization and Its Correlates in the USA and UK." *Culture, Health and Sexuality* 5(2): 103–19.

Ryan, Maureen. 2007. "Spike from 'Buffy' and 'Torchwood's' Captain Jack Harkness—Youza." *Chicago Tribune*, http://featuresblogs.chicagotribune.com/entertainment-tv/2007/07/spike-fr (retrieved 14 July 2007).

Ryan, Michael. 1993. "Foucault's Fallacy." *Strategies* 7: 132–54.

Saewyc, E., L. H. Bearinger, R. W. Blum, and M. D. Resnick. 1999. "Sexual Intercourse, Abuse and Pregnancy among Adolescent Women: Does Sexual Orientation Make a Difference?" *Family Planning Perspectives* 31(3): 127–31.

Sagarin, Edward. 1977. "Sex Deviance: A View from the Window of Middle America." In *Deviants: Voluntary Actors in a Hostile World*, ed. E. Sagarin and F. Montanino. New York: General Learning Press.

Samuels, Ellen. 2003. "My Body, My Closet: Invisible Disability and the Limits of Coming-Out Discourse." *GLQ: A Journal of Lesbian and Gay Studies* 9(1/2): 233–55.

Sanders, T. 2005. "Researching the Online Sex Work Community." In *Virtual Methods: Issues in Social Research on the Internet*, ed. C. Hine. Oxford: Berg.

Sartre, Jean-Paul. 1943. *Being and Nothingness.* Paris: Gallimard.

Savin-Williams, Ritch. 2005. *The New Gay Teenager.* Cambridge, MA: Harvard University Press.

———. 2008. "Then and Now: Recruitment, Definition, Diversity, and Positive Attributes of Same-Sex Populations." *Developmental Psychology* 44(1): 135–38.

Schur, Edwin M. 1971. *Labeling Deviant Behavior: Its Sociological Implications*. New York: Harper and Row.

Schutz, Alfred. 1944. "The Stranger: An Essay in Social Psychology." *American Journal of Sociology* 49(6): 499–507.

Sedgwick, Eve Kosofsky. 1990. *Epistemology of the Closet*. Los Angeles: University of California Press.

———. 1993. "Axiomatic." In *The Cultural Studies Reader*, ed. S. During. London: Routledge.

Seidman, Steven. 1993. "Identity and Politics in a 'Postmodern' Gay Culture: Some Historical and Conceptual Notes." In *Fear of a Queer Planet: Queer Politics and Social Theory*, ed. M. Warner. Minneapolis: University of Minnesota Press.

———. 2001. "From Identity to Queer Politics: Shifts in Normative Heterosexuality and the Meaning of Citizenship." *Citizenship Studies* 5(3): 321–28.

Seidman, S., C. Meeks, and F. Traschen. 1999. "Beyond the Closet? The Changing Social Meaning of Homosexuality in the US." *Sexualities* 2: 9–34.

Sewell, William H. 1992. "A Theory of Structure: Duality, Agency, and Transformation." *American Journal of Sociology* 98(1):1–29.

Sheff, Elisabeth. 2006. "Poly-Hegemonic Masculinities." *Sexualities* 9(5): 621–42.

———. 2008. "The Privilege of Perversities: Race and Socio-economic Status among Polyamorists and Kinksters." Paper courtesy of the author.

Shuster, Rebecca. 1987. "Sexuality as a Continuum: The Bisexual Identity." In *Lesbian Psychologies: Explorations and Challenges*, ed. Boston Lesbian Psychologies Collective. Chicago: University of Illinois Press.

Sieber, J. E. 1993. "The Ethics and Politics of Sensitive Research." In *Researching Sensitive Topics*, ed. C. M. Renzetti and R. M. Lee. London: Sage.

Simmel, Georg. 1971. *On Individuality and Social Forms: Selected Writings*. Chicago: University of Chicago Press.

Simpson, Mark. 2006. "Curioser and Curioser: The Strange 'Disappearance' of Male Bisexuality." MarkSimpson.com www.marksimpson.com/blog/2006/04/26/curiouser-and-curiouser-the-strange-disappearance-of-male-bisexuality (retrieved 26 October, 2009).

Singer, Joy. 1996. "For Better or for Worse: How the Law and Politics of Gay Marriage Affect Polys." *Loving More* 8: 4–6.

Smart, Jeffrey. 1994. "Coming IN." *Brother Sister*, 22 April, p. 9.

Soja, Edward, and Barbara Hooper. 1993. "The Spaces That Difference Makes: Some Notes on the Geographical Margins of the New Cultural Politics." In *Place and the Politics of Identity*, ed. M. Keith and S. Pile. London: Routledge.

Squires, Judith. 1992. "Editorial." *New Formations* 18: v–vii.

Stallybrass, Peter, and Allon White. 1986. *The Politics and Poetics of Transgression*. London: Methuen.

Stonequist, Everett V. 1961. *The Marginal Man: A Study in Personality and Culture Conflict*. New York: Russell and Russell.

Strassberg, Maura I. 2003. *The Challenge of Postmodern Polygamy: Considering Polyamory*. https://culsnet.law.capital.edu/LawReview/backIssues/31-3/Strassberg14.pdf (retrieved 10 April 2003).

Summermoon, Margot. 1998. "A Letter to . . . My Children." *Loving More* 15: 33.

Suzuki, Kazuko. 1999. "Pornography or Therapy? Japanese Girls Creating the Yaoi Phenomenon." In *Millennium Girls: Today's Girls around the World*, ed. Sherrie Inness. London: Rowman & Littlefield.

Talbot, David. 1992. "Unspeakable Pleasures." In *Love without Limits: The Quest for Sustainable Intimate Relationships*, ed. D. Anapol. San Rafael, CA: IntiNet Resource Center.

Talburt, Susan. 2010. "'After-Queer': Subjunctive Pedagogies." *International Journal of Qualitative Studies in Education* 23(1): 49–64.

Taormino, Tristan. 2008. *Opening Up: A Guide to Creating and Sustaining Open Relationships*. San Francisco, CA: Cleis Press.

Tatchell, Peter. 2002. "Equality Is Not Enough." *Sydney Star Observer*, Thursday 7 February: 9.

Thompson, Elisabeth Morgan. 2006. "Girl Friend or Girlfriend? Same-Sex Friendships and Bisexual Images as a Context for Flexible Sexual Identity among Young Women." In *Bisexual Women: Friendships and Social Organization*, ed. M. Paz Galupo. New York: Harrington Park Press.

Thompson, Elisabeth Morgan, and Elisabeth M. Morgan. 2008. "'Mostly Straight' Young Women: Variations in Sexual Behavior and Identity Development." *Developmental Psychology* 44(1): 15–21.

Thorn, Matthew. 2004. "Girls and Women Getting Out of Hand: The Pleasure and Politics of Japan's Amateur Comics Community." In *Fanning the Flames: Fans and Consumer Culture in Contemporary Japan*, ed. William W. Kelly. Albany: State University of New York Press.

Thorson, Allison R. 2009. "Adult Children's Experiences with Their Parent's Infidelity: Communicative Protection and Access Rules in the Absence of Divorce." *Communication Studies* 60(1): 32–48.

Thrupkaew, Noy. 2009. "Fan/tastic Voyage: A Journey into the Wide, Wild World of Slash Fiction." *Bitch Magazine: Feminist Response to Pop Culture*, http://bitchmagazine.org/article/fan-tastic-voyage (retrieved 6 March 2009).

Tor, Maria. 2002. "Freedman Speaks against Bisexual Discrimination." *Cavalier Daily*, University of Virginia, 6 February, www.skottfreedman.com/lectures reviews.html (retrieved 3 April 2002).

Townley, Ben. 2005. "Bisexual Women 'Pressured to Be Lesbians.'" Gay.com, http://UK.gay.com/headlines/8773 (retrieved 1 December 2005).

Trask, Robyn. 2007. "PolyParents, PolyKids." *Loving More* 37: 16–17.

Travers, M. A., and C. O'Brien. 1997. "The Complexities of Bisexual Youth Identities." In *Pride and Prejudice: Working with Lesbian, Gay and Bisexual Youth*, ed. M. Schneider. Toronto, ON: Central Toronto Youth Services.

Trinh, T. Minh-ha. 1990a. "Cotton and Iron." In *Out There: Marginalization and Contemporary Cultures*, ed. R. Ferguson, M. Gever, M. T. Trinh, and C. West. Cambridge, MA: MIT Press.

———. 1990b. "Not You/Like You: Post-colonial Women and the Interlocking Questions of Identity and Difference." In *Making Face, Making Soul: Haciendo Caras*, ed. G. Anzaldua. San Francisco, CA: Aunt Lute.

———. 1991. *When the Moon Waxes Red*. New York: Routledge.

———. 1992. *Framer Framed*. New York: Routledge.

Trudinger, Mark, and Ron Frey. 1995–1996. "When the One and Only, Isn't." *XY: Men, Sex, Politics* 5(4): 14–17.

Turney, Carl. 1993. "Polyfidelity: Relationships of the Future." In *Conscious Living,* February/March, pp. 26–27.

Udis-Kessler, Amanda. 1990. "Bisexuality in an Essentialist World: Toward an Understanding of Biphobia." In *Bisexuality: A Reader and Sourcebook,* ed. T. Geller. Ojai, CA: Times Change Press.

Udry, J. R., and K. Chantala. 2002. "Risk Assessment of Adolescents with Same-Sex Relationships." *Journal of Adolescent Health* 31: 84–92.

Unitarian Universalists for Polyamory Awareness. 2004. *Introduction to Polyamory for UUs.* Unitarian Universalist Association of Congregations, www.uua.org/programs/ministry/mfc/news.html (retrieved 30 March 2004).

Usher, R., I. Bryant, and R. Johnston. 1997. *Adult Education and the Postmodern.* London: Routledge.

Valadez, Gilbert, and Anne Rene Elsbree. 2005. "Queer Coyotes: Transforming Education to Be More Accepting, Affirming, and Supportive of Queer Individuals." *Journal of Latinos and Education* 4(3): 171–92.

Valentine, Johnny. 2004. *One Dad, Two Dads, Brown Dads, Blue Dads.* Los Angeles, CA: Alyson Books.

Valverde, Mariana. 2006. "A New Entity in the History of Sexuality: The Respectable Same-Sex Couple." *Feminist Studies* 32: 155–62.

Van Den Abbeele, Georges. 1992. *Travel as Metaphor: From Montaigne to Rousseau.* Minneapolis: University of Minnesota Press.

Vassallo, Glenn. 2002. "Bisexual Activism in Australia." Paper given at Seventh International Conference on Bisexuality, 25–28 October, University of Technology, Sydney.

Volpp, Serna Yuan. 2010. "What about the 'B' in LGB: Are Bisexual Women's Mental Health Issues Same or Different?" *Journal of Gay and Lesbian Health* 14(1): 41–51.

Walston, Jasmine. 2001. "Polyamory: An Exploratory Study of Responsible Multi-Partnering." Paper given to the Institute of 21st-Century Relationships Conference. Courtesy of the author.

Wark, McKenzie. 1997. "Bisexual Mediations: Beyond the Third Term." In *Sex in Public: Australian Sexual Cultures,* ed. J. J. Matthews. Sydney: Allen & Unwin.

Warner, J., E. McKeown, M. Griffin, K. Johnson, A. Ramsay, C. Cort, and M. King. 2004. "Rates and Predictors of Mental Health in Gay Men, Lesbians, and Bisexual Men and Women: Results from a Survey Based in England and Wales." *British Journal of Psychiatry* 185: 479–85.

Warner, Michael. 1999. *The Trouble with Normal: Sex, Politics, and the Ethics of Queer Life.* New York: The Free Press.

Watson, Janet. 2008. "Representations of Bisexuality in Australian Film." *Journal of Bisexuality* 8(1/2): 97–114.

Watson, J., and M. A. Watson. 1982. "Children of Open Marriages: Parental Disclosure and Perspectives." *Alternative Lifestyles* 5(1): 54–62.

Weber, Adam. 2002. "Survey Results: Who Are We? And Other Interesting Impressions." *Loving More* 30: 4–6.

Weeks, Jeffrey. 1987. "Questions of Identity." In *The Cultural Construction of Sexuality*, ed. P. Caplan. London: Tavistock.

———. 1995. "History, Desire, Identities." In *Conceiving Sexuality: Approaches to Sex Research in a Postmodern World*, ed. Richard G. Parker and John H. Gagnon. New York: Routledge.

———. 1998. "The Sexual Citizen." *Theory, Culture and Society* 15(3–4): 35–52.

Weinberg, Martin S., Colin J. Williams, and Douglas W. Pryor. 1994. *Dual Attraction: Understanding Bisexuality*. New York: Oxford University Press.

Weise, Elizabeth Reba. 1992. *Closer to Home: Bisexuality and Feminism*. Seattle, WA: Seal Press.

Weitzman, Geri D. 2006. "Therapy with Clients Who Are Bisexual and Polyamorous." *Journal of Bisexuality* 6(1/2): 138–64.

———. 2007. "Counseling Bisexuals in Polyamorous Relationships." In *Becoming Visible: Counseling Bisexuals across the Lifespan*, ed. Beth A. Firestein. New York: Columbia University Press.

West, Celeste. 1996. *Lesbian Polyfidelity*. San Francisco, CA: Booklegger Publishing.

White, Valerie. 2007. "Thinking about Children." *Loving More* 37: 12–13.

Whitney, Catherine. 1990. *Uncommon Lives: Gay Men and Straight Women*. New York: Plume.

Wilkinson, Lili. 2009. *Pink*. Sydney: Allen & Unwin.

Williams, Hameed (Herukbuti) S. 2008. "A Bisex-Queer Critique of Same-Sex Marriage Advocacy." *Journal of Bisexuality* 7(3): 313–18.

Winslow, Ben. 2006. "Children of 'Plural Families' to Rally." *Deseret News*, www.deseretnews.com/article/1,5143,645191989,00.html (retrieved 24 December 2006).

Wold, Cheryl, George R. Seage III, William R. Lenderking, Kenneth H. Mayer, Bin Cai, Timothy Heeren, and Robert Goldstein. 1998. "Unsafe Sex in Men Who Have Sex with Both Men and Women." *Journal of Acquired Immune Deficiency Syndromes and Human Retrovirology* 17(4): 361–67.

Woledge, Elizabeth. 2005. "Decoding Desire: From Kirk and Spock to K/S." *Social Semiotics* 15(2): 235–50.

Wood, Andrea. 2006. "'Straight' Women, Queer Texts: Boy-Love Manga and the Rise of a Global Counterpublic." *WSQ: Women's Studies Quarterly* 34(1/2): 394–414.

Wood, Margaret Mary. 1934. *The Stranger: A Study in Social Relationships*. New York: Columbia University Press.

Woolson, Constance Fenimore. 1876/1994. "Felipa." In *Two Friends and Other Nineteenth Century Lesbian Stories by American Women Writers*, ed. S. Koppelman. New York: Meridian.

Worley, Virginia. 2006. "Revolution in the Everyday: *Metissage* as Place of Education." *Discourse: Studies in the Cultural Politics of Education* 27(4): 515–31.

Worth, Heather. 2003. "The Myth of the Bisexual Infector? HIV Risk and Men Who Have Sex with Men." *Journal of Bisexuality* 3(2): 71–88.

Wright, Janet M. 2001. "'Aside from One Little, Tiny Detail, We Are So Incredibly Normal': Perspectives of Children in Lesbian Step Families." In *Queer Families, Queer Politics: Challenging Culture and the State*, ed. Mary Bernstein and Renate Reimann. New York: Columbia University Press.

Yescavage, K., and J. Alexander. 2003. "Seeing What We Want to See: Searching for Bisexual Representation in 'Threesome' Films." *Journal of Bisexuality* 3(2): 109–27.

Yip, A. K. T. 2008. "Researching Lesbian, Gay and Bisexual Christians and Muslims: Some Thematic Reflections." *Sociological Research Online* 13(1), www.socres online.org.uk/13/1/5.html (retrieved 30 April 2008).

Yoshizaki, Amanda. 1992. "Breaking the Rules: Constructing a Bisexual Feminist Marriage." In *Closer to Home: Bisexuality and Feminism*, ed. E. R. Weise. Seattle, WA: Seal Press.

Young, Iris. 1990a. "The Ideal of Community and the Politics of Difference." In *Feminism/Postmodernism*, ed. L. J. Nicholson. New York: Routledge.

———. 1990b. *Justice and the Politics of Difference*. Princeton, NJ: Princeton University Press.

Young, R., H. Sweeting, and P. West. 2006. "Prevalence of Deliberate Self Harm and Attempted Suicide within Contemporary Goth Youth Subculture: Longitudinal Cohort Study." *British Medical Journal* 332: 1058–61.

Yuval-Davis, Nira. 1994. "Women, Ethnicity and Empowerment." *Feminism and Psychology* 4(1): 179–97.

Zanghellini, Aleardo. 2009. "'Boys Love' in Anime and Manga: Japanese Subcultural Production and Its End Users." *Continuum: Journal of Media and Cultural Studies* 23(3): 279–94.

Zell, Morning Glory. 1992. "A Bouquet of Lovers." In *Love without Limits*, ed. D. M. Anapol. San Rafael, CA: IntiNet Resource Center.

Zell, Morning Glory, and Oberon Zell. 1996. "The Spirit of Adventure." *Loving More* 8: 8–9.

Zerubavel, Eviatar. 1991. *The Fine Line: Making Distinctions in Everyday Life*. Chicago: University of Chicago Press.

Zinik, Gary. 1985. "Identity Conflict or Adaptive Flexibility? Bisexuality Reconsidered." *Journal of Homosexuality* 11(1/2): 7–19.

Zipkin, Dvora. 1992. "Why Bi?" In *Closer to Home: Bisexuality and Feminism*, ed. E. R. Weise. Seattle, WA: Seal Press.

Index

About the Author

Maria Pallotta-Chiarolli is senior lecturer in the School of Health and Social Development at Deakin University, Melbourne, Australia. Dr. Maria Pallotta-Chiarolli writes, teaches, and researches on social justice, diversity, and equity issues in education and health. Her primary areas of interest are cultural diversity, gender diversity, sexual diversity, and family diversity.

Maria is also an external faculty member of Saybrook Graduate School and Research Center, San Francisco; the honorary patron of PFLAG (Parents and Friends of Lesbians and Gays) Victoria in Australia; and founding member of AGMC Inc (Australian GLBTIQ Multicultural Council), which is a member of FECCA (Federation of Ethnic Communities' Council of Australia).

Apart from academic chapters, research monographs, and journal articles, Maria's publications include *Someone You Know*, Australia's first AIDS biography; *Girls Talk: Young Women Speak Their Hearts and Minds*, which involved researching with culturally and sexually diverse girls and young women; and *Tapestry*, a biographical narrative on five generations of Maria's Italian family. *Tapestry* was short-listed for the NSW Premier's Award in the Ethnic Affairs Commission category and in the Children's Book Council Non-Fiction Award. Maria has also written *When Our Children Come Out: How to Support Gay, Lesbian, Bisexual and Transgendered Young People*, which is being translated into Spanish, and the following three books co-researched and written with Dr. Wayne Martino: *Boys' Stuff: Boys Talking about What Matters*, which was short-listed for four awards (a Western Australian Premier's Award, the Australian Book Design Award, a Human Rights Award, and was highly commended in the Australian Award for Excellence in Educational Publishing); *So What's a Boy? Issues of Masculinity and Schooling*,

277

which has been translated into Spanish; and *"Being Normal Is the Only Thing to Be": Adolescent Perspectives on Gender in Schools*.

Maria's latest publication is a young adult novel, *Love You Two*, which explores sexual and family diversity, and is Australia's first novel that includes polyamorous and bisexual relationships. It has been shortlisted as a finalist in the Lambda Literary Book Awards. The novel is based on her research with U.S. and Australian polyfamilies and women in relationships with bisexual men. Her forthcoming book is *Outside Belonging: Women in Relationships with Bisexual Men*.